NYSTCE®

NYSTCE®

Library of Congress Cataloging-in-Publication Data:
Pass the NYSTCE.—1st ed.
      p. cm.
ISBN: 978-1-57685-630-7
1. Teachers—Certification—New York (State).
2. Teaching—New York (State)—Examinations—Study guides.
LB1763.N7P37 2007
379.1'5709747—dc22

                            2007011133

Printed in the United States of America

9 8 7 6 5 4 3 2

First Edition

ISBN: 978-1-57685-630-7

"NYSTCE®," "New York State Teacher Certification Examinations™," and the "NYSTCE®" logo are trademarks of the New York State Education Department and National Evaluation Systems, Inc. (NES®).

"NES®" and its logo are registered trademarks of National Evaluation Systems, Inc.™

For more information or to place an order, contact LearningExpress at:
    2 Rector Street
    26th Floor
    New York, NY 10006

Or visit us at:
    www.learnatest.com

About the Contributors

Deborah Eldridge is a professor and chairperson of the Department of Curriculum and Teaching at Montclair State University. She writes and researches on topics related to literacy and teacher education.

Cindy Lassonde is an assistant professor in the Elementary Education and Reading Department at SUNY College at Oneonta, where she teaches undergraduate and graduate courses in literacy. She lives in Schoharie, New York.

Dennis Showers is a professor of education at SUNY Geneseo and a former high school science teacher. He has worked with teachers across the United States and in 12 other countries, including Russia, Chile, and Australia.

Lauren Starkey is a writer and editor specializing in educational and reference works. She also leads workshops on writing and test preparation for students, businesspeople, and artists. Lauren lives in Essex, Vermont, with her husband, three children, and a pug.

Contents

1 ▶ How to Use This Book

CHAPTER SUMMARY

If you have made the decision to pursue a career as a teacher in New York State, you know that one of the requirements is to obtain certification by successfully completing a core of New York State Teacher Certification Examinations, otherwise referred to as the NYSTCE®. These tests measure teacher candidates' skills and knowledge to ensure New York State teachers demonstrate the ability to effectively perform the vast and demanding responsibilities of being a teacher in the state's public schools.

This book is designed to provide the practice, guidance, and support you will need to tackle the Liberal Arts and Sciences Test (LAST), the Elementary and Secondary Assessment of Teaching Skills—Written tests (ATS-W), the Content Specialty Tests (CSTs), and the Assessment of Teaching Skills—Performance (ATS-P). *NYSTCE* contains all the information you need to improve your scores on these tests in the shortest amount of time possible. This chapter serves as a guide for using this book effectively, so you get the most out of your time and effort.

▶ The Book

In this book, you'll find:

- a chapter discussing the benefits of teaching in New York.
- a chapter explaining the basic requirements to teach in New York public schools
- three chapters about the NYSTCE, complete with test descriptions; breakdowns of the subareas on each test; and information about test registration, fees, and scoring
- a chapter to help with study skills and test anxiety
- chapters that review core reading, mathematics, and writing skills
- four full-length practice exams, complete with answers and explanations
- online links and other useful resources

You may want to begin with Chapter 2, "Making the Decision to Become a Teacher." This chapter discusses the benefits of teaching in New York State. It includes points and information that teacher candidates should know, consider, and expect before they decide to pursue a teaching career. You will read examples of what teachers receive and say about their salary, time off, benefits, and personal job satisfaction in various regions and locations. The chapter ends with some specific information on working in the New York City area.

Chapter 3, "Teaching in New York," gets into the specifics of certification and testing. You can use this chapter as a resource to learn about the levels of certification, traditional and alternative routes to certification, and supplemental certifications and endorsements. This chapter will also tell you about the NYSTCE requirements and other pertinent information, such as fingerprinting and maintaining certification. Finally, Chapter 3 ends with a list of useful websites, books, and other valuable resources.

Chapters 4, 5, and 6 describe the exams that collectively make up the NYSTCE. Chapter 4 is about the Liberal Arts and Sciences Test (LAST). Chapter 5 is about the Elementary Assessment of Teaching Skills—Written (ATS-W) and the Secondary Assessment of Teaching Skills—Written (ATS-W). Chapter 6 is about the Content Specialty Test (CST) and Assessment of Teaching Skills—Performance (ATS-P). This group of chapters describes the length, timing, what to bring to the test, registration information, test fees and sites, dates, and scoring information. The specific subareas that appear on the tests are also provided.

Chapter 7, "The LearningExpress Test Preparation System," teaches you how to prepare for any test effectively using LearningExpress's proven test-taking strategies. You will learn to:

- set up a personalized study plan, utilizing the lessons and tests in this book
- use your study time efficiently
- make educated guesses when you are unsure of an answer
- overcome test anxiety

After you have mastered these skills, move on to the three skills review chapters. These review chapters are great tools for studying for the NYSTCE, and each includes examples and explanations that will help you practice as you learn. You should read all of the review chapters, putting emphasis on the subjects that are typically problematic for you.

Chapter 8, "Reading Skills Review," is designed to review the reading skills you will need to pass the LAST, ATS-W, and CST. Because you will be timed on test day, you will learn how to be an "active" reader. In other words, this chapter shows you how to read passages to quickly spot the differences between the main ideas and supporting ideas and to pinpoint key concepts in a reading passage. Also, you will learn to skim through the less important information, so that unnecessary and irrelevant information will not bog you down.

The reading review also demonstrates how to make logical inferences, draw likely conclusions, and gauge an author's attitude based on the information given in a reading passage. And, like each of the review chapters in this book, there are several practice questions allowing you to apply what you have just learned. There's nothing like having a lot of practice to make you feel confident when you go into the real exam.

Chapter 9, "Mathematics Skills Review," covers math basics in a clear and concise manner. Most test takers are intimidated by math questions, so the review is designed to bolster your confidence. It covers mathematical terms, arithmetic, algebraic foundations and equations, percentages, ratios, measurement, and geometry. Plus, you will learn strategies for solving word problems, analyzing data, interpreting graphs and tables, spotting trends and patterns, and recognizing various ways to solve problems. Because many problems you will face on the LAST will require a combination of math skills to get the correct answer, you should review the examples throughout the chapter.

The Writing Skills Review in Chapter 10 is an efficient crash course in writing. This chapter covers the basics in the areas of grammar, mechanics, word usage, and sentence structure. For the constructed-response assignment, you will find useful writing strategies so that you can compose a clear, well-organized essay, effectively stating your objective.

After you have mastered the test-taking strategies in Chapter 7 and reviewed the reading, mathematics, and writing skills in Chapters 8, 9, and 10, respectively, try taking the first full-length LAST practice exam in Chapter 11. After scoring it, you can refer back to Chapters 8, 9, and 10 to review the particular skills that were problematic for you on the first practice exam. Assess your personal strengths and weaknesses, and focus your time where you need it most.

Next, you will move on to the ATS-W practice exams in Chapters 12 and 13. Chapter 12 is the Elementary ATS-W Practice Exam, which consists of 80 multiple-choice questions with distracters and full-answer explanations and one practice essay with sample responses and evaluations at two different levels (strong and weak). Chapter 13 is the Secondary ATS-W Practice Exam, which contains the same components as Chapter 12, except, obviously, at the secondary level.

In Chapter 14, you will find the final full-length LAST practice exam. By taking this test, you will hone your test-taking skills, continue to diagnose your weakest areas, and discover where you might still need improvement. Try taking this test under timed conditions—just like the real exam.

▶ The Online Practice Test

You have the option of taking one of the practice exams found in this book on your computer. *NYSTCE* gives you free online access to a full-length practice LAST. The online test offers you practice with the official tests' format, content, and timing, and includes instant scoring with detailed answer explanations. See the insert at the back of this book for complete details.

▶ Practice for Success

You already have two valuable tools for passing the tests—this book and online practice tests—now the rest is up to you. Ultimately, you will have to rely on yourself to succeed. Remain disciplined, follow your study schedule, and do not give up. Most importantly—practice, practice, practice. Plenty of practice will improve your skills and build your confidence.

Good luck!

2 ▶ Making the Decision to Become a Teacher

CHAPTER SUMMARY

Teaching can be a very rewarding career. A teacher is in a position to open the minds of his or her students and get them excited about their potential in life. If your reasons for wanting to be a teacher, however, are primarily because you want summers off or because you like children, you might want to reconsider your career choice. To make an informed decision, there are several important facts discussed in this chapter that you should know and carefully consider before you decide to pursue teaching. These aren't meant to be warnings or imply negativity by any means. Some will say the following are the best parts about teaching. See what you think.

Professional Words of Wisdom

"I decided to go into teaching because I wanted to be able to make a difference in someone's life and, in turn, in the world. While I enjoyed the office job I held, I just didn't feel like people would even notice if I weren't there day in and day out shuffling papers. Just about anyone could have taken my place. When I became a teacher, I realized spending time with my students every day meant a lot to me . . . and to them. Every day we gave each other little pieces of ourselves as we learned from each other. I wasn't shuffling papers anymore; I was shaping minds and hearts into caring, knowledgeable human beings. I found my purpose."

—*Cindy Lassonde, Southern Tier Region*

▶ Fact #1: Teaching Is a Career

Teaching isn't a job that you "leave at the office" when you go home at the end of the day. More often than not, nights and weekends are spent preparing for the next day, correcting papers, meeting with families, or attending professional development workshops and seminars to update your teaching skills.

Summers and breaks aren't what they appear to be to those outside of education, either. More and more often, teachers are teaching summer school or attending workshops during what used to be their summer break. For example, one of the fastest-growing professional development organizations, the National Writing Project, involves a six-week summer institute in which educators study and collaborate to improve writing instruction. With heightened expectations for teachers and students at the state and federal levels, teachers use "time off" during the school year and summer to update their knowledge and classroom practices more often than not.

National Writing Project

www.nwp.org

Professional Words of Wisdom

What should every prospective educator know about the realities of choosing a teaching career?

"You cannot change the world; just do your best to make it a little bit better."

—*Tony B., special education teacher, Goshen*

"No one can help you to 'like' this work or to become proficient at it unless you are prepared to learn how to do it well. Professional development opportunities help, of course, but there is something to be said for the young teacher who takes responsibility for learning how to do it well because he or she believes it matters to the community that is served."

—*Linda Lee Boesl, English teacher, Pittsford Sutherland High School*

"Be prepared for a job that does not end at 3:00 P.M.! I spend endless hours researching and preparing for new and exciting lessons."

—*Sean Pope, Bedford Central School District*

▶ Fact #2: Teachers Are Professionals

Teachers are expected to be models of upstanding citizens and professionals by the community. A teacher is more than an employee. You will be held responsible and accountable for your behavior inside and outside of the classroom. You won't be able to just not show up for work. Who will take care of your class if you do? When you are ill or have to miss work for any reason, you are expected to make plans for a substitute teacher. Often teachers will say it's easier to go to work not feeling well than to prepare every minute of the school day for a substitute. Some will say, too, that the loyalty they feel toward their students makes them feel responsible to be there for their students every day because they know the students and their educational needs best. With being a teacher comes the feelings and expectations of accountability and responsibility for doing a job well.

Part of being a professional also includes being a lifelong learner. Just like a physician has to stay updated on the latest medical procedures and pharmaceuticals, a teacher must read professional journals; attend classes and workshops; and collaborate with colleagues to be on top of the latest methods, research, and strategies. Students count on educators to know what the latest research says about how to teach reading, for example, in order to make the best use of the time and resources allotted.

Professional Words of Wisdom

What sort of person should NOT choose teaching as a career?

"Impatient people who lack compassion should not become teachers."
—Harry K., fourth grade teacher, Rockland

"Stay away if you don't have a sense of humor."
—Xiomara, creative writing teacher, Brooklyn

"Someone who thinks that teaching is from 8:30 A.M.–3:30 P.M., September to June should not become a teacher. If you're going to teach, you have to realize from day one that your workday will start at 6:00 A.M. and sometimes go until 1:00 A.M. You also have to realize that you don't leave the kids on the last day of school; you will worry and think about them every day during the summer."
—Natalie, math teacher, The Bronx

"Someone who has always imagined being 'the sage on the stage,' or who is in need of an audience should not become a teacher."
—Linda Lee Boesl, English teacher, Pittsford Sutherland High School

"Who should definitely not become a teacher? Someone looking for a gig from 7:30 A.M.–3:00 P.M. with summers off while they're working on their novel, band, or whatever in their *free* time."
—Sean Pope, Bedford Central School District

▶ Fact #3: Teaching Is Caring

Think about your favorite teacher. What do you remember about him or her? Do you remember certain projects you enjoyed and ways that teacher made you feel accepted? Teaching involves more than imparting knowledge. You will be a listener, a mediator, a friend, a disciplinarian, an authoritarian, a facilitator, and a caregiver. When a student isn't doing homework, you may find it is because something is going on at home that the student is having trouble dealing with. Another student might not speak in class because he or she doesn't want to take the risk of being made fun of by others. An effective teacher knows what is going on in his or her students' lives that influences learning, and the teacher knows how to work with the students to encourage cognitive growth and maturity.

A teacher doesn't stand in front of the room and hand out knowledge. There is much more to teaching than meets the eye. You should be prepared to invest part of yourself in your students in order to gain their trust and respect. This takes trust on your part. If you aren't the kind of person who feels comfortable talking with families and students as they seek guidance from you, you might want to reconsider teaching. Teachers who sincerely care about their students, their families, and the school community will find ways to effectively meet the needs of learners.

▶ Fact #4: Teachers Are Skilled Communicators

Effective teachers are skilled at expressing themselves orally and in writing. You should feel comfortable speaking in front of groups. Your public speaking won't just be confined to the students in your classroom; at the very least, in your career you'll also on numerous occasions be required to speak in front of families gathered at Open House and fellow faculty members at staff meetings. Just as important as your speaking skills, your writing skills should also serve as a model for students, families, and colleagues. Strong vocabulary, grammar, and composition skills are essential.

At the PreK–12 level, communicating with families may be a big part of your responsibilities. You should practice communicating with families in ways that are sensitive yet honest. For example, you cannot tell a student's father the student is succeeding at a particular level when he or she is not. However, you will need to express the student's needs in a way that does not offend or alarm the father. Teachers are expected to be knowledgeable about how to speak with family members effectively and sensitively.

Professional Words of Wisdom

What's the biggest mistake many new teachers make?

"I've noticed that many new teachers often put too much pressure on themselves when preparing for their initial observations. The school has already recognized something in you and has given you a job; just plan well and realize it's the administration's job to critique you with both suggestions for improvement as well as praise."

—*Manny D., middle school social studies teacher, Syracuse*

"Jumping on the first job that is offered to them. Take the time to find a position in a school with a strong, supportive administration. Look for an administration that is focused on education, that values the individuality of its students and staff, provides structured mentoring for new teachers, has a strong disciplinary policy in place, and has a strong PTA."

—*Kim G., kindergarten teacher, Orchard Park*

"Without a doubt, it's picking the wrong battles. In my first teaching job working with inner-city students 14–16 years old, I spent my first week trying to break up every little squabble and fight as soon as it started. It didn't take me long to realize I was pouring water in the ocean. No matter how many times I tried to stay ahead of the game, it always wound up passing me by again. I finally learned to let some things just go, and it actually turned out much better for me and the students."

—*Tony B., special education teacher, Goshen*

▶ Benefits of Teaching in New York State

There are many benefits that come with being a teacher in New York State. As stated earlier in this chapter, the first benefit to consider is the personal satisfaction that comes with making a difference in a child's and sometimes a family's lives. By teaching children, you can change their lives forever and empower them to be potentially productive members of our society. In the process, as a teacher you can also change your own life, as your students teach you, and cause you to reflect.

Professional Words of Wisdom

What do you enjoy most about being a teacher?

"Never having the same day twice—there's always something different going on so you don't ever get bored."

—Patrick, chemistry teacher, Nyack

"The mornings, about half an hour before the students get there, when the blackboard is clean and the day is wide open before you, are one of the best times of teaching. That's the possible hour, when today holds the promise of everything you want it to be."

—Natalie, math teacher, The Bronx

"I like establishing a community of trust, a constructivist classroom in which the students become more and more independent . . . as readers and thinkers and participants in discussion."

—Linda Lee Boesl, English teacher, Pittsford Sutherland High School

"I really enjoy inspiring kids to overcome their lives rather than being sucked into the same cycle they grew up with."

—Xiomara, creative writing teacher, Brooklyn

"The daily rewards—when the 'light' goes on in a child's mind and they get it."

—Kim G., kindergarten teacher, Orchard Park

A teacher can be proud to say he or she teaches in New York State because our state has high standards for teacher certification and for all of its students. The state recently reformed and revitalized its educational system by revamping teacher preparation programs and PreK–12 learning standards. The New York State Education Department (NYSED) continues to review and reevaluate its criteria, assessments, and standards as it provides support to public school districts. Professional development programs and mentoring are now mandated and supported by the state.

Other advantages of teaching in the Empire State are the salary and related benefits. New York ranks third among all of the states in teaching salary and fourth for average beginning teacher salary. According to the NYSED, the average teaching salary in New York State is just more than $55,000, which, according to the American

Federation of Teaching's 2005 salary survey, ranks New York sixth in the nation. In comparison, here are average salaries for various regions of the nation:

California	$57,604
Florida	$43,095
Montana	$38,485
Texas	$41,009
Wisconsin	$43,099

Health insurance and retirement benefits are also advantages. School districts usually offer multiple options to consider for health insurance, from personal and family plans to health maintenance organizations (HMOs) and preferred provider organizations (PPOs). As for retirement benefits, the New York State Retirement System is one of the largest public retirement systems in the United States. The system provides retirement, death, and disability benefits to eligible teachers and administrators.

For More Information

New York State Education Department: www.highered.nysed.gov
New York State Retirement System: www.nystrs.org
Teacher Salaries Nationwide: www.aft.org/salary/2005/download/AFT2005SalarySurvey.pdf

If you plan to teach while you are pursuing your master's degree, you will be happy to hear that New York State has more than 100 teacher preparation institutions with high-quality graduate programs. Also, many school districts and institutions offer alternative preparation programs, such as the Career Changer program in which candidates with subject matter expertise can be recommended for teacher certification after meeting certain requirements. One of the more popular alternative preparation programs in the state is the New York City Teaching Fellows Program. More information about the Fellows Program is found in Chapter 3.

For More Information

Official Certification Website: www.highered.nysed.gov/tcert/certificate

Finally, whether you want to teach in a small town, rural school district, the suburbs, or a large, urban school, New York offers diverse opportunities and locations for teachers. The North Country Region offers the Adirondack Mountains and industries related to natural resources, such as timber. The Central and Western New York Regions have abundant agricultural communities, and the Mid-Hudson Region is a mix of forests and farmlands, urban areas, and small villages along the river valley. Take your pick!

Professional Words of Wisdom

"I am lucky; I have taught in both a typical 'inner-city' area in The Bronx, as well as a relatively affluent suburb. It allowed me to really see what I suspected all along: Despite their backgrounds, when you really get down to it, kids are kids."

—*Tony B., special education teacher, Goshen*

"Before moving upstate, I taught in the Lower East Side of Manhattan for a number of years. I find that small town schools lack the diversity that really adds to every student's and teacher's life, and big city schools often frustratingly lack the resources to allow a teacher to perform to the best of his or her abilities."

—*Manny D., middle school social studies teacher, Syracuse*

▶ Teaching in New York City

If you are looking for an exciting, rewarding, and perhaps somewhat challenging place to teach, you may want to look into teaching in New York City.

Professional Words of Wisdom

Teachers who work in New York City say:

"I teach in Brooklyn, where the students bring to the table a host of problems and a unique perspective on life. Those kids are the best: full of attitude, but also full of life. They understand certain literature in a way that others can't; when they read *To Kill a Mockingbird* or *Othello*, they know what it is to be an outsider, to have the system work against you, so they can jump into the stories in a way that more sheltered kids can't."

—*Xiomara, creative writing teacher, Brooklyn*

"The problems with teaching in an inner-city school are not problems of what to teach or how to teach it; so much as they are problems of how to build a wall around the students so they can learn despite the life surrounding them. Building that wall is a challenge, but if you succeed, the rewards are incredible."

—*Natalie, math teacher, The Bronx*

"The diversity that comes hand in hand with teaching in New York City makes my job great. I have had the privilege of teaching some truly wonderful and gifted young people who were genuinely characters. The mix of cultures and personalities always makes for an interesting classroom. A serious disadvantage, however, is the lack of parental support, and perhaps even worse, support from my own administration. Still, with all the drawbacks, I couldn't imagine teaching or living anywhere else."
—*Marco, middle school ELA teacher, Manhattan*

With more than one million students and 1,300 public schools, the New York City student population is one of the most diverse and vibrant in the world. Students represent a variety of experiences, ethnicities, strengths, and needs.

Teaching in New York City offers opportunities that teaching and living in other regions do not. New York City, the largest metropolis in the United States, is known throughout the world as a center for finance, industry, fashion, technology, publishing, and the arts and entertainment. The city's approximately eight million residents can take advantage of unparalleled cultural events and entertainment facilities. Sports enthusiasts can take in professional baseball, hockey, football, and basketball games, or run in the New York City Marathon. Theater-goers have a choice of a number of Broadway and off-Broadway theaters as well as a variety of dance and music companies and Radio City Music Hall. Residents can join the millions of visitors each year who are attracted to the city's wealth of museums, shops, and art galleries. Also, the city is home to top research universities where teachers can pursue graduate and postgraduate degrees.

Working in such a large metropolis, teachers will also experience unique challenges that reflect the realities of city life. For example, schools are crowded. The average elementary class size ranges from 20 to 32 students. The average middle and high-school class sizes range from 28 to 34 students. This, along with a shortage of teachers, can make it difficult to meet the needs of all students and dedicate the necessary time needed to assess students and plan for instruction. Many New York City schools are high-needs schools, meaning students may not perform well on high-stakes standardized tests and the schools are located in high-poverty communities. Teaching in high-needs schools takes dedication and a caring attitude.

As a New York City teacher, you may choose to live in one of the outlying rural or suburban areas and commute into the city on the region's extensive highway system. Or, you may be part of the one-third of the city's college-educated adults who live in one of the five boroughs. The city's system of mass transportation is well-developed and maintained to support employees' and students' needs. Of course, like any large city, you will experience traffic delays, especially during the rush hours when people are going to and leaving work. You will have to plan your commute accordingly.

With this variety of special events and cultural offerings, imagine what it might be like being a teacher in New York City. New York City offers one-of-a-kind resources, challenges, and opportunities for teachers who want to experience and learn from diverse cultures and offer these experiences to their students. There are hundreds of neighborhoods that are rich with the city's diversity.

3 ▶ Teaching in New York

CHAPTER SUMMARY

New York State certification is required for all teachers employed in state public schools. The Office of Teaching Initiatives issues classroom teaching certificates as verification that an individual has completed the required academic degree and coursework and has successfully met specific requirements for assessment and experience. All the information in this chapter was obtained from and can be found in greater detail at the New York State Department of Education, Office of Higher Education's website and the New York State Teacher Certification Examinations' official website. Both sites provide invaluable information for prospective educators in New York State, and it is highly recommended that you visit both sites as a starting point for your NYSTCE prep.

For More Information

New York State Department of Education, Office of Higher Education:
www.highered.nysed.gov/tcert/certificate/index.html
New York State Teacher Certification Examinations: www.nystce.nesinc.com

► Traditional Routes to Certification

Most commonly, teacher candidates are high-school graduates who continue on to a New York State teacher-preparation college or university (or a state that has reciprocity with New York) and then are recommended by the institution for certification. If a candidate graduated from a teacher-preparation program in another state, he or she should apply to the State Education Department for Interstate Reciprocity. To complete this traditional route, the candidate then has to pass the LAST, ATS-W, and the appropriate CST. Some candidates also have to submit the ATS-P video, which is described in full in Chapter 6.

Once a candidate has completed a teacher-education program from a New York college, the institution will use the TEACH Online Services to recommend the candidate. The candidate should set up an account with TEACH and contact the institution for further instructions. If he or she is being recommended by a college, the candidate must first satisfy testing and fingerprinting requirements before the certificate can be issued.

For More Information

TEACH Online Services: www.highered.nysed.gov/tcert/teach

► Alternate Teaching Programs Leading to Certification

The purpose of Alternate Teaching Programs (ATPs) is to prepare teachers rapidly for entry into teaching in areas where there are shortages. ATPs are an important, although small, source of qualified teachers and have been proven effective. ATPs, offered by some colleges that partner with local schools, typically feature an accelerated but rigorous 200-hour program, paid employment, mentoring, and classes, as well as other college and school district support.

Candidates must also pass certification tests. ATPs are aimed at professionals with bachelor's degrees in fields other than teaching who are seeking a second career in teaching. The ATPs are designed for candidates with a strong academic background in the subject they will teach. For example, the candidate must have achieved a 3.0 cumulative grade point average in a bachelor's or graduate program or have alternate approval by an officer designated by the ATP.

While ATPs meet the same requirements as traditional programs, typically they do so in a shorter, condensed timeframe. After candidates have completed the initial training and have successfully completed the required NYSTCEs, they are issued a State Transitional B teaching certificate. Based on the ATP and the candidate's qualifications, certification covers only a specific subject or grade. This certificate is valid for up to three years, as long as the candidate is in an Alternate Teaching Certification (ATC) program and is teaching in a partner school. The candidate is placed in a school in which he or she teaches under the supervision of school-based mentors and college supervisors. During this time span, the candidate is paid by the school district. The candidate also is expected to complete coursework in a teacher-education program during this time. The training is intense and rigorous. Once the candidate has completed the ATC program, he or she can be recommended by the supervising college for initial or professional certification. At that point, the candidate is certified to teach in any New York State school; he or she is not limited to teaching only in ATP schools.

As mentioned previously, the goal of these programs is to prepare candidates to teach in difficult-to-staff content areas (e.g., mathematics, sciences, and languages other than English) and certain geographic areas that experience shortages of qualified teachers (e.g., New York City). Candidates with qualifying bachelor's or graduate degrees who are interested in teaching in these areas should consider looking into the Transitional B certification route.

The largest alternative certification program in the country, the New York City Teaching Fellows Program addresses the city's chronic teaching shortage. The program draws mainly recent college graduates and mid-career professionals to teach in the underperforming schools of the nation's largest school system. In the 2006–2007 academic year, statistics from the program indicate that one in ten of the approximately 78,000 New York City public school teachers is a Teaching Fellow. Once an applicant has been accepted as a Fellow, he or she will teach in a high-need school under professional supervision; matriculate into a subsidized master's program that qualifies the Fellow for certification in a particular subject area; receive the same salary and benefits as other New York City teachers; and, upon successful completion of the program, be eligible to teach (www.nycteachingfellows.org). Other programs exist in upstate New York and New York City. TEACH Online Services has a list of college/school district partnerships that are participating in ATPs. You can access the list at www.highered.nysed.gov/ocue/ATCcontactlist.htm.

▶ Levels of Certification

The two levels of teaching certification most commonly sought are initial and professional. The initial certificate is an entry-level certificate for classroom teachers. It is issued in specific subjects (i.e., biology, childhood education, literacy, math, etc.) and grade levels (i.e., birth through grade 6, grades 5 through 12, or prekindergarten through grade 12). The initial certificate is valid for five years and leads to professional certification.

The professional certificate is also issued in specific subjects and grade levels. Professional certification is continuously valid once required professional development hours have been met on a five-year cycle.

There are two other levels of teaching certification that may pertain to your status: provisional and permanent. Provisional certification was initially the entry-level certificate sought by classroom teachers; however, as of February 2, 2004, provisional certification has been replaced by initial certification. Some teachers may still be working through permanent certification through this old system, however, since provisional certification, which leads to permanent certification, is valid for five years. Until February 2009, some teachers will still be working toward their permanent certification. By the way, permanent certification is valid for the life of the teacher unless it is revoked by the New York State Education Department. Besides the validity requirements, one of the main differences between provisional/permanent versus initial/professional certification is that teachers seeking permanent certification must complete and successfully pass the Assessment of Teaching Skills—Performance video (ATS-P).

When applying for any level of teaching certification, you must select a particular category, title, and type. There are four categories from which to choose: Classroom Teacher, Classroom Teacher—Foreign Languages, or one of the Classroom Teacher Extensions categories, which contain titles that extend the span of grade levels or subject areas. There is also an Other Extensions certificate area that contains titles that extend certification to include American Sign Language, gifted education, bilingual education, and an Other School Service certificate area that contains titles for supplemental teaching services, such as teaching in adult education. After choosing the category, you will need to specify the subject area and grade levels.

Next, you must select a title from a list of possibilities that will be generated depending on which category you have chosen. For example, if you chose Classroom Teacher, Childhood Education, Birth–Grade 6, the title would be Nursery, Kindergarten and Grades 1–6.

Finally, you will select the type. Based on what you have chosen so far, you will be given a choice of certification types, such as initial or professional certification.

▶ Supplemental Certifications

Besides initial and professional certification, there are several supplemental certifications:

- **Annotation Certificate**—an attachment to regular certification. This certificate recognizes the candidate has skills and knowledge beyond those required for regular certification.
- **Extension (Subject) Certificate**—also an attachment to regular certification. This authorizes the candidate to teach an additional grade, population, or subject that he or she is not certified to teach.
- **Conditional Initial Certificate**—issued to candidates who hold certification from a state honored by the Interstate Reciprocity Agreement but have not met the New York State testing requirements yet. The holder of this certificate has up to two years to qualify for the initial certificate.
- **Supplementary Certificate**—allows certified classroom teachers to teach in another subject in an area in which shortages exist. This certificate requires certain semester hour and test prerequisites.
- **Transitional A Certificate**—allows individuals who have not met initial certification requirements but who have occupational experience in agriculture, health, or a trade to teach in the classroom. This certificate is valid for three years.
- **Transitional B Certificate**—discussed previously, is valid for three years while the candidate matriculates through an alternative teacher certification program. This certification is issued to the school district to allow the district to employ such candidates.
- **Transitional C Certificate**—similar to Transitional B except that the candidate is enrolled in a graduate-level alternative teacher certification program.

Some candidates may qualify for additional certification without meeting and completing all the requirements that must be met by first-time applicants. Candidates should check the exact requirements for additional certification that pertain to their certification.

► Testing Information

The NYSTCE program includes a number of tests to measure the candidate's understanding of liberal arts and science, theory and practice, and various content areas relevant to the candidate's certification. As criterion-referenced tests, the NYSTCEs are designed to measure the teacher candidate's skills as compared to an established standard, not to how well other candidates perform. The New York State Commissioner of Education establishes the passing score for each test based on recommendations of state teachers. Candidates may retake any test they do not pass.

The NYSTCE program includes the Liberal Arts and Sciences Test (LAST), the Elementary and Secondary Assessments of Teaching Skills—Written (ATS-W), and the Content Specialty Tests (CSTs). As mentioned previously, if you are seeking permanent certification, the program may also include the Assessment of Teaching Skills—Performance (ATS-P).

If you are a college student, it is recommended that you space out the tests over your college years so you can adequately prepare for each. This will also allow time to retake any tests you may not pass. For example, you may want to take the LAST in your sophomore or junior year, the CSTs in your junior or senior year, and the ATS-W in your senior year.

Following are brief descriptions of the LAST, ATS-W, CST, and ATS-P. More in-depth information appears in Chapters 4, 5, and 6 of this book.

The Liberal Arts and Sciences Test (LAST)
The LAST tests five subareas:

- Scientific, Mathematical, and Technological Processes
- Historical and Social Scientific Awareness
- Artistic Expression and the Humanities
- Communication and Research Skills
- Written Analysis and Expression

The test is made up of multiple-choice questions and a written assignment. Candidates will be asked to demonstrate conceptual and analytical skills, multicultural awareness, and critical thinking and communication skills. See Chapter 4 for information on the LAST.

The Elementary Assessment of Teaching Skills—Written (ATS-W) Examination and The Secondary Assessment of Teaching Skills—Written (ATS-W) Examination
The Elementary and Secondary Assessments of Teaching Skills aim to measure the candidate's professional and pedagogical knowledge. The Elementary Assessment covers the Early Childhood (birth through grade 2) and Childhood (grades 1 through 6) levels. The Secondary Assessment covers knowledge at the Middle Childhood (grades 5 through 9) and Adolescence (grades 7 through 12) levels. These tests are made up of multiple-choice questions and a written assignment. See Chapter 5 for more information on these tests.

The Content Specialty Tests (CSTs)

The CSTs test knowledge and skills in the candidate's chosen content area of certification. They are composed of multiple-choice questions and written assignments. Several tests also include recorded listening and speaking components. See Chapter 6 for information on this group of tests.

The Assessment of Teaching Skills—Performance (ATS-P)

Remember, the ATS-P is only required for teachers with provisional certification seeking permanent certification in PreK–6, secondary academic titles in grades 7 through 12, and English Speakers of Other Languages with effective dates between September 2, 1993 and February 1, 2004. Candidates issued an initial certificate on or after February 2, 2004 do not have to take the ATS-P.

The ATS-P consists of a 20- to 30-minute video-recorded sample of a candidate teaching in an actual classroom setting. It is recommended you tape yourself one or two years after you have been teaching. See Chapter 6 for more information on the ATS-P.

► Other Important Information

Fingerprinting

All teacher candidates who apply for certification must also be cleared by a criminal history background check. This check, cleared through the New York State Education Department, includes fingerprinting. This background check applies to all prospective employees of public school districts, boards of cooperative educational services (BOCES), and charter schools. For candidates cleared by the New York City Board of Education after July 1, 1990, clearance to the Education Department is satisfied.

Complete information and all necessary forms can be downloaded at the Office of School Personnel Review and Accountability website. If you do not have Internet access or cannot print out the forms, fingerprint cards are available at several locations:

- your local school district, BOCES, or charter school
- colleges with teacher preparation programs
- or by sending a request to the Office of School Personnel Review and Accountability (OSPRA) at:

Fingerprint Processing
NYS Education Department
P.O. Box 7352
Albany, NY 12224

Fingerprint packets consist of fingerprint information and instructions and two fingerprint cards. There is a $99 processing fee.

Office of School Personnel Review and Accountability:
www.highered.nysed.gov/tcert/ospra/index.html

Maintaining Certification

Teachers with professional certification must complete 175 hours of acceptable professional development every five years. It is recommended the teacher check with the school district in which he or she is teaching to verify the acceptability of all professional development activities before attending. These hours must be documented and kept on file for at least seven years. Keep track of:

- the program title
- the number of hours accrued
- the name of the provider
- verification of your attendance
- the date and location of the event

If you work in a public school district, the school will report your professional development hours to the state. If you do not work in a public school, you are responsible for reporting.

▶ Useful Resources

For complete information on teaching certification, visit the New York State Education Division, Office of Higher Education website at www.highered.nysed.gov/tcert/certificate/index.html.

To apply for certification, check the status of your application, verify or change your personal profile or professional development record, apply for fingerprint clearance or view your certification records, go to TEACH Online Services at www.highered.nysed.gov/tcert/teach/index.html. (TEACH is an online database system.)

For complete information on certification testing requirements, visit the New York State Teacher Certification Examinations website at www.nystce.nesinc.com. On this site, you will also be able to obtain test-preparation materials, register online, and retrieve unofficial scores.

4 ▶ The LAST

CHAPTER SUMMARY

All of the NYSTCE is designed to ensure that you are prepared with the skills and knowledge you will need to be a successful and effective teacher at the subject and grade level for which you are seeking certification. This chapter will familiarize you with the NYSTCE that tests your knowledge and understanding of the liberal arts and sciences. In this chapter, you will learn all about the Liberal Arts and Sciences Test (LAST): what it consists of, how to go about registering and preparing for it, and how the test is scored. This chapter includes a complete listing of the five subareas of the test, their associated objectives, and focus statements about each. Multiple-choice and writing components of the test are explained.

▶ Test Description

The LAST assesses knowledge and skills in five different sections, referred to as *subareas.* Each subarea is broken down into several objectives, which provide more detail about the knowledge and skills the LAST will assess. Finally, each objective contains examples of content through focus statements. The following subareas, objectives, and focus statements are also available online at www.nystce.nesinc.com.

Subarea I. Scientific, Mathematical, and Technological Processes

Objective 1: Use mathematical reasoning in problem-solving situations to arrive at logical conclusions and to analyze the problem-solving process. Examples include analyzing problem solutions and missing components, determining what the next step might be in a problem, and evaluating the logic in claims based on probability or statistics.

Objective 2: Understand connections between mathematical representations and ideas; use mathematical terms and representations to organize, interpret, and communicate information. Examples include interpreting data from graphs, diagrams, and equations; using multiple representations to relay information; and understanding the use of tables and graphs in forms such as newspapers.

Objective 3: Apply knowledge of numerical, geometric, and algebraic relationships in problem-solving and mathematical contexts. Examples include using numbers in equivalent forms, such as fractions, decimals, and integers; applying algorithms; using ratios; using scales and geometric formulas; and using algebraic formulas and equations.

Objective 4: Understand major concepts, principles, and theories in science and technology; use that understanding to analyze phenomena in the natural world and to interpret information presented in illustrated or written form. Examples include representing scientific theory in graphic form, relating scientific principles to natural phenomena, using design processes, applying technological skills to evaluate how systems meet environmental needs, and analyzing recent scientific discoveries in relation to scientific principles.

Objective 5: Understand the historical development and cultural contexts of mathematics, science, and technology; the relationships and common themes that connect mathematics, science, and technology; and the impact of mathematics, science, and technology on human societies. Examples include analyzing the effects of science and technology as related to our history, society, and the environment; knowing how mathematical models are used to comprehend environmental, scientific, and social phenomena; and analyzing how scientific knowledge affects our lives.

Objective 6: Understand and apply skills, principles, and procedures associated with inquiry and problem solving in the sciences. Examples include using nonquantitative methods, such as case studies, to examine a problem; forming research questions; inferring scientific principles that contribute to scientific developments; showing familiarity with databases and spreadsheets; and understanding scientific inquiry and the components of experimental design.

Subarea II. Historical and Social Scientific Awareness

Objective 7: Understand the interrelatedness of historical, geographic, cultural, economic, political, and social issues and factors. Examples include assessing ways human work and beliefs have affected our society, inferring aspects of group interactions, analyzing factors that influence the forming of values and attitudes, and assessing the implications of political views.

Objective 8: Understand principles and assumptions underlying historical or contemporary arguments, interpretations, explanations, or developments. Examples include recognizing assumptions that help to inform the positions of political parties, inferring political principles, analyzing the assumptions U.S. policies are based upon, and recognizing the ideas underlying interpretations of past events.

Objective 9: Understand different perspectives and priorities underlying historical or contemporary arguments, interpretations, explanations, or developments. Examples include analyzing opinions of participants from various cultures regarding a world event, recognizing the implicit priorities related to given public policy positions, determining multiple perspectives within the United States regarding contemporary and historical issues, and recognizing the motives that inform various points of view.

Objective 10: Understand and apply skills, principles, and procedures associated with inquiry, problem solving, and decision making in history and the social sciences. Examples include assessing sources of information and determining whether conclusions are supported by evidence, analyzing research results to identify potential problems with the methodological approach used, determining the relevance of information for supporting or not supporting a point of view, and evaluating appropriate uses of specific sources to meet informational needs.

Objective 11: Understand and interpret visual representations of historical and social scientific information. Examples include relating graphic representations to public policy decisions; translating graphic and written information; interpreting social or historical scientific information provided in multiple charts, graphs, diagrams, or maps; and inferring important information based on visual forms.

Subarea III. Artistic Expression and the Humanities

Objective 12: Understand and analyze elements of form and content in works from the visual and performing arts from different periods and cultures. Examples include identifying the elements of repetition of shapes, focal point, motif, perspective, rhythm, and symmetry; determining how balance is achieved in the visual or performing arts; identifying the mood, theme, or tone of a piece; and determining how elements affect audience perceptions of a work of art.

Objective 13: Analyze and interpret works from the visual and performing arts representing different periods and cultures and understand the relationship of works of art to their social and historical contexts. Examples include comparing and contrasting modes, themes, and techniques; identifying art from various movements and time periods; and understanding art as a way to communicate concepts and expressions.

Objective 14: Understand forms and themes used in literature from different periods and cultures. Examples include identifying various genres of fiction and nonfiction; distinguishing the theme in a passage; understanding the meaning behind figurative language; and recognizing how imagery, allegory, metaphor, and other literary elements are used to interpret a passage.

Objective 15: Analyze and interpret literature from different periods and cultures and understand the relationship of works of literature to their social and historical contexts. Examples include analyzing how parts of a passage contribute to the whole; comparing and contrasting the mood of multiple passages; distinguishing features of various literary periods, features, and traditions; and recognizing how text communicates various levels of meaning.

Objective 16: Analyze and interpret examples of religious or philosophical ideas from various periods of time and understand their significance in shaping societies and cultures. Examples include identifying religious traditions in given world regions, recognizing beliefs underlying religious or philosophical writings, analyzing the societal implications of religious ideas, and comparing and contrasting concepts in multiple passages that reflect opposing traditions.

Subarea IV. Communication and Research Skills

Objective 17: Derive information from a variety of sources (e.g., magazine articles, essays, websites). Examples include recognizing the main idea and accurate summary or outline of a passage, organizing information from a website, understanding relationships in a passage, and recognizing information that is supportive of the main idea.

Objective 18: Analyze and interpret written materials from a variety of sources. Examples include identifying the writer's purpose, making conclusions based on information presented, interpreting figurative language, and comparing/contrasting views in multiple excerpts.

Objective 19: Use critical-reasoning skills to assess an author's treatment of content in written materials from a variety of sources. Examples include analyzing the structure of an argument and instances of faulty reasoning; interpreting word choice, content, and phrasing of a literary passage to determine purpose, point of view, and position; determining relevance of facts to a writer's argument; and distinguishing between what is fact and what is opinion in a passage.

Objective 20: Analyze and evaluate the effectiveness of expression in a written paragraph or passage according to the conventions of edited American English. Examples include revising written text to correct grammar, sentence construction, unity, coherence, and organization of text.

Objective 21: Demonstrate the ability to locate, retrieve, organize, and interpret information from a variety of traditional and electronic sources. Examples include demonstrating familiarity with encyclopedias, bibliographies, databases, and other reference tools; knowing differences between primary sources and secondary sources; forming research questions; knowing how to retrieve information from CD-ROMs, newspapers, and other resources; interpreting quantitative forms for representing data; creating coherent outlines to organize information; and determining reliability of information.

Subarea V. Written Analysis and Expression (constructed-response assignment)

Objective 22: Prepare an organized, developed composition in edited American English in response to instructions regarding audience, purpose, and content. Examples include expressing thoughts in various genres, such as stating an opinion, comparing and contrasting conflicting views, proposing a solution to a stated problem, and synthesizing information.

▶ The Test Format

The LAST consists of approximately 80 multiple-choice questions and one written constructed response. The number of test questions relates directly to the number of objectives within a subarea. The more objectives there are within a subarea, the more test questions appear in that subarea. For example, Subarea I makes up about 23% of the test; Subareas II, III, and IV, about 19% each; and Subarea V, about 20%.

Answer all the questions in the multiple-choice section of the LAST. It is better to guess than to leave an answer blank.

You must complete the written section of the LAST in order to pass. If you do not complete it or it is otherwise unscoreable, you will not pass. To be scoreable, the written assignment must:

- be related to the assigned topic
- be legible
- be written in the required language
- contain a sufficient amount of original work

Past test takers recommend that you should do the constructed response essay first while you are still fresh. Writing a complex essay after you have gone through 80 multiple-choice items can make the task more difficult. Complete all items. There is no penalty for getting a multiple-choice item incorrect, so even if you are not sure about an answer, eliminate the options you are most sure are not correct and make your best guess among the options that remain.

► Registering for the Test

You may register for the LAST online, by mail, or, only during the emergency registration period, by telephone. Check the testing schedule well in advance before registering by going to the NYSTCE website at www.nystce.nesinc.com. There are different registration fees depending on whether you meet the regular registration date, the late date, or the emergency date. To register online, go to the NYSTCE website and click on "Register Now." Payment must be made by credit, debit, or check card. To register by mail, use the registration form found in the *NYSTCE Registration Bulletin* or order the form online at the NYSTCE website. Mail the completed form—with your check, cashier's check, or money order—to the address on the form. If you are one of those wait-until-the-last-minute people, there is a third option of registering by telephone. There is an additional fee for this option, and due to space, staff, and time constraints, your request may not even be available. Telephone registration, allowed only during the emergency registration dates that immediately precede the test session, is available by calling 413-256-2882.

Before you register, visit the NYSTCE website to familiarize yourself with the registration process and to select a test date and site. Then, gather the information you will need:

- payment information (i.e., credit card number)
- personal information (i.e., Social Security number)
- your institution's code
- the test date and area you prefer

While alternative testing arrangements are available, the candidate must complete additional documentation ahead of time to request this option.

After your registration has been processed, you will receive confirmation in the form of an admission ticket that you must bring with you the day of the test. Check the information on the ticket for accuracy. If any information is wrong, call 413-256-2882 right away. Keep a copy of this admission ticket for your personal file because it contains the identification number that you will need to access your test score.

For More Information

Official site of the NYSTCE test developer: www.nystce.nesinc.com
Telephone registration number (allowed only during the emergency registration dates): 413-256-2882

▶ The Test Sites

Following is a list of test sites; however, not all sites are used for each test date. You should check the NYSTCE website to find out which dates the LAST is given at each site. The sites include:

- Albany
- Binghamton
- Buffalo
- Cortland
- Geneseo
- Hackensack, NJ
- Long Island (Nassau and Suffolk Counties)
- New Paltz
- Niagara
- New York City (The Bronx, Brooklyn, Manhattan, Queens, and Staten Island)
- Plattsburgh
- Potsdam
- Rochester
- Syracuse
- Toronto, Ontario
- Westchester County
- Puerto Rico

What to Bring on Test Day

Be sure to bring the following to the test:

- your admission ticket
- three or four sharpened no. 2 pencils with erasers
- official identification that contains a recent photograph of you
- another form of identification (does not have to contain a photograph)

What *Not* to Bring on Test Day

Smoking, visitors, and weapons are not allowed. Also, these items are prohibited:

- cell phones and other electronic devices, such as PDAs, computers, spell-checkers, and calculator watches
- packages and totes, such as backpacks
- written materials, such as books
- food or drinks

▶ Test Fees

The registration fee for the LAST is $88. Additional fees will be charged above and beyond this base fee in these situations:

Late Registration	$30
Emergency Registration	$70
Out-of-State Testing	$70

There are also fees for changing your registration date or location ($20), obtaining additional copies of your test results ($15 for each additional report), and rescoring of the test ($30). You will also be charged if your credit card or check payment does not clear ($20).

▶ The Test Schedule

The LAST is administered only during the morning session, from 7:45 A.M. to 12:30 P.M. Test dates are available on the NYSTCE website.

You will be given four hours to complete the LAST. You will be in control of the amount of time you spend on each section and the order in which you complete the sections of the test. But, at the end of the four hours, you will be required to turn in your materials no matter what. It may take you less than four hours to complete, but arrange your schedule to dedicate the full four hours to the test that day. You shouldn't make any other commitments during those four hours.

It is recommended that as you go through the test questions, you should skip ones that you do not know the answer to right away. Do not spend time trying to figure out answers. Move on. However, be sure that when you do skip a question on the question sheet, you also skip that question's corresponding row of answer choices on the answer sheet. Circle or otherwise identify the questions you skip on the test booklet so you can easily return to them the second time through.

▶ Scoring Information

Your LAST score is a cumulative score representing all subareas of the test, including all multiple-choice questions and the constructed-response assignment. Your total score will fall between 100 and 300. A passing score for the LAST is any score of 220 or above.

5 ▶ The ATS-W

CHAPTER SUMMARY

All of the NYSTCE is designed to ensure that you are prepared with the skills and knowledge you will need to be a successful and effective teacher at the subject and grade level for which you are seeking certification. This chapter will familiarize you with the NYSTCE that tests your pedagogical knowledge and skills at the elementary or secondary level, depending on which certification you are working toward. In this chapter, you will learn all about two tests: the Elementary Assessment of Teaching Skills—Written (ATS-W) and the Secondary Assessment of Teaching Skills—Written (ATS-W). From here on, we will refer to them both as the ATS-W because everything about them is the same—registration, test structure, fees, and so on—except that one includes elementary content and the other secondary. In this chapter you will learn what they consist of, how to go about registering and preparing for them, and how the tests are scored. This chapter includes a complete listing of the four subareas of the tests, associated objectives, and focus statements. Multiple-choice and writing components of the tests are explained.

▶ Test Description

The ATS-W assesses knowledge and skills in four subareas. Each subarea is broken down into several objectives, which provide more detail about the knowledge and skills the ATS-W will assess. Finally, each objective contains examples of content through focus statements. The subareas, objectives, and focus statements are the same across both the elementary and secondary tests. The following subareas, objectives, and focus statements are also available online at www.nystce.nesinc.com.

Subarea 1. Student Development and Learning

Objective 1: Understand human development, including developmental processes and variations, and use this understanding to promote student development and learning. Examples include knowledge of the major theories of human development from birth to grade 6; recognizing how a child's development in one domain affects learning in other domains; identifying milestones of physical, linguistic, emotional, and moral development; applying understanding of development to evaluate instructional goals; and selecting instructional approaches to promote development.

Objective 2: Understand learning processes and use this understanding to promote student development and learning. Examples include analyzing the interaction between development and learning and the processes students use to construct meaning; demonstrating an understanding of various types of learning strategies and how learners use them; analyzing factors that influence learning and adapting instruction to promote learning; recognizing how a teacher's and students' roles affect learning; recognizing strategies for promoting learning and students' ownership in relation to their learning.

Objective 3: Understand how factors in the home, school, and community may affect students' development and readiness to learn; use this understanding to create a classroom environment within which all students can develop and learn. Examples include recognizing the impact of sociocultural factors and how students' health and safety may affect learning; recognizing the significance of the home environment; analyzing how structures in the school, such as tracking, may affect students' self-concept and learning; identifying strategies for promoting student learning by taking advantage of positive factors in the home, school, and community; analyzing ways that peer interactions promote or hinder a student's success in school; demonstrating knowledge of peer-related issues for students and the interrelated nature of these issues; and recognizing how behaviors related to peer issues can affect development and learning.

Objective 4: Understand language and literacy development and use this knowledge in all content areas to develop the listening, speaking, reading, and writing skills of students, including students for whom English is not their primary language. Examples include identifying factors that influence language acquisition; identifying stages of second-language acquisition; identifying approaches in promoting English Language Learners' development of English language proficiency; recognizing the role of oral language development, vocabulary development, the alphabetic principle, phonemic awareness, and phonological skills in the development of literacy; understanding evidence-based instructional strategies; recognizing similarities and differences between literacy development of native English speakers and English Language Learners; and selecting instructional strategies that promote students' uses of literacy skills as learning tools.

Objective 5: Understand diverse student populations and use knowledge of diversity within the school and the community to address the needs of all learners, to create a sense of community among students, and to promote students' appreciation of and respect for individuals and groups. Examples include demonstrating knowledge of how to promote a sense of community among groups in the classroom; recognizing strategies for working with diverse student populations; promoting students' understanding and appreciation of diversity to enhance learning; and recognizing that classroom environments that respect diversity promote learning.

Objective 6: Understand the characteristics and needs of students with disabilities, developmental delays, and exceptional abilities (including gifted and talented students); use this knowledge to help students reach their highest levels of achievement and independence. Examples include demonstrating knowledge of types of disabilities, exceptional abilities, and developmental delays; evaluating, selecting, creating, and modifying materials to address needs; identifying teacher requirements associated with referring students with special needs and working with Individualized Education Plans (IEPs); and demonstrating an understanding of service delivery models and strategies to ensure all students participate in all classroom activities.

Subarea II. Instruction and Assessment

Objective 7: Understand how to structure and manage a classroom to create a safe, healthy, and secure learning environment. Examples include analyzing relationships between student learning and classroom management; demonstrating understanding of socialization strategies; organizing a daily schedule that capitalizes on developmental characteristics of learners; evaluating and managing transitions; and analyzing the effects of spatial arrangements on student learning and behavior.

Objective 8: Understand curriculum development and apply knowledge of factors and processes in curricular decision making. Examples include demonstrating knowledge of classroom curricular decision making; evaluating curriculum resources for their effectiveness in addressing the needs of students; modifying curricula based on learner characteristics; and integrating curricula.

Objective 9: Understand the interrelationship between assessment and instruction and how to use formal and informal assessment to learn about students, plan instruction, monitor student understanding in the context of instruction, and make effective instructional modifications. Examples include understanding the integration of assessment and instruction; demonstrating knowledge of basic assessment approaches; showing knowledge of various purposes for assessments; knowing how to use and interpret rubrics; and recognizing strategies for creating and modifying lessons based on assessment results.

Objective 10: Understand instructional planning and apply knowledge of planning processes to design effective instruction that promotes the learning of all students. Examples include recognizing factors to consider in planning instruction; applying information about specific planning factors to define lesson objectives, select instructional approaches, and develop specific lesson plans; using assessment before, during, and after instruction; identifying the prior knowledge required by a student for a given lesson; analyzing a lesson in terms of organization and feasibility; and collaborating to implement instruction.

Objective 11: Understand various instructional approaches and use this knowledge to facilitate student learning. Examples include analyzing how specific instructional approaches relate to learners; recognizing strategies for varying the teacher's role as related to the instructional approach used; promoting productive small-group interactions; and comparing instructional approaches according to student outcomes.

Objective 12: Understand principles and procedures for organizing and implementing lessons and use this knowledge to promote student learning and achievement. Examples include evaluating various strategies for organizing and implementing a lesson; organizing instruction to include multiple strategies for teaching content; evaluating instructional materials; and adjusting lessons in response to student performance and feedback.

Objective 13: Understand the relationship between student motivation and achievement and how motivational principles and practices can be used to promote and sustain student cooperation in learning. Examples include comparing motivational strategies; analyzing effects of intrinsic and extrinsic motivational strategies; recognizing factors that promote or hinder student motivation; recognizing direct engagement in learning; enhancing student interest; using play to benefit learning; and recognizing the importance of encouragement and peer relationships in sustaining students' interest.

Objective 14: Understand communication practices that are effective in promoting student learning and creating a climate of trust and support in the classroom and how to use a variety of communication modes to support instruction. Examples include analyzing how classroom communication is influenced by factors such as culture, gender, and age; analyzing teacher–student interactions, purposes for questioning, and how communication may be adjusted to enhance student learning.

Objective 15: Understand uses of technology, including instructional and assistive technology, in teaching and learning; apply this knowledge to use technology effectively and to teach students how to use technology to enhance their learning. Examples include demonstrating an understanding of how to effectively use technology and assistive technology in the classroom; recognizing issues pertaining to the use of technology in the classroom, such as privacy and security; addressing equity issues related to technology; and evaluating technologically produced products.

Subarea III. The Professional Environment

Objective 16: Understand the history, philosophy, and role of education in New York State and the broader society. Examples include analyzing relationships between society and education; understanding the historical foundations of education in the United States; working collaboratively and cooperatively with colleagues; comparing centralized models and school-based decision making; and demonstrating knowledge of the roles of the components of the New York State education system.

Objective 17: Understand how to reflect productively on one's own teaching practice and how to update one's professional knowledge, skills, and effectiveness. Examples include reflecting on one's teaching strengths and weaknesses; working effectively with colleagues to increase one's skills or understanding; and knowing how to respond to feedback from others.

Objective 18: Understand the importance of and apply strategies for promoting productive relationships and interactions among the school, home, and community to enhance student learning. Examples include initiating and maintaining effective communication among colleagues and families; using a variety of strategies to work with families to reinforce learning; and using community resources to enhance learning.

Objective 19: Understand reciprocal rights and responsibilities in situations involving interactions between teachers and students, parents/guardians, community members, colleagues, school administrators, and other school personnel. Examples include understanding laws related to students' rights; knowing a teacher's rights and responsibilities in certain situations; knowing the family's rights and responsibilities in certain situations; and understanding the appropriateness of a teacher's response to a family, especially when dealing with a difference in opinion.

Subarea IV. Instruction and Assessment: Constructed-Response Item

The content addressed by the writing assignment comes from Subarea II, Objectives 7 through 15.

▶ The Test Format

The ATS-W consists of approximately 80 multiple-choice questions and one written constructed response. The number of test questions relates directly to the number of objectives within a subarea. The more objectives there are within a subarea, the more test questions appear in that subarea. For example, Subarea I makes up about 25% of the test; Subarea II, about 38%; Subarea III, about 17%; and Subarea IV, about 20%.

Answer all the questions in the multiple-choice section of the ATS-W. It is better to guess than to leave an answer blank.

You must complete the written section of the ATS-W in order to pass. If you do not complete it or it is otherwise unscoreable, you will not pass. To be scoreable, the written assignment must:

- be related to the assigned topic
- be legible
- be in the required language
- contain a sufficient amount of original work

Past test takers recommend that you should do the constructed-response essay first while you are still fresh. Writing a complex essay after you have gone through 80 multiple-choice items can make the task more difficult. Complete all items. There is no penalty for getting a multiple-choice item incorrect, so even if you are not sure about an answer, eliminate the options you are most sure are not correct and make your best guess among the options that remain.

▶ Registering for the Test

You may register for the ATS-W online, by mail, or, only during the emergency registration period, by telephone. Check the testing schedule well in advance before registering by going to the NYSTCE website at www.nystce.nesinc.com. There are different registration fees depending on whether you meet the regular registration date, the late date, or the emergency date. To register online, go to the NYSTCE website and click on "Register Now." Payment must be made by credit, debit, or check card. To register by mail, use the registration form found in the *NYSTCE Registration Bulletin* or order the form online at the NYSTCE website. Mail the completed form—with your check, cashier's check, or money order—to the address on the form. If you are one of those wait-until-the-last-minute people, there is a third option of registering by telephone. There is an additional fee for this option, and due to space, staff, and time constraints, your request may not even be available. Telephone registration, allowed only during the emergency registration dates that immediately precede the test session, is available by calling 413-256-2882.

Before you register, visit the NYSTCE website to familiarize yourself with the registration process and to select a test date and site. Then, gather the information you will need:

- payment information (i.e., credit card number)
- personal information (i.e., Social Security number)
- your institution's code
- the test date and area you prefer

While alternative testing arrangements are available, the candidate must complete additional documentation ahead of time to request this option.

After your registration has been processed, you will receive confirmation in the form of an admission ticket that you must bring with you the day of the test. Check the information on the ticket for accuracy. If any information is wrong, call 413-256-2882 right away. Keep a copy of this admission ticket for your personal file because it contains the identification number that you will need to access your test score.

For More Information

Official site of the NYSTCE test developer: www.nystce.nesinc.com
Telephone registration number (allowed only during the emergency registration dates): 413-256-2882

▶ The Test Sites

Following is a list of test sites; however, not all sites are used for each test date. You should check the NYSTCE website to find out which dates the ATS-W is given at each site. The sites include:

- Albany
- Binghamton
- Buffalo
- Cortland
- Geneseo
- Hackensack, NJ
- Long Island (Nassau and Suffolk Counties)
- New Paltz

- Niagara
- New York City (The Bronx, Brooklyn, Manhattan, Queens, and Staten Island)
- Plattsburgh
- Potsdam
- Rochester
- Syracuse
- Toronto, Ontario
- Westchester County
- Puerto Rico

What to Bring on Test Day

Be sure to bring the following to the test:

- your admission ticket
- three or four sharpened no. 2 pencils with erasers
- official identification that contains a recent photograph of you
- another form of identification (does not have to contain a photograph)

What *Not* to Bring on Test Day

Smoking, visitors, and weapons are not allowed. Also, these items are prohibited:

- cell phones and other electronic devices, such as PDAs, computers, spell-checkers, and calculator watches
- packages and totes, such as backpacks
- written materials, such as books
- food or drinks

▶ Test Fees

The registration fee for the ATS-W is $88. Additional fees will be charged above and beyond this base fee in these situations:

Late Registration	$30
Emergency Registration	$70
Out-of-State Testing	$70

There are also fees for changing your registration date or location ($20), obtaining additional copies of your test results ($15 for each additional report), and rescoring of the test ($30). You will also be charged if your credit card or check payment does not clear ($20).

▶ The Test Schedule

The ATS-W is administered only during the afternoon session, from 1:00 P.M. to 5:45 P.M. Test dates are available on the NYSTCE website.

You will be given four hours to complete the ATS-W. You will be in control of the amount of time you spend on each section and the order in which you complete the sections of the test. But, at the end of the four hours, you will be required to turn in your materials no matter what. It may take you less than four hours to complete, but arrange your schedule to dedicate the full four hours to the test that day. You shouldn't make any other commitments during those four hours.

It is recommended that as you go through the test questions, you should skip ones that you do not know the answer to right away. Do not spend time trying to figure out answers. Move on. However, be sure that when you do skip a question on the question sheet, you also skip that question's corresponding row of answer choices on the answer sheet. Circle or otherwise identify the questions you skip on the test booklet so you can easily return to them the second time through.

▶ Scoring Information

Your ATS-W score is a cumulative score representing all subareas of the test, including all multiple-choice questions and the constructed-response assignment. Your total score will fall between 100 and 300. The passing score for the ATS-W is any score of 220 or above.

6▶ The CST and ATS-P

CHAPTER SUMMARY

All of the NYSTCE are designed to ensure that you are prepared with the skills and knowledge you will need to be a successful and effective teacher at the subject and grade level for which you are seeking certification. This chapter will familiarize you with the group of Content Specialty Tests (CSTs) and the Assessment of Teaching Skills—Performance (ATS-P) video. In this chapter, you will learn who must take these tests, what they consist of, how to go about registering and preparing for them, and how the tests are scored.

For More Information

Information about these tests has been accessed from the NYSTCE Test Frameworks, available online at www.nystce.nesinc.com/index.asp, and the NYSTCE Preparation Guides, available at www.nystce.nesinc.com/NY_viewSG_opener.asp.

▶ Who Must Take the CST and ATS-P?

If you received provisional certification effective before February 2, 2004 in the areas of PreK–6, secondary academic titles for grades 7–12, or English to Speakers of Other Languages, you must pass the CST in the content area of the certification and the ATS-P to obtain permanent certification. If you are applying for initial certification, effective after February 2, 2004, you will not need to take the ATS-P. See descriptions of provisional, permanent, initial, and professional certifications in Chapter 3.

▶ Which CST Do I Take?

There are 29 content-specific tests. How do you know which one is the right one for you? To determine which CST is required to achieve the certification you desire, it is recommended that you first visit the Search Certification Requirements website. After submitting the requested information (the subject, grade, certificate title, and certificate type), this tool will list all the tests, including the specific CST you will need to pass for certification. Once you know which CST is right for you, go to the NYSTCE website to download the appropriate NYSTCE Test Framework and Preparation Guide in your content area. These resources provide in-depth information about each CST.

Each CST assesses knowledge and skills in several subareas. Each subarea is broken down into several objectives, which provide more detail about the knowledge and skills that particular CST will assess. Finally, each objective contains examples of content through focus statements. The subareas, objectives, and focus statements are different across each CST.

▶ Test Descriptions

The CSTs measure content area knowledge and skills in the candidate's field of certification. Each CST is typically made up of 70 to 90 multiple-choice selected-response questions and one or two constructed-response writing assignments. There are several exceptions, however. Several tests—the group of Modern Languages Other than English and the Music CSTs—have taped listening and speaking components along with a writing task. The American Sign Language CST includes a proficiency component in which candidates view a video of American Sign Language and then respond to a set of questions. For this test, candidates also will respond in American Sign Language in the isolation of an individual testing room.

The content areas, test field number, and subareas assessed in each field follow. To obtain a list of objectives tested in each subarea, as mentioned previously, download the appropriate NYSTCE Test Framework available online at the official website.

For More Information

Official NYSTCE website: www.nystce.nesinc.com
Search Certification Requirements website:
http://eservices.nysed.gov/teach/certhelp/CertRequirementHelp.do#cfocus

Agriculture (068)—agricultural education and career development; plant science; animal science; agricultural business management, economics, and marketing; agricultural mechanics and technology; agriculture and the environment; and a constructed response on agricultural education and career development

American Sign Language (061)—receptive comprehension, linguistics of American Sign Language, deaf culture, and a productive proficiency

Biology (006)—foundations of scientific inquiry, cell biology and biochemistry, genetics and evolution, biological unity and diversity and life processes, human biology, ecology, and a constructed response on foundations of scientific inquiry

Blind and Visually Impaired (062)—understanding blindness and visual impairments, assessing students and developing individualized education programs, promoting student development and learning, promoting students' communication and literacy skills, professional practice, and a constructed response on promoting students' communication and literacy skills

Business and Marketing (069)—business management; marketing; accounting; business technology and information systems; economics, entrepreneurship, and international business; quantitative analysis, consumer economics, and career development; and a constructed response on business management

Chemistry (007)—foundations of scientific inquiry; matter and atomic structure; energy, chemical bonds, and molecular structure; chemical reactions; stoichiometry and solutions; interactions of chemistry and the environment; and a constructed response on foundations of scientific inquiry

Dance (070)—dance elements and skills; creating and performing dance; anatomy, health, and dance in everyday life; dance and culture; and a constructed response on responding to and analyzing dance

Deaf and Hard of Hearing (063)—understanding students who are deaf and hard of hearing, assessing students and developing individualized education programs, promoting student development and learning, working in the professional environment, and a constructed response on promoting student development and learning

Earth Science (008)—foundations of scientific inquiry, space systems, atmospheric systems, geological systems, water systems, and a constructed response on geological systems

Educational Technology Specialist (071)—foundations of educational computing and technology, professional applications of technology, integrating technology into education, technology leadership and resource management, and a constructed response on integrating technology into education

English (003)—listening and speaking, writing, reading, fundamentals of literature, language and literature (a section on language and another on the history of literature), and a constructed response on fundamentals of literature

English to Speakers of Other Languages (ESOL) (022)—foundations of ESOL instruction, developing English language proficiency across the curriculum, the ESOL program, and a constructed response on developing English language proficiency across the curriculum

Family and Consumer Sciences (072)—individual and family health and wellness; human development and parenting; interpersonal and family relationships; nutrition, food science, and food production; consumer skills and resource management; workplace skills and careers; and a constructed response on human development and parenting

Gifted Education (064)—understanding students with gifts and talents, assessment and evaluation of students with gifts and talents, promoting student development and learning, working in the professional environment, and a constructed response on promoting student development and learning

Health Education (073)—personal health and fitness, maintaining a safe and healthy environment, health-related resources and skills, the health education program, and a constructed response on health-related resources and skills

Latin (010)—reading comprehension and appreciation, language structures, cultural understanding, and two constructed responses: writing and oral reading

Library Media Specialist (074)—the library media program, library media resources, information literacy skills, program administration and leadership, and a constructed response on information literacy skills

Literacy (065)—foundations of literacy, reading instruction and assessment, the role of the literacy professional, and a constructed response on reading instruction and assessment

Mathematics (004)—mathematical reasoning and communication; algebra; trigonometry and calculus; measurement and geometry; data analysis, probability, statistics, and discrete mathematics; and a constructed response on algebra

Modern Languages Other Than English—Using a somewhat different format, the Modern Languages Other Than English CSTs have taped listening and speaking components along with a writing task.

Cantonese (011), Greek (014), Hebrew (015), Japanese (017), Mandarin (018), and Russian (019) subareas—a constructed response on each of the following: listening comprehension, reading comprehension, language structures, cultural understanding, written expression, and oral expression

French (012), German (013), Italian (016), and Spanish (020) subareas—multiple-choice selected responses on listening comprehension, reading comprehension, language structures, and cultural understanding, and two constructed responses: written expression and oral expression

Multi-Subject (002)—English language arts, mathematics, science and technology, social studies, the fine arts, health and fitness, family and consumer science and career development, and a constructed response on the foundations of reading

Music (075)—music theory, music performance, listening skills, music history and culture, and a constructed response on music history and culture. The music CST has taped listening and speaking components along with a writing task.

Physical Education (076)—physical fitness and health, lifelong movement activities and sports, personal growth and development, the physical education program, and a constructed response on physical fitness and health

Physics (009)—foundations of scientific inquiry; mechanics and thermodynamics; electricity and magnetism; waves, sound, and light; Quantum Theory and the atom; and a constructed response on foundations of scientific inquiry

Social Studies (005)—history; geography; economics; civics, citizenship, and government; social studies skills; and a constructed response on history

Students with Disabilities (060)—understanding and evaluating students with disabilities, promoting student learning and development in a collaborative learning community, working in a collaborative professional environment, and a constructed response on promoting student learning and development in a collaborative learning community

Technology Education (077)—fundamentals of technology, communication systems, power and energy systems, manufacturing and construction systems, transportation systems, bio-related systems, and a constructed response on fundamentals of technology

Theatre (078)—creating, performing, and producing theatre; theatre tools, media, and techniques; theatre and culture; responding to and analyzing theatre; and a constructed response on theatre tools, media, and techniques

Visual Arts (079)—visual arts materials and processes, principles and elements of art and design, visual arts and culture, aesthetic and interdisciplinary connections, and a constructed response on visual arts and culture

► Registering for the CST

You may register for the CST online, by mail, or, only during the emergency registration period, by telephone. Check the testing schedule well in advance before registering by going to the NYSTCE website at www.nystce.nesinc.com. There are different registration fees depending on whether you meet the regular registration date, the late date, or the emergency date. To register online, go to the NYSTCE website and click on "Register Now." Payment must be made by credit, debit, or check card. To register by mail, use the registration form found in the *NYSTCE Registration Bulletin* or order the form online at the NYSTCE website. Mail the completed form—with your check, cashier's check, or money order—to the address on the form. If you are one of those wait-until-the-last-minute people, there is a third option of registering by telephone. There is an additional fee for this option, and due to space, staff, and time constraints, your request may not even be available. Telephone registration, allowed only during the emergency registration dates that immediately precede the test session, is available by calling 413-256-2882.

Before you register, visit the NYSTCE website to familiarize yourself with the registration process and to select a test date and site. Then, gather the information you will need:

- payment information (i.e., credit card number)
- personal information (i.e., Social Security number)
- your institution's code
- the test date and area you prefer

While alternative testing arrangements are available, the candidate must complete additional documentation ahead of time to request this option.

After your registration has been processed, you will receive confirmation in the form of an admission ticket that you must bring with you the day of the test. Check the information on the ticket for accuracy. If any information is wrong, call 413-256-2882 right away. Keep a copy of this admission ticket for your personal file because it contains the identification number that you will need to access your test score.

▶ The Test Sites

Following is a list of test sites; however, not all sites are used for each test date. You should check the NYSTCE website to find out which dates the CST is given at each site. The sites include:

- Albany
- Binghamton
- Buffalo
- Cortland
- Geneseo
- Hackensack, NJ
- Long Island (Nassau and Suffolk Counties)
- New Paltz
- Niagara
- New York City (The Bronx, Brooklyn, Manhattan, Queens, and Staten Island)
- Plattsburgh
- Potsdam
- Rochester
- Syracuse
- Toronto, Ontario
- Westchester County
- Puerto Rico

What to Bring on Test Day

Be sure to bring the following to the test:

- your admission ticket
- three or four sharpened no. 2 pencils with erasers
- official identification that contains a recent photograph of you
- another form of identification (does not have to contain a photograph)

Also, for some CSTs you are allowed to bring a scientific calculator (chemistry and physics) or an approved graphing calculator (mathematics).

What *Not* to Bring on Test Day

Smoking, visitors, and weapons are not allowed. Also, these items are prohibited:

- cell phones and other electronic devices, such as PDAs, computers, spell-checkers, and calculator watches
- packages and totes, such as backpacks

- written materials, such as books
- food or drinks

▶ Test Fees

The registration fee for the CST is $88. Additional fees will be charged above and beyond this base fee in these situations:

Late Registration	$30
Emergency Registration	$70
Out-of-State Testing	$70

There are also fees for changing your registration date or location ($20), obtaining additional copies of your test results ($15 for each additional report), and rescoring of the test ($30). You will also be charged if your credit card or check payment does not clear ($20).

▶ The Test Schedule

The CST is administered either during the morning session, from 7:45 A.M. to 12:30 P.M., or the afternoon sessions, from 1:00 P.M. to 5:45 P.M. Test dates are available on the NYSTCE website.

You will be given four hours to complete the CST. You will be in control of the amount of time you spend on each section and the order in which you complete the sections of the test. But, at the end of the four hours, you will be required to turn in your materials no matter what. It may take you less than four hours to complete, but arrange your schedule to dedicate the full four hours to the test that day. You shouldn't make any other commitments during those four hours.

It is recommended that as you go through the test questions, you should skip ones that you do not know the answer to right away. Do not spend time trying to figure out answers. Move on. However, be sure that when you do skip a question on the question sheet, you also skip that question's corresponding row of answer choices on the answer sheet. Circle or otherwise identify the questions you skip on the test booklet so you can easily return to them the second time through.

▶ Scoring Information

Your CST score is a cumulative score representing all subareas of the test, including all multiple-choice questions and the constructed-response assignment. Your total score will fall between 100 and 300. The passing score for the CST is any score of 220 or above.

► The ATS-P

The ATS-P consists of a 20- to 30-minute video-recorded sample of a candidate teaching in an actual classroom setting. It is recommended that you tape yourself one or two years after you have begun teaching. You can find the objectives for the ATS-P online in *NYSTCE Assessment of Teaching Skills—Performance Information Guide for 2006–2007*, which can be accessed at www.nystce.nesinc.com/NY_infoguide_opener.asp.

It is important that the 20- to 30-minute video depict a complete lesson with a beginning and an ending, involve regularly scheduled students, include direct instruction as well as non–whole-group instruction, and clearly show yourself speaking and teaching. Along with the videotape, you should complete and submit a *Context of Instruction Form* and a *Candidate Identification Form*. You will receive these forms upon registering for the ATS-P.

► Registering for the ATS-P

ATS-P registration is unlike any of the other NYSTCE. You do not register to take the test on a certain day at a certain location. Instead, you register either online or via mail only (telephone registration is not an option), complete the video and forms on your own, and then send the video in for scoring. See the *Registering for the CST* section in this chapter for specific information on how to register online and by mail.

The schedule for the ATS-P is based on set deadlines for submission. You should check the deadline schedule online at the official NYSTCE website for dates that fit your needs.

Soon after registering, you will receive a packet of information in the mail. This packet will include a manual that describes all the procedures and includes all the forms you will need. Read this manual very carefully, as it contains all the information you will need to successfully complete the ATS-P. Submissions that do not follow the guidelines in the manual will be rated "Requirements Not Met." There are no refunds issued if this happens. You will just need to register and try again.

► Test Fee for the ATS-P

The registration fee for the ATS-P is $145.

► Scoring the ATS-P

The videos are scored holistically based on the five objectives previously listed. Videos will be scored as:

- "Pass" if teaching performance reflects satisfactory skills
- "Not Pass" if teaching performance does not reflect the teaching skills described in the objectives
- "Requirements Not Met" if teaching performance does not provide sufficient evidence to judge the candidate's skills. This rating may be given if, for example, the video is faulty or the procedures from the manual were not followed.

7 ▶ The LearningExpress Test Preparation System

CHAPTER SUMMARY

Taking the NYSTCE can be tough. It demands a lot of preparation if you want to achieve top scores. Your future depends on your passing the exams. The LearningExpress Test Preparation System, developed exclusively for LearningExpress by leading test experts, gives you the discipline and attitude you need to be successful.

Fact: taking the New York State Teacher Certification Exams is not easy, and neither is getting ready for them. Your future career as a teacher depends on your getting passing scores, but there are all sorts of pitfalls that can keep you from doing your best on your exams. Here are some of the obstacles that can stand in the way of your success:

- being unfamiliar with the format of the exams
- being paralyzed by test anxiety
- leaving your preparation to the last minute
- not preparing at all!
- not knowing vital test-taking skills: how to pace yourself through the exams, how to use the process of elimination, and when to guess
- not being in tip-top mental and physical shape
- messing up on test day by arriving late at the test site, having to work on an empty stomach, or shivering through the exam because the room is cold

What's the common denominator in all these test-taking pitfalls? One word: control. Who's in control, you or the exam?

Here's some good news: The LearningExpress Test Preparation System puts you in control. In nine easy-to-follow steps, you will learn everything you need to know to make sure that you are in charge of your preparation and your performance on the exams. Other test takers may let the test get the better of them; other test takers may be unprepared or out of shape, but not you. You will have taken all the steps you need to take to get high scores on the NYSTCE.

Here's how the LearningExpress Test Preparation System works: Nine easy steps lead you through everything you need to know and do to get ready to master your exams. Each of the steps includes both reading about the step and one or more activities. It's important that you do the activities along with the reading, or you won't be getting the full benefit of the system. Each step tells you approximately how much time that step will take you to complete.

Step 1: Get Information	50 minutes
Step 2: Conquer Test Anxiety	20 minutes
Step 3: Make a Plan	30 minutes
Step 4: Learn to Manage Your Time	10 minutes
Step 5: Learn to Use the Process of Elimination	20 minutes
Step 6: Know When to Guess	20 minutes
Step 7: Reach Your Peak Performance Zone	10 minutes
Step 8: Get Your Act Together	10 minutes
Step 9: Do It!	10 minutes
Total	**3 hours**

We estimate that working through the entire system will take you approximately three hours, though it's perfectly OK if you work faster or slower. If you take an afternoon or evening, you can work through the whole LearningExpress Test Preparation System in one sitting. Otherwise, you can break it up, and do just one or two steps a day for the next several days. It's up to you—remember, you are in control.

▶ Step 1: Get Information

Time to complete: 50 minutes
Activity: Read Chapters 4–6

Knowledge is power. The first step in the LearningExpress Test Preparation System is finding out everything you can about the tests that comprise the NYSTCE. Once you have your information, the next steps in the LearningExpress Test Preparation System will show you what to do about it.

Part A: Straight Talk about the NYSTCE

Why do you have to take these rigorous exams, anyway? It's simply an attempt to be sure you have the knowledge and skills necessary for a teacher.

It's important for you to remember that your scores on the NYSTCE do not determine how smart you are or even whether you will make a good teacher. There are all kinds of things exams like this can't test, like whether you have the drive, determination, and dedication to be a teacher. Those kinds of things are hard to evaluate, while tests are easy to evaluate.

This is not to say that the exams aren't important! The knowledge tested on the exams is knowledge you will need to do your job. And your ability to enter the profession you've trained for depends on your passing these exams. And that's why you are here—using the LearningExpress Test Preparation System to achieve control over the exams.

Part B: What's on the Test

If you haven't already done so, stop here and read Chapters 4–6 of this book, which give you an overview of the exams. Then, go to the official NYSTCE website, www.nystce.nesinc.com, and read the most up-to-date information about your exams directly from the test developers.

▶ Step 2: Conquer Test Anxiety

Time to complete: 20 minutes
Activity: Take the Test Anxiety Test

Having complete information about the exams is the first step in getting control of them. Next, you have to overcome one of the biggest obstacles to test success: test anxiety. Test anxiety not only impairs your performance on an exam, but also keeps you from preparing! In Step 2, you will learn stress management techniques that will help you succeed on your exams. Learn these strategies now, and practice them as you work through the exams in this book, so they will be second nature to you by exam day.

Combating Test Anxiety

The first thing you need to know is that a little test anxiety is a good thing. Everyone gets nervous before a big exam—and if that nervousness motivates you to prepare thoroughly, so much the better. It's said that Sir Laurence Olivier, one of the foremost British actors of the last century, felt ill before every performance. His stage fright didn't impair his performance; in fact, it probably gave him a little extra edge—just the kind of edge you need to do well, whether on a stage or in an examination room.

On page 48 is the Test Anxiety Test. Stop and answer the questions to find out whether your level of test anxiety is something you should worry about.

Test Anxiety Test

You only need to worry about test anxiety if it is extreme enough to impair your performance. The following questionnaire will provide a diagnosis of your level of test anxiety. In the blank before each statement, write the number that most accurately describes your experience.

0 = Never   1 = Once or twice   2 = Sometimes   3 = Often

_____ I have gotten so nervous before an exam that I simply put down the books and didn't study for it.

_____ I have experienced disabling physical symptoms such as vomiting and severe headaches because I was nervous about an exam.

_____ I have simply not shown up for an exam because I was scared to take it.

_____ I have experienced dizziness and disorientation while taking an exam.

_____ I have had trouble filling in the little circles because my hands were shaking too hard.

_____ I have failed an exam because I was too nervous to complete it.

_____ **Total: add up the numbers in the blanks above.**

Your Test Anxiety Score

Here are the steps you should take, depending on your score. If you scored:

Below 3, your level of test anxiety is nothing to worry about; it's probably just enough to give you that little extra edge.

Between 3 and 6, your test anxiety may be enough to impair your performance, and you should practice the stress management techniques listed in this section to try to bring your test anxiety down to manageable levels.

Above 6, your level of test anxiety is a serious concern. In addition to practicing the stress management techniques listed in this section, you may want to seek additional, personal help by contacting your academic counselor. Tell the counselor that you have a level of test anxiety that sometimes keeps you from being able to take the exam. The counselor may be willing to help you or may suggest someone else you should talk to.

Stress Management before the Test

If you feel your level of anxiety getting the best of you in the weeks before a test, here is what you need to do to bring the level down again:

- **Get prepared.** There's nothing like knowing what to expect and being prepared for it to put you in control of test anxiety. That's why you are reading this book. Use it faithfully, and remind yourself that you are better prepared than most of the people taking the test.

- **Practice self-confidence.** A positive attitude is a great way to combat test anxiety. This is no time to be humble or shy. Stand in front of the mirror and say to your reflection, "I am prepared. I am full of self-confidence. I am going to ace this test. I know I can do it." Say it into a tape recorder and play it back once a day. If you hear it often enough, you will believe it.

- **Fight negative messages**. Every time someone starts telling you how hard the exam is or how it's almost impossible to get a high score, start saying your self-confidence messages. Don't listen to the negative messages. Turn on your tape recorder and listen to your self-confidence messages.
- **Visualize**. Imagine yourself reporting for duty on your first day as a teacher or in your teacher training program. Visualizing success can help make it happen—and it reminds you of why you are doing all this work in preparing for the exam.
- **Exercise**. Physical activity helps calm your body down and focus your mind. Besides, being in good physical shape can actually help you do well on the exam. Go for a run, lift weights, go swimming—and do it regularly.

Stress Management on Test Day

There are several ways you can bring down your level of test anxiety on test day. They will work best if you practice them in the weeks before the test, so you know which ones work best for you:

- **Practice deep breathing**. Take a deep breath while you count to five. Hold it for a count of one, then let it out on a count of five. Repeat several times.
- **Move your body**. Try rolling your head in a circle. Rotate your shoulders. Shake your hands from the wrist. Many people find these movements very relaxing.
- **Visualize again**. Think of the place where you are most relaxed: lying on the beach in the sun, walking through the park, or whatever. Now, close your eyes and imagine you are actually there. If you practice in advance, you will find that you only need a few seconds of this exercise to experience a significant increase in your sense of well-being.

When anxiety threatens to overwhelm you right there during the exam, there are still things you can do to manage the stress level:

- **Repeat your self-confidence messages**. You should have them memorized by now. Say them quietly to yourself, and believe them!
- **Visualize one more time**. This time, visualize yourself moving smoothly and quickly through the test answering every question right and finishing just before time is up. Like most visualization techniques, this one works best if you have practiced it ahead of time.
- **Find an easy question**. Find an easy question, and answer it. Getting even one question finished gets you into the test-taking groove.
- **Take a mental break**. Everyone loses concentration once in a while during a long test. It's normal, so you shouldn't worry about it. Instead, accept what has happened. Say to yourself, "Hey, I lost it there for a minute. My brain is taking a break." Put down your pencil, close your eyes, and do some deep breathing for a few seconds. Then you will be ready to go back to work.

Try these techniques ahead of time, and see if they work for you!

▶ Step 3: Make a Plan

Time to complete: 30 minutes
Activity: Construct a study plan

Maybe the most important thing you can do to get control of yourself and your exam is to make a study plan. Too many people fail to prepare simply because they fail to plan. Spending hours on the day before the exam poring over sample test questions not only raises your level of test anxiety, it also is simply no substitute for careful preparation and practice over time.

Don't fall into the cram trap. Take control of your preparation time by mapping out a study schedule. On the following pages are two sample schedules, based on the amount of time you have before you take your exams. If you are the kind of person who needs deadlines and assignments to motivate you for a project, here they are. If you are the kind of person who doesn't like to follow other people's plans, you can use the suggested schedules here to construct your own.

Even more important than making a plan is making a commitment. You have to set aside some time every day for study and practice. Try for at least 20 minutes a day. Twenty minutes daily will do you much more good than two hours on Saturday.

Don't put off your study until the day before an exam. Start now. A few minutes a day, with half an hour or more on weekends, can make a big difference in your score.

Schedule A: The 30-Day Plan

If you have at least a month before you take the LAST or ATS-W, you have plenty of time to prepare—as long as you don't waste it! If you have less than a month, turn to Schedule B.

TIME	PREPARATION
Days 1–4	Skim over any study materials you may have. Make a note of 1) areas you expect to be emphasized on the exam, and 2) areas you don't feel confident in. On Day 4, concentrate on those areas.
Day 5	If you are preparing for the LAST, take the first practice exam in Chapter 11. If you are preparing for the ATS-W, take the appropriate exam in this book (Chapter 12 or 13).
Day 6	Score the practice exam. Identify two areas that you will concentrate your studies on.
Days 7–10	Study one of the areas you identified as your weak point. Don't forget, for LAST preparation there is a Reading Skills Review in Chapter 8, a Mathematics Skills Review in Chapter 9, and a Writing Skills Review in Chapter 10. Review one of these chapters in detail to improve your score on the next practice LAST.
Days 11–14	Study the other area you identified as your weak point.
Day 15	If you are preparing for the LAST, take the second practice exam in Chapter 14. If you are preparing for the ATS-W, take the appropriate exam that we offer online.
Day 16	Score the second practice exam. Identify another area to concentrate your studies on.
Days 17–21	Study the one area you identified for review.
Days 22–29	Take an overview of all your study materials, consolidating your strengths and improving on your weaknesses.
Day before the exam	Relax. Do something unrelated to the exam and go to bed at a reasonable hour.

Schedule B: The Ten-Day Plan

If you have two weeks or less before you take the LAST or ATS-W, use this ten-day schedule to help you make the most of your time.

TIME	PREPARATION
Day 1	Take the appropriate practice exam in this book and score it using the answer key at the end. Note which topics you need to review most.
Day 2	Review one area that gave you trouble on the practice exam. If you are preparing for the LAST, use the Reading Skills Review in Chapter 8, the Mathematics Skills Review in Chapter 9, and the Writing Skills Review in Chapter 10. Review one of these chapters in detail to improve your score on the next practice test.
Day 3	Review another area that gave you trouble on your practice exam.
Day 4	If you are preparing for the LAST, take the second practice exam in Chapter 14 and score it. If you are preparing for the ATS-W, take the practice test we offer online and note your scores.
Day 5	If your score on the second practice exam doesn't show improvement on the two areas you studied, review them. If you did improve in those areas, choose a new weak area to study today.
Days 6–7	Continue to use the review chapters to improve some skills and reinforce others.
Days 8–10	Use your last study days to brush up on any areas that are still giving you trouble. Use the resources in this book and from your classes.
Day before the exam	Relax. Do something unrelated to the exam and go to bed at a reasonable hour.

▶ Step 4: Learn to Manage Your Time

Time to complete: 10 minutes to read, many hours of practice!
Activity: Practice these strategies as you take the sample tests in this book

Steps 4, 5, and 6 of the LearningExpress Test Preparation System put you in charge of your exam by showing you test-taking strategies that work. Practice these strategies as you take the sample tests in this book, and then you will be ready to use them on test day.

First, you will take control of your time on the exams. It's a terrible feeling to know there are only five minutes left when you are only three-quarters of the way through a test. Here are some tips to keep that from happening to you:

- **Follow directions**. Read the directions carefully and ask questions before the exam begins if there's anything you don't understand.
- **Pace yourself**. Use your watch or the clock in the testing room to keep track of the time you have left.
- **Keep moving**. Don't waste time on one question. If you don't know the answer, skip the question and move on. You can always go back to it later.
- **Don't rush**. Though you should keep moving, rushing won't help. Try to keep calm and work methodically and quickly.

► Step 5: Learn to Use the Process of Elimination

Time to complete: 20 minutes
Activity: Complete the worksheet on Using the Process of Elimination

After time management, your next most important tool for taking control of your exam is using the process of elimination wisely. It's standard test-taking wisdom that you should always read all the answer choices before choosing your answer. This helps you find the right answer by eliminating wrong answer choices. And, sure enough, that standard wisdom applies to your exam, too.

You should always use the process of elimination on tough questions, even if the right answer jumps out at you. Sometimes the answer that jumps out isn't right after all. You should always proceed through the choices in order. You can start with choice **a** and eliminate any choices that are clearly incorrect.

If you are taking the test on paper, like the practice exams in this book, it's good to have a system for marking good, bad, and maybe answers. We're recommending this one:

X = bad
✔ = good
? = maybe

If you don't like these marks, devise your own system. Just make sure you do it long before test day—while you're working through the practice exams in this book—so you won't have to worry about it just before the exam.

Even when you think you are absolutely clueless about a question, you can often use the process of elimination to get rid of one answer choice. If so, you are better prepared to make an educated guess, as you will see in Step 6. More often, the process of elimination allows you to get down to only two possibly right answers. Then you are in a strong position to guess. And sometimes, even though you don't know the right answer, you find it simply by getting rid of the wrong ones.

Try using your powers of elimination on the questions in the worksheet Using the Process of Elimination on page 54. The questions aren't about teaching; they're just designed to show you how the process of elimination works. The answer explanations for this worksheet show one possible way you might use the process to arrive at the right answer.

The process of elimination is your tool for the next step, which is knowing when to guess.

Use the process of elimination to answer the following questions.

1. Ilsa is as old as Meghan will be in five years. The difference between Ed's age and Meghan's age is twice the difference between Ilsa's age and Meghan's age. Ed is 29. How old is Ilsa?
    a. 4
    b. 10
    c. 19
    d. 24

2. "All drivers of commercial vehicles must carry a valid commercial driver's license whenever operating a commercial vehicle." According to this sentence, which of the following people need NOT carry a commercial driver's license?
    a. a truck driver idling his engine while waiting to be directed to a loading dock
    b. a bus operator backing her bus out of the way of another bus in the bus lot
    c. a taxi driver driving his personal car to the grocery store
    d. a limousine driver taking the limousine to her home after dropping off her last passenger of the evening

3. Smoking tobacco has been linked to
    a. increased risk of stroke and heart attack.
    b. all forms of respiratory disease.
    c. increasing mortality rates over the past ten years.
    d. juvenile delinquency.

4. Which of the following words is spelled correctly?
    a. incorrigible
    b. outragous
    c. domestickated
    d. understandible

Answers

Here are the answers, as well as some suggestions as to how you might have used the process of elimination to find them.

1. **d.** You should have eliminated choice **a** right off the bat. Ilsa can't be four years old if Meghan is going to be Ilsa's age in five years. The best way to eliminate other answer choices is to try plugging them into the information given in the problem. For instance, for choice **b**, if Ilsa is 10, then Meghan must be 5. The difference in their ages is 5. The difference between Ed's age, 29, and Meghan's age, 5, is 24. Is 24 two times 5? No. Then choice **b** is wrong. You could eliminate choice **c** in the same way and be left with choice **d**.

2. **c.** Note the word *not* in the question, and go through the answers one by one. Is the truck driver in choice **a** "operating a commercial vehicle?" Yes, idling counts as "operating," so he needs to have a commercial driver's license. Likewise, the bus operator in choice **b** is operating a commercial vehicle; the question doesn't say the operator has to be on the street. The limo driver in choice **d** is operating a commercial vehicle, even if it doesn't have a passenger in it. However, the cabbie in choice **c** is *not* operating a commercial vehicle, but his own private car.

3. **a.** You could eliminate choice **b** simply because of the presence of the word *all*. Such absolutes hardly ever appear in correct answer choices. Choice **c** looks attractive until you think a little about what you know—aren't *fewer* people smoking these days, rather than more? So how could smoking be responsible for a higher mortality rate? (If you didn't know that *mortality rate* means the rate at which people die, you might keep this choice as a possibility, but you would still be able to eliminate two answers and have only two to choose from.) And choice **d** is not logical, so you could eliminate that one, too. And you are left with the correct choice, **a**.

4. **a.** How you used the process of elimination here depends on which words you recognized as being spelled incorrectly. If you knew that the correct spellings were *outrageous*, *domesticated*, and *understandable*, then you were home free. You probably knew that at least one of those words was wrong!

▶ Step 6: Know When to Guess

Time to complete: 20 minutes
Activity: Complete the worksheet on Your Guessing Ability

Armed with the process of elimination, you are ready to take control of one of the big questions in test taking: Should I guess? The first and main answer is: *Yes*. Some exams have what's called a "guessing penalty," in which a fraction of your wrong answers is subtracted from your right answers, but the NYSTCE does NOT work like that. The number of questions you answer correctly yields your raw score. So you have nothing to lose and everything to gain by guessing.

Your Guessing Ability

The following are ten really hard questions. You are not supposed to know the answers. Rather, this is an assessment of your ability to guess when you don't have a clue. Read each question carefully, just as if you did expect to answer it. If you have any knowledge at all of the subject of the question, use that knowledge to help you eliminate wrong choices.

1. September 7 is Independence Day in
   a. India.
   b. Costa Rica.
   c. Brazil.
   d. Australia.

2. Which of the following is the formula for determining the momentum of an object?
   a. $p = mv$
   b. $F = ma$
   c. $P = IV$
   d. $E = mc^2$

3. Because of the expansion of the universe, the stars and other celestial bodies are all moving away from each other. This phenomenon is known as
   a. Newton's first law.
   b. the big bang.
   c. gravitational collapse.
   d. Hubble flow.

4. American author Gertrude Stein was born in
   a. 1713.
   b. 1830.
   c. 1874.
   d. 1901.

5. Which of the following is NOT one of the Five Classics attributed to Confucius?
   a. the *I Ching*
   b. the *Book of Holiness*
   c. the *Spring and Autumn Annals*
   d. the *Book of History*

6. The religious and philosophical doctrine that holds that the universe is constantly in a struggle between good and evil is known as
   a. Pelagianism.
   b. Manichaeanism.
   c. Neo-Hegelianism.
   d. Epicureanism.

7. The third chief justice of the U.S. Supreme Court was
   a. John Blair.
   b. William Cushing.
   c. James Wilson.
   d. John Jay.

8. Which of the following is the poisonous portion of a daffodil?
   a. the bulb
   b. the leaves
   c. the stem
   d. the flowers

9. The winner of the Masters golf tournament in 1953 was
   a. Sam Snead.
   b. Cary Middlecoff.
   c. Arnold Palmer.
   d. Ben Hogan.

10. The state with the highest per capita personal income in 1980 was
    a. Alaska.
    b. Connecticut.
    c. New York.
    d. Texas.

Answers

Check your answers against the correct answers below.

1. c.
2. a.
3. d.
4. c.
5. b.
6. b.
7. b.
8. a.
9. d.
10. a.

▶ How Did You Do?

You may have simply gotten lucky and actually known the answer to one or two questions. In addition, your guessing was more successful if you were able to use the process of elimination on any of the questions. Maybe you didn't know who the third chief justice was (question 7), but you knew that John Jay was the first. In that case, you would have eliminated choice **d** and therefore improved your odds of guessing right from one in four to one in three.

According to probability, you should get $2\frac{1}{2}$ answers correct, so getting either two or three right would be average. If you got four or more right, you may be a really terrific guesser. If you got one or none right, you may be a really bad guesser.

Keep in mind, though, that this is only a small sample. You should continue to keep track of your guessing ability as you work through the sample questions in this book. Circle the numbers of questions you guess on as you make your guess; or, if you don't have time while you take the practice exams, go back afterward and try to remember which questions you guessed at. Remember, on an exam with four answer choices, your chances of getting a right answer is one in four. So keep a separate "guessing" score for each exam. How many questions did you guess on? How many did you get right? If the number you got right is at least one-fourth of the number of questions you guessed on, you are at least an average guesser, maybe better—and you should always go ahead and guess on the real exam. If the number you got right is significantly lower than one-fourth of the number you guessed on, you would, frankly, be safe in guessing anyway, but maybe you would feel more comfortable if you guessed only selectively, when you can eliminate a wrong answer or at least have a good feeling about one of the answer choices.

▶ Step 7: Reach Your Peak Performance Zone

Time to complete: 10 minutes to read; weeks to complete!
Activity: Complete the Physical Preparation Checklist

To get ready for a challenge like a big exam, you have to take control of your physical, as well as your mental, state. Exercise, proper diet, and rest will ensure that your body works with, rather than against, your mind on test day, as well as during your preparation.

Exercise

If you don't already have a regular exercise program going, the time during which you are preparing for an exam is actually an excellent time to start one. And if you are already keeping fit—or trying to get that way—don't let the pressure of preparing for an exam fool you into quitting now. Exercise helps reduce stress by pumping wonderful good-feeling hormones called **endorphins** into your system. It also increases the oxygen supply throughout your body, including your brain, so you will be at peak performance on test day.

A half hour of vigorous activity—enough to raise a sweat—every day should be your aim. If you are really pressed for time, every other day is OK. Choose an activity you like and get out there and do it. Jogging with a friend always makes the time go faster, or take a radio.

But don't overdo it. You don't want to exhaust yourself. Moderation is the key.

Diet

First of all, cut out the junk. Go easy on caffeine and nicotine, and eliminate alcohol and any other drugs from your system at least two weeks before the exam.

What your body needs for peak performance is simply a balanced diet. Eat plenty of fruits and vegetables, along with protein and carbohydrates. Foods that are high in lecithin (an amino acid), such as fish and beans, are especially good "brain foods."

The night before the exam, you might "carbo-load" the way athletes do before a contest. Eat a big plate of spaghetti, rice and beans, or whatever your favorite carbohydrate is.

Rest

You probably know how much sleep you need every night to be at your best, even if you don't always get it. Make sure you do get that much sleep, though, for at least a week before the exam. Moderation is important here, too. Extra sleep will just make you groggy.

If you are not a morning person and your exam will be given in the morning, you should reset your internal clock so that your body doesn't think you are taking an exam at 3:00 A.M. You have to start this process well before the exam. The way it works is to get up half an hour earlier each morning, and then go to bed half an hour earlier that night. Don't try it the other way around; you will just toss and turn if you go to bed early without having gotten up early. The next morning, get up another half an hour earlier, and so on. How long you will have to do this depends on how late you are used to getting up. Use the Physical Preparation Checklist on the next page to make sure you are in top form.

Physical Preparation Checklist

For the week before the exam, write down what physical exercise you engaged in and for how long and what you ate for each meal. Remember, you are trying for at least half an hour of exercise every other day (preferably every day) and a balanced diet that's light on junk food.

Exam minus 7 days
Exercise: _____ for ____ minutes
Breakfast: _____
Lunch: _____
Dinner: _____
Snacks: _____

Exam minus 6 days
Exercise: _____ for ____ minutes
Breakfast: _____
Lunch: _____
Dinner: _____
Snacks: _____

Exam minus 5 days
Exercise: _____ for ____ minutes
Breakfast: _____
Lunch: _____
Dinner: _____
Snacks: _____

Exam minus 4 days
Exercise: _____ for ____ minutes
Breakfast: _____
Lunch: _____
Dinner: _____
Snacks: _____

Exam minus 3 days
Exercise: _____ for ____ minutes
Breakfast: _____
Lunch: _____
Dinner: _____
Snacks: _____

Exam minus 2 days
Exercise: _____ for ____ minutes
Breakfast: _____
Lunch: _____
Dinner: _____
Snacks: _____

Exam minus 1 day
Exercise: _____ for ____ minutes
Breakfast: _____
Lunch: _____
Dinner: _____
Snacks: _____

▶ Step 8: Get Your Act Together

Time to complete: 10 minutes to read; time to complete will vary
Activity: Complete the Final Preparations worksheet

You are in control of your mind and body; you are in charge of test anxiety, your preparation, and your test-taking strategies. Now it's time to take charge of external factors, like the testing site and the materials you need to take the exam.

Find Out Where the Exam Is and Make a Trial Run

Do you know how to get to the testing site? Do you know how long it will take to get there? If not, make a trial run, preferably on the same day of the week at the same time of day. Make note on the Final Preparations worksheet of the amount of time it will take you to get to the exam site. Plan on arriving 30–45 minutes early so you can get the lay of the land, use the bathroom, and calm down. Then figure out how early you will have to get up that morning, and make sure you get up that early every day for a week before the exam.

Gather Your Materials

The night before the exam, lay out the clothes you will wear and the materials you have to bring with you to the exam. Plan on dressing in layers; you won't have any control over the temperature of the examination room. Have a sweater or jacket you can take off if it's warm. Use the checklist on the Final Preparations worksheet to help you pull together what you will need.

Don't Skip Breakfast

Even if you don't usually eat breakfast, do so on exam morning. A cup of coffee doesn't count. Don't eat doughnuts or other sweet foods, either. A sugar high will leave you with a sugar low in the middle of the exam. A mix of protein and carbohydrates is best: Cereal with milk or eggs with toast will do your body a world of good.

Final Preparations

Getting to the Exam Site

Location of exam: _____

Date: _____

Departure time: _____

Do I know how to get to the exam site? Yes _____ No _____
If no, make a trial run.

Time it will take to get to exam site: _____

Things to Lay Out the Night Before

Clothes I will wear   _____

Sweater/jacket   _____

Watch   _____

Photo ID   _____

No. 2 pencils   _____

Calculator   _____

_____   _____

_____   _____

▶ Step 9: Do It!

Time to complete: 10 minutes, plus test-taking time
Activity: Ace the LAST or ATS-W!

Fast forward to exam day. You are ready. You made a study plan and followed through. You practiced your test-taking strategies while working through this book. You are in control of your physical, mental, and emotional state. You know when and where to show up and what to bring with you. In other words, you are better prepared than most of the other people taking the exam. You are psyched.

Just one more thing. When you are done with the exam, you will have earned a reward. Plan a celebration. Call up your friends and plan a party, or have a nice dinner for two—whatever your heart desires. Give yourself something to look forward to.

And then do it. Go into the exam, full of confidence, armed with test-taking strategies you have practiced until they're second nature. You are in control of yourself, your environment, and your performance on the exam. You are ready to succeed. So do it. Go in there and ace the exam. And look forward to your future career as a teacher!

8 ▶ Reading Skills Review

CHAPTER SUMMARY

Reading comprehension is an important skill to have in life and on tests. This chapter covers the most essential reading and reading comprehension strategies for success. You will learn to become an active reader, to understand the difference between the main idea and supporting ideas, and to recognize information that is implied, but not stated in a passage. These skills will help you on the NYSTCE.

Developing strong reading comprehension skills is crucial for success as a prospective teacher. This chapter will help strengthen your ability to understand written passages and demonstrate insight and discrimination about what you read. The LAST, ATS-W, and CSTs contain passages of varying lengths: long passages of about 200 words, shorter passages of approximately 100 words, and short statements of a few sentences. Passages may also include forms and other visual representations that you will be asked to comprehend. Multiple-choice questions follow each passage, visual representation, or statement.

The topics presented in the NYSTCE reflect a range of subjects, from teaching methods and strategies across content areas, to science, mathematics, technology, history, social sciences, artistic expression, the humanities, communication, and research skills and processes. Although you do not need any specialized knowledge or a background in the subject to answer the questions, you do need to show that you can extract information from the passage. Some questions will focus on the explicit information offered: its main purpose, supporting details, and organization. Other questions will ask you to interpret and evaluate the assumptions that are implicit in the text's underlying message, arguments, and logic.

▶ Types of Questions

Some of the questions on the LAST, ATS-W, and CSTs focus on *what* information is presented in a passage, others deal with *how* information is presented. The questions fall into two basic categories: literal comprehension and critical and inferential comprehension.

Literal Comprehension

Literal comprehension questions measure your ability to understand the literal content of a passage. You might be asked to identify the main purpose of a passage, locate a fact or detail, describe how the passage is organized, or define how a word is used in a passage. There are four types of literal comprehension questions:

1. **Main Idea**. For this question type, you need to be able to identify the main idea of the passage or a specific paragraph in the passage.

    Examples
    - The views expressed in this selection are most consistent with . . . ?
    - The passage is primarily concerned with . . . ?
    - Which of the following best describes a central aspect of Mel's daily ritual?

2. **Supporting Idea**. This question type asks you to summarize a supporting idea in the passage. You will need to be able to locate specific information in the passage, such as a fact, figure, or name.

    Examples
    - According to the charts, how many people in the United States have Type II diabetes?
    - The passage states that a lunar eclipse occurs when . . . ?
    - Which of the following is NOT mentioned as one of the reasons for the Cuban Missile Crisis?
    - Use the following information to answer the questions that follow.

3. **Organization**. In this type of question, you will be asked to recognize how a reading passage is organized. Organization questions may ask you to identify how a passage uses transitions and key phrases or how ideas within a passage relate to each other.

    Examples
    - Which of the following best describes the theme of the passage?
    - This passage is most likely taken from a . . . (newspaper column, textbook, etc.)?
    - The phrase "the contrast in meaning and tone" refers to the contrast between . . . ?
    - Why is the word *indescribably* used in sentence 4?

4. **Vocabulary**. This question type asks you to determine the meaning of a word.

   Examples

   - Which of the following words, if substituted for the word *indelible* in the passage, would introduce the LEAST change in the meaning of the sentence?
   - The word *protest* in the passage could best be replaced by . . . ?
   - Which of the following is the best meaning of the word *experience* as it is used in the passage?

▶ Critical and Inferential Comprehension

Whereas literal comprehension questions are straightforward, critical and inferential comprehension questions ask you to read between the lines of a text. These questions are about what is *implied* in the passage or statement. They ask you to identify the author's assumptions and attitudes and evaluate the weaknesses and strengths of the author's argument or logic. Critical and inferential comprehension questions include three types:

1. **Evaluation**. This question type asks you to evaluate the strengths and weaknesses of the argument presented in a passage. Evaluation questions will ask you to judge whether something is fact or opinion, or whether the evidence presented supports the message of the passage.

   Examples

   - In order to evaluate the validity of the author's claim regarding Jackson Pollock, it would be most helpful to know which of the following?
   - Which of the following is NOT mentioned in the passage as a weakness in the new law?
   - Which of the following numbered sentences of the passage expresses a fact rather than an opinion?
   - Use the reproduction to answer the following questions.

2. **Inferences**. This type of question asks you to make an inference (draw a logical conclusion) based on the content of the passage. Inference questions may ask you to determine an author's underlying assumptions or attitude toward the subject of the passage.

   Examples

   - Which of the following is an unstated assumption made by the author of the passage?
   - It can be inferred from the passage that the art of Picasso and Matisse differ in all of the following ways EXCEPT . . .
   - The author would be LEAST likely to agree with which of the following statements?

3. **Generalizations**. This question type requires you to apply the ideas of a passage to new situations, recognize similar situations, and draw conclusions about the content of the passage. Many of the questions found on the ATS-W are generalization questions.

Examples

- Which of the following conclusions about rainfull is best supported by information in the graphs?
- Which of the following conclusions can you make based on the passage?
- Given the information in the passage, what appeared to be an important post-World War II trend in the United States?
- Which of the following would be considered primary sources?
- Which of these strategies . . . ?

Now that you have a better idea of what to expect on the exams, you can begin to review some reading comprehension skills and test-taking strategies. By honing these skills, you will be better equipped to understand reading passages and to do your best on the exams.

▶ Reading Skill Builders

Reading may seem like a passive activity—after all, you are sitting, looking at words on a page. However, to improve your reading comprehension you need to read *actively,* meaning that you need to interact with the text. Incorporate these active-reading techniques into your study plan for the NYSTCE. Each time you read a magazine, newspaper, or book, sharpen your reading comprehension skills using these strategies:

- **Skim ahead**. Scan the text *before* you read. Look at how the text is organized: How is it broken into sections? In what order are the topics presented? Note key words and ideas that are highlighted in boldface type or in bulleted lists.
- **Jump back**. Review the text after you read. By looking at summaries, headings, and highlighted information, you increase your ability to remember information and make connections between ideas.
- **Look up new words**. Keep a dictionary on hand as you read. Look up unfamiliar words and list them with their definitions in a notebook or make flash cards. To help you remember new words, connect them to something in your life or reading. Make a point to use new words in your writing and conversation. By increasing your vocabulary, you build your reading comprehension.
- **Highlight key ideas**. As you read, highlight or underline key terms, main ideas, or concepts that are new to you. Be selective—if you highlight too much of the text, nothing will stand out for you on the page. (If you don't own the book, use a notebook to jot down information.)
- **Take notes**. Note taking can help you remember material, even if you never look at your notes again. That's because it's a muscle activity and using your muscles can actually aid your memory. Record your questions, observations, and opinions as you read. Write down the main idea of the passage, the author's point of view, and whether you agree with the author.
- **Make connections**. When you connect two ideas, you improve your chances of remembering the material. For example, if you are reading about a current presidential race, you may note how it is similar to or different from past elections. How have circumstances changed? You may also connect the topic to your own experience: How did you feel about the past election versus the current race?

▶ Locate the Main Idea

When tests ask you to find the main idea of a passage, they are asking you to determine an overall feeling or thought that a writer wants to convey about the subject. To find the main idea, think about a **general statement** that brings together all of the ideas in a paragraph or passage. Look out for statements that are too specific—a main idea must be broad enough to contain all of the concepts presented in a passage. Test takers often confuse the main idea of a passage with its main topic. The topic is the **subject**—what the passage is about. The main idea is what the author wants to express *about* the subject.

Main Topic versus Main Idea

Topic/subject: what the passage is about
Main idea: what the author wants to say about a subject

Textbook writing and the passages on the NYSTCE often follow a basic pattern of **general idea → specific idea**. In other words, a writer states the main idea (makes a general claim about the subject) and then provides evidence for it through, specific details and facts. Do you always find main ideas in the first sentence of the passage? The answer is no; although a first sentence may contain the main idea, an author may decide to build up to the main point. In that case, you may find the main idea in the last sentence of an introductory paragraph, or even in the last paragraph of the passage.

Read the following paragraph and answer the practice question that follows:

Experts say that if you feel drowsy during the day, even during boring activities, you haven't had enough sleep. If you routinely fall asleep within five minutes of lying down, you probably have severe sleep deprivation, possibly even a sleep disorder. Microsleep, or a very brief episode of sleep in an otherwise awake person, is another mark of sleep deprivation. In many cases, people are not aware that they are experiencing microsleeps. The widespread practice of "burning the candle at both ends" in western industrialized societies has created so much sleep deprivation that what is really abnormal sleepiness is now almost the norm.
Source: National Institute of Neurological Disorders and Stroke, National Institutes of Health, www.ninds.nih.gov

What is the main point of this passage?

a. If you fall asleep within five minutes every time you lie down, you are sleep deprived.

b. If you experience enough microsleeps, you can attain the sleep you need to function.

c. Sleep deprivation is a pervasive problem in the United States and other western nations.

d. If trends in sleep deprivation continue, our society will experience grave consequences.

e. Sleep deprivation is responsible for approximately 100,000 car accidents each year.

Choice **a** is a true statement, but too specific to be a main idea. Choice **b** is a false statement. Choice **d** is a speculative statement that is not implied in the passage, and choice **e** is a detail or fact that is not supported by the information in the paragraph. Only choice **c** represents a general or "umbrella" statement that covers all of the information in the paragraph. Notice that in the sample passage, the author does not present the main idea in the first sentence, but rather builds up to the main point, which is expressed in the last sentence of the paragraph.

▶ Find Essential Facts

Some of the literal comprehension questions on the NYSTCE will ask you to identify a paraphrase or rewording of supporting details. How can you distinguish a main idea from a supporting idea? Unlike main ideas, supporting ideas present facts or **specific information**. They often answer the questions *what? when? why?* or *how?*

How can you locate a supporting detail in a passage that is 200 words long? One thing you don't have to do is memorize the passage. This test does not require that you have perfect recall. Instead, it measures your ability to read carefully and know where to look for specific information. Here are some tips for finding supporting details:

- **Look for language clues.** Writers often use transitional words or phrases to signal that they are introducing a fact or supporting idea. As you read, keep your eyes open for these common phrases:

for example	for instance	in particular
in addition	furthermore	some
other	specifically	such as

- **Focus on key words from the question.** Questions often contain two or three important words that signal what information to look for in the passage. For example, a question following a passage about the American car industry reads, "The passage states that hybrid automobiles work best if. . . ." The key words are *hybrid automobiles* and *best.* They tell you to look for a sentence that contains the phrase *hybrid automobiles* and describes an optimal situation. Instead of rereading the passage, *skim* through the paragraphs looking for the key word. Keep in mind that the passage may use a slightly different wording than the key word. As you scan, look for words that address the same idea.

■ **Pay attention to the structure of the passage**. Take note of how the passage is organized as you read. Does the author begin with or build to the main point? Is information presented chronologically? Where does the author offer evidence to back up the main point? Understanding how a passage is structured can help you locate the information you need. Read on for more about common organizational models.

Read the following paragraph, focusing on its main idea and the details that support the main idea. Then, answer the practice questions that follow.

The history of microbiology begins with a Dutch haberdasher named Antoni van Leeuwenhoek, a man of no formal scientific education. In the late 1600s, Leeuwenhoek, inspired by the magnifying lenses used by drapers to examine cloth, assembled some of the first microscopes. He developed a technique for grinding and polishing tiny, convex lenses, some of which could magnify an object up to 270 times. After scraping some plaque from between his teeth and examining it under a lens, Leeuwenhoek found tiny squirming creatures, which he called "animalcules." His observations, which he reported to the Royal Society of London, are among the first descriptions of living bacteria.

1. What inspired Leeuwenhoek's invention of the microscope?
   a. his training in science
   b. the great microbiologists of his era
   c. the lenses used by the practitioners of his profession
   d. the desire to observe bacteria
   e. the common practice of teeth scraping

2. In which sentence does the author give Leeuwenhoek's description of living bacteria?
   a. sentence 1
   b. sentence 2
   c. sentence 3
   d. sentence 4
   e. sentence 5

Answers

1. c. The first paragraph provides the supporting detail to answer this question. Leeuwenhoek, a haberdasher, was "inspired by the magnifying lenses used by drapers to examine cloth." One of the key words from the question—*inspired*—leads you to the location of the detail in the passage. Choice **a** is refuted by a detail presented in the line: "a man of no formal scientific education." Choice **b** is untrue, because the first sentence of the passage states that "the history of microbiology begins" with Leeuwenhoek. Choice **d** is also incorrect, because Leeuwenhoek did not know *what* he would discover under his microscope, and choice **e** is a silly choice used as a distracter.

2. **d.** You can find Leeuwenhoek's description of bacteria in sentence 4: "tiny squirming creatures, which he called 'animalcules.' " You may have been tricked into selecting choice **e**, because of its repetition of the phrase "description of living bacteria," from sentence 5. Be sure to always refer back to the passage when answering a question—do not rely on your memory. Choice **e** is incorrect, because it does not refer to Leeuwenhoek's own description, but rather the significance of his observation. This question highlights the importance of taking note of where crucial details are located in a passage. Again, do not try to memorize or learn facts or details, but have an idea about where to find them.

▶ All about Organization

Organization questions on the NYSTCE ask you to identify how a passage is structured. You need to be able to recognize organizational patterns, common transitional phrases, and how ideas relate within a passage. Understanding the structure of a passage can also help you locate concepts and information, such as the main idea or supporting details.

To organize their ideas effectively, writers rely on one of several basic organizational patterns. The four most common strategies are:

- chronological order
- order of importance
- comparison and contrast
- cause and effect

Chronological order arranges events by the order in which they happened, from beginning to end. Textbooks, instructions and procedures, essays about personal experiences, and magazine feature articles may use this organizing principle. Passages organized by chronology offer language cues—in the form of transitional words or phrases—to signal the passage of time and link one idea or event to the next. Here are some of the most common chronological transitions:

first, second, third, etc.	before	after	next	now
then	when	as soon as	immediately	suddenly
soon	during	while	meanwhile	later
in the meantime	at last	eventually	finally	afterward

Order of importance organizes ideas by rank instead of by time. Instead of describing what happened next, this pattern presents what is most, or least, important. The structure can work two ways: writers can either organize their ideas by increasing importance (least important idea → most important idea) or by decreasing importance (most important idea → least important idea).

Newspaper articles follow the principle of decreasing importance; they cover the most important information in the first sentence or paragraph (the *who, what, when, where,* and *why* about an event). As a result, readers can get the facts of an event without reading the entire article. Writing that is trying to persuade its readers or make an argument often uses the pattern of increasing importance. By using this structure, a writer creates a snowball effect, building and building upon the idea. "Saving the best for last" can create suspense for the reader and leave a lasting impression of the writer's main point.

Just as a chronological arrangement uses transitions, so does the order of importance principle. Keep your eyes open for the following common transitional words and phrases:

first and foremost	most important	more important	moreover
above all	first, second, third	last but not least	finally

Comparison and contrast arranges two things or ideas side by side to show the ways in which they are similar or different. This organizational model allows a writer to analyze two things or ideas and determine how they measure up to one another. For example, this description of the artists Pablo Picasso and Henri Matisse uses comparison and contrast:

The grand old lions of modernist innovation, Picasso and Matisse, originated many of the most significant developments of twentieth-century art (comparison). However, although they worked in the same tradition, they each had a different relationship to painting (contrast). For example, Picasso explored signs and symbols in his paintings, whereas Matisse insisted that the things represented in his paintings were merely things: the oranges on the table of a still life were simply oranges on the table (contrast).

Writers use two basic methods to compare and contrast ideas. In the **point-by-point** method, each aspect of idea A is followed by a comparable aspect of idea B, so that a paragraph resembles this pattern: ABABABAB. In the **block** method, a writer presents several aspects of idea A, followed by several aspects of idea B. The pattern of the block method looks like this: AAAABBBB.

Again, transitions can signal whether a writer is using the organizing principle of comparison and contrast. Watch for these common transitions:

Transitions Showing Similarity

similarly	in the same way	likewise
like	in a like manner	just as
and	also	both

Transitions Showing Difference

but	on the other hand	yet
however	on the contrary	in contrast
conversely	whereas	unlike

Cause and effect arranges ideas to explain why an event took place (cause) and what happened as a result (effect). Sometimes one cause has several effects, or an effect may have several causes. For example, a historian writing about World War I might investigate several causes of the war (assassination of the heir to the Austro-Hungarian throne, European conflicts over territory and economic power), and describe the various effects of the war (ten million soldiers killed, weakened European powers, enormous financial debt).

Key words offer clues that a writer is describing cause and effect. Pay attention to these words as you read:

Words Indicating Cause

because	created by
since	caused by

Words Indicating Effect

therefore	so
hence	consequently
as a result	

A writer might also describe a **contributing** cause, which is a factor that *helps* to make something happen but can't make that thing happen by itself. On the opposite end of the spectrum is a **sufficient** cause, which is an event that, by itself, is strong enough to make the event happen. Often an author will offer an opinion about the cause or effect of an event. In that case, readers must judge the validity of the author's analysis. Are the author's ideas logical? Do the ideas support the conclusions?

Read the following excerpt and answer the practice question.

When Rosa Parks refused to give up her seat to a white person in Montgomery, Alabama, and was arrested in December 1955, she set off a chain of events that generated a momentum the civil rights movement had never before experienced. Local civil rights leaders were hoping for such an opportunity to test the city's segregation laws. Deciding to boycott the buses, the African-American community soon formed a new organization to supervise the boycott, the Montgomery Improvement Association (MIA). The young pastor of the Dexter Avenue Baptist Church, Reverend Martin Luther King, Jr., was chosen as the first MIA leader. The boycott, more successful than anyone hoped, led to a 1956 Supreme Court decision banning segregated buses.
Source: Excerpt from the Library of Congress, "The African American Odyssey: A Quest for Full Citizenship."

The author implies that the action and arrest of Rosa Parks directly resulted in
  a. the 1956 Supreme Court decision banning segregated buses.
  b. Martin Luther King, Jr.'s ascendancy as a civil rights leader.
  c. the formation of the civil rights movement in Montgomery, Alabama.
  d. the bus boycott in Montgomery, Alabama.
  e. the birth of a nationwide struggle for civil rights.

The answer is choice **d**. According to the passage, Rosa Parks's action directly inspired local civil rights leaders to institute the Montgomery bus boycott. Although Rosa Parks's action may have been a *contributing* factor to King's emergence as a civil rights leader (choice **b**) and the Supreme Court's later decision to ban segregated buses (choice **a**), it was not the *direct* cause of these events, according to the passage. Choice **c** is incorrect because the passage makes clear that a local civil rights movement already existed and was not the result of Rosa Parks's refusal to give up her bus seat. Likewise, choice **e** is incorrect. Rosa Parks's action may have furthered the national civil rights movement, but it was not its direct cause.

▶ Strategies for Vocabulary Questions

If you encounter an unfamiliar word when you are reading, you may likely grab a dictionary and look it up. During the NYSTCE, however, you can't use a dictionary to check the meaning of new words. However, you can use a number of strategies to figure out what a word means.

Vocabulary questions measure your word power, but they also evaluate an essential reading comprehension skill, which is your ability to determine the meaning of a word from its **context**. The sentences that surround the word offer important clues about its meaning. For example, see if you can figure out the meaning of the word *incessant* from this context:

The incessant demands of the job are too much for me. The responsibilities are endless!

The word *incessant* most nearly means
  a. inaccessible.
  b. difficult.
  c. unceasing.
  d. compatible.
  e. manageable.

The best choice is **c**. The sentence, *The responsibilities are endless*, restates the phrase in the first sentence, *incessant demands*. This restatement, or elaboration, suggests the meaning of *incessant*: continuing or following without interruption.

If the context of an unfamiliar word does not restate its meaning, try these two steps to figure out what the word means:

1. **Is the word positive or negative?** Using the context of the passage, determine whether the unfamiliar word is a positive or negative term. If a word is used in a positive context, you can eliminate the answer choices that are negative. In the preceding example, you can guess that the word *incessant* is used negatively. The phrase, *too much for me*, suggests that the demands of the job are overwhelming and negative. Thus, you can eliminate choices **d** and **e** because they represent positive terms.
2. **Replace the vocabulary word** with the remaining answer choices, one at a time. Does the answer choice make sense when you read the sentence? If not, eliminate the answer choice. In the previous example, choice **a**, *inaccessible*, simply does not make sense in the sentence. Choice **b**, *difficult*, is too general to be a likely synonym. Only choice **c**, *unceasing*, makes sense in the context.

▶ Fact vs. Opinion

Just because something is in print does not mean that it is fact. Most writing contains some **bias**—the personal judgment of a writer. Sometimes a writer's beliefs unknowingly affect how he or she writes about a topic. In other cases, a writer deliberately attempts to shape the reader's reaction and position. For example, a writer may present only one perspective about a subject or include only facts that support his or her point of view. Critical and inferential questions on the NYSTCE—specifically evaluation questions—will ask you to judge the strengths or weaknesses of an author's argument. You will be required to distinguish between fact and opinion, and decide whether the supporting details, or evidence, effectively back up the author's main point.

To separate fact from opinion, consider these differences:

- A **fact** is a statement that can be verified by a reliable source.
- An **opinion** is a statement about the beliefs or feelings of a person or group.

When determining whether a statement is factual, consider whether a source gives researched, accurate information. The following is an example of a factual statement—it can be supported by the recent national census:

The U.S. population is growing older—in fact, adults over age 65 are the fastest-growing segment of today's population.

Opinions, on the other hand, reflect judgments that may or may not be true. Opinions include speculation or predictions of the future that cannot be proven at the present time. The following statement represents an opinion—it offers a belief about the future. Others may disagree with the prediction:

Many believe that the population boom among elderly Americans will create a future healthcare crisis.

Language clues can alert you to a statement that reflects an opinion. Look for these common words that introduce opinions:

likely	should/could	say
possibly	think	charge
probably	believe	attest

Exhibit A—Evidence

Most writing presents *reasonable opinions,* based on fact: A writer asserts an opinion and supports it with facts or other evidence. A writer can use different types of evidence to build an argument—some forms of proof are more reliable than other types. When you read, look for the forms of evidence listed below and consider how accurate each might be:

observations

interviews

surveys and questionnaires

experiments

personal experience

expert opinions

▶ Reading between the Lines

Inference questions on the NYSTCE will ask you to make an inference, or draw a logical conclusion, about what you read. Sometimes a writer does not explicitly state the main idea or offer a conclusion. The reader must infer the writer's meaning. To determine a writer's underlying assumptions or attitude, you need to look for clues in the context of the passage. One revealing clue to the writer's meaning is word choice.

Word choice, also called diction, is the specific language the writer uses to describe people, places, and things. Word choice includes these forms:

- particular words or phrases a writer uses
- the way words are arranged in a sentence
- repetition of words or phrases
- inclusion of particular details

Consider how word choice affects the following two sentences:

  a. Lesson preparation benefits a teacher's performance in the classroom.
  b. Lesson preparation improves a teacher's performance in the classroom.

The only difference between the two sentences is that sentence **a** uses *benefits,* and sentence **b** uses *improves.* Both sentences state that lesson preparation has a positive influence on a teacher's performance in the classroom. However, sentence **a** is stronger because of word choice: *to benefit* means to be useful or advantageous, whereas *to improve* means to enhance in value. The writer of sentence **b** believes that preparation is not only useful, it actually increases a teacher's effectiveness. The writer doesn't have to spell this out for you, because the word choice makes the position clear.

▶ Denotation and Connotation

Even words with similar dictionary definitions (**denotations**) have different suggested meanings (**connotations**). Consider the different implied meanings of the following word pairs:

- slim/thin
- perilous/dangerous
- rich/wealthy

Although they are nearly synonyms, these word pairs suggest varying degrees and have subtle differences in their effect. The word *slim* suggests fitness and grace. *Thin* is more neutral, or possibly negative, implying someone may be too skinny to be healthy. *Perilous* suggests a greater threat of harm than the term *dangerous:* it has a more ominous connotation and implies a more life-threatening situation. The subtle difference between *rich* and *wealthy* is again, one of degree: *rich* implies having enough to fulfill normal needs; *wealthy* suggests an established and elevated societal class.

▶ Euphemism and Dysphemism

Writers also reveal their attitude toward a subject through the use of euphemism or dysphemism. Here is a quick definition of the terms:

- **euphemism**—a neutral or positive expression used in place of a negative one
- **dysphemism**—a negative expression substituted for a neutral or positive one

A euphemism is the substitution of an agreeable description of something that might be unpleasant. In contrast, a dysphemism is an offensive, disagreeable, or disparaging expression that describes something neutral or agreeable.

For example, a student who fails a test might use a euphemistic statement when reporting the grade to his or her parents:

"I didn't do very well on the test."

The student might feel more comfortable using a dysphemism when talking to his or her classmates:

"I bombed on that test. I tanked!"

Another example might be the sentence, "I've been fired." A euphemism for this statement is "I've been let go," whereas a dysphemism for the statement is, "I've been axed."

▶ Style

Just as word choice can alert you to a writer's underlying message, so can other aspects of a writer's style. **Style** is the distinctive way in which a writer uses language to inform or promote an idea. In addition to word choice, a writer's style consists of three basic components:

- sentence structure
- degree of detail or description
- degree of formality

When you read a magazine, newspaper, or book, consider how the writer uses sentences. Does the writer use short, simple sentences or long, complex sentences, packed with clauses and phrases? Writers use different **sentence structures** to create different effects: they may make short declarative statements in order to persuade readers or long descriptions to create a flow that pleases the reader's ear.

Degree of detail refers to how specific an author is in describing something. For example, a writer may use a general term (dog, beach, government) or specific terms (German Shepherd, Crane's Beach, British Parliament). In evaluating the strength of a writer's argument, consider whether terms are too general to provide adequate evidence.

Degree of formality refers to how formal or casual the writer's language is. Technical jargon or terminology is an example of formal language. Colloquial phrases and slang are examples of casual language. Writers create distance and a sense of objectivity when they use formal language, whereas slang expresses familiarity. The degree of formality a writer uses should be appropriate to the purpose and message. For example, a business missive that uses slang is likely to put off its audience, whereas a novel aimed at teenage readers may use slang to appeal to its audience.

▶ Emotional Language

When writers want to persuade a reader of something, they may rely on emotional language. Emotional language targets a reader's emotions—fears, beliefs, values, prejudices—instead of appealing to a reader's reason or critical thinking. Just as advertising often uses emotional language to sell a product, writers use emotional appeals to sell an idea. Here are five techniques to look out for as you read:

- **Bandwagon**. The basic message of a bandwagon appeal is that "everyone else is doing something, so you should, too." It appeals to the reader's desire to join the crowd or be on the winning team. Examples from advertising include: "Americans buy more of our brand than any other brand," or "the toothpaste picky parents choose."
- **Common Man**. In this approach, writers try to convince a reader that their message is just plain old common sense. Colloquial language or phrases and common jokes are examples of this technique.
- **Generalities**. In this approach, writers use words or phrases that evoke deep emotions and carry strong associations for most people. By doing so, a writer can appeal to readers' emotions so that they will accept the message without evaluating it. Generalities are vague so that readers supply their own interpretations and do not ask further questions. Examples of generalities are *honor, peace, freedom,* or *home.*
- **Labeling or name calling**. This method links a negative label, name, or phrase to a person, group, or belief. Name calling can be a direct attack that appeals to hates or fears, or it can be indirect, appealing to a sense of ridicule. Labels can evoke deep emotions, such as *communist* or *terrorist.* Others can be negatively charged, depending on the situation: *yuppie, slacker, reactionary.*
- **Testimonial**. In advertising, athletes promote a range of products, from cereal to wristwatches. Likewise, a writer may use a public figure, expert, or other respected person to endorse an idea or support the writer's argument. Because readers may respect or admire the person, they may be less critical and more willing to accept an idea.

Tone Makes Meaning

You can detect a writer's tone—the mood or attitude as conveyed through language—from a writer's choices about point of view, language use, and style. LAST and CST questions will sometimes ask you to evaluate and summarize a writer's tone. When you read material in preparation for the exams, always think about the tone of each passage. Here are some common words that describe tone:

cheerful	apologetic	sarcastic
complimentary	critical	playful
hopeful	humorous	authoritative
gloomy	ironic	indifferent

▶ Point of View

One strategy that writers use to convey their meaning to readers is through **point of view**. Point of view is the person or perspective through which the writer channels the information and ideas. It determines *who* is speaking to the reader. Depending on the writer's intentions, he or she may present a **subjective** point of view (a perspective based on thoughts, feelings, and experiences), or an **objective** one (one that discounts the writer's personal feelings and attempts to offer an unbiased view). Understanding the point of view of a passage will help you answer questions that ask you to identify an author's assumptions or attitude. Here are three approaches to point of view:

First-person point of view expresses the writer's personal feelings and experiences directly to the reader using these pronouns: *I, me, mine; we, our, us.* The first person creates a sense of intimacy between the reader and writer because it expresses a *subjective* point of view.

This excerpt from Kate Simon's 1982 memoir, *Bronx Primitive*, provides an example of first-person perspective:

> Instead of a city of silver rivers and golden bridges, America turned out to be Uncle David's flat on Avenue C in which my father had first lived when he came to America. We walked up several flights of dark stairs and knocked on a door pasted over with glazed patterned paper of connecting rectangles and circles in blue and red and green, whose lines I liked to trace with my eye while the others talked.

Second-person point of view is another personal perspective in which the writer speaks directly to the reader, addressing the reader as *you.* Writers use the second person to give directions or to make the reader feel directly involved with the argument or action of their message. The following excerpt uses the second person:

> Next week you will begin reading what most critics label the first science fiction novel: Mary Shelley's *Frankenstein*. Understanding what makes this novel a work of science fiction can help you understand why it has so much power.

Third-person point of view expresses an impersonal point of view by presenting the perspective of an outsider (a "third person") who is not directly involved with the action. Writers use the third person to establish distance from the reader and present a seemingly *objective* point of view. The third person uses these pronouns: *he, him, his; she, her, hers; it, its; and they, them, theirs.* Most NYSTCE passages are written in the third person. The following is an example of the third-person perspective:

> The Sami are an indigenous people living in the northern parts of Norway, Sweden, Finland, and Russia's Kola peninsula. Originally, the Sami religion was animistic; that is, for them, nature and natural objects had a conscious life, a spirit.

▶ Practice

Read the following passage from Frank McCourt's 1996 memoir *Angela's Ashes* to answer the practice questions. Consider the writer's choice of words, style, and point of view and how it affects the message presented in the text.

We go to school through lanes and back streets so that we won't meet the respectable boys who go to the Christian Brothers' School or the rich ones who go to the Jesuit school, Crescent College. The Christian Brothers' boys wear tweed jackets, warm woolen sweaters, shirts, ties, and shiny new boots. We know they're the ones who will get jobs in the civil service and help the people who run the world. The Crescent College boys wear blazers and school scarves tossed around their necks and over their shoulders to show they're cock o' the walk. They have long hair which falls across their foreheads and over their eyes so that they can toss their quaffs like Englishmen. We know they're the ones who will go to university, take over the family business, run the government, run the world. We'll be the messenger boys on bicycles who deliver their groceries or we'll go to England to work on the building sites. Our sisters will mind their children and scrub their floors unless they go off to England, too. We know that. We're ashamed of the way we look and if boys from the rich schools pass remarks we'll get into a fight and wind up with bloody noses or torn clothes. Our masters will have no patience with us and our fights because their sons go to the rich schools and, "Ye have no right to raise your hands to a better class of people so ye don't."

1. The *we* the author uses throughout the passage refers to
  a. his family.
  b. the poor children in his neighborhood.
  c. the children who attend rich schools.
  d. the author and his brother.
  e. the reader and writer.

2. The passage suggests that the author goes to school
  a. in shabby clothing.
  b. in a taxi cab.
  c. in warm sweaters and shorts.
  d. on a bicycle.
  e. to become a civil servant.

3. The word *pass* as used in the passage means
  a. to move ahead of.
  b. to go by without stopping.
  c. to be approved or adopted.
  d. to utter.
  e. to come to an end.

4. The author quotes his schoolmasters saying, "Ye have no right to raise your hands to a better class of people so ye don't" in order to

   a. demonstrate how strict his schoolmasters were.

   b. contrast his school to the Christian Brothers' School and Crescent College.

   c. show how his teachers reinforced class lines.

   d. prove that the author thought his teacher was mean.

   e. show how unfair his schoolmasters were.

Answers

1. b. When talking about school, so the reference must be to school-aged children. In addition, the passage contrasts the *we*'s with the *respectable boys* and the *rich ones,* so the *we*'s are neither wealthy nor respected.

2. a. The author and his classmates *go to school through lanes and back streets* to avoid the students who go to school dressed in warm and *respectable* clothing. He also states that they are *ashamed of the way we look,* implying that they are poorly dressed.

3. d. The boys would get into fights if the rich boys were to utter derogatory words or *pass remarks.*

4. c. While the quote here does show how the author's schoolmasters talked, it has a more important function: to show that his schoolmasters reinforced the class system by telling the author and his classmates to stay in their place and not challenge the existing class structure.

▶ Test-Taking Tips

Now that you have reviewed the components that will help you understand and analyze what you read, you are ready to consider some specific test-taking strategies. The following techniques will help you read the NYSTCE passages quickly and effectively and answer the multiple-choice questions strategically so that you can boost your score.

   Reading passages for a test is different than reading at home. For one thing, you have a time limit. The time you spend reading each passage detracts from the time you have to answer questions. Here are some basic guidelines for keeping you moving through the test in a time-efficient way:

- **Spend no more than two minutes on a question**. Circle difficult questions and return to them if you have time.
- **Skim and answer short passages quickly**. Short passages have only one or two questions, so you should move through them with speed. Give yourself a bit more time for long passages that are followed by more than two questions.
- **Guess, if necessary**. The NYSTCE does not penalize for wrong answers. Make sure to answer each question, even if you think you might return to it later.
- **Circle, underline, and make notes**. You can write in your test booklet, so be sure to mark up the passage as you read. Scribble down quick notes that will help you answer the questions.
- **Target the first part of the passage**. The first third of many reading passages is packed with essential information. Often you can answer main-idea questions based on the information at the start of

a passage. Likewise, for longer passages of 200 words, you will often find what each paragraph is about from its first two sentences.

- **Locate details, but don't learn them**. Detail-heavy portions of passages can be dense and difficult to read. Don't spend precious time rereading and absorbing details—just make sure you know where to find them in the passage. That way you can locate a detail if a question asks about it.

▶ Eliminating Wrong Answers

Test makers use "distracters" in test questions that can confuse you into choosing an incorrect answer. Familiarizing yourself with some of the common distraction techniques that test makers use will increase your chances of eliminating wrong answers and selecting the right answer.

- **The choice that does too little**. This distracter type often follows main idea questions. The answer choice makes a true statement, but it is too narrow, too specific to be a main idea of the passage. It zeros in on select elements or supporting ideas of a passage instead of expressing a main idea.
- **The choice that does too much**. This distracter also relates to main idea questions. Unlike the type discussed previously, this answer choice goes too far, or beyond the scope of the passage. It may be a true statement, but cannot be supported by what the author expresses in the text.
- **The close, but not close enough, choice**. This type of answer is very close to the correct answer, but is wrong in some detail.
- **The off-topic choice**. Test takers often find this answer choice the easiest to spot and eliminate. It may have nothing at all to do with the passage itself.
- **The irrelevant choice**. This option uses language found in the text—elements, ideas, phrases, words— but does not answer the question correctly. These distracters are tricky because test designers "bait" them with a good deal of information from the passage.
- **The contradictory choice**. This answer may in fact be opposite or nearly opposite to the correct answer. If two of the answer choices seem contrary to each other, there is a good chance that one of these choices will be correct.
- **The choice that is too broad**. This distracter relates to supporting detail questions. Although it may be a true statement, it is too general and does not address the specifics the question is looking for.

▶ Look Out for Absolutes

Reading comprehension questions that use words that represent absolutes should alert you to the likely presence of clever distracters among the answer choices. Two or more answers may be close contenders—they may reflect language from the passage and be true in general principle, but not true in *all* circumstances. Beware of these commonly used absolutes in reading questions:

best	most closely	always	all
primarily	most nearly	never	none

Types of Readers

How you approach a reading passage may show what kind of reader you are. Each of the following approaches has some merit. When you practice reading passages as part of your study plan, experiment with some of these different styles to see what works best for you.

- The **concentrator** reads the passage thoroughly before looking at the questions. By concentrating on the passage, you can locate answers quickly if you don't already know the answer.
- The **skimmer** skims the passage before looking at the questions. Once you understand how the passage is arranged, you can go back and find the answers.
- The **cautious reader** reads the questions and answer choices first. Because you know what questions to expect, you can be on the lookout as you read the passage.
- The **game player** reads the questions first and answers them by guessing. By guessing the answers, you become familiar with the questions and can recognize the answers when you read the passage.
- The **educated guesser** reads the questions first, but not the answers. When you find the answer in the passage, you can quickly look among the answer choices for the right one.
- The **efficiency expert** reads the questions first, looking for key words that indicate where an answer is located. By doing this, you can skim the passage for answers instead of reading the whole passage.

▶ Five-Step Approach to Answering Reading Questions

If you feel daunted by the task of quickly reading and understanding dense passages, here is a quick approach that you can use. Feel free to adapt it to your style or change the order of the steps, but try to incorporate each of the five steps somewhere in your process.

Step 1—Preview

To get an idea of the content and organization of a passage, begin by skimming it. With practice, you will quickly discern topic sentences and key adjectives. Often, the first two sentences in a paragraph are topic sentences—they will tell you what a paragraph is about. If the passage is several paragraphs long, read the first and last sentence of each paragraph. You can't depend 100% on this technique, though; use your judgment to determine if a sentence is truly a topic sentence.

Step 2—Skim the Questions

Quickly take in the question or questions that follow a passage, marking important words and phrases. Don't bother reading the multiple-choice answers. You simply want to gather clues about what to look for when you read.

Step 3—Read Actively

Although you do not want to memorize or analyze the passage, you do need to read it. Keep your pencil handy to mark the passage as you read, looking for information that applies to the questions you skimmed. Circle or underline topic sentences, main ideas, or phrases that reveal the author's point of view. Check important names, dates, or difficult words. Mark transitions and phrases, such as *however, on the other hand, most importantly, but,* or *except* that help you to follow the author's direction or the organization of the passage.

As you read, ask yourself some of the following questions:

- What is the main theme or idea in the passage?
- What is the author's purpose or goal?
- How do ideas in the passage relate to the main idea?
- What is the tone or mood of the passage? Informative? Critical? Playful?
- How is the passage structured?

Step 4—Review the Passage

After actively reading the passage, take a few seconds to look over the main idea, the topic sentences, or other elements you have marked. Ask yourself what you have just read. Your goal is not to understand the passage thoroughly, but rather to get the gist of it. Quickly summarize it in your own words.

Don't get hung up on difficult phrasing or technical elements in the passage that you might not even need to know. Instead of focusing on absorbing specific details, just know the location of details in the passage. Remember, you can refer back to the passage several times while answering the questions. Focus on the general direction, main ideas, organization, purpose, and point of view of the passage, rather than learning details.

Step 5—Answer the Questions

Now it's time to answer the questions. Base your answers only on what is stated and implied in the passage. Some answer choices will try to trick you with information that is beyond the scope of the passage. Read *all* multiple-choice answers before rushing to choose one. Eliminate and mark off as many choices as possible. If you eliminate all of the answer choices but two, reach your decision quickly between the remaining two. After you have timed yourself working with the practice tests in this book, you will have a good idea of your time limitations.

▶ Using the Five-Step Approach

This practice applies the five-step approach to a sample passage. You may want to review the five-step approach before you begin.

Sample Passage

Read the following passage to answer questions 1 and 2.

In his famous study of myth, *The Hero With a Thousand Faces,* Joseph Campbell writes about the archetypal hero who has ventured outside the boundaries of the village and, after many trials and adventures, has returned with the boon that will save or enlighten his fellows. Like Carl Jung, Campbell believes that the story of the hero is part of the collective unconscious of all humankind. He likens the returning hero to the sacred or tabooed personage described by James Frazier in *The Golden Bough.* Such an individual must, in many instances of myth, be insulated from the rest of society, "not merely for his own sake but for the sake of others; for since the virtue of holiness is, so to say, a powerful explosive which the smallest touch can detonate, it is necessary in the interest of the general safety to keep it within narrow bounds."

There is much similarity between the archetypal hero who has journeyed into the wilderness and the poet who has journeyed into the realm of imagination. Both places are dangerous and full of wonders, and both, at their deepest levels, are journeys that take place into the kingdom of the unconscious mind, a place that, in Campbell's words, "goes down into unsuspected Aladdin caves. There not only jewels but dangerous jinn abide . . ."

1. Based on the passage, which of the following best describes the story that will likely be told by Campbell's returning hero and Frazier's sacred or tabooed personage?
   a. a radically mind-altering story
   b. a story that will terrify people to no good end
   c. a warning of catastrophe to come
   d. a story based on a dangerous lie
   e. a parable aimed at establishing a religious movement

2. Which of the following is the most accurate definition of the word *boon* as it is used in the passage?
   a. present
   b. blessing
   c. charm
   d. prize
   e. curse

You can answer these questions by following the five-step approach explained in the previous lesson.

Preview

Read the first sentence of each paragraph: "In his famous study of myth . . ." and "There is much similarity . . ." Because of the length of the sentences in each passage, you may or may not wish to read the ending sentences in each paragraph. Underline the topic sentences.

Skim the Questions

Now, skim the questions and mark them.

- Based on the passage, which of the following best describes the story that will likely be told by Campbell's returning hero and Frazier's sacred or tabooed personage? An important word in this question is *story*. Also note the use of the absolute, *best*. This means that more than one answer choice may be true, but only one is the best answer. Circle or mark these terms. You may also notice that this is an inference question; it asks you to infer something based on the information of the passage.
- Which of the following is the most accurate definition of the word *boon* as it is used in the passage? This is a vocabulary question that measures your literal comprehension. The most important elements in this question are *definition* and *boon*. Mark these words. Again, note that the question asks for the *most accurate* definition—more than one answer choice may apply, but only one offers the best answer.

Read Actively

Now, read actively, marking the passage. The following marked passage is an example of which things you might choose to circle or underline in the passage:

In his famous study of myth, *The Hero With a Thousand Faces*, Joseph Campbell writes about the archetypal hero who has ventured outside the boundaries of the village and, after many **trials** and **adventures,** has returned with the **boon** that will **save** or **enlighten** his fellows. Like Carl Jung, Campbell believes that the story of the hero is part of the collective unconscious of all humankind. He likens the returning **hero** to the **sacred or tabooed personage** described by James Frazier in *The Golden Bough*. (**comparison here**) Such an individual must, in many instances of myth, be insulated from the rest of society, "not merely for his own sake but for the sake of others; for since the virtue of holiness is, so to say, a powerful explosive which the smallest touch can detonate, it is necessary in the interest of the general safety to keep it within narrow bounds."

There is much similarity between the archetypal hero who has journeyed into the wilderness and the poet who has journeyed into the realm of imagination. (**comparison here**) Both places are **dangerous** and **full of wonders**, and both, at their deepest levels, are journeys that take place into the kingdom of the **unconscious mind**, a place that, in Campbell's words, "goes down into unsuspected Aladdin caves. There not only jewels but dangerous jinn abide . . ."

Like many reading comprehension passages, the sample text features topic sentences that begin each paragraph. Then, the paragraphs become detail-heavy. Although you may have marked different terms in the sample passage, you should underscore the word *boon* in the first sentence, because it applies to the second question. The information you need to infer the answer to the first question (the story that is likely told by Campbell's hero and Frazier's sacred or tabooed personage) is also contained in the first paragraph. The quotation at the end of the first paragraph is dense and somewhat difficult to read and understand. Don't bother rereading difficult parts of a passage—in this case, you can answer the questions without completely comprehending the quotation.

Your system of marking this passage may vary. You may underline topic sentences, circle words that cue important details, or put a star beside words that indicate the author's attitude or purpose. The important thing is to mark the passage in a way that will help you answer the questions.

Depending on the answers you are seeking, you may jot down notes or make observations as you read:

- Regarding the main idea, it seems that the author is proposing that the act of creating is similar to the journey undertaken by Campbell's mythic hero—both make a kind of passage and return with a vital message for others. (This would apply to a question that asks you to summarize the main idea.)
- The passage uses comparison to describe Campbell's study of myth: it compares Jung and Campbell, Campbell and Frazier, and the hero and the poet. (This would apply to a question about organization of the passage.)
- The author cites quotes by Campbell to support the main idea. (This would apply to an evaluation question in which you are asked to look at the strengths and weaknesses of the author's argument.)
- The tone of the passage is measured and analytical. (This would apply to a question about the author's attitude or point of view.)

Review the Passage

Take a few seconds to summarize in your own words what the passage is about. Look again at how you have marked the passage.

The passage is about Joseph Campbell's mythic hero and how his journey and return home relate to the experience of a poet.

Answer the Questions

Look again at question 1:

1. Based on the passage, which of the following best describes the story that will likely be told by Campbell's returning hero and Frazier's sacred or tabooed personage?
   a. a radically mind-altering story
   b. a story that will terrify people to no good end
   c. a warning of catastrophe to come
   d. a story based on a dangerous lie
   e. a parable aimed at establishing a religious movement

The passage states that the hero's tale will *save* and *enlighten* his fellows, but that it will also be *dangerous*. Choice **a** is the best answer. You can infer from the information of the passage that such a story would surely be radically mind-altering. Choice **b** is directly contradicted in the passage. If the hero's tale would terrify people to no good end, it could not possibly be enlightening. There is nothing in the passage to imply that the tale is a warning of catastrophe, a dangerous lie, or a parable (choices **c**, **d**, and **e**).

Now, look again at question 2:

2. Which of the following is the most accurate definition of the word *boon* as it is used in the passage?
   a. present
   b. blessing
   c. charm
   d. prize
   e. curse

Even if you don't know the dictionary definition of the word *boon,* you can determine its meaning from the context of the passage. You can determine that *boon* is a positive term because the passage states that the hero's boon *will save or enlighten his fellows.* Therefore, you can eliminate choice **e**, *curse,* which is negative. You can also guess from the context of the passage that a boon is likely to be intangible, and not a concrete *present, charm,* or *prize* (choices **a**, **c**, and **d**). Choice **b** offers the most accurate definition of boon, which is a timely benefit, favor, or blessing.

Now, take the skills you have learned or honed in this review and apply them to the practice tests.

9 ▶ Mathematics Skills Review

CHAPTER SUMMARY

This chapter covers the math skills you need to know for the NYSTCE. First, you will learn about question types, and then you will learn about arithmetic, measurement, algebra, geometry, and data analysis.

The NYSTCE measures those mathematical skills and concepts that a New York State educator needs to teach math effectively in state public schools. Many of the problems require the integration of multiple skills and broad knowledge to achieve a solution. The exams cover several types of questions, and several types of math. Before you start reviewing math concepts, you should familiarize yourself specifically with Subarea 1 of the LAST. Subarea 1 is outlined in Chapter 4. This subarea is where you will find the bulk of the NYSTCE objectives related to mathematical processes and knowledge. However, it is recommended that you review the math skills presented in this chapter to prepare for your CST as well, as questions throughout these two exams—the LAST and CST—may involve reading and interpreting charts, graphs, and other visual representations to respond to content-related questions.

There are two types of skills you should know: conceptual knowledge and procedural knowledge.

Conceptual Knowledge refers to your ability to understand number and operation sense. You must have an understanding of the basic ideas of numbers, number properties, and operations defined on numbers (whole numbers, fractions, and decimals).

Some question types include:

- **Order**. These questions require an understanding of order among whole numbers, fractions, and decimals.
- **Equivalence**. These questions require an understanding that numbers can be represented in more than just one way.
- **Numeration and place value**. These questions require an understanding of how numbers are named, place value, and order of value.
- **Number properties**. These questions require an understanding of the properties of whole numbers.
- **Operation properties**. These questions require an understanding of the properties (commutative, associative, and distributive) of the basic operations (addition, subtraction, multiplication, and division).

Procedural Knowledge refers to your ability to understand the procedures necessary to represent quantitative relationships. These questions also show your ability to plan, solve, interpret, or complete operations to solve math problems.

Some question types include:

- **Computation**. These questions require an ability to perform computations; change the result of a computation to fit the context of a problem; and recognize what is needed to solve a problem.
- **Estimation**. These questions require an ability to estimate and to determine the validity of an estimate.
- **Ratio, proportion, and percent**. These questions require an ability to solve problems dealing with ratio, proportion, and percent.
- **Probability**. These questions require an ability to evaluate numbers used to express simple probability and to determine the probability of a possible outcome.
- **Equations**. These questions require an ability to solve simple equations and inequalities and to guess the result of changing aspects of a problem.
- **Algorithmic thinking**. These questions require an ability to understand an algorithmic view (i.e., you must follow procedure, understand different ways to solve a problem, identify or evaluate a procedure, and recognize patterns).

Representations of Quantitative Information refers to your ability to understand graphical displays of quantitative information, to extract information, to recognize if statements based on information are valid or not, to understand relationships in and extrapolate data, and to display a given set of information graphically. These types of questions are sprinkled throughout the NYSTCE.

Some question types include:

- **Interpretation**. These questions require an ability to read and interpret displays of information, including bar graphs, line graphs, pie charts, pictographs, tables, scatter plots, schedules, simple flowcharts, and diagrams. You must also have the ability to recognize relationships and understand statistics.

- **Trends**. These questions require an ability to recognize, compare, contrast, and predict based on given information.
- **Inferences**. These questions require an ability to make conclusions or inferences from given data.
- **Patterns**. These questions require an ability to understand patterns in data, including variation.
- **Connections**. These questions require an ability to understand the relationships between numerical values, the rules relating table values. You must be able to select a graph accurately representing a set of data.

Measurement and Informal Geometry refers to your ability to understand measurement, both U.S. customary and metric systems, and properties and relationships in geometry. At least half the questions will focus on informal geometry.

Some question types include:

- **Systems of measurement**. These questions require an ability to demonstrate basic understanding of the U.S. customary and metric systems of measurement. You should be able to convert from one unit to another and recognize correct units for making measurements.
- **Measurement**. These questions require an ability to recognize the measurements needed to solve a problem. You must also be able to solve for area, volume, and length, including using formulas, estimation, and rates, and comparisons.
- **Geometric properties**. These questions require an ability to use geometric properties and relationships in real-life applications.

Formal Mathematical Reasoning refers to your ability to use logic.
Some question types include:

- **Logical connectives and quantifiers**. These questions require an ability to interpret statements that use *and, or, if . . . then*, as well as *some, all*, or *none*.
- **Validity of arguments**. These questions require an ability to use reasoning to determine the validity of an argument.
- **Generalization**. These questions require an ability to understand generalization.

Now that you know more about the question types, following are the math skills you will need to review to succeed. Examples and sample questions are provided to help you study.

▶ Arithmetic

This section covers the basics of mathematical operations and their sequence. It also reviews variables, integers, fractions, decimals, and square roots.

Numbers and Symbols

Numbers and the Number Line

- **Counting numbers** (or natural numbers): $1, 2, 3, \ldots$
- **Whole numbers** include the counting numbers and zero: $0, 1, 2, 3, 4, 5, 6, \ldots$
- **Integers** include the whole numbers and their opposites. Remember, the opposite of zero is zero: $\ldots -3, -2, -1, 0, 1, 2, 3, \ldots$
- **Rational numbers** are all numbers that can be written as fractions, where the numerator and denominator are both integers, but the denominator is not zero. For example, $\frac{2}{3}$ is a rational number, as is $\frac{-6}{5}$. The decimal form of these numbers is either a terminating (ending) decimal, such as the decimal form of $\frac{3}{4}$ which is 0.75; or a repeating decimal, such as the decimal form of $\frac{1}{3}$ which is $0.3333333\ldots$
- **Irrational numbers** are numbers that cannot be expressed as terminating or repeating decimals (i.e., nonrepeating, nonterminating decimals such as π, $\sqrt{2}$, $\sqrt{12}$).

The number line is a graphical representation of the order of numbers. As you move to the right, the value increases. As you move to the left, the value decreases.

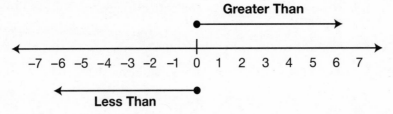

If we need a number line to reflect certain rational or irrational numbers, we can estimate where they should be.

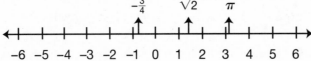

Comparison Symbols

The following table will illustrate some comparison symbols:

=	is equal to	$5 = 5$
≠	is not equal to	$4 \neq 3$
>	is greater than	$5 > 3$
≥	is greater than or equal to	$x \geq 5$ (x can be 5 or any number > 5)
<	is less than	$4 < 6$
≤	is less than or equal to	$x \leq 3$ (x can be 3 or any number < 3)

Symbols of Addition

In addition, the numbers being added are called **addends**. The result is called a **sum**. The symbol for addition is called a **plus** sign. In the following example, 4 and 5 are addends and 9 is the sum:

$$4 + 5 = 9$$

Symbols of Subtraction

In subtraction, the number being subtracted is called the **subtrahend**. The number being subtracted FROM is called the **minuend**. The answer to a subtraction problem is called a **difference**. The symbol for subtraction is called a **minus** sign. In the following example, 15 is the minuend, 4 is the subtrahend, and 11 is the difference:

$$15 - 4 = 11$$

Symbols of Multiplication

When two or more numbers are being multiplied, they are called **factors**. The answer that results is called the **product**. In the following example, 5 and 6 are factors and 30 is their product:

$$5 \times 6 = 30$$

There are several ways to represent multiplication in the above mathematical statement.

- A dot between factors indicates multiplication:
  $5 \cdot 6 = 30$
- Parentheses around any one or more factors indicate multiplication:
  $(5)6 = 30$, $5(6) = 30$, and $(5)(6) = 30$.

- Multiplication is also indicated when a number is placed next to a variable: $5a = 30$. In this equation, 5 is being multiplied by a.

Symbols of Division

In division, the number being divided BY is called the **divisor**. The number being divided INTO is called the **dividend**. The answer to a division problem is called the **quotient**.

There are a few different ways to represent division with symbols. In each of the following equivalent expressions, 3 is the divisor and 8 is the dividend:

$$8 \div 3, \; 8/3, \; \frac{8}{3}, \text{ and } 3\overline{)8}$$

Prime and Composite Numbers

A positive integer that is greater than the number 1 is either prime or composite, but not both.

- A **prime** number is a number that has exactly two factors: 1 and itself.

    Examples
    2, 3, 5, 7, 11, 13, 17, 19, 23 . . .

- A **composite** number is a number that has more than two factors.

    Examples
    4, 6, 8, 9, 10, 12, 14, 15, 16 . . .

- The number 1 is neither prime nor composite since it has only one factor.

Operations

Addition

Addition is used when it is necessary to combine amounts. It is easiest to add when the addends are stacked in a column with the place values aligned. Work from right to left, starting with the ones column.

    Example
    Add $40 + 129 + 24$.

1. Align the addends in the ones column. Because it is necessary to work from right to left, begin to add starting with the ones column. Because the ones column totals 13, and 13 equals 1 ten and 3 ones, write the 3 in the ones column of the answer, and regroup or "carry" the 1 ten to the next column as a 1 over the tens column so it gets added with the other tens.

$$
\begin{array}{r}
1\\
40\\
129\\
+\ \ 24\\
\hline
3
\end{array}
$$

2. Add the tens column, including the regrouped 1.

$$
\begin{array}{r}
1\\
40\\
129\\
+\ \ 24\\
\hline
93
\end{array}
$$

3. Then add the hundreds column. Because there is only one value, write the 1 in the answer.

$$
\begin{array}{r}
1\\
40\\
129\\
+\ \ 24\\
\hline
193
\end{array}
$$

Subtraction

Subtraction is used to find the difference between amounts. It is easiest to subtract when the minuend and subtrahend are in a column with the place values aligned. Again, just as in addition, work from right to left. It may be necessary to regroup.

Example

If Becky has 52 clients, and Claire has 36, how many more clients does Becky have?

1. Find the difference between their client numbers by subtracting. Start with the ones column. Because 2 is less than the number being subtracted (6), regroup or "borrow" a ten from the tens column. Add the regrouped amount to the ones column. Now subtract 12 − 6 in the ones column.

$$
\begin{array}{r}
4\,1\\
\cancel{5}\cancel{2}\\
-\ \ 36\\
\hline
6
\end{array}
$$

2. Regrouping 1 ten from the tens column left 4 tens. Subtract 4 − 3 and write the result in the tens column of the answer. Becky has 16 more clients than Claire. Check by addition: 16 + 36 = 52.

$$
\begin{array}{r}
\overset{4\,1}{\cancel{5}2} \\
-\ \ 36 \\
\hline
16
\end{array}
$$

Multiplication

In multiplication, the same amount is combined multiple times. For example, instead of adding 30 three times, 30 + 30 + 30, it is easier to simply multiply 30 by 3. If a problem asks for the product of two or more numbers, the numbers should be multiplied to arrive at the answer.

Example

A school auditorium contains 54 rows, each containing 34 seats. How many seats are there in total?

1. In order to solve this problem, you could add 34 to itself 54 times, but we can solve this problem easier with multiplication. Line up the place values vertically, writing the problem in columns. Multiply the number in the ones place of the top factor (4) by the number in the ones place of the bottom factor (4): $4 \times 4 = 16$. Because 16 = 1 ten and 6 ones, write the 6 in the ones place in the first partial product. Regroup or carry the ten by writing a 1 above the tens place of the top factor.

$$
\begin{array}{r}
\overset{1}{}\ \ \\
34 \\
\times\ \ 54 \\
\hline
6
\end{array}
$$

2. Multiply the number in the tens place in the top factor (3) by the number in the ones place of the bottom factor (4); $4 \times 3 = 12$. Then add the regrouped amount 12 + 1 = 13. Write the 3 in the tens column and the one in the hundreds column of the partial product.

$$
\begin{array}{r}
\overset{1}{}\ \ \\
34 \\
\times\ \ 54 \\
\hline
136
\end{array}
$$

3. The last calculations to be done require multiplying by the tens place of the bottom factor. Multiply 5 (tens from bottom factor) by 4 (ones from top factor); $5 \times 4 = 20$, but because the 5 really represents a number of tens, the actual value of the answer is 200 ($50 \times 4 = 200$). Therefore, write the two zeros under the ones and tens columns of the second partial product and regroup or carry the 2 hundreds by writing a 2 above the tens place of the top factor.

$$
\begin{array}{r}
\overset{2}{}\ \ \\
34 \\
\times\ \ 54 \\
\hline
136 \\
00
\end{array}
$$

4. Multiply 5 (tens from bottom factor) by 3 (tens from top factor); $5 \times 3 = 15$, but since the 5 and the 3 each represent a number of tens, the actual value of the answer is 1,500 ($50 \times 30 = 1,500$). Add the two additional hundreds carried over from the last multiplication: $15 + 2 = 17$ (hundreds). Write the 17 in front of the zeros in the second partial product.

$$
\begin{array}{r}
^2 \\
34 \\
\times\ \ 54 \\
\hline
136 \\
1,700 \\
\end{array}
$$

5. Add the partial products to find the total product:

$$
\begin{array}{r}
^2 \\
34 \\
\times\ \ 54 \\
\hline
136 \\
+\ \ 1,700 \\
\hline
1,836 \\
\end{array}
$$

Note: It is easier to perform multiplication if you write the factor with the greater number of digits in the top row. In this example, both factors have an equal number of digits, so it does not matter which is written on top.

Division

In division, the same amount is subtracted multiple times. For example, instead of subtracting 5 from 25 as many times as possible, $25 - 5 - 5 - 5 - 5 - 5$, it is easier to simply divide, asking how many 5s are in 25; $25 \div 5$.

Example

At a road show, three artists sold their beads for a total of $54. If they share the money equally, how much money should each artist receive?

1. Divide the total amount ($54) by the number of ways the money is to be split (3). Work from left to right. How many times does 3 divide 5? Write the answer, 1, directly above the 5 in the dividend, because both the 5 and the 1 represent a number of tens. Now multiply: Because $1(\text{ten}) \times 3(\text{ones}) = 3(\text{tens})$, write the 3 under the 5, and subtract; $5(\text{tens}) - 3(\text{tens}) = 2(\text{tens})$.

$$
\begin{array}{r}
1\ \ \ \\
3\overline{)54} \\
-3\ \ \ \\
\hline
2\ \ \ \\
\end{array}
$$

2. Continue dividing. Bring down the 4 from the ones place in the dividend. How many times does 3 divide 24? Write the answer, 8, directly above the 4 in the dividend. Because $3 \times 8 = 24$, write 24 below the other 24 and subtract $24 - 24 = 0$.

$$
\begin{array}{r}
18 \\
3\overline{)54} \\
-3\!\downarrow \\
\hline
24 \\
-24 \\
\hline
0
\end{array}
$$

Remainders

If you get a number other than zero after your last subtraction, this number is your remainder.

Example

9 divided by 4.

$$
\begin{array}{r}
2 \\
4\overline{)9} \\
-8 \\
\hline
1
\end{array}
$$

1 is the remainder.

The answer is 2 r1. This answer can also be written as $2\frac{1}{4}$ because there was one part left over out of the four parts needed to make a whole.

Working with Integers

Remember, an integer is a whole number or its opposite. Here are some rules for working with integers:

Adding

Adding numbers with the same sign results in a sum of the same sign:

(positive) + (positive) = positive   and   (negative) + (negative) = negative

When adding numbers of different signs, follow this two-step process:

1. Subtract the positive values of the numbers. Positive values are the values of the numbers without any signs.
2. Keep the sign of the number with the larger positive value.

Example

$-2 + 3 =$

1. Subtract the positive values of the numbers: $3 - 2 = 1$.
2. The number 3 is the larger of the two positive values. Its sign in the original example was positive, so the sign of the answer is positive. The answer is positive 1.

Example

$8 + -11 =$

1. Subtract the positive values of the numbers: $11 - 8 = 3$.
2. The number 11 is the larger of the two positive values. Its sign in the original example was negative, so the sign of the answer is negative. The answer is negative 3.

Subtracting

When subtracting integers, change all subtraction signs to addition signs and change the sign of the number being subtracted to its opposite. Then follow the rules for addition.

Examples

$(+10) - (+12) = (+10) + (-12) = -2$
$(-5) - (-7) = (-5) + (+7) = +2$

Multiplying and Dividing

A simple method for remembering the rules of multiplying and dividing is that if the signs are the same when multiplying or dividing two quantities, the answer will be positive. If the signs are different, the answer will be negative.

(positive) $\times$ (positive) = positive
$\dfrac{\text{(positive)}}{\text{(positive)}} = $ positive

(positive) $\times$ (negative) = negative
$\dfrac{\text{(positive)}}{\text{(negative)}} = $ negative

(negative) $\times$ (negative) = positive
$\dfrac{\text{(negative)}}{\text{(negative)}} = $ positive

Examples

$(10)(-12) = -120$
$-5 \times -7 = 35$
$-\dfrac{12}{3} = -4$
$\dfrac{15}{3} = 5$

Sequence of Mathematical Operations

There is an order in which a sequence of mathematical operations must be performed:

P: Parentheses/Grouping Symbols. Perform all operations within parentheses first. If there is more than one set of parentheses, begin to work with the innermost set and work toward the outside. If more than one operation is present within the parentheses, use the remaining rules of order to determine which operation to perform first.

E: Exponents. Evaluate exponents.

M/D: Multiply/Divide. Work from left to right in the expression.

A/S: Add/Subtract. Work from left to right in the expression.

This order is illustrated by the following acronym PEMDAS, which can be remembered by using the first letter of each of the words in the phrase: **P**lease **E**xcuse **M**y **D**ear **A**unt **S**ally.

Example

$$\frac{(5+3)^2}{4} + 27$$
$$= \frac{(8)^2}{4} + 27$$
$$= \frac{64}{4} + 27$$
$$= 16 + 27$$
$$= 43$$

Properties of Arithmetic

There are several properties of mathematics:

- **Commutative Property**: This property states that the result of an arithmetic operation is not affected by reversing the order of the numbers. Multiplication and addition are operations that satisfy the commutative property.

  ### *Examples*

  $5 \times 2 = 2 \times 5$
  $5a = a5$
  $b + 3 = 3 + b$

  However, neither subtraction nor division is commutative, because reversing the order of the numbers does not yield the same result.

  ### *Examples*

  $5 - 2 \neq 2 - 5$
  $6 \div 3 \neq 3 \div 6$

- **Associative Property**: If parentheses can be moved to group different numbers in an arithmetic problem without changing the result, then the operation is associative. Addition and multiplication are associative.

  Examples

  $2 + (3 + 4) = (2 + 3) + 4$

  $2(ab) = (2a)b$

- **Distributive Property**: When a value is being multiplied by a sum or difference, multiply that value by each quantity within the parentheses. Then, take the sum or difference to yield an equivalent result.

  Examples

  $5(a + b) = 5a + 5b$

  $5(100 - 6) = (5 \times 100) - (5 \times 6)$

  This second example can be proved by performing the calculations:

  $$5(94) = 5(100 - 6)$$
  $$= 500 - 30$$
  $$470 = 470$$

Additive and Multiplicative Identities and Inverses

- The **additive identity** is the value which, when added to a number, does not change the number. For all of the sets of numbers defined previously (counting numbers, integers, rational numbers, etc.), the additive identity is 0.

  Examples

  $5 + 0 = 5$

  $-3 + 0 = -3$

  Adding 0 does not change the values of 5 and −3, so 0 is the additive identity.

- The **additive inverse** of a number is the number which, when added to the number, gives you the additive identity.

  Example

  What is the additive inverse of −3?

This means, "What number can I add to −3 to give me the additive identity (0)?"

−3 + ___ = 0

−3 + 3 = 0

The answer is 3.

- The **multiplicative identity** is the value which, when multiplied by a number, does not change the number. For all of the sets of numbers defined previously (counting numbers, integers, rational numbers, etc.) the multiplicative identity is 1.

Examples

$5 \times 1 = 5$

$-3 \times 1 = -3$

Multiplying by 1 does not change the values of 5 and −3, so 1 is the multiplicative identity.

- The **multiplicative inverse** of a number is the number which, when multiplied by the number, gives you the multiplicative identity.

Example

What is the multiplicative inverse of 5?

This means, "What number can I multiply 5 by to give me the multiplicative identity (1)?"

$5 \times \underline{\quad} = 1$

$5 \times \frac{1}{5} = 1$

The answer is $\frac{1}{5}$.

There is an easy way to find the multiplicative inverse. It is the **reciprocal**, which is obtained by reversing the numerator and denominator of a fraction. In the above example, the answer is the reciprocal of 5; 5 can be written as $\frac{5}{1}$, so the reciprocal is $\frac{1}{5}$.

Some numbers and their reciprocals:

4	$\frac{1}{4}$
$\frac{2}{3}$	$\frac{3}{2}$
$-\frac{6}{5}$	$-\frac{5}{6}$
$\frac{1}{6}$	6

Note: Reciprocals do not change sign.

Note: The additive inverse of a number is the opposite of the number; the multiplicative inverse is the reciprocal.

Factors and Multiples

Factors

Factors are numbers that can be divided into a larger number without a remainder.

Example

$12 \div 3 = 4$

The number 3 is, therefore, a factor of the number 12. Other factors of 12 are 1, 2, 4, 6, and 12. The common factors of two numbers are the factors that both numbers have in common.

Examples

The factors of 24 = 1, 2, 3, 4, 6, 8, 12, and 24.
The factors of 18 = 1, 2, 3, 6, 9, and 18.

From the previous examples, you can see that the common factors of 24 and 18 are 1, 2, 3, and 6. From this list it can also be determined that the *greatest* common factor of 24 and 18 is 6. Determining the **greatest common factor** (GCF) is useful for simplifying fractions.

Example

Simplify $\frac{16}{20}$

The factors of 16 are 1, 2, 4, 8, and 16. The factors of 20 are 1, 2, 4, 5, and 20. The common factors of 16 and 20 are 1, 2, and 4. The greatest of these, the GCF, is 4. Therefore, to simplify the fraction, both numerator and denominator should be divided by 4.

$$\frac{16 \div 4}{20 \div 4} = \frac{4}{5}$$

Multiples

Multiples are numbers that can be obtained by multiplying a number x by a positive integer.

Example

$5 \times 7 = 35$

The number 35 is, therefore, a multiple of the number 5 and of the number 7. Other multiples of 5 are 5, 10, 15, 20, etc. Other multiples of 7 are 7, 14, 21, 28, etc.

The common multiples of two numbers are the multiples that both numbers share.

Example
Some multiples of 4 are: 4, 8, 12, 16, 20, 24, 28, 32, 36 . . .
Some multiples of 6 are: 6, 12, 18, 24, 30, 36, 42, 48 . . .

Some common multiples are 12, 24, and 36. It can also be determined that the *least* common multiple of the numbers 4 and 6 is 12, because this number is the smallest number that appeared in both lists. The **least common multiple**, or LCM, is used when performing addition and subtraction of fractions to find the least common denominator.

Example (using denominators 4 and 6 and LCM of 12)

$$\frac{1}{4} + \frac{5}{6} = \frac{1(3)}{4(3)} + \frac{5(2)}{6(2)}$$
$$= \frac{3}{12} + \frac{10}{12}$$
$$= \frac{13}{12}$$
$$= 1\frac{1}{12}$$

Decimals

The most important thing to remember about decimals is that the first place value to the right of the decimal point is the tenths place. The place values are as follows:

1	2	6	8	•	3	4	5	7
THOUSANDS	HUNDREDS	TENS	ONES	DECIMAL POINT	TENTHS	HUNDREDTHS	THOUSANDTHS	TEN THOUSANDTHS

In expanded form, this number can also be expressed as:

$1,268.3457 = (1 \times 1,000) + (2 \times 100) + (6 \times 10) + (8 \times 1) + (3 \times .1) + (4 \times .01) + (5 \times .001) + (7 \times .0001)$

Adding and Subtracting Decimals

Adding and subtracting decimals is very similar to adding and subtracting whole numbers. The most important thing to remember is to line up the decimal points. Zeros may be filled in as placeholders when all numbers do not have the same number of decimal places.

Example

What is the sum of 0.45, 0.8, and 1.36?

$$
\begin{array}{r}
^{1\ 1}\ \\
0.45 \\
0.80 \\
+\ 1.36 \\
\hline
2.61
\end{array}
$$

Take away 0.35 from 1.06.

$$
\begin{array}{r}
^{0\ 1}\ \\
\cancel{1}.06 \\
-0.35 \\
\hline
0.71
\end{array}
$$

Multiplication of Decimals

Multiplication of decimals is exactly the same as multiplication of integers, except one must make note of the total number of decimal places in the factors.

Example

What is the product of 0.14 and 4.3?

First, multiply as usual (do not line up the decimal points):

$$
\begin{array}{r}
4.3 \\
\times\,.14 \\
\hline
172 \\
+\,430 \\
\hline
602
\end{array}
$$

Now, to figure out the answer, 4.3 has one decimal place and .14 has two decimal places. Add in order to determine the total number of decimal places the answer must have to the right of the decimal point. In this problem, there are a total of three (1 + 2) decimal places. When finished multiplying, start from the right side of the answer, and move to the left the number of decimal places previously calculated.

.602

In this example, 602 turns into .602 because there have to be three decimal places in the answer. If there are not enough digits in the answer, add zeros in front of the answer until there are enough.

Example

Multiply 0.03 × 0.2.

$$
\begin{array}{r}
.03 \\
\times\ \ .2 \\
\hline
6
\end{array}
$$

There are three total decimal places in the problem; therefore, the answer must contain three decimal places. Starting to the right of 6, move left three places. The answer becomes 0.006.

Dividing Decimals

Dividing decimals is a little different from integers for the setup, and then the regular rules of division apply. It is easier to divide if the divisor does not have any decimals. In order to accomplish that, simply move the decimal place to the right as many places as necessary to make the divisor a whole number. If the decimal point is moved in the divisor, it must also be moved in the dividend in order to keep the answer the same as the original problem; 4 ÷ 2 has the same solution as its multiples 8 ÷ 4 and 28 ÷ 14, etc. Moving a decimal point in a division problem is equivalent to multiplying a numerator and denominator of a fraction by the same quantity, which is the reason the answer will remain the same.

If there are not enough decimal places in the answer to accommodate the required move, simply add zeros until the desired placement is achieved. Add zeros after the decimal point to continue the division until the decimal terminates, or until a repeating pattern is recognized. The decimal point in the quotient belongs directly above the decimal point in the dividend.

Example

What is $.425\overline{)1.53}$?

First, to make .425 a whole number, move the decimal point 3 places to the right: 425.
Now, move the decimal point 3 places to the right for 1.53: 1,530.
The problem is now a simple long division problem.

$$
\begin{array}{r}
3.6 \\
425.\overline{)1,530.0} \\
-1,275\downarrow \\
\hline
2,550 \\
-2,550 \\
\hline
0
\end{array}
$$

Comparing Decimals

Comparing decimals is actually quite simple. Just line up the decimal points and then fill in zeros at the end of the numbers until each one has an equal number of digits.

Example

Compare .5 and .005.

Line up decimal points.
.5
.005

Add zeros.
.500
.005

Now, ignore the decimal point and consider, which is bigger: 500 or 5?
500 is definitely bigger than 5, so .5 is larger than .005.

Rounding Decimals

It is often inconvenient to work with very long decimals. Often it is much more convenient to have an approximation for a decimal that contains fewer digits than the entire decimal. In this case, we **round** decimals to a certain number of decimal places. There are numerous options for rounding:

To the nearest integer: zero digits to the right of the decimal point
To the nearest tenth: one digit to the right of the decimal point (tenths unit)
To the nearest hundredth: two digits to the right of the decimal point (hundredths unit)

In order to round, we look at two digits of the decimal: the digit we are rounding to, and the digit to the immediate right. If the digit to the immediate right is less than 5, we leave the digit we are rounding to alone, and omit all the digits to the right of it. If the digit to the immediate right is 5 or greater, we increase the digit we are rounding by one, and omit all the digits to the right of it.

Example

Round $\frac{3}{7}$ to the nearest tenth and the nearest hundredth.

Dividing 3 by 7 gives us the repeating decimal .428571428571.... If we are rounding to the nearest tenth, we need to look at the digit in the tenths position (4) and the digit to the immediate right (2). Because 2 is less than 5, we leave the digit in the tenths position alone, and drop everything to the right of it. So, $\frac{3}{7}$ to the nearest tenth is .4.

To round to the nearest hundredth, we need to look at the digit in the hundredths position (2) and the digit to the immediate right (8). Because 8 is more than 5, we increase the digit in the hundredths position by 1, giving us 3, and drop everything to the right of it. So, $\frac{3}{7}$ to the nearest hundredth is .43.

Fractions

To work well with fractions, it is necessary to understand some basic concepts.

Simplifying Fractions

Rule:

$$\frac{ac}{bc} = \frac{a}{b}$$

- To simplify fractions, identify the greatest common factor (GCF) of the numerator and denominator and divide both the numerator and denominator by this number.

Example

Simplify $\frac{63}{72}$

The GCF of 63 and 72 is 9, so divide 63 and 72 each by 9 to simplify the fraction:

$$\frac{63 \div 9 = 7}{72 \div 9 = 8}$$

$$\frac{63}{72} = \frac{7}{8}$$

Adding and Subtracting Fractions

Rules:

To add or subtract fractions with the same denominator:

$$\frac{a}{b} \pm \frac{c}{b} = \frac{a \pm c}{b}$$

To add or subtract fractions with different denominators:

$$\frac{a}{b} \pm \frac{c}{d} = \frac{ad \pm cb}{bd}$$

- To add or subtract fractions with like denominators, just add or subtract the numerators and keep the denominator.

Examples

$$\frac{1}{7} + \frac{5}{7} = \frac{6}{7} \text{ and } \frac{5}{8} - \frac{2}{8} = \frac{3}{8}$$

- To add or subtract fractions with unlike denominators, first find the least common denominator or LCD. The LCD is the smallest number divisible by each of the denominators.

For example, for the denominators 8 and 12, 24 would be the LCD because 24 is the smallest number that is divisible by both 8 and 12: $8 \times 3 = 24$, and $12 \times 2 = 24$.

Using the LCD, convert each fraction to its new form by multiplying both the numerator and denominator by the appropriate factor to get the LCD, and then follow the directions for adding/subtracting fractions with like denominators.

Example

$$\frac{1}{3} + \frac{2}{5} = \frac{1(5)}{3(5)} + \frac{2(3)}{5(3)}$$
$$= \frac{5}{15} + \frac{6}{15}$$
$$= \frac{11}{15}$$

Multiplication of Fractions

Rule:

$$\frac{a}{b} \times \frac{c}{d} = \frac{a \times c}{b \times d}$$

- Multiplying fractions is one of the easiest operations to perform. To multiply fractions, simply multiply the numerators and the denominators.

Example

$$\frac{4}{5} \times \frac{6}{7} = \frac{24}{35}$$

If any numerator and denominator have common factors, these may be simplified before multiplying. Divide the common multiples by a common factor. In the example below, 3 and 6 are both divided by 3 before multiplying.

Example

$$\frac{\overset{1}{\cancel{3}}}{5} \times \frac{1}{\underset{2}{\cancel{6}}} = \frac{1}{10}$$

Dividing Fractions

Rule:

$$\frac{a}{b} \div \frac{c}{d} = \frac{a}{b} \times \frac{d}{c} = \frac{a \times d}{b \times c}$$

- Dividing fractions is equivalent to multiplying the dividend by the reciprocal of the divisor. When dividing fractions, simply multiply the dividend by the divisor's reciprocal to get the answer.

Example

(dividend) ÷ (divisor)

$$\frac{1}{4} \div \frac{1}{2}$$

Determine the reciprocal of the divisor:

$$\frac{1}{2} \rightarrow \frac{2}{1}$$

Multiply the dividend ($\frac{1}{4}$) by the reciprocal of the divisor ($\frac{2}{1}$) and simplify if necessary.

$$\frac{1}{4} \div \frac{1}{2} = \frac{1}{4} \times \frac{2}{1}$$

$$= \frac{2}{4}$$

$$= \frac{1}{2}$$

Comparing Fractions

Rules:

If $\frac{a}{b} = \frac{c}{d}$, then $ad = bc$

If $\frac{a}{b} < \frac{c}{d}$, then $ad < bc$

If $\frac{a}{b} > \frac{c}{d}$, then $ad > bc$

Sometimes it is necessary to compare the size of fractions. This is very simple when the fractions are familiar or when they have a common denominator.

Examples
$\frac{1}{2} < \frac{3}{4}$ and $\frac{11}{18} > \frac{5}{18}$

- If the fractions are not familiar and/or do not have a common denominator, there is a simple trick to remember. Multiply the numerator of the first fraction by the denominator of the second fraction. Write this answer under the first fraction. Then multiply the numerator of the second fraction by the denominator of the first one. Write this answer under the second fraction. Compare the two numbers. The larger number represents the larger fraction.

Examples
Which is larger: $\frac{7}{11}$ or $\frac{4}{9}$?

Cross multiply:

$7 \times 9 = 63 \qquad 4 \times 11 = 44$

$63 > 44$, therefore,

$\frac{7}{11} > \frac{4}{9}$

Compare $\frac{6}{18}$ and $\frac{2}{6}$.
Cross multiply:

$6 \times 6 = 36 \qquad 2 \times 18 = 36$

$36 = 36$, therefore,

$\frac{6}{18} = \frac{2}{6}$

Converting Decimals to Fractions

- To convert a nonrepeating decimal to a fraction, the digits of the decimal become the numerator of the fraction, and the denominator of the fraction is a power of 10 that contains that number of digits as zeros.

Example
Convert .125 to a fraction.

The decimal .125 means 125 *thousandths*, so it is 125 parts of 1,000. An easy way to do this is to make 125 the numerator, and because there are three digits in the number 125, the denominator is 1 with three zeros, or 1,000:

$$.125 = \frac{125}{1,000}$$

Then we just need to reduce the fraction:

$$\frac{125}{1,000} = \frac{125 \div 125}{1,000 \div 125} = \frac{1}{8}$$

- When converting a repeating decimal to a fraction, the digits of the repeating pattern of the decimal become the numerator of the fraction, and the denominator of the fraction is the same number of 9s as digits.

Example
Convert $.\overline{3}$ to a fraction.

You may already recognize $.\overline{3}$ as $\frac{1}{3}$. The repeating pattern, in this case 3, becomes our numerator. There is one digit in the pattern, so 9 is our denominator.

$$.\overline{3} = \frac{3}{9} = \frac{3 \div 3}{9 \div 3} = \frac{1}{3}$$

Example
Convert $.\overline{36}$ to a fraction.

The repeating pattern, in this case 36, becomes our numerator. There are two digits in the pattern, so 99 is our denominator:

$$.\overline{36} = \frac{36}{99} = \frac{36 \div 9}{99 \div 9} = \frac{4}{11}$$

Converting Fractions to Decimals

- To convert a fraction to a decimal, simply treat the fraction as a division problem.

Example
Convert $\frac{3}{4}$ to a decimal.

$$4\overline{)3.00} = .75$$

So, $\frac{3}{4}$ is equal to .75.

Converting Mixed Numbers to and from Improper Fractions

Rule:

$$a\frac{b}{c} = \frac{ac + b}{c}$$

- A mixed number is a number greater than 1 which is expressed as a whole number joined to a proper fraction. Examples of mixed numbers are $5\frac{3}{8}$, $2\frac{1}{3}$, and $-4\frac{5}{6}$. To convert from a mixed number to an improper fraction (a fraction where the numerator is greater than the denominator), multiply the whole number and the denominator and add the numerator. This becomes the new numerator. The new denominator is the same as the original.

Note: If the mixed number is negative, temporarily ignore the negative sign while performing the conversion, and just make sure you replace the negative sign when you're done.

   Example
   Convert $5\frac{3}{8}$ to an improper fraction.

   Using the prior formula, $5\frac{3}{8} = \frac{5 \times 8 + 3}{8} = \frac{43}{8}$

   Example
   Convert $-4\frac{5}{6}$ to an improper fraction.

   Temporarily ignore the negative sign and perform the conversion: $4\frac{5}{6} = \frac{4 \times 6 + 5}{6} = \frac{29}{6}$
   The final answer includes the negative sign: $-\frac{29}{6}$

- To convert from an improper fraction to a mixed number, simply treat the fraction like a division problem, and express the answer as a fraction rather than a decimal.

   Example
   Convert $\frac{23}{7}$ to a mixed number.

   Perform the division: $23 \div 7 = 3\frac{2}{7}$

Percents

Percents are always "out of 100." 45% means 45 out of 100. Therefore, to write percents as decimals, move the decimal point two places to the left (to the hundredths place).

$$45\% = \frac{45}{100} = 0.45$$

$$3\% = \frac{3}{100} = 0.03$$

$$124\% = \frac{124}{100} = 1.24$$

$$0.9\% = \frac{.9}{100} = \frac{9}{1,000} = 0.009$$

Here are some conversions you should be familiar with:

Fraction	Decimal	Percentage
$\frac{1}{2}$	.5	50%
$\frac{1}{4}$	.25	25%
$\frac{1}{3}$	.333 . . .	$33.\overline{3}\%$
$\frac{2}{3}$	.666 . . .	$66.\overline{6}\%$
$\frac{1}{10}$	.1	10%
$\frac{1}{8}$	.125	12.5%
$\frac{1}{6}$	.1666 . . .	$16.\overline{6}\%$
$\frac{1}{5}$	.2	20%

Absolute Value

The absolute value of a number is the distance of that number from zero. Distances are always represented by positive numbers, so the absolute value of any number is positive. Absolute value is represented by placing small vertical lines around the value: $|x|$.

Examples

The absolute value of seven: $|7|$.

The distance from seven to zero is seven, so $|7| = 7$.

The absolute value of negative three: $|-3|$.

The distance from negative three to zero is three, so $|-3| = 3$.

Exponents

Positive Exponents

A positive exponent indicates the number of times a base is used as a factor to attain a product.

> *Example*
> Evaluate 2^5.
>
> 2 is the base and 5 is the exponent. Therefore, 2 should be used as a factor 5 times to attain a product:
>
> $$2^5 = 2 \times 2 \times 2 \times 2 \times 2 = 32$$

Zero Exponent

Any non-zero number raised to the zero power equals 1.

> *Examples*
> $5^0 = 1$ $70^0 = 1$ $29{,}874^0 = 1$

Negative Exponents

A base raised to a negative exponent is equivalent to the reciprocal of the base raised to the positive exponent (absolute value of the exponent).

> *Examples*
> $5^{-1} = \frac{1}{5}$
> $7^{-2} = \left(\frac{1}{7}\right)^2 = \frac{1}{49}$
> $\left(\frac{2}{3}\right)^{-2} = \left(\frac{3}{2}\right)^2 = \frac{9}{4}$

Exponent Rules

- When multiplying identical bases, you add the exponents.

> *Examples*
> $2^2 \times 2^4 \times 2^6 = 2^{12}$
> $a^2 \times a^3 \times a^5 = a^{10}$

■ When dividing identical bases, you subtract the exponents.

   Examples

   $\dfrac{2^7}{2^3} = 2^4$ $\dfrac{a^9}{a^4} = a^5$

■ If a base raised to a power (in parentheses) is raised to another power, you multiply the exponents together.

   Examples

   $(3^2)^7 = 3^{14}$ $(g^4)^3 = g^{12}$

Perfect Squares

5^2 is read "5 to the second power," or, more commonly, "5 squared." Perfect squares are numbers that are second powers of other numbers. Perfect squares are always zero or positive, because when you multiply a positive or a negative by itself, the result is always positive. The perfect squares are $0^2, 1^2, 2^2, 3^2 \ldots$

   Perfect squares: 0, 1, 4, 9, 16, 25, 36, 49, 64, 81, 100 . . .

Perfect Cubes

5^3 is read "5 to the third power," or, more commonly, "5 cubed." (Powers higher than three have no special name.) Perfect cubes are numbers that are third powers of other numbers. Perfect cubes, unlike perfect squares, can be both positive or negative. This is because when a negative is multiplied by itself three times, the result is negative. The perfect cubes are $0^3, 1^3, 2^3, 3^3 \ldots$

   Perfect cubes: 0, 1, 8, 27, 64, 125 . . .

   ■ Note that 64 is both a perfect square and a perfect cube.

Square Roots

The square of a number is the product of the number and itself. For example, in the statement $3^2 = 3 \times 3 = 9$, the number 9 is the square of the number 3. If the process is reversed, the number 3 is the square root of the number 9. The symbol for square root is $\sqrt{}$ and is called a **radical**. The number inside of the radical is called the **radicand**.

   Example

   $5^2 = 25$, therefore $\sqrt{25} = 5$

Because 25 is the square of 5, it is also true that 5 is the square root of 25.

The square root of a number might not be a whole number. For example, the square root of 7 is 2.645751311. . . . It is not possible to find a whole number that can be multiplied by itself to equal 7. Square roots of non-perfect squares are irrational.

Cube Roots

The cube of a number is the product of the number and itself for a total of three times. For example, in the statement $2^3 = 2 \times 2 \times 2 = 8$, the number 8 is the cube of the number 2. If the process is reversed, the number 2 is the cube root of the number 8. The symbol for cube root is the same as the square root symbol, except for a small three $\sqrt[3]{}$. It is read as "cube root." The number inside of the radical is still called the radicand, and the three is called the index. (In a square root, the index is not written, but it has an index of 2.)

> *Example*
> $5^3 = 125$, therefore $\sqrt[3]{125} = 5$.

Like square roots, the cube root of a number might be not be a whole number. Cube roots of non-perfect cubes are irrational.

Probability

Probability is the numerical representation of the likelihood of an event occurring. Probability is always represented by a decimal or fraction between 0 and 1; 0 meaning that the event will never occur, and 1 meaning that the event will always occur. The higher the probability, the more likely the event is to occur.

A **simple event** is one action. Examples of simple events are: drawing one card from a deck, rolling one die, flipping one coin, or spinning a hand on a spinner once.

Simple Probability

The probability of an event occurring is defined as the number of desired outcomes divided by the total number of outcomes. The list of all outcomes is often called the **sample space**.

$$P(\text{event}) = \frac{\text{\# of desired outcomes}}{\text{total number of outcomes}}$$

> *Example*
> What is the probability of drawing a king from a standard deck of cards?

There are four kings in a standard deck of cards. So, the number of desired outcomes is 4. There are a total of 52 ways to pick a card from a standard deck of cards, so the total number of outcomes is 52. The probability of drawing a king from a standard deck of cards is $\frac{4}{52}$. So, P(king) = $\frac{4}{52}$.

> *Example*
> What is the probability of getting an odd number on the roll of one die?

There are three odd numbers on a standard die: 1, 3, and 5. So, the number of desired outcomes is three. There are six sides on a standard die, so there are a total of six possible outcomes. The probability of rolling an odd number on a standard die is $\frac{3}{6}$. So, P(odd) $= \frac{3}{6}$.

Note: It is not necessary to reduce fractions when working with probability.

Probability of an Event Not Occurring

The sum of the probability of an event occurring and the probability of the event *not* occurring = 1. Therefore, if we know the probability of the event occurring, we can determine the probability of the event *not* occurring by subtracting from 1.

Example

If the probability of rain tomorrow is 45%, what is the probability that it will *not* rain tomorrow?

45% = .45, and 1 − .45 = .55 or 55%. The probability that it will not rain is 55%.

Probability Involving the Word *Or*

Rule:

P(event A *or* event B) = P(event A) + P(event B) − P(overlap of event A and B)

When the word *or* appears in a simple probability problem, it signifies that you will be adding outcomes. For example, if we are interested in the probability of obtaining a king or a queen on a draw of a card, the number of desired outcomes is 8, because there are 4 kings and 4 queens in the deck. The probability of event A (drawing a king) is $\frac{4}{52}$, and the probability of drawing a queen is $\frac{4}{52}$. The overlap of event A and B would be any cards that are both a king and a queen at the same time, but there are no cards that are both a king and a queen at the same time. So, the probability of obtaining a king or a queen is $\frac{4}{52} + \frac{4}{52} - \frac{0}{52} = \frac{8}{52}$.

Example

What is the probability of getting an even number or a multiple of 3 on the roll of a die?

The probability of getting an even number on the roll of a die is $\frac{3}{6}$, because there are three even numbers (2, 4, 6) on a die and a total of six possible outcomes. The probability of getting a multiple of 3 is $\frac{2}{6}$, because there are two multiples of 3 (3, 6) on a die. But because the outcome of rolling a 6 on the die is an overlap of both events, we must subtract $\frac{1}{6}$ from the result so we don't count it twice.

P(even *or* multiple of 3) = P(even) + P(multiple of 3) − P(overlap)
$$= \frac{3}{6} + \frac{2}{6} - \frac{1}{6} = \frac{4}{6}$$

Compound Probability

A **compound event** is performing two or more simple events in succession. Drawing two cards from a deck, rolling three dice, flipping five coins, having four babies, are all examples of compound events.

This can be done "with replacement" (probabilities do not change for each event) or "without replacement" (probabilities change for each event).

The probability of event A followed by event B occurring is P(A) $\times$ P(B). This is called the **counting principle** for probability.

Note: In mathematics, the word *and* usually signifies addition. In probability, however, *and* signifies multiplication and *or* signifies addition.

Example

You have a jar filled with 3 red marbles, 5 green marbles, and 2 blue marbles. What is the probability of getting a red marble followed by a blue marble, with replacement?

"With replacement" in this case means that you will draw a marble, note its color, and then replace it back into the jar. This means that the probability of drawing a red marble does not change from one simple event to the next.

Note that there are a total of 10 marbles in the jar, so the total number of outcomes is 10.

$$P(\text{red}) = \frac{3}{10} \text{ and } P(\text{blue}) = \frac{2}{10} \text{ so P(red followed by blue) is } \frac{3}{10} \times \frac{2}{10} = \frac{6}{100}$$

If the problem was changed to say "without replacement," that would mean you are drawing a marble, noting its color, but not returning it to the jar. This means that for the second event, you no longer have a total number of 10 outcomes, you only have 9 because you have taken one red marble out of the jar. In this case:

$$P(\text{red}) = \frac{3}{10} \text{ and } P(\text{blue}) = \frac{2}{9} \text{ so P(red followed by blue) is } \frac{3}{10} \times \frac{2}{9} = \frac{6}{90}$$

Statistics

Statistics is the field of mathematics that deals with describing sets of data. Often, we want to understand trends in data by looking at where the center of the data lies. There are a number of ways to find the center of a set of data.

Mean

When we talk about average, we usually are referring to the **arithmetic mean** (usually just called the **mean**). To find the mean of a set of numbers, add all of the numbers together and divide by the quantity of numbers in the set.

Average = (sum of set) ÷ (quantity of set)

Example

Find the average of 9, 4, 7, 6, and 4.

$$\frac{9+4+7+6+4}{5} = \frac{30}{5} = 6$$

The mean, or average, of the set is 6.

(Divide by 5 because there are 5 numbers in the set.)

Median

Another center of data is the median. It is literally the "center" number if you arrange all the data in ascending or descending order. To find the median of a set of numbers, arrange the numbers in ascending or descending order and find the middle value.

- If the set contains an odd number of elements, then simply choose the middle value.

  Example

  Find the median of the number set: 1, 5, 4, 7, 2.

  First arrange the set in order—1, 2, 4, 5, 7—and then find the middle value. Because there are five values, the middle value is the third one: 4. The median is 4.

- If the set contains an even number of elements, simply average the two middle values.

  Example

  Find the median of the number set: 1, 6, 3, 7, 2, 8.

  First arrange the set in order—1, 2, 3, 6, 7, 8—and then find the middle values, 3 and 6. Find the average of the numbers 3 and 6: $\frac{3+6}{2} = \frac{9}{2} = 4.5$. The median is 4.5.

Mode

Sometimes when we want to know the average, we just want to know what occurs most often. The **mode** of a set of numbers is the number that appears the greatest number of times.

  Example

  For the number set 1, 2, 5, 9, 4, 2, 9, 6, 9, 7, the number 9 is the mode because it appears the most frequently.

▶ Measurement

This section will review the basics of measurement systems used in the United States (sometimes called customary measurement) and other countries, methods of performing mathematical operations with units of measurement, and the process of converting between different units.

The use of measurement enables a connection to be made between mathematics and the real world. To measure any object, assign a number and a unit of measure. For instance, when a fish is caught, it is often weighed in ounces and its length measured in inches. The following lesson will help you become more familiar with the types, conversions, and units of measurement.

Types of Measurements

The types of measurements used most frequently in the United States are listed here:

Units of Length

12 inches (in.) = 1 foot (ft.)

3 feet = 36 inches = 1 yard (yd.)

5,280 feet = 1,760 yards = 1 mile (mi.)

Units of Volume

8 ounces* (oz.) = 1 cup (c.)

2 cups = 16 ounces = 1 pint (pt.)

2 pints = 4 cups = 32 ounces = 1 quart (qt.)

4 quarts = 8 pints = 16 cups = 128 ounces = 1 gallon (gal.)

Units of Weight

16 ounces* (oz.) = 1 pound (lb.)

2,000 pounds = 1 ton (T.)

Units of Time

60 seconds (sec.) = 1 minute (min.)

60 minute = 1 hour (hr.)

24 hours = 1 day

7 days = 1 week

52 weeks = 1 year (yr.)

12 months = 1 year

365 days = 1 year

*Notice that ounces are used to measure the dimensions of both volume and weight.

Converting Units

When performing mathematical operations, it may be necessary to convert units of measure to simplify a problem. Units of measure are converted by using either multiplication or division.

- To convert from a larger unit into a smaller unit, *multiply* the given number of larger units by the number of smaller units in only one of the larger units:

(given number of the larger units) $\times$ (the number of smaller units per larger unit) = answer in smaller units

For example, to find the number of inches in 5 feet, multiply 5, the number of larger units, by 12, the number of inches in one foot:

5 feet = _?_ inches

5 feet $\times$ 12 (the number of inches in a single foot) = 60 inches: 5 ft. $\times \frac{12 \text{ in.}}{1 \text{ ft.}}$ = 60 in.

Therefore, there are 60 inches in 5 feet.

Example
Change 3.5 tons to pounds.

3.5 tons = _?_ pounds

3.5 tons $\times \frac{2{,}000 \text{ pounds}}{1 \text{ ton}}$ = 7,000 pounds

Therefore, there are 7,000 pounds in 3.5 tons.

- To change a smaller unit to a larger unit, *divide* the given number of smaller units by the number of smaller units in only one of the larger units:

$$\frac{\text{given number of smaller units}}{\text{the number of smaller units per larger unit}} = \text{answer in larger units}$$

For example, to find the number of pints in 64 ounces, divide 64, the number of smaller units, by 16, the number of ounces in one pint.

64 ounces = _?_ pints

$$\frac{64 \text{ ounces}}{16 \text{ ounces per pint}} = 4 \text{ pints}$$

Therefore, 64 ounces equals four pints.

Example
Change 32 ounces to pounds.

32 ounces = _?_ pounds

$$\frac{32 \text{ ounces}}{16 \text{ ounces per pound}} = 2 \text{ pounds}$$

Therefore, 32 ounces equals two pounds.

Basic Operations with Measurement

You may need to add, subtract, multiply, and divide with measurement. The mathematical rules needed for each of these operations with measurement follow.

Addition with Measurements

To add measurements, follow these two steps:

1. Add like units.
2. Simplify the answer by converting smaller units into larger units when possible.

> *Example*
>
> Add 4 pounds 5 ounces to 20 ounces.

$$
\begin{array}{ll}
4 \text{ lb. } 5 \text{ oz.} & \text{Be sure to add ounces to ounces.} \\
+\ \ \ 20 \text{ oz.} & \\
\hline
4 \text{ lb. } 25 \text{ oz.} &
\end{array}
$$

Because 25 ounces is more than 16 ounces (1 pound), simplify by dividing by 16:

$$
\begin{array}{r}
1 \text{ lb. r } 9 \text{ oz.} \\
16 \text{ oz.}{\overline{)25 \text{ oz.}}} \\
-16 \text{ oz.} \\
\hline
9 \text{ oz.}
\end{array}
$$

Then add the 1 pound to the 4 pounds:

4 pounds 25 ounces = 4 pounds + 1 pound 9 ounces = 5 pounds 9 ounces

Subtraction with Measurements

1. Subtract like units if possible.
2. If not, regroup units to allow for subtraction.
3. Write the answer in simplest form.

For example, 6 pounds 2 ounces subtracted from 9 pounds 10 ounces.

$$
\begin{array}{ll}
9 \text{ lb. } 10 \text{ oz.} & \text{Subtract ounces from ounces.} \\
-\ 6 \text{ lb. } 2 \text{ oz.} & \text{Then subtract pounds from pounds.} \\
\hline
3 \text{ lb. } 8 \text{ oz.} &
\end{array}
$$

Sometimes, it is necessary to regroup units when subtracting.

> *Example*
>
> Subtract 3 yards 2 feet from 5 yards 1 foot.

Because 2 feet cannot be taken from 1 foot, regroup 1 yard from the 5 yards and convert the 1 yard to 3 feet. Add 3 feet to 1 foot. Then subtract feet from feet and yards from yards:

$$\overset{4}{\cancel{5}} \text{ yd. } \overset{4}{\cancel{1}} \text{ ft.}$$
$$-\quad 3 \text{ yd. } 2 \text{ ft.}$$
$$\overline{\quad 1 \text{ yd. } 2 \text{ ft.}}$$

5 yards 1 foot − 3 yards 2 feet = 1 yard 2 feet

Multiplication with Measurements

1. Multiply like units if units are involved.
2. Simplify the answer.

Example

Multiply 5 feet 7 inches by 3.

$$
\begin{array}{r}
5 \text{ ft. } 7 \text{ in.} \\
\times \qquad 3 \\
\hline
15 \text{ ft. } 21 \text{ in.}
\end{array}
$$

Multiply 7 inches by 3, then multiply 5 feet by 3. Keep the units separate.

Because 12 inches = 1 foot, simplify 21 inches.

15 ft. 21 in. = 15 ft. + 1 ft. 9 in. = 16 ft. 9 in.

Example

Multiply 9 feet by 4 yards.

First, decide on a common unit: either change the 9 feet to yards, or change the 4 yards to feet. Both options are explained here:

Option 1:
To change yards to feet, multiply the number of feet in a yard (3) by the number of yards in this problem (4).

3 feet in a yard • 4 yards = 12 feet

Then multiply: 9 feet $\times$ 12 feet = 108 square feet.

(**Note:** feet • feet = square feet = ft^2)

Option 2:
To change feet to yards, divide the number of feet given (9), by the number of feet in a yard (3).

9 feet ÷ 3 feet in a yard = 3 yards

Then multiply 3 yards by 4 yards = 12 square yards.

(**Note:** yards • yards = square yards = yd^2)

Division with Measurements

1. Divide into the larger units first.
2. Convert the remainder to the smaller unit.
3. Add the converted remainder to the existing smaller unit if any.
4. Divide into smaller units.
5. Write the answer in simplest form.

Example

Divide 5 quarts 4 ounces by 4.

1. Divide into the larger unit:

$$
\begin{array}{r}
1 \text{ qt. r } 1 \text{ qt.} \\
4\overline{)5 \text{ qt.}} \\
\underline{-4 \text{ qt.}} \\
1 \text{ qt.}
\end{array}
$$

2. Convert the remainder:

   1 qt. = 32 oz.

3. Add remainder to original smaller unit:

   32 oz. + 4 oz. = 36 oz.

4. Divide into smaller units:

   36 oz. ÷ 4 = 9 oz.

5. Write the answer in simplest form:

   1 qt. 9 oz.

Metric Measurements

The metric system is an international system of measurement also called the **decimal system**. Converting units in the metric system is much easier than converting units in the customary system of measurement. However, making conversions between the two systems is much more difficult. The basic units of the metric system are the meter, gram, and liter. Here is a general idea of how the two systems compare:

Metric System	Customary System
1 meter	A meter is a little more than a yard; it is equal to about 39 inches
1 gram	A gram is a very small unit of weight; there are about 30 grams in one ounce.
1 liter	A liter is a little more than a quart.

Prefixes are attached to the basic metric units listed previously to indicate the amount of each unit. For example, the prefix *deci* means one-tenth ($\frac{1}{10}$); therefore, one decigram is one-tenth of a gram, and one decimeter is one-tenth of a meter. The following six prefixes can be used with every metric unit:

Kilo	Hecto	Deka	Deci	Centi	Milli
(k)	(h)	(dk)	(d)	(c)	(m)
1,000	100	10	$\frac{1}{10}$	$\frac{1}{100}$	$\frac{1}{1,000}$

Examples

- 1 hectometer = 1 hm = 100 meters
- 1 millimeter = 1 mm = $\frac{1}{1,000}$ meter = .001 meter
- 1 dekagram = 1 dkg = 10 grams
- 1 centiliter = 1 cL* = $\frac{1}{100}$ liter = .01 liter
- 1 kilogram = 1 kg = 1,000 grams
- 1 deciliter = 1 dL* = $\frac{1}{10}$ liter = .1 liter

*Notice that liter is abbreviated with a capital letter—L.

The chart below illustrates some common relationships used in the metric system:

Length	Weight	Volume
1 km = 1,000 m	1 kg = 1,000 g	1 kL = 1,000 L
1 m = .001 km	1 g = .001 kg	1 L = .001 kL
1 m = 100 cm	1 g = 100 cg	1 L = 100 cL
1 cm = .01 m	1 cg = .01 g	1 cL = .01 L
1 m = 1,000 mm	1 g = 1,000 mg	1 L = 1,000 mL
1 mm = .001 m	1 mg = .001 g	1 mL = .001 L

Conversions within the Metric System

An easy way to do conversions with the metric system is to move the decimal point either to the right or left because the conversion factor is always ten or a power of ten. Remember, when changing from a large unit to a smaller unit, multiply. When changing from a small unit to a larger unit, divide.

Making Easy Conversions within the Metric System

When multiplying by a power of ten, move the decimal point to the right, as the number becomes larger. When dividing by a power of ten, move the decimal point to the left, as the number becomes smaller.

To change from a larger unit to a smaller unit, move the decimal point to the right.

$\rightarrow$

kilo hecto deka UNIT deci centi milli

$\leftarrow$

An easy way to remember the metric prefixes is to remember the mnemonic: "King Henry Died of Drinking Chocolate Milk." The first letter of each word represents a corresponding metric heading from Kilo down to Milli: "King"—Kilo, "Henry"—Hecto, "Died"—Deka, "of"—original Unit, "Drinking"—Deci, "Chocolate"—Centi, and "Milk"—Milli.

To change from a smaller unit to a larger unit, move the decimal point to the left.

Example

Change 520 grams to kilograms.

1. Be aware that changing grams to kilograms is going from small units to larger units and, thus, requires that the decimal point move to the left.
2. Beginning at the UNIT (for grams), note that the kilo heading is three places away. Therefore, the decimal point will move three places to the left.

k h dk UNIT d c m

3. Move the decimal point from the end of 520 to the left three places.
520
←
.520
Place the decimal point before the 5: .520
The answer is 520 grams = .520 kilograms.

Example

Ron's supply truck can hold a total of 20,000 kilograms. If he exceeds that limit, he must buy stabilizers for the truck that cost $12.80 each. Each stabilizer can hold 100 additional kilograms. If he wants to pack 22,300,000 grams of supplies, how much money will he have to spend on the stabilizers?

1. First, change 2,300,000 grams to kilograms.

kg hg dkg g dg cg mg

2. Move the decimal point three places to the left: 22,300,000 g = 22,300.000 kg = 22,300 kg.
3. Subtract to find the amount over the limit: 22,300 kg − 20,000 kg = 2,300 kg.
4. Because each stabilizer holds 100 kilograms and the supplies exceed the weight limit of the truck by 2,300 kilograms, Ron must purchase 23 stabilizers: 2,300 kg ÷ 100 kg per stabilizer = 23 stabilizers.
5. Each stabilizer costs $12.80, so multiply $12.80 by 23: $12.80 × 23 = $294.40.

▶ Algebra

This section will help in mastering algebraic equations by reviewing variables, cross multiplication, algebraic fractions, reciprocal rules, and exponents. Algebra is arithmetic using letters, called **variables**, in place of numbers. By using variables, the general relationships among numbers can be easier to see and understand.

Algebra Terminology

A **term** of a polynomial is an expression that is composed of variables and their exponents, and coefficients. A **variable** is a letter that represents an unknown number. Variables are frequently used in equations, formulas, and in mathematical rules to help illustrate numerical relationships. When a number is placed next to a variable, indicating multiplication, the number is said to be the **coefficient** of the variable.

Examples

$8c$ 8 is the coefficient to the variable c.

$6ab$ 6 is the coefficient to both variables, a and b.

Three Kinds of Polynomials

- **Monomials** are single terms that are composed of variables and their exponents and a positive or negative coefficient. The following are examples of monomials: x, $5x$, $-6y^3$, $10x^2y$, 7, 0.
- **Binomials** are two non-like monomial terms separated by + or − signs. The following are examples of binomials: $x + 2$, $3x^2 - 5x$, $-3xy^2 + 2xy$.
- **Trinomials** are three non-like monomial terms separated by + or − signs. The following are examples of trinomials: $x^2 + 2x - 1$, $3x^2 - 5x + 4$, $-3xy^2 + 2xy - 6x$.
- Monomials, binomials, and trinomials are all examples of **polynomials**, but we usually reserve the word polynomial for expressions formed by more than three terms.
- The **degree** of a polynomial is the largest sum of the terms' exponents.

Examples

- The degree of the trinomial $x^2 + 2x - 1$ is 2, because the x^2 term has the highest exponent of 2.
- The degree of the binomial $x + 2$ is 1, because the x term has the highest exponent of 1.
- The degree of the binomial $-3x^4y^2 + 2xy$ is 6, because the x^4y^2 term has the highest exponent sum of 6.

Like Terms

If two or more terms have exactly the same variable(s), and these variables are raised to exactly the same exponents, they are said to be **like terms**. Like terms can be simplified when added and subtracted.

Examples

$7x + 3x = 10x$

$6y^2 - 4y^2 = 2y^2$

$3cd^2 + 5c^2d$ cannot be simplified. Because the exponent of 2 is on d in $3cd^2$ and on c in $5c^2d$, they are not like terms.

The process of adding and subtracting like terms is called **combining** like terms. It is important to combine like terms carefully, making sure that *the variables are exactly the same.*

Algebraic Expressions

An algebraic expression is a combination of monomials and operations. The difference between algebraic expressions and algebraic equations is that algebraic expressions are evaluated at different given values for variables, while algebraic equations are solved to determine the value of the variable that makes the equation a true statement.

There is very little difference between expressions and equations, because equations are nothing more than two expressions set equal to each other. Their usage is subtly different.

> ### Example
> A mobile phone company charges a $39.99 a month flat fee for the first 600 minutes of calls, with a charge of $.55 for each minute thereafter.
>
> Write an algebraic expression for the cost of a month's mobile phone bill:
> $39.99 + $.55$x$, where x represents the number of additional minutes used.
>
> Write an equation for the cost (C) of a month's mobile phone bill:
> $C = $39.99 + $.55$x$, where x represents the number of additional minutes used.

In the previous example, you might use the expression $39.99 + $.55$x$ to determine the cost if you are given the value of x by substituting the value for x. You could also use the equation $C = $39.99 + $.55$x$ in the same way, but you can also use the equation to determine the value of x if you were given the cost.

Simplifying and Evaluating Algebraic Expressions

We can use the mobile phone company example to illustrate how to simplify algebraic expressions. Algebraic expressions are evaluated by a two-step process: substituting the given value(s) into the expression, and then simplifying the expression by following the order of operations (PEMDAS).

> ### Example
> Using the cost expression $39.99 + $.55$x$, determine the total cost of a month's mobile phone bill if the owner made 700 minutes of calls.
> Let x represent the number of minutes over 600 used, so in order to find out the difference, subtract $700 - 600$; $x = 100$ minutes over 600 used.

Substitution: Replace *x* with its value, using parentheses around the value.

$39.99 + $.55*x*

$39.99 + $.55(100)

Evaluation: PEMDAS tells us to evaluate Parentheses and Exponents first. There is no operation to perform in the parentheses, and there are no exponents, so the next step is to multiply, and then add.

$39.99 + $.55(100)

$39.99 + $55 = $94.99

The cost of the mobile phone bill for the month is $94.99.

You can evaluate algebraic expressions that contain any number of variables, as long as you are given all of the values for all of the variables.

Simple Rules for Working with Linear Equations

A linear equation is an equation whose variables' highest exponent is 1. It is also called a **first-degree equation**. An equation is solved by finding the value of an unknown variable.

1. The equal sign separates an equation into two sides.
2. Whenever an operation is performed on one side, the same operation must be performed on the other side.
3. The first goal is to get all of the variable terms on one side and all of the numbers (called **constants**) on the other side. This is accomplished by *undoing* the operations that are attaching numbers to the variable, thereby isolating the variable. The operations are always done in reverse "PEMDAS" order: start by adding/subtracting, then multiply/divide.
4. The final step often will be to divide each side by the coefficient, the number in front of the variable, leaving the variable alone and equal to a number.

Example

$$5m + 8 = 48$$
$$-8 = -8$$
$$5m = 40$$
$$\frac{5m}{5} = \frac{40}{5}$$
$$m = 8$$

Undo the addition of 8 by subtracting 8 from both sides of the equation. Then "undo" the multiplication by 5 by dividing by 5 on both sides of the equation. The variable, *m*, is now isolated on the left side of the equation, and its value is 8.

Checking Solutions to Equations

To check an equation, substitute the value of the variable into the original equation.

Example

To check the solution of the previous equation, substitute the number 8 for the variable m in $5m + 8 = 48$.

$$5(8) + 8 = 48$$
$$40 + 8 = 48$$
$$48 = 48$$

Because this statement is true, the answer $m = 8$ must be correct.

Isolating Variables Using Fractions

Working with equations that contain fractions is almost exactly the same as working with equations that do not contain variables, except for the final step. The final step when an equation has no fractions is to divide each side by the coefficient. When the coefficient of the variable is a fraction, you will instead multiply both sides by the reciprocal of the coefficient. Technically, you could still divide both sides by the coefficient, but that involves division of fractions, which can be trickier.

Example

$$\frac{2}{3}m + \frac{1}{2} = 12$$
$$-\frac{1}{2} = -\frac{1}{2}$$
$$\frac{2}{3}m = 11\frac{1}{2}$$
$$\frac{3}{2} \cdot \frac{2}{3}m = 11\frac{1}{2} \cdot \frac{3}{2}$$
$$\frac{3}{2} \cdot \frac{2}{3}m = \frac{23}{2} \cdot \frac{3}{2}$$
$$m = \frac{69}{4}$$

Undo the addition of $\frac{1}{2}$ by subtracting $\frac{1}{2}$ from both sides of the equation. Multiply both sides by the reciprocal of the coefficient. Convert the $11\frac{1}{2}$ to an improper fraction to facilitate multiplication. The variable m is now isolated on the left side of the equation, and its value is $\frac{69}{4}$.

Equations with More Than One Variable

Equations can have more than one variable. Each variable represents a different value, although it is possible that the variables have the same value.

Remember that like terms have the same variable and exponent. All of the rules for working with variables apply in equations that contain more than one variable, but you must remember not to combine terms that are not alike.

Equations with more than one variable cannot be "solved," because if there is more than one variable in an equation there is usually an infinite number of values for the variables that would make the equation true. Instead, we are often required to "solve for a variable," which instead means to isolate that variable on one side of the equation.

Example
Solve for y in the equation $2x + 3y = 5$.

There are an infinite number of values for x and y that satisfy the equation. Instead, we are asked to isolate y on one side of the equation.

$$2x + 3y = 5$$
$$-2x = -2x$$
$$\frac{3y}{3} = \frac{-2x + 5}{3}$$
$$y = \frac{-2x + 5}{3}$$

Cross Multiplying
Because algebra uses percents and proportions, it is necessary to learn how to cross multiply. You can solve an equation that sets one fraction equal to another by **cross multiplication**. Cross multiplication involves setting the cross products of opposite pairs of terms equal to each other.

Example

$$\frac{x}{10} = \frac{70}{100}$$
$$100x = 700$$
$$\frac{100x}{100} = \frac{700}{100}$$
$$x = 7$$

Algebraic Fractions
Working with algebraic fractions is very similar to working with fractions in arithmetic. The difference is that algebraic fractions contain algebraic expressions in the numerator and/or denominator.

Example
A hotel currently has only one-fifth of their rooms available. If x represents the total number of rooms in the hotel, find an expression for the number of rooms that will be available if another tenth of the total rooms are reserved.

Because x represents the total number of rooms, $\frac{x}{5}$ (or $\frac{1}{5}x$) represents the number of available rooms. One-tenth of the total rooms in the hotel would be represented by the fraction $\frac{x}{10}$. To find the new number of available rooms, find the difference: $\frac{x}{5} - \frac{x}{10}$.
Write $\frac{x}{5} - \frac{x}{10}$ as a single fraction.

Just like in arithmetic, the first step is to find the LCD of 5 and 10, which is 10. Then change each fraction into an equivalent fraction that has 10 as a denominator.

$$\frac{x}{5} - \frac{x}{10} = \frac{x(2)}{5(2)} - \frac{x}{10}$$
$$= \frac{2x}{10} - \frac{x}{10}$$
$$= \frac{x}{10}$$

$\frac{x}{10}$ rooms will be available after another tenth of the rooms are reserved.

Reciprocal Rules

There are special rules for the sum and difference of reciprocals. The reciprocal of 3 is $\frac{1}{3}$ and the reciprocal of x is $\frac{1}{x}$.

- If x and y are not 0, then $\frac{1}{x} + \frac{1}{y} = \frac{y}{xy} + \frac{x}{xy} = \frac{y+x}{xy}$.
- If x and y are not 0, then $\frac{1}{x} - \frac{1}{y} = \frac{y}{xy} - \frac{x}{xy} = \frac{y-x}{xy}$.

Translating Words into Numbers

The most important skill needed for word problems is being able to translate words into mathematical operations. The following will be helpful in achieving this goal by providing common examples of English phrases and their mathematical equivalents.

Phrases meaning addition: *increased by; sum of; more than; exceeds by.*

Examples

A number increased by five: $x + 5$.

The sum of two numbers: $x + y$.

Ten more than a number: $x + 10$.

Phrases meaning subtraction: *decreased by; difference of; less than; fewer than; diminished by.*

Examples

10 less than a number: $x - 10$.

The difference of two numbers: $x - y$.

Phrases meaning multiplication: *times; times the sum/difference; product; of.*

Example

Three times a number: $3x$.

Twenty percent of 50: $20\% \times 50$.

Five times the sum of a number and three: $5(x + 3)$.

Phrases meaning "equals": *is; result is.*

Example

15 is 14 plus 1: $15 = 14 + 1$.

10 more than 2 times a number is 15: $2x + 10 = 15$.

Assigning Variables in Word Problems

It may be necessary to create and assign variables in a word problem. To do this, first identify any knowns and unknowns. The known may not be a specific numerical value, but the problem should indicate something about its value. Then let x represent the unknown you know the least about.

Examples

Max has worked for three more years than Ricky.

Unknown: Ricky's work experience $= x$

Known: Max's experience is three more years $= x + 3$

Heidi made twice as many sales as Rebecca.

Unknown: number of sales Rebecca made $= x$

Known: number of sales Heidi made is twice Rebecca's amount $= 2x$

There are six less than four times the number of pens than pencils.

Unknown: the number of pencils $= x$

Known: the number of pens $= 4x - 6$

Todd has assembled five more than three times the number of cabinets that Andrew has.

Unknown: the number of cabinets Andrew has assembled $= x$

Known: the number of cabinets Todd has assembled is five more than three times the number

Andrew has assembled $= 3x + 5$

Percentage Problems

To solve percentage problems, determine what information has been given in the problem and fill this information into the following template:

_____ is ____% of _____

Then translate this information into a one-step equation and solve. In translating, remember that *is* translates to = and *of* translates to ×. Use a variable to represent the unknown quantity.

Examples

A) Finding a percentage of a given number:

In a new housing development there will be 50 houses. 40% of the houses must be completed in the first stage. How many houses are in the first stage?

1. Translate.

_____ is 40% of 50.

x is .40 × 50.

2. Solve.

$x = .40 × 50$

$x = 20$

20 is 40% of 50. There are 20 houses in the first stage.

B) Finding a number when a percentage is given:

40% of the cars on the lot have been sold. If 24 were sold, how many total cars are there on the lot?

1. Translate.

24 is 40% of _____

$24 = .40 × x$

2. Solve.

$$\frac{24}{.40} = \frac{.40x}{.40}$$

$60 = x$

24 is 40% of 60. There were 60 total cars on the lot.

C) Finding what percentage one number is of another:

Matt has 75 employees. He is going to give 15 of them raises. What percent of the employees will receive raises?

1. Translate.

15 is _____% of 75.

$15 = x × 75$

2. Solve.

$$\frac{15}{75} = \frac{75x}{75}$$

$$.20 = x$$

$$20\% = x$$

15 is 20% of 75. Therefore, 20% of the employees will receive raises.

Problems Involving Ratio

A **ratio** is a comparison of two quantities measured in the same units. It is symbolized by the use of a colon—$x{:}y$. Ratios can also be expressed as fractions ($\frac{x}{y}$) or using words (x to y).

Ratio problems are solved using the concept of multiples.

Example

A bag contains 60 screws and nails. The ratio of the number of screws to nails is 7:8. How many of each kind are there in the bag?

From the problem, it is known that 7 and 8 share a multiple and that the sum of their products is 60. Whenever you see the word *ratio* in a problem, place an "x" next to each of the numbers in the ratio, and those are your unknowns.

Let $7x$ = the number of screws.

Let $8x$ = the number of nails.

Write and solve the following equation:

$$7x + 8x = 60$$

$$\frac{15x}{15} = \frac{60}{15}$$

$$x = 4$$

Therefore, there are $(7)(4) = 28$ screws and $(8)(4) = 32$ nails.

Check: $28 + 32 = 60$ screws, $\frac{28}{32} = \frac{7}{8}$.

Problems Involving Variation

Variation is a term referring to a constant ratio in the change of a quantity.

- Two quantities are said to vary directly if their ratios are constant. Both variables change in an equal direction. In other words, two quantities vary directly if an increase in one causes an increase in the other. This is also true if a decrease in one causes a decrease in the other.

Example

If it takes 300 new employees a total of 58.5 hours to train, how many hours of training will it take for 800 employees?

Because each employee needs about the same amount of training, you know that the hours vary directly. Therefore, you can set the problem up the following way:

$$\frac{\text{employees}}{\text{hours}} \rightarrow \frac{300}{58.5} = \frac{800}{x}$$

Cross multiply to solve:

$$(800)(58.5) = 300x$$
$$\frac{46{,}800}{300} = \frac{300x}{300}$$
$$156 = x$$

Therefore, it would take 156 hours to train 800 employees.

■ Two quantities are said to vary inversely if their products are constant. The variables change in opposite directions. This means that as one quantity increases, the other decreases, or as one decreases, the other increases.

Example

If two people plant a field in six days, how many days will it take six people to plant the same field? (Assume each person is working at the same rate.)

As the number of people planting increases, the days needed to plant decreases. Therefore, the relationship between the number of people and days varies inversely. Because the field remains constant, the two products can be set equal to each other.

$$2 \text{ people} \times 6 \text{ days} = 6 \text{ people} \times x \text{ days}$$
$$2 \times 6 = 6x$$
$$\frac{12}{6} = \frac{6x}{6}$$
$$2 = x$$

Thus, it would take six people two days to plant the same field.

Rate Problems

In general, there are three different types of rate problems likely to be encountered in the workplace: cost per unit, movement, and work-output. **Rate** is defined as a comparison of two quantities with different units of measure.

$$\text{Rate} = \frac{x \text{ units}}{y \text{ units}}$$

Examples

$$\frac{\text{dollars}}{\text{hour}}, \frac{\text{cost}}{\text{pound}}, \frac{\text{miles}}{\text{hour}}$$

Cost Per Unit

Some problems will require the calculation of unit cost.

>   ### Example
>
>   If 100 square feet cost $1,000, how much does 1 square foot cost?
>
> $$\frac{\text{Total cost}}{\text{\# of square feet}} = \frac{\$1,000}{100\ \text{ft}^2}$$
>
> $$= \$10 \text{ per square foot}$$

Movement

In working with movement problems, it is important to use the following formula:

$$(\text{Rate})(\text{Time}) = \text{Distance}$$

>   ### Example
>
>   A courier traveling at 15 mph traveled from his base to a company in $\frac{1}{4}$ of an hour less than it took when the courier traveled 12 mph. How far away was his drop off?

First, write what is known and unknown.

Unknown: time for courier traveling 12 mph $= x$

Known: time for courier traveling 15 mph $= x - \frac{1}{4}$.

Then, use the formula $(\text{Rate})(\text{Time}) = \text{Distance}$ to find expressions for the distance traveled at each rate:

12 mph for x hours $=$ a distance of $12x$ miles

15 miles per hour for $x - \frac{1}{4}$ hours $=$ a distance of $15x - \frac{15}{4}$ miles.

The distance traveled is the same, therefore, make the two expressions equal to each other:

$$12x = 15x - 3.75$$
$$-15x = -15x$$
$$\frac{-3x}{-3} = \frac{-3.75}{-3}$$
$$x = 1.25$$

Be careful, 1.25 is not the distance; it is the time. Now you must plug the time into the formula $(\text{Rate})(\text{Time}) = \text{Distance}$. Either rate can be used.

$12x = \text{distance}$

$12(1.25) = \text{distance}$

$15 \text{ miles} = \text{distance}$

Work-Output

Work-output problems are word problems that deal with the rate of work. The following formula can be used on these problems:

(Rate of Work)(Time Worked) = Job or Part of Job Completed

Example

Danette can wash and wax two cars in 6 hours, and Judy can wash and wax the same two cars in 4 hours. If Danette and Judy work together, how long will it take to wash and wax one car?

Because Danette can wash and wax two cars in 6 hours, her rate of work is $\frac{2\,\text{cars}}{6\,\text{hours}}$, or one car every 3 hours. Judy's rate of work is therefore, $\frac{2\,\text{cars}}{4\,\text{hours}}$, or one car every 2 hours. In this problem, making a chart will help:

	Rate	**Time**	**=**	**Part of job completed**
Danette	$\frac{1}{3}$	x	=	$\frac{1}{3}x$
Judy	$\frac{1}{2}$	x	=	$\frac{1}{2}x$

Because they are both working on only one car, you can set the equation equal to one: Danette's part + Judy's part = 1 car:

$$\frac{1}{3}x + \frac{1}{2}x = 1$$

Solve by using 6 as the LCD for 3 and 2 and clear the fractions by multiplying by the LCD:

$$6(\tfrac{1}{3}x) + 6(\tfrac{1}{2}x) = 6(1)$$
$$2x + 3x = 6$$
$$\frac{5x}{5} = \frac{6}{5}$$
$$x = 1\tfrac{1}{5}$$

Thus, it will take Judy and Danette $1\frac{1}{5}$ hours to wash and wax one car.

Patterns and Functions

The ability to detect patterns in numbers is a very important mathematical skill. Patterns exist everywhere in nature, business, and finance.

When you are asked to find a pattern in a series of numbers, look to see if there is some common number you can add, subtract, multiply, or divide each number in the pattern by to give you the next number in the series.

For example, in the sequence 5, 8, 11, 14 . . . you can add three to each number in the sequence to get the next number in the sequence. The next number in the sequence is 17.

Example

What is the next number in the sequence $\frac{3}{4}$, 3, 12, 48?

Each number in the sequence can be multiplied by the number 4 to get the next number in the sequence: $\frac{3}{4} \times 4 = 3, 3 \times 4 = 12, 12 \times 4 = 48$, so the next number in the sequence is $48 \times 4 = 192$.

Sometimes it is not that simple. You may need to look for a combination of multiplying and adding, dividing and subtracting, or some combination of other operations.

Example

What is the next number in the sequence 0, 1, 2, 5, 26?

Keep trying various operations until you find one that works. In this case, the correct procedure is to square the term and add 1: $0^2 + 1 = 1, 1^2 + 1 = 2, 2^2 + 1 = 5, 5^2 + 1 = 26$, so the next number in the sequence is $26^2 + 1 = 677$.

Properties of Functions

A **function** is a relationship between two variables x and y where for each value of x, there is one and only one value of y. Functions can be represented in four ways:

- a table or chart
- an equation
- a word problem
- a graph

For example, the following four representations are equivalent to the same function:

Word Problem
Javier has one more than two times the
number of books Susanna has.

Equation

$y = 2x + 1$

Graph

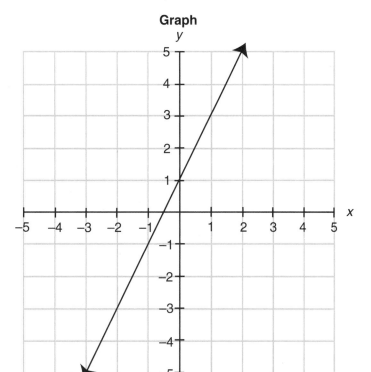

Table

x	y
-3	-5
-2	-3
-1	-1
0	1
1	3
2	5

Helpful hints for determining if a relation is a function:

■ If you can isolate y in terms of x using only one equation, it **is** a function.
■ If the equation contains y^2, it will **not** be a function.
■ If you can draw a vertical line anywhere on a graph such that it touches the graph in more than one place, it is **not** a function.
■ If there is a value for x that has more than one y-value assigned to it, it is **not** a function.

x	y
5	2
3	−1
2	0
6	1
5	4

x	y
−2	5
−1	6
0	7
1	8
2	9

x	y
−2	3
−1	3
0	3
1	3
2	3

In this table, the
x-value of 5 has **two**
corresponding *y*-values,
2 and 4. Therefore,
it is **not** a function.

In this table, every
x-value
{−2, −1, 0, 1, 2, 3}
has **one** corresponding
y-value. This **is**
a function.

In this table, every
x-value
{−2, −1, 0, 1, 2, 3}
has **one** corresponding
y-value, even though
that value is 3
in every case.
This **is** a function.

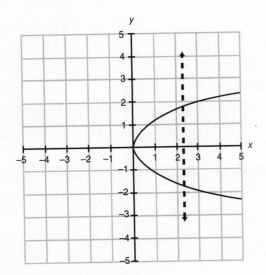

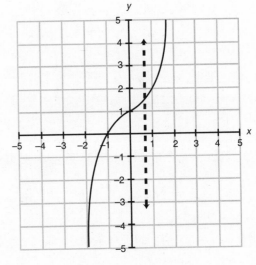

In this graph, there
is at least one vertical
line that can be drawn
(the dotted line) that intersects
the graph in more than one
place. This is **not** a function.

In this graph, there is no
vertical line that can be drawn
that intersects the graph
in more than one place.
This **is** a function.

Examples

$x = 5$ 　　　　Contains no variable y, so you cannot isolate y. This is **not** a function.

$2x + 3y = 5$ 　　Isolate y:

$$2x + 3y = 5$$
$$-2x \qquad -2x$$
$$\frac{3y}{3} = \frac{-2x + 5}{3}$$
$$y = -\frac{2}{3x} + \frac{5}{3}$$

This is a **linear function**, of the form $y = mx + b$.

$x^2 + y^2 = 36$ 　Contains y^2, so it is **not** a function.

$|y| = 5$ 　　　　There is no way to isolate y with a single equation; therefore, it is **not** a function.

Function Notation

Instead of using the variable y, often you will see the variable $f(x)$. This is shorthand for "function of x" to automatically indicate that an equation is a function. This can be confusing; $f(x)$ does not indicate two variables f and x multiplied together, it is a notation that means the single variable y.

Although it may seem that $f(x)$ is not an efficient shorthand (it has more characters than y), it is a very eloquent way to indicate that you are being given expressions to evaluate. For example, if you are given the equation $f(x) = 5x - 2$, and you are being asked to determine the value of the equation at $x = 2$, you need to write "evaluate the equation $f(x) = 5x - 2$ when $x = 2$." This is very wordy. With function notation, you only need to write "determine $f(2)$." The x in $f(x)$ is replaced with a 2, indicating that the value of x is 2. This means that $f(2) = 5(2) - 2 = 10 - 2 = 8$.

All you need to do when given an equation $f(x)$ and told to evaluate $f(value)$, replace the *value* for every occurrence of x in the equation.

Example

Given the equation $f(x) = 2x^2 + 3x + 1$, determine $f(0)$ and $f(-1)$.

$f(0)$ means replace the value 0 for every occurrence of x in the equation and evaluate.
$$f(0) = 2(0)^2 + 3(0) + 1$$
$$= 0 + 0 + 1$$
$$= 1$$
$f(-1)$ means replace the value -1 for every occurrence of x in the equation and evaluate.
$$f(0) = 2(-1)^2 + 3(-1) + 1$$
$$= 2(1) + -3 + 1$$
$$= 2 - 3 + 1$$
$$= 0$$

Families of Functions

There are a number of different types, or families, of functions. Each function family has a certain equation and its graph takes on a certain appearance. You can tell what type of function an equation is by just looking at the equation or its graph.

These are the shapes that various functions have. They can appear thinner or wider, higher or lower, or upside down.

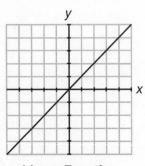

Linear Function
$f(x) = mx + b$
$y = mx + b$

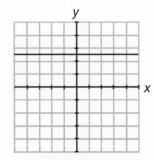

Constant Function
$f(x) = c$
$y = c$
The equation contains no variable x.

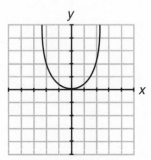

Quadratic Function
$f(x) = ax^2 + bx + c$
$y = ax^2 + bx + c$
This is the function name for a parabola.

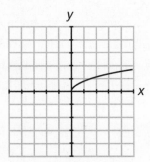

Square Root Function
The equation has to contain a square root symbol.

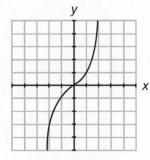

Cubic Function
$f(x) = ax^3 + bx^2 + cx + d$
$y = ax^3 + bx^2 + cx + d$

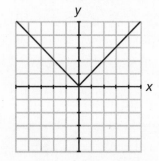

Absolute Value Function
The equation has to have an absolute value symbol in it.

Systems of Equations

A system of equations is a set of two or more equations with the same solution. Two methods for solving a system of equations are substitution and elimination.

Substitution

Substitution involves solving for one variable in terms of another and then substituting that expression into the second equation.

Example

$2p + q = 11$ and $p + 2q = 13$

- First, choose an equation and rewrite it, isolating one variable in terms of the other. It does not matter which variable you choose:
$2p + q = 11$ becomes $q = 11 - 2p$.

- Second, substitute $11 - 2p$ for q in the other equation and solve:
$p + 2(11 - 2p) = 13$
$p + 22 - 4p = 13$
$22 - 3p = 13$
$22 = 13 + 3p$
$9 = 3p$
$p = 3$

- Now, substitute this answer into either original equation for p to find q:
$2p + q = 11$
$2(3) + q = 11$
$6 + q = 11$
$q = 5$

- Thus, $p = 3$ and $q = 5$.

Elimination

The elimination method involves writing one equation over another and then adding or subtracting the like terms on the same sides of the equal sign so that one letter is eliminated.

Example

$x - 9 = 2y$ and $x - 3 = 5y$

- Rewrite each equation in the same form:
$x - 9 = 2y$ becomes $x - 2y = 9$ and $x - 3 = 5y$ becomes $x - 5y = 3$.

- If you subtract the two equations, the "x" terms will be eliminated, leaving only one variable.
Subtract:
$x - 2y = 9$
$-(x - 5y = 3)$
$\frac{3y}{3} = \frac{6}{3}$
$y = 2$ is the answer.

■ Substitute 2 for y in one of the original equations and solve for x:

$x - 9 = 2y$

$x - 9 = 2(2)$

$x - 9 = 4$

$x - 9 + 9 = 4 + 9$

$x = 13$

■ The answer to the system of equations is $y = 2$ and $x = 13$.

If the variables do not have the same or opposite coefficients as in the previous example, adding or subtracting will not eliminate a variable. In this situation, it is first necessary to multiply one or both of the equations by some constant or constants so that the coefficients of one of the variables are the same or opposite. There are many different ways you can choose to do this.

Example

$3x + y = 13$

$x + 6y = -7$

We need to multiply one or both of the equations by some constant that will give equal or opposite coefficients of one of the variables. One way to do this is to multiply every term in the second equation by -3.

$3x + y = 13$

$-3(x + 6y = -7) \;\rightarrow\; -3x - 18y = 21$

Now, if you add the two equations, the "x" terms will be eliminated, leaving only one variable. Continue as in the previous example.

$3x + y = 13$

$-3x - 18y = 21$

$\dfrac{-17y}{-17} = \dfrac{34}{-17}$

$y = -2$ is the answer.

■ Substitute -2 for y in one of the original equations and solve for x.

$3x + y = 13$

$3x + (-2) = 13$

$3x + (-2) + 2 = 13 + 2$

$3x = 15$

$x = 5$

■ The answer to the system of equations is $y = -2$ and $x = 5$

Inequalities

Linear inequalities are solved in much the same way as simple equations. The most important difference is that when an inequality is multiplied or divided by a negative number, the inequality symbol changes direction.

> **Example**
>
> $10 > 5$ so $(10)(-3) < (5)(-3)$
>
> $-30 < -15$

Solving Linear Inequalities

To solve a linear inequality, isolate the letter and solve the same way as you would in a linear equation. Remember to reverse the direction of the inequality sign if you divide or multiply both sides of the equation by a negative number.

> **Example**
>
> If $7 - 2x > 21$, find x.

- Isolate the variable:

$$7 - 2x > 21$$
$$\underline{-7 \qquad -7}$$
$$-2x > 14$$

- Because you are dividing by a negative number, the direction of the inequality symbol changes direction:

$$\frac{-2x}{-2} > \frac{14}{-2}$$
$$x < -7$$

- The answer consists of all real numbers less than -7.

Solving Compound Inequalities

To solve an inequality that has the form $c < ax + b < d$, isolate the letter by performing the same operation on each part of the equation.

> **Example**
>
> If $-10 < -5y - 5 < 15$, find y.

- Add five to each member of the inequality:

$$-10 + 5 < -5y - 5 + 5 < 15 + 5 = 5 < -5y < 20$$

- Divide each term by -5, changing the direction of both inequality symbols:

$$\frac{-5}{-5} < -\frac{5y}{-5} < \frac{20}{-5} = 1 > y > -4$$

The solution consists of all real numbers less than 1 and greater than -4.

► Geometry

This section will familiarize you with the properties of angles, lines, polygons, triangles, and circles, as well as the formulas for area, volume, and perimeter.

Geometry is the study of shapes and the relationships among them. Basic concepts in geometry will be detailed and applied in this section. The study of geometry always begins with a look at basic vocabulary and concepts. Therefore, a list of definitions and important formulas is provided.

Geometry Terms

Area	the space inside a two-dimensional figure
Circumference	the distance around a circle
Chord	a line segment that goes through a circle, with its endpoints on the circle
Congruent	lengths, measures of angles, or size of figures are equal
Diameter	a chord that goes directly through the center of a circle—the longest line segment that can be drawn in a circle
Hypotenuse	the longest side of a right triangle, always opposite the right angle
Leg	either of the two sides of a right triangle that make the right angle
Perimeter	the distance around a figure
π (pi)	the ratio of any circle's circumference to its diameter. Pi is an irrational number, but most of the time it is ok to approximate π with 3.14.
Radius	a line segment from the center of a circle to a point on the circle (half of the diameter)
Surface Area	the sum of the areas of all of a three-dimensional figure's faces
Volume	the space inside a three-dimensional figure

Coordinate Geometry

Coordinate geometry is a form of geometrical operations in relation to a coordinate plane. A **coordinate plane** is a grid of square boxes divided into four quadrants by both a horizontal (x) axis and a vertical (y) axis. These two axes intersect at one coordinate point, (0,0), the **origin**. A coordinate point, also called an **ordered pair**, is a specific point on the coordinate plane with the first number representing the horizontal placement and the second number representing the vertical placement. Coordinate points are given in the form of (x,y).

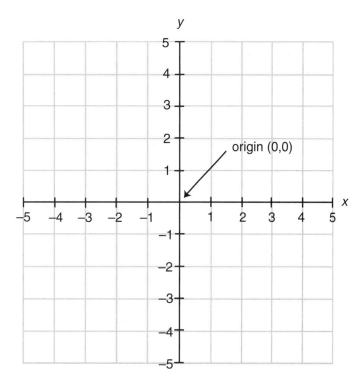

Graphing Ordered Pairs (Points)

- The x-coordinate is listed first in the ordered pair and tells you how many units to move to either the left or to the right. If the x-coordinate is positive, move to the right. If the x-coordinate is negative, move to the left.
- The y-coordinate is listed second and tells you how many units to move up or down. If the y-coordinate is positive, move up. If the y-coordinate is negative, move down.

Example
Graph the following points: (2,3), (3,–2), (–2,3), and (–3,–2).

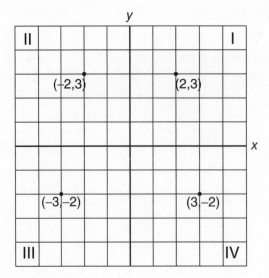

- Notice that the graph is broken up into four quadrants with one point plotted in each one. Here is a chart to indicate which quadrants contain which ordered pairs based on their signs:

Points	Sign of Coordinates	Quadrant
(2,3)	(+,+)	I
(−2,3)	(−,+)	II
(−3,−2)	(−,−)	III
(3,−2)	(+,−)	IV

Lines, Line Segments, and Rays

A **line** is a straight geometric object that goes on forever in both directions. It is infinite in length, and is represented by a straight line with an arrow at both ends. Lines can be labeled with one letter (usually in italics) or with two capital letters near the arrows. **Line segments** are portions of lines. They have two endpoints and a definitive length. Line segments are named by their endpoints. **Rays** have an endpoint and continue straight in one direction. Rays are named by their endpoint and one point on the ray.

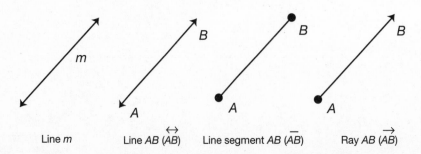

Line *m*   Line *AB* ($\overleftrightarrow{AB}$)   Line segment *AB* ($\overline{AB}$)   Ray *AB* ($\overrightarrow{AB}$)

Parallel and Perpendicular Lines

Parallel lines (or line segments) are a pair of lines, that if extended, would never intersect or meet. The symbol ∥ is used to denote that two lines are parallel. **Perpendicular lines** (or line segments) are lines that intersect to form right angles, and are denoted with the symbol ⊥.

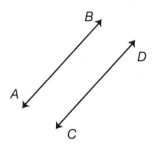

Parallel Lines *AB* and *CD*

$$\overset{\leftrightarrow}{AB} \parallel \overset{\leftrightarrow}{CD}$$

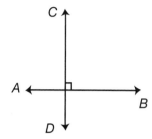

Perpendicular Lines *AB* and *CD*

$$\overset{\leftrightarrow}{AB} \perp \overset{\leftrightarrow}{CD}$$

Lengths of Horizontal and Vertical Segments

Two points with the same *y*-coordinate lie on the same horizontal line and two points with the same *x*-coordinate lie on the same vertical line. The distance between a horizontal or vertical segment can be found by taking the absolute value of the difference of the two points.

> ### Example
> Find the lengths of line segments $\overline{AB}$ and $\overline{BC}$.

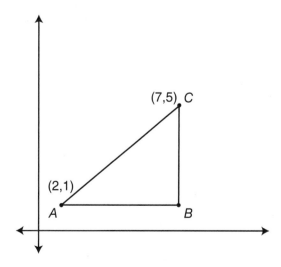

$$|2 - 7| = 5 = AB$$
$$|1 - 5| = 4 = BC$$

Distance of Coordinate Points

The distance between any two points is given by the formula $d = \sqrt{(x_2 - x_1)^2 + (y_2 - y_1)^2}$, where (x_1, y_1) represents the coordinates of one point and (x_2, y_2) is the other. The subscripts are used to differentiate between the two different coordinate pairs.

Example

Find the distance between points $A(-3, 5)$ and $B(1, -4)$.

Let (x_1, y_1) represent point A and let (x_2, y_2) represent point B. This means that $x_1 = -3$, $y_1 = 5$, $x_2 = 1$, and $y_2 = -4$. Substituting these values into the formula gives us:

$$d = \sqrt{(x_2 - x_1)^2 + (y_2 - y_1)^2}$$
$$d = \sqrt{(1 - (-3))^2 + (-4 - 5)^2}$$
$$d = \sqrt{(4)^2 + (-9)^2}$$
$$d = \sqrt{16 + 81}$$
$$d = \sqrt{97}$$

Midpoint

The midpoint of a line segment is a point located at an equal distance from each endpoint. This point is in the exact center of the line segment, and is said to be **equidistant** from the segment's endpoints.

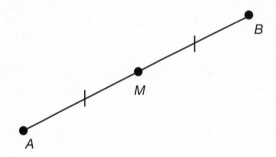

M is the midpoint of $\overline{AB}$

In coordinate geometry, the formula for finding the coordinates of the midpoint of a line segment whose endpoints are (x_1, y_1) and (x_2, y_2) is given by $M = (\frac{x_1 + x_2}{2}, \frac{y_1 + y_2}{2})$.

Example

Determine the midpoint of the line segment $\overline{AB}$ with $A(-3, 5)$ and $B(1, -4)$.

Let (x_1, y_1) represent point A and let (x_2, y_2) represent point B. This means that $x_1 = -3$, $y_1 = 5$, $x_2 = 1$, and $y_2 = -4$. Substituting these values into the formula gives us:

$$M = (\frac{-3+1}{2}, \frac{5+(-4)}{2})$$

$$M = (-\frac{2}{2}, \frac{1}{2})$$

$$M = (-1, \frac{1}{2})$$

Note: There is no such thing as the midpoint of a line, as lines are infinite in length.

Slope

The **slope** of a line (or line segment) is a numerical value given to show how steep a line is. A line or segment can have one of four types of slope (positive, negative, zero, or undefined).

- A line with a **positive slope** increases from the bottom left to the upper right on a graph.
- A line with a **negative slope** decreases from the upper left to the bottom right on a graph.
- A horizontal line is said to have a **zero slope**.
- A vertical line is said to have **no slope** (undefined).
- Parallel lines have **equal slopes**.
- Perpendicular lines have slopes that are negative reciprocals of each other.

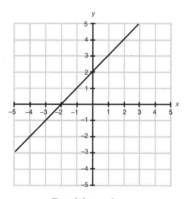

Positive slope

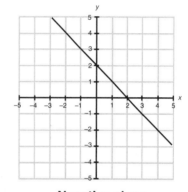

Negative slope

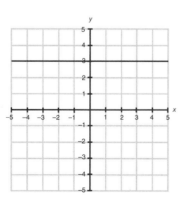

Zero slope

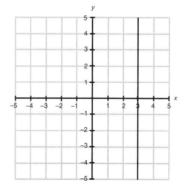

Undefined (no) slope

The slope of a line can be found if you know the coordinates of any two points that lie on the line. It does not matter which two points you use. It is found by writing the change in the y-coordinates of any two points on the line, over the change in the corresponding x-coordinates. (This is also known as the *rise* over the *run*.)

The formula for the slope of a line (or line segment) containing points (x_1, y_1) and (x_2, y_2): $m = \frac{y_2 - y_1}{x_2 - x_1}$.

Example

Determine the slope of the line joining points $A(-3,5)$ and $B(1,-4)$.

Let (x_1, y_1) represent point A and let (x_2, y_2) represent point B. This means that $x_1 = -3$, $y_1 = 5$, $x_2 = 1$, and $y_2 = -4$. Substituting these values into the formula gives us:

$$m = \frac{y_2 - y_1}{x_2 - x_1}$$
$$m = \frac{-4 - 5}{1 - (-3)}$$
$$m = \frac{-9}{4}$$

Example

Determine the slope of the line in the following graph.

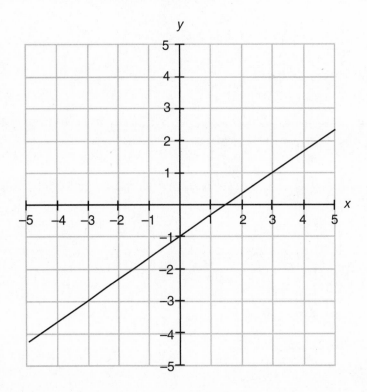

Two points that can be easily determined on the graph are $(3,1)$ and $(0,-1)$. Let $(3,1) = (x_1, y_1)$, and let $(0,-1) = (x_2, y_2)$. This means that $x_1 = 3$, $y_1 = 1$, $x_2 = 0$, and $y_2 = -1$. Substituting these values into the formula gives us:

$$m = \frac{-1-1}{0-3}$$
$$m = \frac{-2}{-3} = \frac{2}{3}$$

Note: If you know the slope and at least one point on a line, you can find the coordinates of other points on the line. Simply move the required units determined by the slope. For example, from (8,9), given the slope $\frac{7}{5}$, move up seven units and to the right five units. Another point on the line, thus, is (13,16).

Determining the Equation of a Line

The equation of a line is given by $y = mx + b$ where:

- y and x are variables such that every coordinate pair (x,y) is on the line
- m is the **slope** of the line
- b is the **y-intercept**, the y-value at which the line intersects (or intercepts) the y-axis

In order to determine the equation of a line from a graph, determine the slope and y-intercept and substitute it in the appropriate place in the general form of the equation.

Example

Determine the equation of the line in the following graph.

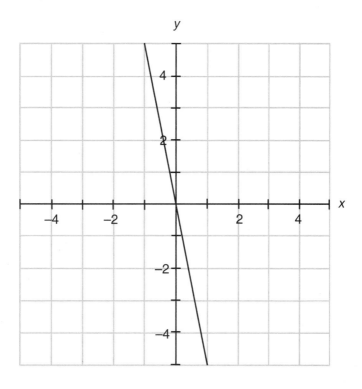

In order to determine the slope of the line, choose two points that can be easily determined on the graph. Two easy points are (−1,4) and (1,−4). Let (−1,4) = (x_1, y_1), and let (1,−4) = (x_2, y_2). This means that $x_1 = -1$, $y_1 = 4$, $x_2 = 1$, and $y_2 = -4$. Substituting these values into the formula gives us: $m = \frac{-4-4}{1-(-1)} = \frac{-8}{2} = -4$.

Looking at the graph, we can see that the line crosses the y-axis at the point (0,0). The y-coordinate of this point is 0. This is the y-intercept.

Substituting these values into the general formula gives us $y = -4x + 0$, or just $y = -4x$.

Example

Determine the equation of the line in the following graph.

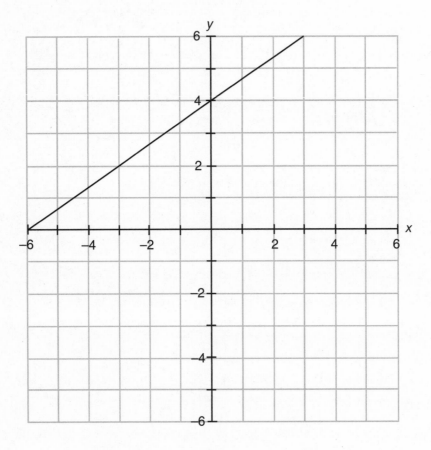

Two points that can be easily determined on the graph are (−3,2) and (3,6). Let (−3,2) = (x_1,y_1), and let (3,6) = (x_2,y_2). Substituting these values into the formula gives us:
$m = \frac{6-2}{3-(-3)} = \frac{4}{6} = \frac{2}{3}$.

We can see from the graph that the line crosses the y-axis at the point (0,4). This means the y-intercept is 4.

Substituting these values into the general formula gives us $y = \frac{2}{3}x + 4$.

Angles

Naming Angles

An **angle** is a figure composed of two rays or line segments joined at their endpoints. The point at which the rays or line segments meet is called the **vertex** of the angle. Angles are usually named by three capital letters, where the first and last letter are points on the end of the rays, and the middle letter is the vertex.

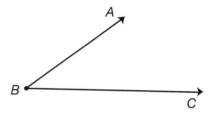

This angle can be named either $\angle ABC$ or $\angle CBA$, but because the vertex of the angle is point B, letter B must be in the middle.

We can sometimes name an angle by its vertex, as long as there is no ambiguity in the diagram. For example, in this angle we may call the angle $\angle B$, because there is only one angle in the diagram that has B as its vertex.

But, in the following diagram, there are a number of angles that have point B as their vertex, so we must name each angle in the diagram with three letters.

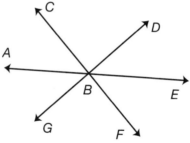

Angles may also be numbered (not measured) with numbers written between the sides of the angles, on the interior of the angle, near the vertex.

Classifying Angles

The unit of measure for angles is the degree.

Angles can be classified into the following categories: acute, right, obtuse, and straight.

- An **acute angle** is an angle that measures between 0 and 90°.

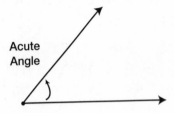

- A **right angle** is an angle that measures exactly 90°. A right angle is symbolized by a square at the vertex.

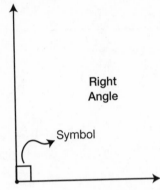

- An **obtuse angle** is an angle that measures more than 90°, but less than 180°.

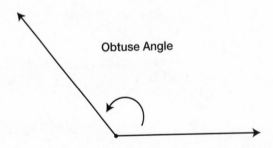

- A **straight angle** is an angle that measures 180°. Thus, both of its sides form a line.

Straight Angle

Special Angle Pairs

- **Adjacent angles** are two angles that share a common vertex and a common side. There is no numerical relationship between the measures of the angles.

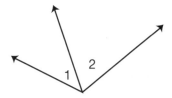

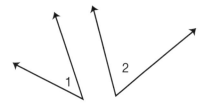

Adjacent angles ∠1 and ∠2   Nonadjacent angles ∠1 and ∠2

- A **linear pair** is a pair of adjacent angles whose measures add to 180°.

- **Supplementary angles** are any two angles whose sum is 180°. A linear pair is a special case of supplementary angles. A linear pair is always supplementary, but supplementary angles do not have to form a linear pair.

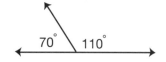

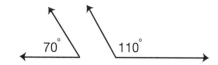

Linear pair (also supplementary)   Supplementary angles (but not a linear pair)

- **Complementary angles** are two angles whose sum measures 90°. Complementary angles may or may not be adjacent.

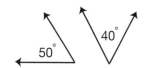

Adjacent complementary angles   Nonadjacent complementary angles

Example

Two complementary angles have measures $2x°$ and $3x + 20°$. What are the measures of the angles?

Because the angles are complementary, their sum is 90°. We can set up an equation to let us solve for x:

$2x + 3x + 20 = 90$

$5x + 20 = 90$

$5x = 70$

$x = 14$

Substituting $x = 14$ into the measures of the two angles, we get $2(14) = 28°$ and $3(14) + 20 = 62°$. We can check our answers by observing that $28 + 62 = 90$, so the angles are indeed complementary.

Example

One angle is 40 more than 6 times its supplement. What are the measures of the angles?

Let $x =$ one angle.

Let $6x + 40 =$ its supplement.

Because the angles are supplementary, their sum is 180°. We can set up an equation to let us solve for x:

$x + 6x + 40 = 180$

$7x + 40 = 180$

$7x = 140$

$x = 20$

Substituting $x = 20$ into the measures of the two angles, we see that one of the angles is 20° and its supplement is $6(20) + 40 = 160°$. We can check our answers by observing that $20 + 160 = 180$, proving that the angles are supplementary.

Note: A good way to remember the difference between supplementary and complementary angles is that the letter c comes before s in the alphabet; likewise "90" comes before "180" numerically.

Angles of Intersecting Lines

Important mathematical relationships between angles are formed when lines intersect. When two lines intersect, four smaller angles are formed.

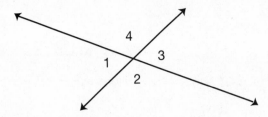

Any two adjacent angles formed when two lines intersect form a linear pair, therefore they are supplementary. In this diagram, $\angle 1$ and $\angle 2$, $\angle 2$ and $\angle 3$, $\angle 3$ and $\angle 4$, and $\angle 4$ and $\angle 1$ are all examples of linear pairs.

Also, the angles that are opposite each other are called **vertical angles**. Vertical angles are angles who share a vertex and whose sides are two pairs of opposite rays. Vertical angles are congruent. In this diagram, $\angle 1$ and $\angle 3$ are vertical angles, so $\angle 1 \cong \angle 3$; $\angle 2$ and $\angle 4$ are congruent vertical angles as well.

Note: Vertical angles is a name given to a special angle pair. Try not to confuse this with right or perpendicular angles, which often have vertical components.

Example

Determine the value of *y* in the following diagram:

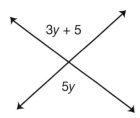

The angles marked $3y + 5$ and $5y$ are vertical angles, so they are congruent and their measures are equal. We can set up and solve the following equation for *y*:

$$3y + 5 = 5y$$
$$5 = 2y$$
$$2.5 = y$$

Replacing *y* with the value 2.5 gives us the $3(2.5) + 5 = 12.5$ and $5(2.5) = 12.5$. This proves that the two vertical angles are congruent, with each measuring 12.5°.

Parallel Lines and Transversals

Important mathematical relationships are formed when two parallel lines are intersected by a third, nonparallel line called a **transversal**.

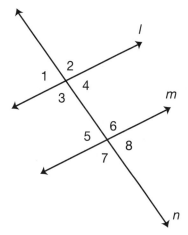

In the previous diagram, parallel lines *l* and *m* are intersected by transversal *n*. Supplementary angle pairs and vertical angle pairs are formed in this diagram, too.

Supplementary Angle Pairs		Vertical Angle Pairs
∠1 and ∠2	∠2 and ∠4	∠1 and ∠4
∠4 and ∠3	∠3 and ∠1	∠2 and ∠3
∠5 and ∠6	∠6 and ∠8	∠5 and ∠8
∠8 and ∠7	∠7 and ∠5	∠6 and ∠7

Other congruent angle pairs are formed:

- Alternate interior angles are angles on the **interior** of the parallel lines, on **alternate** sides of the transversal: $\angle 3$ and $\angle 6$; $\angle 4$ and $\angle 5$.
- Corresponding angles are angles on **corresponding** sides of the parallel lines, on **corresponding** sides of the transversal: $\angle 1$ and $\angle 5$; $\angle 2$ and $\angle 6$; $\angle 3$ and $\angle 7$; $\angle 4$ and $\angle 8$.

Example

In the following diagram, line l is parallel to line m. Determine the value of x.

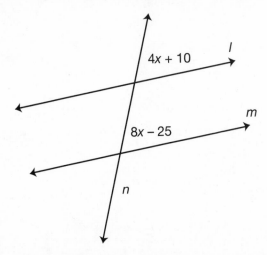

The two angles labeled are **corresponding** angle pairs, because they are located on top of the parallel lines and on the same side of the transversal (same relative location). This means that they are congruent, and we can determine the value of x by solving the equation:

$$4x + 10 = 8x - 25$$
$$10 = 4x - 25$$
$$35 = 4x$$
$$8.75 = x$$

We can check our answer by replacing the value 8.75 in for x in the expressions $4x + 10$ and $8x - 25$:

$$4(8.75) + 10 = 8(8.75) - 25$$
$$45 = 45$$

Note: If the diagram showed the two angles were a vertical angle pair or alternate interior angle pair, the problem would be solved in the same way.

Area, Circumference, and Volume Formulas

Here are the basic formulas for finding area, circumference, and volume. They will be discussed in detail in the following sections.

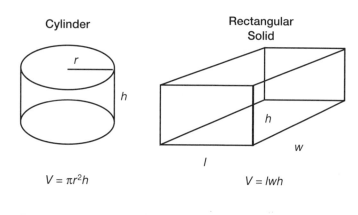

Circle

$C = 2\pi r$
$A = \pi r^2$

Rectangle

$A = lw$

Triangle

$A = \frac{1}{2}bh$

Cylinder

$V = \pi r^2 h$

Rectangular Solid

$V = lwh$

C =	Circumference	w =	Width
A =	Area	h =	Height
r =	Radius	v =	Volume
l =	Length	b =	Base

Triangles

The sum of the measures of the three angles in a triangle always equals 180°.

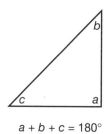

$a + b + c = 180°$

Exterior Angles

An **exterior angle** can be formed by extending a side from any of the three vertices of a triangle. Here are some rules for working with exterior angles:

- An exterior angle and an interior angle that share the same vertex are supplementary. In other words, exterior angles and interior angles form straight lines with each other.
- An exterior angle is equal to the sum of the nonadjacent interior angles.
- The sum of the exterior angles of a triangle equals 360°.

Example

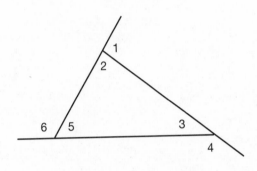

$$m\angle 1 + m\angle 2 = 180° \quad m\angle 1 = m\angle 3 + m\angle 5$$
$$m\angle 3 + m\angle 4 = 180° \quad m\angle 4 = m\angle 2 + m\angle 5$$
$$m\angle 5 + m\angle 6 = 180° \quad m\angle 6 = m\angle 3 + m\angle 2$$
$$m\angle 1 + m\angle 4 + m\angle 6 = 360°$$

Classifying Triangles

It is possible to classify triangles into three categories based on the number of congruent (indicated by the symbol $\cong$) sides. Sides are congruent when they have equal lengths.

Scalene Triangle	Isosceles Triangle	Equilateral Triangle
no sides congruent	more than two congruent sides	all sides congruent

It is also possible to classify triangles into three categories based on the measure of the greatest angle:

Acute Triangle	Right Triangle	Obtuse Triangle
greatest angle is acute	greatest angle is 90°	greatest angle is obtuse

Angle-Side Relationships

Knowing the angle-side relationships in isosceles, equilateral, and right triangles is helpful.

- In isosceles triangles, congruent angles are opposite congruent sides.

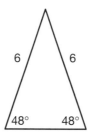

- In equilateral triangles, all sides are congruent and all angles are congruent. The measure of each angle in an equilateral triangle is always 60°.

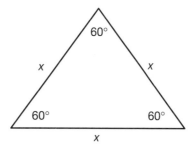

- In a right triangle, the side opposite the right angle is called the **hypotenuse** and the other sides are called **legs**. The box in the 90° angle symbolizes that the triangle is, in fact, a right triangle.

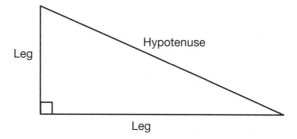

Pythagorean Theorem

The **Pythagorean theorem** is an important tool for working with right triangles. It states: $a^2 + b^2 = c^2$, where a and b represent the legs and c represents the hypotenuse.

This theorem makes it easy to find the length of any side as long as the measure of two sides is known. So, if leg $a = 1$ and leg $b = 2$ in the following triangle, it is possible to find the measure of the hypotenuse, c.

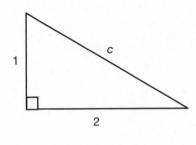

$$a^2 + b^2 = c^2$$
$$1^2 + 2^2 = c^2$$
$$1 + 4 = c^2$$
$$5 = c^2$$
$$\sqrt{5} = c$$

Pythagorean Triples

Sometimes, the measures of all three sides of a right triangle are integers. If three integers are the lengths of a right triangle, we call them **Pythagorean triples**. Some popular Pythagorean triples are:

3, 4, 5

5, 12, 13

8, 15, 17

9, 40, 41

The smaller two numbers in each triple represent the length of the legs, and the largest number represents the length of the hypotenuse.

Multiples of Pythagorean Triples

Whole-number multiples of each triple are also triples. For example, if we multiply each of the lengths of the triple 3, 4, 5 by 2, we get 6, 8, 10. This is also a triple.

Example

If given a right triangle with sides measuring 6, x, and a hypotenuse 10, what is the value of x?

3, 4, 5 is a Pythagorean triple, and a multiple of that is 6, 8, 10. Therefore, the missing side length is 8.

Comparing Triangles

Triangles are said to be congruent (indicated by the symbol $\cong$) when they have exactly the same size and shape. Two triangles are congruent if their corresponding parts (their angles and sides) are congruent. Sometimes it is easy to tell if two triangles are congruent by looking at them. However, in geometry, it must be able to be proven that the triangles are congruent.

There are a number of ways to prove that two triangles are congruent:

Side-Side-Side (SSS)   If the three sides of one triangle are congruent to the three corresponding sides of another triangle, the triangles are congruent.

Side-Angle-Side (SAS)   If two sides and the included angle of one triangle are congruent to the corresponding two sides and included angle of another triangle, the triangles are congruent.

Angle-Side-Angle (ASA)   If two angles and the included side of one triangle are congruent to the corresponding two angles and included side of another triangle, the triangles are congruent.

Used less often but also valid:

Angle-Angle-Side (AAS)   If two angles and the non-included side of one triangle are congruent to the corresponding two angles and non-included side of another triangle, the triangles are congruent.

Hypotenuse-Leg (Hy-Leg)   If the hypotenuse and a leg of one right triangle are congruent to the hypotenuse and leg of another right triangle, the triangles are congruent.

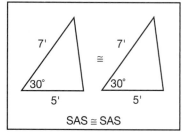
SAS ≅ SAS

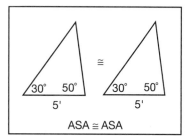
ASA ≅ ASA

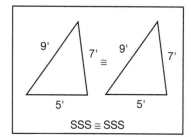
SSS ≅ SSS

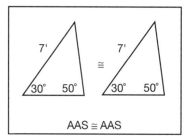
AAS ≅ AAS

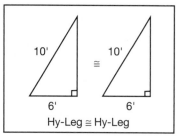
Hy-Leg ≅ Hy-Leg

Example

Determine if these two triangles are congruent.

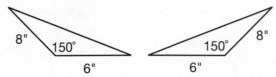

Although the triangles are not aligned the same way, there are two congruent corresponding sides, and the angle between them (150°) is congruent. Therefore, the triangles are congruent by the SAS postulate.

Example

Determine if these two triangles are congruent.

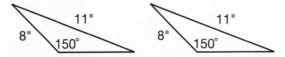

Although the triangles have two congruent corresponding sides, and a corresponding congruent angle, the 150° angle is not included between them. This would be "SSA," but SSA is not a way to prove that two triangles are congruent.

Area of a Triangle

Area is the amount of space inside a two-dimensional object. Area is measured in square units, often written as *unit²*. So, if the length of a triangle is measured in feet, the area of the triangle is measured in *feet²*.

A triangle has three sides, each of which can be considered a **base** of the triangle. A perpendicular line segment drawn from a vertex to the opposite base of the triangle is called the **altitude**, or the **height**. It measures how tall the triangle stands.

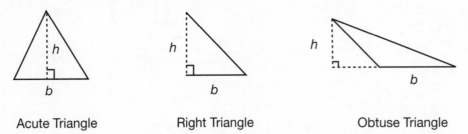

Acute Triangle   Right Triangle   Obtuse Triangle

It is important to note that the height of a triangle is not necessarily one of the sides of the triangle. The correct height for the following triangle is 8, not 10. The height will always be associated with a line segment (called an **altitude**) that comes from one vertex (angle) to the opposite side and forms a right angle (signified by the box). In other words, the height must always be perpendicular to (form a right angle with) the base. Note that in an obtuse triangle, the height is outside the triangle, and in a right triangle the height is one of the sides.

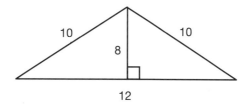

The formula for the area of a triangle is given by $A = \frac{1}{2}bh$, where b is the base of the triangle, and h is the height.

Example

Determine the area of the following triangle.

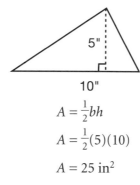

$$A = \frac{1}{2}bh$$

$$A = \frac{1}{2}(5)(10)$$

$$A = 25 \text{ in}^2$$

Volume Formulas

A **prism** is a three-dimensional object that has matching polygons as its top and bottom. The matching top and bottom are called the **bases** of the prism. The prism is named for the shape of the prism's base, so a **triangular prism** has congruent triangles as its bases.

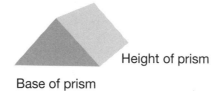

Height of prism

Base of prism

Note: This can be confusing. The **base** of the prism is the shape of the polygon that forms it; the **base** of a triangle is one of its sides.

Volume is the amount of space inside a three-dimensional object. Volume is measured in cubic units, often written as $unit^3$. So, if the edge of a triangular prism is measured in feet, the volume of it is measured in $feet^3$.

The volume of ANY prism is given by the formula $V = A_b h$, where A_b is the area of the prism's base, and h is the height of the prism.

Example

Determine the volume of the following triangular prism:

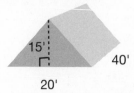

The area of the triangular base can be found by using the formula $A = \frac{1}{2}bh$, so the area of the base is $A = \frac{1}{2}(15)(20) = 150$. The volume of the prism can be found by using the formula $V = A_b h$, so the volume is $V = (150)(40) = 6,000$ cubic feet.

A **pyramid** is a three-dimensional object that has a polygon as one base, and instead of a matching polygon as the other, there is a point. Each of the sides of a pyramid is a triangle. Pyramids are also named for the shape of their (non-point) base.

The volume of a pyramid is determined by the formula $\frac{1}{3}A_b h$.

Example

Determine the volume of a pyramid whose base has an area of 20 square feet and stands 50 feet tall.

Because the area of the base is given to us, we only need to replace the appropriate values into the formula.

$V = \frac{1}{3}A_b h$

$V = \frac{1}{3}(20)(50)$

$V = 33\frac{1}{3}$

The pyramid has a volume of $33\frac{1}{3}$ cubic feet.

Polygons

A polygon is a closed figure with three or more sides; for example, triangles, rectangles, pentagons, etc.

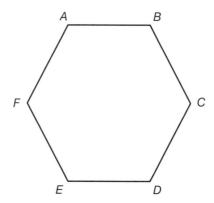

Shape	Number of Sides
Circle	0
Triangle	3
Quadrilateral (square/rectangle)	4
Pentagon	5
Hexagon	6
Heptagon	7
Octagon	8
Nonagon	9
Decagon	10

Terms Related to Polygons

- **Vertices** are corner points, also called **endpoints**, of a polygon. The vertices in the previous polygon are A, B, C, D, E, and F and they are always labeled with capital letters.
- A **regular polygon** has congruent sides and congruent angles.
- An **equiangular polygon** has congruent angles.

Interior Angles

To find the sum of the interior angles of any polygon, use this formula:

$S = 180(x - 2)°$, where x = the number of sides of the polygon.

Example

Find the sum of the interior angles in the following polygon.

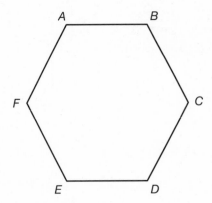

The polygon is a pentagon that has 5 sides, so substitute 5 for *x* in the formula:

$S = (5 - 2) \times 180°$

$S = 3 \times 180°$

$S = 540°$

Exterior Angles

Similar to the exterior angles of a triangle, the sum of the exterior angles of any polygon equals 360°.

Similar Polygons

If two polygons are similar, their corresponding angles are congruent and the ratios of the corresponding sides are in proportion.

Example

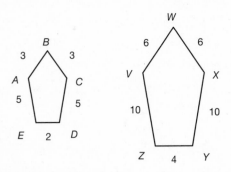

$\angle A = \angle V = 140°$
$\angle B = \angle W = 60°$
$\angle C = \angle X = 140°$
$\angle D = \angle Y = 100°$
$\angle E = \angle Z = 100°$

$$\frac{AB}{VW} \quad \frac{BC}{WX} \quad \frac{CD}{XY} \quad \frac{DE}{YZ} \quad \frac{EA}{ZV}$$

$$\frac{3}{6} = \frac{3}{6} = \frac{5}{10} = \frac{5}{10} = \frac{2}{4}$$

These two polygons are similar because their angles are congruent and the ratios of the corresponding sides are in proportion.

Quadrilaterals

A **quadrilateral** is a four-sided polygon. Because a quadrilateral can be divided by a diagonal into two triangles, the sum of its interior angles will equal 180 + 180 = 360°.

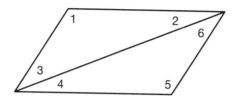

$$m\angle 1 + m\angle 2 + m\angle 3 + m\angle 4 + m\angle 5 + m\angle 6 = 360°$$

Parallelograms

A parallelogram is a quadrilateral with two pairs of parallel sides.

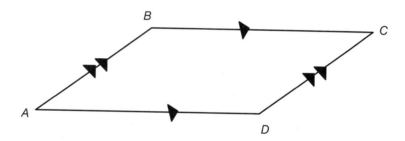

In the previous figure, $\overline{AB} \parallel \overline{CD}$ and $\overline{BC} \parallel \overline{AD}$. Parallel lines are symbolized with matching numbers of triangles or arrows.

A parallelogram has:

- opposite sides that are congruent ($\overline{AB} = \overline{CD}$ and $\overline{BC} = \overline{AD}$)
- opposite angles that are congruent ($m\angle A = m\angle C$ and $m\angle B = m\angle D$)
- consecutive angles that are supplementary ($m\angle A + m\angle B = 180°$, $m\angle B + m\angle C = 180°$, $m\angle C + m\angle D = 180°$, $m\angle D + m\angle A = 180°$)
- diagonals (line segments joining opposite vertices) that bisect each other (divide each other in half)

Special Types of Parallelograms

- A **rectangle** is a parallelogram that has four right angles.

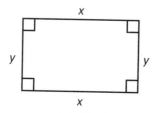

- A **rhombus** is a parallelogram that has four equal sides.

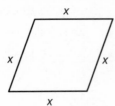

- A **square** is a parallelogram in which all angles are equal to 90° and all sides are congruent. A square is a special case of a rectangle where all the sides are congruent. A square is also a special type of rhombus where all the angles are congruent.

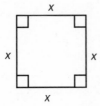

Diagonals of Parallelograms

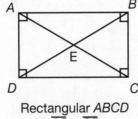

Rectangular *ABCD*
$\overline{AC} \cong \overline{BD}$

Rhombus *ABCD*
$\overline{AC} \perp \overline{BD}$

Square *ABCD*
$\overline{AB} \perp \overline{CD}, \overline{AC} \cong \overline{BD}$

In this diagram, parallelogram *ABCD* has diagonals $\overline{AC}$ and $\overline{BD}$ that intersect at point *E*. The diagonals of a parallelogram bisect each other, which means that $\overline{AE} \cong \overline{EC}$ and $\overline{BE} \cong \overline{ED}$.

In addition, the following properties hold true:

- the diagonals of a rhombus are perpendicular
- the diagonals of a rectangle are congruent
- the diagonals of a square are both perpendicular and congruent

Example

In parallelogram *ABCD*, the diagonal $\overline{AC} = 5x + 10$ and $\overline{BC} = 9x$. Determine the value of *x*.

Because the diagonals of a parallelogram are congruent, the lengths are equal. We can then set up and solve the equation $5x + 10 = 9x$ to determine the value of x.

$5x + 10 = 9x$	Subtract x from both sides of the equation.
$10 = 4x$	Divide both sides of the equation by 4.
$2.5 = x$	

Area and Volume Formulas

The area of any parallelogram can be found with the formula $A = bh$, where b is the base of the parallelogram, and h is the height. The base and height of a parallelogram are defined the same as in a triangle.

Note: Sometimes b is called the length (l) and h is called the width (w) instead. If this is the case, the area formula is $A = lw$.

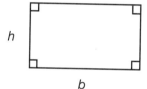 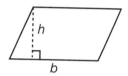

A **rectangular prism** (or **rectangular solid**) is a prism that has rectangles as bases. Recall that the formula for any prism is $V = A_b h$. Because the area of the rectangular base is $A = lw$, we can replace lw for A_b in the formula, giving us the more common, easier to remember formula, $V = lwh$. If a prism has a different quadrilateral-shaped base, use the general prisms formula for volume.

Note: A cube is a special rectangular prism with six congruent squares as sides. This means that you can use the $V = lwh$ formula for it, too.

Rectangular
Solid

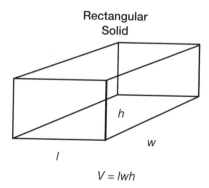

$V = lwh$

Circles

Terminology

A **circle** is formally defined as the set of points a fixed distance from a point. The more sides a polygon has, the more it looks like a circle. If you consider a polygon with 5,000 small sides, it will look like a circle, but a circle is not a polygon. A circle contains 360° around a center point.

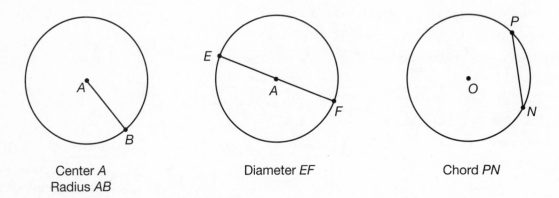

Center *A*   Diameter *EF*   Chord *PN*
Radius *AB*

- The midpoint of a circle is called the **center**.
- The distance around a circle (called **perimeter** in polygons) is called the **circumference**.
- A line segment that goes through a circle, with its endpoints on the circle, is called a **chord**.
- A chord that goes directly through the center of a circle (the longest line segment that can be drawn) in a circle is called the **diameter**.
- The line from the center of a circle to a point on the circle (half of the diameter) is called the **radius**.
- A **sector** of a circle is a fraction of the circle's area.
- An **arc** of a circle is a fraction of the circle's circumference.

Circumference, Area, and Volume Formulas

The area of a circle is $A = \pi r^2$, where r is the radius of the circle. The circumference (perimeter of a circle) is $2\pi r$, or πd, where r is the radius of the circle and d is the diameter.

Example
Determine the area and circumference of the following circle.

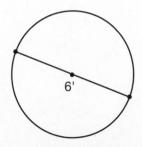

6'

We are given the diameter of the circle, so we can use the formula $C = \pi d$ to find the circumference.

$C = \pi d$

$C = \pi(6)$

$C = 6\pi \approx 18.85$ feet

The area formula uses the radius, so we need to divide the length of the diameter by 2 to get the length of the radius: $6 \div 2 = 3$. Then we can just use the formula.

$A = \pi(3)2$

$A = 9\pi \approx 28.27$ square feet.

Note: *Circumference* is a measure of length, so the answer is measured in *units*, where the *area* is measured in *square units*.

Area of Sectors and Lengths of Arcs

The area of a sector can be determined by figuring out what the percentage of the total area the sector is, and then multiplying by the area of the circle.

The length of an arc can be determined by figuring out what the percentage of the total circumference of the arc is, and then multiplying by the circumference of the circle.

Example

Determine the area of the shaded sector and the length of the arc AB.

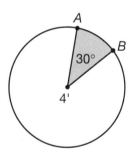

Because the angle in the sector is 30°, and we know that a circle contains a total of 360°, we can determine what fraction of the circle's area it is: $\frac{30°}{360°} = \frac{1}{12}$ of the circle.

The area of the entire circle is $A = \pi r^2$, so $A = \pi(4)^2 = 16\pi$.

So, the area of the sector is $\frac{1}{12} \times 16\pi = \frac{16\pi}{12} = \frac{4}{3}\pi \approx 4.19$ square inches.

We can also determine the length of the arc AB, because it is $\frac{30°}{360°} = \frac{1}{12}$ of the circle's circumference.

The circumference of the entire circle is $C = 2\pi r$, so $C = 2\pi(4) = 8\pi$.

This means that the length of the arc is $\frac{1}{12} \times 8\pi = \frac{8\pi}{12} = \frac{2}{3\pi} \approx 2.09$ inches.

A prism that has circles as bases is called a **cylinder**. Recall that the formula for any prism is $V = A_b h$. Because the area of the circular base is $A = \pi r^2$, we can replace πr^2 for A_b in the formula, giving us $V = \pi r^2 h$, where r is the radius of the circular base, and h is the height of the cylinder.

Cylinder

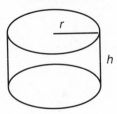

$$V = \pi r^2 h$$

A sphere is a three-dimensional object that has no sides. A basketball is a good example of a sphere. The volume of a sphere is given by the formula $V = \frac{4}{3}\pi r^3$.

Example

Determine the volume of a sphere whose radius is 1.5 feet.

Replace 1.5 feet in for r in the formula $V = \frac{4}{3}\pi r^3$.

$$V = \frac{4}{3}\pi r^3$$

$$V = \frac{4}{3}\pi(1.5)^3$$

$$V = \frac{4}{3}(3.375)\pi$$

$$V = 4.5\pi \approx 14.14$$

The answer is approximately 14.14 cubic feet.

Example

An aluminum can is 6 inches tall and has a base with a radius of 2 inches. Determine the volume the can holds.

Aluminum cans are cylindrical in shape, so replace 2 inches for r and 6 inches for h in the formula $V = \pi r^2 h$.

$$V = \pi r^2 h$$

$$V = \pi(2)^2(6)$$

$$V = 24\pi \approx 75.40 \text{ cubic feet}$$

▶ Data Analysis

Data analysis simply means reading graphs, tables, and other graphical forms. You should be able to:

- read and understand scatter plots, graphs, tables, diagrams, charts, figures, etc.
- interpret scatter plots, graphs, tables, diagrams, charts, figures, etc.
- compare and interpret information presented in scatter plots, graphs, tables, diagrams, charts, figures, etc.
- draw conclusions about the information provided
- make predictions about the data

It is important to read tables, charts, and graphs very carefully. Read all of the information presented, paying special attention to headings and units of measure. This section will cover tables and graphs. The most common types of graphs are scatter plots, bar graphs, and pie graphs. What follows is an explanation of each, with examples for practice.

Tables

All tables are composed of **rows** (horizontal) and **columns** (vertical). Entries in a single row of a table usually have something in common, and so do entries in a single column. Look at the following table that shows how many cars, both new and used, were sold during the particular months.

Month	New Cars	Used Cars
June	125	65
July	155	80
August	190	100
September	220	115
October	265	140

Tables are very concise ways to convey important information without wasting time and space. Just imagine how many lines of text would be needed to convey the same information. With the table, however, it is easy to refer to a given month and quickly know how many total cars were sold. It would also be easy to compare month to month. In fact, practice by comparing the total sales of July with October.

In order to do this, first find out how many cars were sold in each month. There were 235 cars sold in July ($155 + 80 = 235$) and 405 cars sold in October ($265 + 140 = 405$). With a little bit of quick arithmetic it can quickly be determined that 170 more cars were sold during October ($405 - 235 = 170$).

Scatter Plots

Whenever a variable depends continuously on another variable, this dependence can be visually represented in a **scatter plot**. A scatter plot consists of the horizontal (x) axis, the vertical (y) axis, and collected data points for variable y, measured at variable x. The variable points are often connected with a line or a curve. A graph often contains a legend, especially if there is more than one data set or more than one variable. A legend is a key for interpreting the graph. Much like a legend on a map lists the symbols used to label an interstate highway, a railroad line, or a city, a legend for a graph lists the symbols used to label a particular data set. Look at the following sample graph. The essential elements of the graph—the x- and y-axis—are labeled. The legend to the right of the graph shows that diamonds are used to represent the variable points in data set 1, while squares are used to represent the variable points in data set 2. If only one data set exists, the use of a legend is not essential.

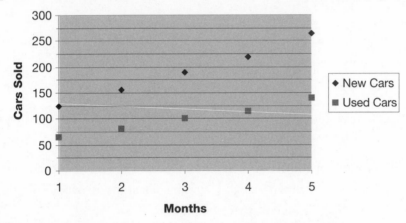

(**Note:** This data was used in the previous example for tables.)

The x-axis represents the months after new management and promotions were introduced at an automobile dealership. The y-axis represents the number of cars sold in the particular month after the changes were made. The diamonds reflect the New Cars sold and the squares show the number of Used Cars sold. What conclusions can be drawn about the sales? Note that the new and used car sales are both increasing each month at a pretty steady rate. The graph also shows that New Cars increase at a higher rate and that there are many more New Cars sold per month.

Try to look for scatter plots with different trends—including:

- increase
- decrease
- rapid increase, followed by leveling off
- slow increase, followed by rapid increase
- rise to a maximum, followed by a decrease
- rapid decrease, followed by leveling off
- slow decrease, followed by rapid decrease
- decrease to a minimum, followed by a rise
- predictable fluctuation (periodic change)
- random fluctuation (irregular change)

Bar Graphs

Whereas scatter plots are used to show change, **bar graphs** are often used to indicate an amount or level of occurrence of a phenomenon for different categories. Consider the following bar graph. It illustrates the number of employees who were absent due to illness during a particular week in two different age groups.

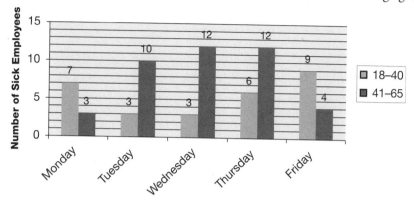

In this bar graph, the categories are the days of the week, and the frequency represents the number of employees who are sick. It can be immediately seen that younger employees are sick before and after the weekend. There is also an inconsistent trend for the younger employees with data ranging all over the place. During mid-week the older crowd tends to stay home more often.

How many people on average are sick in the 41–65 age group? To find the average you first must find out how many illnesses occur each week in the particular age group. There are a total of 41 illnesses for a five-day period ($3 + 10 + 12 + 12 + 4 = 41$). To calculate the average, just divide the total illnesses by the number of days for a total of 8.2 illnesses ($\frac{41}{5} = 8.2$), or more realistically, 8 absences per day.

Pictographs

Pictographs are very similar to bar graphs, but instead of bars indicating frequency, small icons are assigned a key value indicating frequency.

Number of Students at the Pep Rally	
Freshmen	🚹🚹🚹🚹🚹🚹🚹🚹🚹🚹🚹🚹
Sophmores	🚹🚹🚹🚹🚹🚹
Juniors	🚹🚹🚹🚹🚹
Seniors	🚹🚹🚹

Key: 🚹 indicates 10 people

In this pictograph, the key indicates that every icon represents 10 people, so it is easy to determine that there were $12 \times 10 = 120$ freshmen, $5.5 \times 10 = 55$ sophomores, $5 \times 10 = 50$ juniors, and $3 \times 10 = 30$ seniors.

Pie Charts and Circle Graphs

Pie charts are often used to show what percent of a total is taken up by different components of that whole. This type of graph is representative of a whole and is usually divided into percentages. Each section of the chart represents a portion of the whole, and all of these sections added together will equal 100% of the whole. The following chart shows the three styles of model homes in a new development and what percentage of each there is.

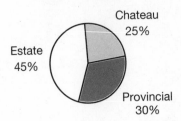

The chart shows the different models of homes. Find the percentage of Estate homes. In order to find this percentage, look at the pie chart. The categories add up to 100% (25 + 30 + 45 = 100). From the actual chart you can visually see that 45% of the homes are done in the Estate model.

Broken-Line Graphs

Broken-line graphs illustrate a measurable change over time. If a line is slanted up, it represents an increase, whereas a line sloping down represents a decrease. A flat line indicates no change.

In the following broken-line graph, the number of delinquent payments is charted for the first quarter of the year. Each week the number of outstanding bills is summed and recorded.

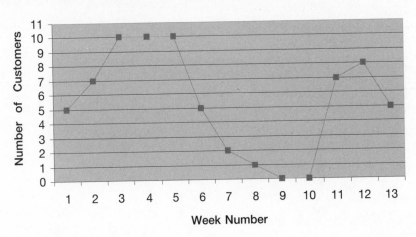

There is an increase in delinquency for the first two weeks and then it maintains for an additional two weeks. There is a steep decrease after week 5 (initially) until the ninth week, where it levels off again, but this time at 0. The 11th week shows a radical increase followed by a little jump up at week 12, and then a decrease to week 13. It is also interesting to see that the first and last weeks have identical values.

Diagrams

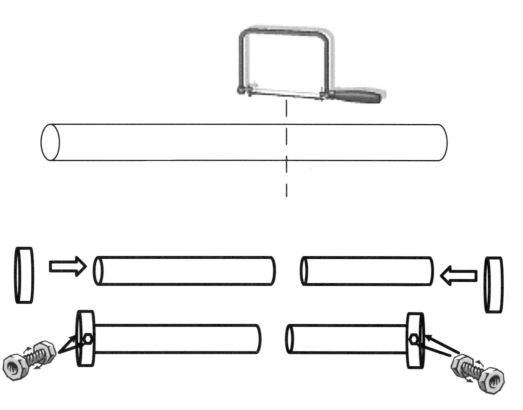

This diagram shows a sequence of events to construct two new objects out of one pipe and a few other parts. First, the instructions show that the pipe must be cut into two pieces with a saw. The next two levels show how the assembly will take place, first adding the end pieces and then bolting in those pieces.

Diagrams could be used to show a sequence of events, a process, an idea, or the relationship between different events or people.

When you see a diagram, first ask what the purpose of it is. What is it trying to illustrate? Then look at the different labeled parts of the diagram. What is the function of each part? How are they interrelated? Take a look at the following diagram.

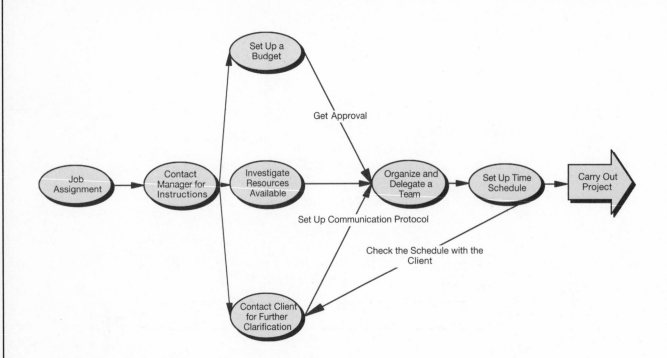

This diagram is a typical chart of how to start a new project. It starts (on the left), by learning about the assignment from the manager and then investigating several aspects of heading a project, including the client, resources, and budget. Once an overall picture is achieved, you will then know how many people will be required for the project in order to create an accurate schedule for the project. There are also reminders and further protocols within the diagram in the links.

Now, take the skills you have learned or honed in this review and apply them to your practice tests.

10 ▶ Writing Skills Review

CHAPTER SUMMARY

Good writing skills are essential to success on the constructed-response questions on the NYSTCE, and of course, are critical to success in your career as a teacher. It's important to be able to communicate ideas clearly and accurately in written English. To help you express yourself effectively, this chapter reviews the elements of good writing: basic grammar, sentence structure, verb and pronoun agreement, and idiomatic expressions.

The NYSTCE assess your writing knowledge and skills in two ways: through multiple-choice questions that measure your ability to identify errors in grammar or sentence structure, and through the constructed-response writing assignments. The LAST will include several multiple-choice questions related to the conventions of writing. The particular CST you take will determine the questions related to writing. For example, the English CST would, of course, include questions directly related to conventions. The LAST, ATS-Ws, and CSTs all contain constructed responses that require you to express yourself effectively in written form.

► Multiple-Choice Questions

On your tests, you'll encounter multiple-choice questions that will measure your knowledge of the basics of grammar, sentence construction, appropriate word choice, and your ability to locate errors. You will be asked to analyze the effectiveness of the expression in a passage according to the conventions of edited American English. You may be asked about language usage or sentence correction. In these types of multiple-choice questions, you must demonstrate your ability to recognize and correct awkward sentence constructions and other grammatical elements. For example:

Answer questions 1 and 2 on the basis of the following passage. This selection is from Willa Cather's short story, *Neighbour Rosicky*.

(1) On the day before Christmas the weather set in very cold; no snow, but a bitter, biting wind that whistled and sang over the flat land and lashed one's face like fine wires. (2) There was baking going on in the Rosicky kitchen all day, and Rosicky sat inside, making over a coat that Albert had outgrown into an overcoat for John. (3) Mary's big red geranium in bloom for Christmas, and a row of Jerusalem cherry trees, full of berries. (4) It was the first year she had ever grown these; Doctor Ed brung her the seeds from Omaha when he went to some medical convention. (5) They reminded Rosicky of plants he had seen in England; and all afternoon, as he stitched, he sat thinking about the two years in London, which his mind usually shrank from even after all this while.

1. Which of the following numbered parts displays nonstandard use of a verb form?
   a. Part 2
   b. Part 3
   c. Part 4
   d. Part 5

2. Which of the following numbered parts contains a nonstandard sentence?
   a. Part 2
   b. Part 3
   c. Part 4
   d. Part 5

Answers
1. c. Part 4 contains a nonstandard verb form, *brung*, as the past-tense form of *to bring*; the correct verb *is brought*. Choices a, b, and d are incorrect because they do not contain nonstandard usages of verbs.
2. b. Part 3 contains a sentence fragment, for there is no main verb in the sentence. Choices a, c, and d are incorrect because they are complete sentences.

▶ Constructed-Response Assignment

This chapter will help you most in your preparation for the constructed-response writing assignments in the NYSTCE. In these tasks, the candidate writes an essay in response to a specific prompt relevant to the purpose of the particular NYSTCE. For example, the CST and LAST constructed responses are content related, while the ATS-W constructed responses are related to teaching methods and strategies.

As explained in Chapters 4, 5, and 6, all of the constructed responses are evaluated using the same scoring scale. This ensures consistency among examinations. The components of the scoring scales reflect the candidate's ability to:

- effectively express the purpose of the essay
- accurately and effectively apply specialized knowledge and skills to the topic
- provide support in the essay through appropriate examples and/or sound reasoning that reflects an understanding of the specialized knowledge

In addition, strong responses to the constructed responses are characterized by:

- a clear focus and unity—the stated task is clearly addressed
- an appropriate expressive approach that is consistent with the writer's audience and purpose
- organization and reasoning—opinions, arguments, and expositions are presented in a structured style
- support and development—evidence and details are provided to support the positions taken
- conventions and mechanics—writing is free from distracting grammar and spelling errors and other writing flaws

Now that you are familiar with the format of the multiple-choice questions and the constructed responses, you are ready to review some of the rules and patterns of English grammar, sentence structure, idioms, and word usage. The last part of this chapter will cover the constructed-response portions of the NYSTCE in more detail: the kinds of writing prompts you can expect, test-taking strategies, and essential information for organizing and creating a clear, well-supported constructed response.

▶ Grammatical Relationships

Many people grimace when faced with grammar exercises, but in order to communicate with others, pass tests, and get your point across in writing, using words and punctuation effectively is a necessary skill. Maybe you're one of the millions of people who, as a student in elementary or high school, found memorizing grammar rules tedious. Maybe you were confused by all of the *exceptions* to those rules. Maybe you thought they would just come naturally as you continued to write and speak.

First, know you are not alone. It is true that some people work very hard to understand the rules, while others seem to have a natural gift for writing. And that's OK; we all have unique talents. Still, it's a fact that most jobs today require good communication skills, including writing. The good news is that grammar and writing skills can be developed with practice. Begin to improve your writing by reviewing this section.

Adjectives and Adverbs

Adjectives and adverbs add spice to writing—they are words that describe, or modify, other words. However, adjectives and adverbs describe different parts of speech. Whereas adjectives modify nouns or pronouns, adverbs modify verbs, adjectives, or other adverbs. For example:

We enjoyed the *delicious* meal.
The chef prepared it *perfectly*.

The first sentence uses the adjective *delicious* to modify the noun *meal*. In the second sentence, the adverb *perfectly* describes the verb *prepared*. Adverbs are easy to spot—most end in *-ly*. However, some of the trickiest adverbs do not end in the typical *-ly* form. The following are problem modifiers to look out for in your writing:

Good/Well—Writers often confuse the adverb *well* with its adjective counterpart, *good*.
Ellie felt *good* about her test results. (*Good* describes the proper noun *Ellie*.)
Ruben performed *well* on the test. (*Well* modifies the verb *performed*.)

Bad/Badly—Similarly, writers confuse the function of these two modifiers. Remember to use the adverb *badly* to describe an action.
Henry felt *bad* after staying up all night before the exam. (*Bad* describes Henry.)
Juliet did *badly* in her first classroom presentation. (*Badly* describes the verb *did*.)

Fewer/Less—These two adjectives are a common pitfall for writers. To distinguish between them, look carefully at the noun modified in the sentence. *Fewer* describes *plural* nouns, or things that can be counted. *Less* describes *singular* nouns that represent a quantity or a degree.
The high school enrolls *fewer* students than it did a decade ago.
Emilia had *less* time for studying than Maggie.

Adjectives that follow verbs can also cause confusion. Although an adjective may come after a verb in a sentence, it may describe a noun or pronoun that comes before the verb. Here is an example:

The circumstances surrounding Shakespeare's authorship seemed strange. (The adjective, *strange*, describes the subject, *circumstances*.)

Take special note of modifiers in sentences that use verbs that deal with the senses: *touch, taste, look, smell,* and *sound*. Here are some examples of sentences that use the same verb, but different modifiers:

Sarah felt sick after her performance review. (The adjective *sick* modifies *Sarah*.)
The archaeologist felt carefully through the loose dirt. (The adverb *carefully* modifies *felt*.)

The judge looked skeptical after the witness testified. (The adjective *skeptical* modifies *judge*.)
The judge looked skeptically at the flamboyant lawyer. (The adverb *skeptically* modifies *looked*.)

Subject-Verb Agreement

They goes together, or *they go together?* You probably don't even have to think about which subject goes with which verb in this clause—your ear easily discerns that the second version is correct. Subject-verb agreement is when the subject of a clause matches the verb *in number.* Singular nouns take singular verbs; plural nouns take plural verbs. However, some instances of subject-verb agreement are tricky. Look out for the following three problem areas on the writing test:

Phrases Following the Subject—Pay close attention to the subject of the sentence. Do not be mis-led by phrases that may follow the subject. These phrases may confuse you into selecting a verb that does not agree with the subject. Find the usage error in this sentence:

Betty Friedan's 1963 book, <u>an exposé</u> of domesticity <u>that challenged</u> long-held American attitudes,
                        A   B

<u>remain</u> an <u>important contribution</u> to feminism.
  C   D

The error is in part C. The singular subject, *book,* needs a singular verb, *remains.* Don't be confused by the plural noun *attitudes,* which is part of a phrase that follows the subject.

Subjects Following the Verb—Be sure to locate the subject of the sentence. Test makers use subjects that come after the verb to confuse you. Sentence constructions that begin with *there is* or *there are* signal that the subject comes after the verb. Which answer gives the correct replacement phrase for the following sentence?

Although the Australian government protects the Great Barrier Reef, <u>there is environmental factors that</u> <u>continue to threaten</u> the world's largest coral reef ecosystem.
  a. there is environmental factors that continue to threaten
  b. environmental factors that continue to threaten
  c. there are environmental factors that continue to threaten
  d. there are environmental factors that continued to threaten
  e. there is environmental factors that would continue to threaten

The answer is **c**. The plural subject *factors* requires a plural form of the verb, *are*. The verb *continue* is in the correct tense in the original sentence, so choices **d** and **e** are incorrect. The deletion of *there are* in choice **b** does not make sense in the sentence, and leaving the word *that* is grammatically incorrect.

Special Singular Nouns—Some words that end in *s*, like *measles, news, checkers, economics, sports,* and *politics,* are often singular despite their plural form, because we think of them as one thing. Keep a watch out for collective nouns—nouns that refer to a number of people or things that form a single unit. These words, such as *audience, stuff, crowd, government, group,* and *orchestra,* need a singular verb. Find the usage error in this sentence:

That <u>rowdy</u> group of drama students <u>were</u> labeled "the anarchists," <u>because</u> they took over the university
     A   B   C

president's office <u>in a protest</u> against the dress code.
              D

The error is in part B. The collective noun, *group,* is the singular subject of the sentence. Notice how the position of the prepositional phrase *of drama students* following the subject is misleading.

Pronoun Agreement

Pronouns are words that take the place of a noun or another pronoun, called an **antecedent**. Just as subjects and verbs must agree in number, pronouns and their antecedents must match *in number*. If an antecedent is singular, the pronoun must be singular. If an antecedent is plural, the pronoun must be plural.

Pronouns also need to match their antecedent in case. **Case** refers to a word's grammatical relationship to other words in a sentence. A pronoun that takes the place of the subject of a sentence should be in the nominative case (*I, you, we, he, she, it, they*), whereas a pronoun that refers to the object in a sentence should be in the objective case (*me, us, you, him, her, it, them*). Here are some examples:

Matteo is funny, but *he* can also be very serious. (subject)
Bernadette hired Will, and she also fired *him.* (object)

In most cases, you will automatically recognize errors in pronoun agreement. The phrase, *Me worked on the project with him* is clearly incorrect. However, some instances of pronoun agreement can be tricky. Review these common pronoun problems:

- **Indefinite pronouns** like *each, everyone, anybody, no one, one, either,* are singular.
  <u>Each</u> of the boys presented *his* science project.
- **Two or more nouns joined by *and*** use a plural pronoun.
  <u>Andy Warhol and Roy Lichtenstein</u> engaged popular culture in *their* art.

- **Two or more singular nouns joined by** *or* use a singular pronoun.
  <u>Francis or Andrew</u> will loan you *his* book.
- **He or she?** In speech, people often use the pronoun *they* to refer to a single person of unknown gender.
  However, this is incorrect—a singular antecedent requires a singular pronoun.
  <u>A person</u> has the right to do whatever <u>he or she</u> wants.

The following table lists some pronouns that are commonly confused with verb contractions or other words. Look out for these errors in the multiple-choice questions.

CONFUSING WORD	QUICK DEFINITION
Its	belonging to it
It's	it is
Your	belonging to you
You're	you are
Their	belonging to them
They're	they are
There	describes where an action takes place
Whose	belonging to whom
Who's	who is *or* who has
Who	refers to people
That	refers to things
Which	introduces clauses that are not essential to the information in the sentence, unless they refer to people. In that case, use *who.*

Try this practice sentence-correction question:

A child who is eager to please will often follow <u>everything that their parents say.</u>

- **a.** everything that their parents say.
- **b.** everything which their parents say.
- **c.** everything that his or her parents say.
- **d.** most everything that their parents say.
- **e.** everything that their parents said.

Choice **c** is the correct answer. The antecedent, *a child,* is singular. Even though you don't know the gender of the child, the possessive pronoun should be *his* or *her* in order to agree in number.

Pronoun Problem—Unclear Reference

When a pronoun can refer to more than one antecedent in a sentence it is called an unclear, or ambiguous, reference. An ambiguous pronoun reference also occurs when there is no apparent antecedent. Look carefully for this common error in your writing—a sentence may read smoothly, but may still contain an unclear reference. Look at the following sentence. Which underlined part contains a usage error?

A regular feature in American newspapers <u>since</u> the early nineteenth century, <u>they</u> use satirical humor to
                                         A   B

<u>visually</u> comment <u>on</u> a current event.
   C   D

The error is in part B. Who or what uses satirical humor? You don't know how to answer, because the pronoun *they* does not have a clear antecedent. If you replace *they* with *political cartoons*, the sentence makes sense.

Verbs—Action Words

A verb is the action word of a sentence. The three basic verb tenses—present, past, and future—let you know when something happens, happened, or will happen. Test makers include some of these common verb trouble spots in their exams.

Shifting Verb Tense—Verb tense should be consistent. If a sentence describes an event in the past, its verbs should all be in the past tense.

Incorrect: When Kate visited Japan, she sees many Shinto temples.

Correct: When Kate visited Japan, she saw many Shinto temples.

Past Tense for Present Conditions—It's incorrect to describe a present condition in the past tense.

Incorrect: My sister met her husband in a cafe. He was very tall.

Correct: My sister met her husband in a cafe. He is very tall.

Incomplete Verbs—Test makers may trick you by including the *-ing* form, or progressive form, of a verb without a helping verb (*is, has, has been, was, had, had been,* etc.). Make sure that verbs are complete and make sense in the sentence.

Incorrect: The major newspapers covering the story throughout the year because of the controversy.

Correct: The major newspapers have been covering the story throughout the year because of the controversy.

Subjunctive Mood—The subjunctive mood of verbs expresses something that is imagined, wished for, or contrary to fact. The subjunctive of *was* is *were*.

Incorrect: If I was a movie star, I would buy a fleet of Rolls Royces.

Correct: If I were a movie star, I would buy a fleet of Rolls Royces.

Find the usage error in the following sentence:

<u>Unhappy</u> about the lack <u>of</u> parking at the old stadium, season ticket holders <u>considering</u> <u>boycotting</u> next
   A   B   C   D
week's game.

The error is in part C. *Considering* needs a helping verb to be complete and to make sense in this sentence. The clause should read *season ticket holders are considering boycotting next week's game.*

▶ Structural Relationships

When you speak, you may leave your sentences unfinished or run your sentences together. Written expression makes a more permanent impression than speech. In writing, sentence fragments, run-on sentences, misplaced modifiers, and dangling modifiers are structural problems that obscure the meaning of a sentence. The parts of sentences need to have a clear relationship to each other to make sense. This section reviews common errors in sentence structure, including comparison mistakes, incorrect use of independent and subordinate clauses, double negatives, and unparallel sentence construction.

Making Comparisons

One common writing problem involves comparisons. When a sentence compares two things or activities, the form, or part of speech, of the two entities must match. A writer can compare two nouns or, alternatively, two verb phrases but should not compare a noun with a verb phrase.

Incorrect: For me, watching a psychological thriller is harder than a horror film.

Correct: For me, watching a psychological thriller is harder than sitting through a horror film.

In the correct version of the sentence, the verb phrase *watching a psychological thriller* matches the form of the verb phrase *sitting through a horror film*. Look at the following sentence. Select the choice that best corrects the usage error in the underlined part.

Even though they were admired by some, <u>the innovations of Lewis Carroll's later novels were</u> not as well received as his *Alice's Adventures in Wonderland.*
  a. the innovations of Lewis Carroll's later novels were
  b. Lewis Carroll's later novels were
  c. the innovations about Lewis Carroll's later novels were
  d. the innovations of Lewis Carroll were
  e. Lewis Carroll was

Choice **b** is the correct answer. The original sentence compared *the innovations* of Carroll's later novels with the book, *Alice's Adventures in Wonderland.* The comparison becomes parallel when you simply compare Lewis Carroll's later novels with his early book. Another way to make the sentence parallel would be to compare the innovations of the later novels with the innovations of the early book.

Sentence Fragments

All inventory at reduced prices! Spectacular savings for you! Although pithy and popular with advertisers, sentence fragments are incomplete sentences that do not accurately communicate an idea. To be complete, a sentence needs more than punctuation at its end—it needs a subject and an active verb. A common fragment error is the use of the *-ing* form of a verb without a helping verb.

Incorrect:	Emily sitting on the sofa, wondering what to do next.
Correct:	Emily was sitting on the sofa, wondering what to do next.

Another common type of sentence fragment is a **subordinate clause** that stands alone. To review, clauses are groups of words that have a subject and a verb. An **independent clause** is one that stands alone and expresses a complete thought. Even though a subordinate clause has a subject and a verb, it does not express a complete thought. It needs an independent clause to support it.

To identify a sentence fragment or subordinate clause, look for the following joining words, called **subordinating conjunctions**. When a clause has a subordinating conjunction, it needs an independent clause to complete an idea.

after	because	once	though	when
although	before	since	unless	where
as, as if	if	that	until	while

Examples

The Canadian goose that built a nest in the pond outside our building.

As if the storm never happened, as if no damage was done.

In the first example, removing the connector *that* would make a complete sentence. In the second example, the subordinate clauses need an independent clause to make logical sense: *As if the storm never happened, as if no damage was done, Esme remained blithely optimistic.* Try to locate the sentence fragment in the following example:

One <u>participant</u> of the civil rights movement <u>explained</u> that <u>in the heated atmosphere</u> of the 1960s,
      A   B   C

<u>sit-in protests effective enough</u> to draw the attention of the nation.
        D

The sentence fragment is found in part D. In this question, the independent clause has a subject (*one participant*) and a verb (*explained*). However, the subordinate clause, beginning with the connector *that*, needs a verb to make sense. Adding the verb *were* completes the thought and fixes the fragment: *that in the heated atmosphere of the 1960s, sit-in protests were effective enough to draw the attention of the nation.*

Run-on Sentences

"Planning ahead and studying for a test builds confidence do you know what I mean?" In speech, you may run your sentences together, but if you do so in writing, you will confuse your reader. In a run-on sentence, two independent clauses run together as one sentence without being separated by punctuation.

There are four ways to correct a run-on sentence. Study how each fix listed here changes the following run-on sentence.

Example
We stopped for lunch we were starving.

1. **Add a period.** This separates the run-on sentence and makes two simple sentences.
   We stopped for lunch. We were starving.
2. **Add a semicolon.**
   We stopped for lunch; we were starving.
3. **Use a comma and a coordinating conjunction** (*and, but, or, for, nor, yet, so*) to connect the two clauses.
   We were starving, **so** we stopped for lunch.
4. **Use a subordinating conjunction** (see page 194 for a list of subordinating conjunctions). By doing this, you turn one of the independent clauses into a subordinating clause.
   Because we were starving, we stopped for lunch.

Be sure to look out for another common form of run-on sentence, the **comma splice**. A comma splice incorrectly uses a comma to separate two independent clauses.

Incorrect: Jacob bought the groceries, Lucy cooked dinner.

You can repair a comma splice in two ways: add a conjunction after the comma or replace the comma with a semicolon.

Correct: Jacob bought the groceries, and Lucy cooked dinner.
                OR
                Jacob bought the groceries; Lucy cooked dinner.

Select the choice that corrects the run-on in the following sentence:

Citizen Kane, Orson Welles's first full-length film, <u>is considered an American classic, however it did not manage</u> to garner the 1941 Academy Award for best picture.
a. is considered an American classic, however it did not manage
b. is considered an American classic. However, it did not manage
c. is considered an American classic however it did not manage
d. is considered an American classic however. It did not manage
e. is considered an American classic because it did not manage

Choice **b** is correct. This original sentence is a run-on because the word *however* is used as if it were a conjunction. The words *however, therefore,* and *then* are not conjunctions, but rather a special kind of adverb that expresses a relationship between two clauses. Called **conjunctive adverbs**, these words cannot join two independent clauses the way a conjunction does. To repair this kind of run-on or comma splice, you can make two sentences (the way that choice **b** does above). Another option for fixing the original sentence is to separate the two main clauses with a semicolon and set the adverb off from the rest of the clause with a comma. Note that you can move the adverb around in its clause without changing the meaning of the sentence.

- *Citizen Kane,* Orson Welles's first full-length film, is considered an American classic; however, it did not manage to garner the 1941 Academy Award for best picture.
- *Citizen Kane,* Orson Welles's first full-length film, is considered an American classic; it did not manage, however, to garner the 1941 Academy Award for best picture.

More about Clauses

When a sentence contains two clauses that are linked in a logical way, they are **coordinated**. Subordinate clauses are joined by a conjunction (*as, after, although, because*) to the independent clause to complete a thought or idea. Problems occur when conjunctions are misused in a way that makes a sentence obscure and lacking in meaning. Notice how in the following example, the conjunction *because* creates a confusing and illogical premise, whereas in the second example, the conjunction *although* sets up a contrast between the two clauses that makes sense.

Unclear: Because he was late again, the teacher let him off with just a warning.
Correct: Although he was late again, the teacher let him off with just a warning.

Another type of mistake is when a sentence has two or more subordinate clauses, but no independent clause. This is a problem with **subordination**. Here is an example:

Incorrect: Since the Industrial Revolution, because people have increased the concentration of carbon dioxide in the atmosphere by 30 percent by burning fossil fuels and cutting down forests.

The previous sentence contains two subordinate clauses: the first introduced by the conjunction *since,* and the second introduced by the conjunction *because.* By removing *because,* you create an independent clause, and the sentence makes sense. Which part of the following sentence can you remove to make the sentence make sense?

When European settlers <u>arrived</u> in North America <u>in the fifteenth century,</u> <u>where</u> they <u>encountered</u>
                                        A   B   C   D
diverse Native American cultures.

If you remove the subordinating conjunction in part C, *where,* the second subordinating clause becomes an independent clause.

Misplaced Modifiers

Modifiers are phrases that describe nouns, pronouns, and verbs. In a sentence, they must be placed as closely as possible to the words they describe. If they are misplaced, you will end up with a sentence that means something other than what you intended. The results can be comical, but the joke may be on you!

Misplaced Modifier:	My uncle told me about feeding cows in the kitchen. (Why are there cows in the kitchen?)
Correct:	In the kitchen, my uncle told me about feeding cows.
Misplaced Modifier:	A huge python followed the man that was slithering slowly through the grass. (Why was the man slithering through the grass?)
Correct:	Slithering through the grass, a huge python followed the man.
	OR
	A huge python that was slithering slowly through the grass followed the man.

Dangling modifiers are phrases, located at the beginning of a sentence and set off by a comma, that mistakenly modify the wrong noun or pronoun. To be correct, modifying phrases at the beginning of a sentence should describe the noun or pronoun (the subject of the sentence) that directly follows the comma.

Dangling Modifier:	Broken and beyond repair, Grandma threw the serving dish away. (Why was Grandma broken?)
Correct:	Broken and beyond repair, the serving dish was thrown away by Grandma.
	OR
	Grandma threw away the serving dish that was broken and beyond repair.

Correct the following sentence:

Subsidized by the federal government, <u>students can get help financing their post-secondary education through the Federal Work-Study Program.</u>

   a. students can get help financing their post-secondary education through the Federal Work-Study Program.

   b. since students finance their post-secondary education through the Federal Work-Study Program.

   c. to students who need help financing their post-secondary education.

   d. financing a post-secondary education is possible through the Federal Work-Study Program.

   e. the Federal Work-Study Program helps students finance their post-secondary education.

The correct answer is **e**. In the original sentence, the modifying phrase incorrectly describes the subject *students*. In choice **d**, the modifying phrasing incorrectly describes financing. Choices **b** and **c** are subordinate clauses, and, therefore, incorrect. Only choice **e** answers the question "What is subsidized by the federal government?" in a way that makes sense.

Double Negatives

When you use two negatives such as *not* or *no* in a sentence, you may think that you are emphasizing your point. In fact, you are obscuring your meaning. As in math, two negatives result in a positive. When you write, "I don't have no money," you are actually saying that you do have money. Always avoid using double negatives—they are considered grammatically incorrect. *No* and *not* are obvious negatives, but be on the lookout for any sentence that doubles up on any of the following words:

no one	neither	nobody	scarcely
nothing	nowhere	hardly	barely

Find the double negative in the following sentence:

<u>Children</u> <u>don't hardly</u> need computers in the classroom <u>in order</u> <u>to learn</u> basic skills like math and
   A   B   C   D
reading.

The double negative is found in part B. The negative verb *don't* and the adverb *hardly* cancel each other out. The double negative obscures the meaning of the sentence. To rewrite the sentence in a way that makes sense, you could remove either word.

Parallel Structure

When a sentence has a parallel structure, it means that its words and phrases follow the same grammatical structure. Parallel structure makes sentences easier to read and helps express ideas clearly. Parallel construction is important in sentences that make lists or describe a series of events. Each part of the list or series must be in the same form, or part of speech, as the others.

Not Parallel: Every day, I went to school, worked part time, and was exercising.
                      (Two verbs are in the past tense; one is a past participle.)

Parallel: Every day, I went to school, worked part time, and exercised.

Not Parallel: We are looking for a teaching assistant who is smart, reliable, and will come on time.
                      (Two characteristics are adjectives, whereas the third consists of a verb phrase.)

Parallel: We are looking for a teaching assistant who is smart, reliable, and punctual.

Parallel construction is also crucial when a sentence uses a *not only/but also* pattern. Review the following examples:

The author not only <u>raised several important questions</u>, but she also <u>made a convincing argument</u>. (Notice how the phrases following the *not only/but also* pattern are in the same form. Each has a verb in the past tense and a noun.)

The contract dispute was a result not only <u>of a breakdown in communication</u> but also <u>of the town's budgetary crisis.</u> (Here the words following the *not only/but also* pattern are in the form of prepositional phrases.)

Select the choice that creates parallel structure in the following sentence:

Expressing yourself clearly and effectively in writing means knowing the basic mechanics of language, eliminating ambiguity, choosing the right words, <u>and correct punctuation.</u>
  a. and correct punctuation.
  b. or correct punctuation
  c. and use correct punctuation.
  d. and having used correct punctuation.
  e. and using correct punctuation.

Choice **e** creates parallel structure because it follows the grammatical pattern of the sentence: a list of phrases beginning with **gerunds** (a gerund is a noun created from the *-ing* form of a verb).

► Idioms and Word Choice

Idioms—words, phrases, or expressions used in everyday language—make up a large part of English. If your native language is not English, the use of idioms may challenge you. That is because idioms often have unusual grammatical structures or have a meaning that does not make sense if you simply add up the meanings of each word. Native English speakers recognize most idioms *by ear*—the words just sound right.

Prepositional Idioms

Prepositions are words that express the relationship in time or space between words in a sentence. They are generally short words, such as *in, on, around, above, between, beside, by, before,* or *with,* that introduce prepositional phrases in a sentence. Review and familiarize yourself with this list of common prepositional idioms:

according to	depend on/upon	next to
afraid of	equal to	of the opinion
anxious about	except for	on top of
apologize to (someone)	fond of	opposite of
apologize for (something)	from now on	prior to
approve of	from time to time	proud of
ashamed of	frown on/upon	regard to
aware of	full of	related to
blame (someone) for	glance at/through	rely on/upon
blame (something) on	grateful to (someone)	respect for
bored with	grateful for (something)	responsible for
capable of	in accordance with	satisfied with
compete with	incapable of	similar to
complain about	in conflict	sorry for
composed of	inferior to	suspicious of
concentrate on	insist on/upon	take care of
concerned with	in the habit of	thank (someone) for
congratulate on	in the near future	tired of
conscious of	interested in	with regard to
consist of	knowledge of	

Keep your ear attuned to the use of prepositional idioms in the following sentence. Which underlined part isn't idiomatic?

The <u>period of</u> intellectual development known as the Renaissance <u>correspond to</u> a <u>time of</u> political
     A   B   C

stability <u>in western</u> <u>Europe</u>.
            D   E

The word combination in part B, *correspond to,* is simply not idiomatic; *corresponded with* is the correct prepositional idiom.

Redundancy and Wordiness

You may be asked to identify redundant or wordy language. Your ability to write concisely and clearly will also be an important part of the constructed-response portion of the test. To eliminate unnecessary repetitions or excessive wordiness, look for words that add no new information to a sentence.

Redundant:	<u>Due to the fact that</u> the circumstances of the case were <u>sensitive in nature</u>, the proceedings were kept confidential.
Correct:	<u>Because</u> the circumstances of the case were <u>sensitive</u>, the proceedings were kept confidential.

Redundant:	Charles <u>returned back</u> to his room <u>at 10:00 A.M. in the morning</u>.
Correct:	Charles <u>returned</u> to his room <u>at 10:00 A.M.</u>

Commonly Confused Words

A misused word can significantly alter the meaning of a sentence. The following list contains some commonly confused words. If you find some that you frequently confuse, study them and practice using them correctly in a sentence.

CONFUSING WORDS	QUICK DEFINITION
accept	recognize
except	excluding
affect (verb)	to influence
effect (noun)	result
effect (verb)	to bring about
all ready	totally prepared
already	by this time

CONFUSING WORDS	QUICK DEFINITION
allude	make indirect reference to
elude	evade
illusion	unreal appearance
all ways	every method
always	forever
among	in the middle of several
between	in an interval separating (two)
assure	to make certain
	(assure someone)
ensure	to make certain
insure	to make certain (financial value)
beside	next to
besides	in addition to
complement	match
compliment	praise
continual	constantly
continuous	uninterrupted
disinterested	no strong opinion either way
uninterested	don't care
elicit	to stir up
illicit	illegal
eminent	well known
imminent	pending
farther	beyond
further	additional
incredible	beyond belief, astonishing
incredulous	skeptical, disbelieving
loose	not tight
lose	unable to find
may be	something could possibly be
maybe	perhaps
overdo	do too much
overdue	late

CONFUSING WORDS	QUICK DEFINITION
persecute	to mistreat
prosecute	to take legal action
personal	individual
personnel	employees
precede	go before
proceed	continue
proceeds	profits
principal (adjective)	main
principal (noun)	person in charge; a sum of interest-earning money
principle	standard
stationary	still, not moving
stationery	writing material
than	in contrast to
then	next
to	on the way to
too	also
weather	climate
whether	if

► Mechanics

Knowing the mechanics of language means getting down to basics—the rules of punctuation and capitalization. Punctuation marks are standardized marks that clarify meaning for your reader, serving as traffic signs that direct the reader to pause, connect, stop, consider, and go. Although most likely you have studied and learned many of the basic rules of punctuation and capitalization, this section will cover some common problem areas, including misuse of commas, semicolons, colons, apostrophes, and capitalization.

Commas

Commas create pauses, clarify meaning, and separate different parts of a sentence. The comma splice is a common misuse of the comma—review this problem on page 195. Remember the six basic rules for using commas as follows.

Use a comma:

1. **To separate independent clauses** joined by a coordinating conjunction, such as *and, but, nor, so, for,* or *or.* Use a comma before the conjunction.

   My instinct was to solve the problem slowly and deliberately, *but* we only had a week before the deadline.

2. **To set off nonessential clauses.** A nonessential clause is one that can be removed from a sentence without changing its meaning.

   My friend Rebecca, *who is active in the local labor union,* is a fifth-grade teacher.

3. **To set off words or phrases that interrupt** the flow of thought in a sentence.

   The certification program, *however,* works well for me.

   Elena Alvarez, *my adviser and mentor,* was present at the meeting.

4. **To set off an introductory element,** such as a word or phrase that comes at the beginning of a sentence.

   Thrilled by the results, Phin presented the study to his colleagues.

5. **To set apart a series of words in a list.** Usually, the last item in a list is preceded by a conjunction. Although a comma is not necessary before the conjunction, it is preferred that you use one.

   Micah, Jose, and Sam attended the conference.

   Micah, Jose and Sam attended the conference.

6. **To separate elements of dates and addresses.** Commas are used to separate dates that include the day, month, and year. Dates that include just the month and year do not need commas. When the name of a city and state are included in an address, set off both with commas.

   Margaret moved to *Portsmouth, New Hampshire,* for the job.

   Maco came to Greensboro on *June 15, 2004,* right after she graduated from the program.

   Maco came to Greensboro in *June 2004* after she graduated from the program.

Semicolons

Review how to use semicolons correctly by using the following guidelines.

1. **Use a semicolon to separate independent clauses** that are not joined by a conjunction.
2. **Use a semicolon to separate independent clauses that contain commas,** even if the clauses are joined by a conjunction.
3. **Use a semicolon to separate independent clauses connected with a conjunctive adverb,** such as *however, therefore, then, thus,* or *moreover.*

Colons

Colons are used to introduce elements and to show an equivalent relationship (almost like an equals sign in math). Follow these guidelines to recognize the correct use of colons:

1. **Use a colon to introduce a list** when the clause before the colon can stand as a complete sentence.

    These are the first-year teachers: Ellen, Ben, and Eliza.

    The first-year teachers are Ellen, Ben, and Eliza. (No colon here.)

2. **Use a colon to introduce a restatement or elaboration** of the previous clause.

    James enjoys teaching *Measure for Measure* each spring: it is his favorite play.

3. **Use a colon to introduce a word, phrase, or clause** that adds emphasis to the main body of the sentence.

    Carrie framed the check: it was the first paycheck she had ever earned.

4. **Use a colon to introduce a formal quotation.**

    Writer Gurney Williams offered this advice to parents: "Teaching creativity to your child isn't like teaching good manners. No one can paint a masterpiece by bowing to another person's precepts about elbows on the table."

Use the punctuation guidelines you have reviewed to find the punctuation error in the following sentence:

Alternative medicine, which includes a range of practices outside of conventional medicine such as
                    A

herbs, homeopathy, massage, yoga, and acupuncture; holds increasing appeal for Americans.
  B   C D

The semicolon in part C does not work because it does not separate two independent clauses. It should be replaced with a comma, setting off the nonessential clause that begins with the word *which*.

Apostrophes

Apostrophes are used to show possession. Consider these eight rules for using apostrophes:

1. **Add *'s* to form the singular possessive,** even when the noun ends in *s:*

    Mr. Summers's essay convinced me.

2. **Add *'s* to plural words not ending in *s.***

    The *children's* ability to absorb foreign language is astounding.

    The workshops focus on working *women's* needs.

3. **Add *'* to plural words ending in *s.***

    The *students'* grades improved each semester.

4. **Add *'s* to indefinite pronouns that show ownership.**

    Everyone's ability level should be considered.

5. **Never use apostrophes with possessive pronouns.**

   This experiment must be *yours.*

6. **Use *'s* to form the plurals of letters, figures, and numbers, as well as expressions of time or money.**

   Mind your *p's* and *q's.*

   The project was the result of a *year's* worth of work.

7. **Add *'s* to the last word of a compound noun, compound subject, or name of a business or institution.**

   The *president-elect's* speech riveted the audience.

   Gabbie and Michael's wedding is in October.

   The *National Science Teachers Association's* meeting will take place next week.

8. **Use apostrophes to show that letters or words are omitted in contractions.**

   Abby *doesn't* (does not) work today.

   Who's (who is) on first?

Capitalization

Capitalization is necessary both for specific words and to start sentences and quotations. The following are six instances when capitalization is needed:

- the first word of the sentence
- proper nouns (names of *specific* people, places, and things)
- the first word of a complete quotation, but not a partial quotation
- the first, last, and any other important words of a title
- languages
- the pronoun *I,* and any contractions made with it

Sometimes knowing when to capitalize a word is tricky. Look for these trouble spots in your writing:

- **Compass directions**, such as *east* or *west,* are not capitalized unless they refer to a specific geographical area.

  The American Civil War was fought between the *North* and the *South.*
- **Family relationships** are not capitalized when they are preceded by a pronoun.

  I met *my mother* for lunch.

  Uncle Russ agreed to babysit, so that I could meet *Mother* for lunch.
- **Seasons and parts of the academic year** are not capitalized.

  I'll register for the course this *fall.*
- **Words modified by proper adjectives** are not capitalized, unless they are part of a proper name.

  Jacob recommended the *Italian restaurant* in his neighborhood.

Find the usage error in the following sentence:

When Thomas Jefferson sent explorers Lewis and Clark into the <u>West,</u> he patterned their mission on the
A

<u>Enlightenments'</u> scientific methods<u>:</u> to observe, collect, document<u>,</u> and classify.
   B   C   D

The usage error is in part B. As a proper noun, *the Enlightenment* is correctly capitalized; however, the apostrophe is misplaced. To show possession, add *'s* to a singular noun. The *West* is correctly capitalized because it refers to a geographical region of the United States.

▶ Introducing the Essay

Essays can intimidate anyone—even teachers. You know you will be asked to write a constructed response, but you don't know your topic beforehand. And you are under pressure: you have limited time to complete the task. Even though this sounds nerve-racking, with preparation, you will be ready to produce your best writing. The good news is that because the time limit is brief, your constructed response doesn't need to be a novel. It should be one to two pages long. Furthermore, because you are provided with a topic, you don't need to spend valuable time deciding what to write about.

What to Expect

The possible writing prompts in the NYSTCE® constructed responses present a statement or passage and ask you to respond to it. Be ready to explain and back up your position or answer with specific reasons and examples from your personal experience, observations, or reading. **Do not write about a topic other than the one provided.** To receive a passing score, you must write in the required language. Your writing must be legible, related to the assigned topic, and contain a sufficient amount of original work.

▶ Steps to a Strong Essay

The pre-writing—or planning—process is essential to developing a clear, organized essay. Because of the time limit, you may be tempted to skip the pre-writing stage. However, the five to ten minutes that you spend planning will be worth it. Pre-writing consists of some quick, basic steps: carefully reading and understanding the writing prompt, formulating a thesis, brainstorming for examples that will support your thesis, and drafting an outline or basic structure for your essay.

Step 1—Create a Clear Thesis

To begin, carefully read the writing prompt. Make sure that you fully understand it. Then, decide what is your position or response: Do you agree or disagree with the statement? Consider to what extent you agree or disagree with the position: Are you in 100% agreement or do you only partly agree with the statement? Your answer to these questions will make up the main idea or **thesis** of your essay. It will form the foundation of your essay and will determine what kind of support, or examples, you will provide.

A strong thesis does not merely repeat or rephrase the question or prompt. It does not state how *others* might respond to it. Rather, it presents *your* point of view.

A thesis statement should:

- answer the question given in the writing prompt
- tell the reader what your subject is
- inform the reader what you think and feel about the subject
- use clear, active language

Don't waste time making your thesis statement a masterpiece. You will be able to grab the reader's attention by clearly stating your purpose in simple words.

Consider the following prompt:

"Focusing on fashion and clothes can distract students from learning. School uniforms should be mandatory for all high school students."
Discuss the extent to which you agree or disagree with this opinion. Support your views with specific reasons and examples from your own experience, observations, or reading.

The following sentences are *not* thesis statements:

- Many private schools already require school uniforms.
- Some students prefer school uniforms, while others detest them.
- Why do schools use uniforms?

The following *are* thesis statements; they relate directly to the prompt:

- School uniforms discourage high school students from learning responsibility and developing individuality.
- School uniforms are effective in creating a positive learning environment.

Remember that you can also impose some conditions on your answer. For example, if you disagree with mandatory school uniforms, you can still qualify your answer: "I disagree that students should be required to wear school uniforms, but I believe a dress code helps create an effective learning atmosphere."

Step 2—Brainstorm for Ideas

Your answer to the question in the writing prompt will form the argument that you present in your essay. Once you have decided what your position will be, you will begin to brainstorm—think up ideas—that support your thesis. Try to generate about three to five reasons that back up your main idea.

Brainstorming is a pre-writing process in which you imagine or write down any ideas that come to mind. To brainstorm effectively, do not judge your ideas initially—simply put them down on paper. If you are stuck for ideas, try these brainstorming strategies:

- Try the **freewriting** technique in which you write nonstop for two minutes. Keep your pen to paper and your hand moving. Doubtlessly, your ideas will emerge.
- **List** as many ideas as you can. Don't edit for grammar or structure; just write down whatever comes to mind.
- Now get selective. Choose three to five of your strongest ideas for your essay.

For example, here's how you might brainstorm supporting ideas for the writing prompt mentioned earlier:

Thesis: Mandatory school uniforms are not effective tools for creating a positive learning environment.

Examples
Why?

Uniforms don't give students the opportunity to make choices.

Uniforms send a message to students that they cannot be trusted.

Students find distractions in class even when they are wearing uniforms.

Teenage years are a time of self-exploration.

Learning isn't only something you read in a book—it's about finding out who you are.

Students need to learn about making good choices.

Personal experience—in my parochial high school, kids wore uniforms.

Lack of trust—couldn't be trusted to do even a simple thing like dressing ourselves.

Found other ways to rebel—smoking, wearing make-up, wearing hair to attract attention.

Distractions in class other than clothes—note writing, gossip, cell phones.

Self-exploration—clothes let teens to try on different identities (sporty, punk, artistic).

Learning about good choices—introduce a forum for students where they can talk about making choices? Encourage kids to talk about how they present themselves when they wear different clothes; talk about choices teens make that can be dangerous; talk about choices adults face.

Step 3—Outline Your Essay

To make sure that your essay is well developed and organized, draft an outline. An outline will help you put your ideas into a logical order and identify any gaps in your supporting details. Essays follow a basic three-part structure:

1. **Introduction:** Present your position or positions to your readers. State your thesis. Effectively and explicitly state the purpose of your response.
2. **Body:** Provide specific support for your thesis through examples and/or sound reasoning that reflects your understanding of the focus of the topic. Be sure to address each component of the question if the prompt includes multiple components.
3. **Conclusion:** Bring closure to your response and restate your thesis.

Your constructed response should follow this basic structure, too. List one point on your outline for each paragraph.

Essay Structure

Where you put your introduction and conclusion is obvious; however, you need a pattern, or structure, to organize the ideas in the body of your essay. In some responses, the paragraphs that comprise your body will be dictated by the specific components of the prompt. Other prompts may be less obvious. In this case, you may use one of these common patterns: **chronological order, comparison and contrast, cause and effect,** and **order of importance.** The following chart lists each organizing principle's key characteristics and effective uses in writing.

ORGANIZATIONAL PATTERN	CHARACTERISTICS	EFFECTIVE USES
Chronological order	Uses time as organizing principle; describes events in the order in which they happened	Historical texts, personal narratives, fiction
Order of importance	Arranges ideas by increasing or decreasing importance instead of time	Persuasive essays, newspaper articles
Comparison and contrast	Places two or more items side by side to show similarities and differences	Comparative essays
Cause and effect	Explains possible reasons why something took place	Historical analysis, analysis of current events

Now it's time to make a detailed outline based on the writing prompt described earlier in the chapter. The outline organizes the supporting ideas by increasing importance. It includes reasons that support the thesis and examples that support each reason. Because this outline is so detailed, it offers a guide for almost every sentence in the body of the essay. When you write your final response, you will use the outline to guide the structure and content as you add examples and connections to support your positions or answers to each component of the prompt.

Introduction:

Thesis: Mandatory school uniforms are not effective tools for creating a positive, learning environment.

Reason 1: When students feel that they are not trusted, they "live down" to expectations.

> *Examples:* Feel need to prove individuality through attention to make-up, hair; draw attention through risky behaviors like smoking; continue to find distractions like gossip, note passing, cell phones

Reason 2: School uniforms discourage self-discovery and individuality.

> *Examples:* Can't try out looks that come with different identities (sporty, punk, artistic); fashion is harmless way to find out "who you are"

Reason 3: Students don't learn to make good choices.

> *Examples:* Students aren't prepared for making decisions, simple (clothes, nutrition) or big (college, jobs, whether or not to engage in risky behaviors, friends, romantic relationships)

Conclusion:

> Robbing students of choice discourages self-discovery and does not prepare students for making decisions. Allow students to make choices about their clothes, but also provide a class or forum for discussing how to make good choices, both big and small.

Target Your Audience

Effective writing pays close attention to its *audience*. Good writers consider their readers: Who are they? What do they know about the subject? What preconceived notions do they have? What will hold their attention?

Unless the NYSTCE constructed response states otherwise in the prompt, you should write to a general audience, meaning your readers are people with a variety of interests and backgrounds. Knowing your audience helps you make key writing decisions about your level of formality and detail. Your level of formality determines whether you will use slang, an informal tone, technical jargon, or formal language in your writing. A good guide for the NYSTCE is a balanced approach:

- Treat your readers with respect.
- Don't put off your readers with language that is too formal or pretentious. Don't try to use big, important-sounding words.
- Avoid jargon (technical or specialized language) unless you define or explain what it means.
- Avoid slang (too informal).
- Aim for a natural tone, without being too informal.

Your level of detail is also based on your audience. Because you are writing for a general audience and not for friends or family, your readers will not be familiar with your background or experiences. For example, if you are arguing against mandatory student uniforms, do not assume that your readers know whether your high school implemented such a rule. Give your readers adequate context by briefly describing your experiences as it applies to your argument.

First Impression—The Introduction

Once you have completed your detailed outline, you are ready to write. Don't dedicate too much time to perfecting the wording of your introduction. Instead, use clear, direct language to introduce your reader to your thesis and focus. A good way to begin is to restate in your own words the quotation given in the prompt and then state your thesis. Here is an example using the prompt discussed earlier:

> Although fashion and clothes can sometimes distract students, mandatory school uniforms are
> not the answer to creating a good learning environment.

Another useful technique for creating a strong introduction is to begin with your thesis and then give a summary of the evidence (supporting details) you will be presenting in the body of your essay. Here is an expanded version of the previous thesis statement:

> Although fashion and clothes can sometimes distract students, mandatory school uniforms are
> not the answer to creating a good learning environment. School uniforms can be a negative influ-
> ence in that they send a message that students can't be trusted to make good choices. High
> school students need to explore different identities through the harmless means of fashion.

Notice how this introduction outlines the first two main points of the essay's body: how mandatory school uniforms (1) send a negative message about students' ability to make decisions, and (2) discourage self-discovery.

Supporting Paragraphs—The Body of the Essay

Working from your detailed outline, begin composing the body of your essay (about three paragraphs long). Treat each of your paragraphs like a mini-essay, with its own thesis (a topic sentence that expresses the main idea of the paragraph) and supporting details (examples). Follow these guidelines for creating supporting paragraphs:

- **Avoid introducing several ideas within one paragraph.** By definition, a paragraph is a group of sentences about the *same* idea.
- **Use at least one detail** or example to back up each main supporting idea.
- **Budget the number of sentences in each paragraph by the amount of time you have left to write the response.** Your essay will be short. If you write too many sentences for each paragraph you may run short on time and space. If you write too few sentences, you may not develop your idea adequately.
- **Use transitions.** Key words and phrases can help guide readers through your essay. You can use these common transitions to indicate the order of importance of your material: *first and foremost, most important, first, second, third, moreover, finally,* and *above all.* Do not use *firstly, secondly,* or *thirdly*—these forms are incorrect and awkward.

Active versus Passive Voice

For precise, direct writing, use the active voice. In English grammar, **voice** expresses a relationship between the verb and the subject of the sentence or its direct object. When you write in the **active voice**, the subject of the sentence causes, or is the source of, the action (verb). When you use the **passive voice**, the subject does not perform the action, but rather is acted upon. Sentences in the passive voice are often wordier and more difficult to understand. Here are some examples of active vs. passive voice:

Active: We suggest that you organize your ideas by importance.

Passive: It is suggested that you organize your ideas by importance. (Note that this sentence does not say *who* performed the action.)

Active: Her brother typed the letter.

Passive: The letter was typed by her brother. (Here the *doer* of the action is the direct object *brother,* not the subject of the sentence, *letter.*)

Sentence Variety

A strong essay will show your ability to manipulate sentence structure for effect. Sentence structure is an important element of style. If all of your sentences have the same pattern, your writing will be monotonous and dull:

School uniforms are negative. They don't boost students' confidence. They don't make students feel trustworthy. They don't let students explore different styles and personalities.

Although these sentences are simple and direct, they are unlikely to captivate a reader. Because they all have the same length and structure, they create a monotonous pattern. Here is the same paragraph, revised to show variety in sentence structure:

School uniforms are negative because they do not boost students' confidence or make them feel trustworthy. Fashion choices allow students to explore different styles and personalities.

Four sentences are reduced to two; the pronoun *they* is no longer repeated; and verb choices are active and varied. You can also create emphasis in your writing through sentence structure. The best place to put sentence elements that you want to emphasize is at the end. What comes lasts lingers longest in the reader's ears.

He is tall, dark, and handsome. (The emphasis is on *handsome.* If *tall* is the most important characteristic, then it should come last.)

You can also use a dash to set off a part of a sentence for emphasis:

He is tall, dark, handsome—and married.

The dash emphasizes the last element, heightening the sense of disappointment the writer is trying to convey.

Your Conclusion

The last paragraph of your essay should sum up your argument. Avoid introducing new ideas or topics. Instead, your concluding paragraph should restate your thesis, but in *new words*. Your conclusion should demonstrate that you covered your topic fully and should convince readers that they have learned something meaningful from your argument. Here's an example:

> School uniforms might be the easy answer: They create conformity and minimize distractions in the classroom. However, in order to teach students how to make good choices when they face tough decisions, school administrators need to invest students with the responsibility to practice everyday choices—like deciding what they wear to school.

The Last Step—Proofread

Plan to take about five minutes to proofread—a time allowance that does not let you substantially revise or rewrite your piece. Much of what happens when you rewrite—like reorganizing your argument or making sure you present adequate support—must occur during the *pre-writing* process, when you are outlining your essay. The goal of proofreading is to give your essay a final polish, by checking your spelling, correcting grammatical errors, and if needed, changing word order or word choice. To proofread, carefully read your essay, paying attention to anything that doesn't sound right. The following checklist outlines some basic grammatical problems to look out for as you proofread. (All of these grammar trouble spots have been explained previously in this chapter.)

- **Make sure nouns and verbs agree.** The subject of the sentence must match the verb in number. If the subject is singular, the verb is singular. If the subject is plural, the verb is plural.
- **Make sure pronouns and antecedents agree.** Pronouns and the nouns they represent, antecedents, must agree in number. If the antecedent is singular, the pronoun is singular; if the antecedent is plural, the pronoun is plural.
- **Check your modifiers.** Look out for modifiers that are easy to confuse like *good/well, bad/badly, fewer/less.* Remember: adjectives modify nouns and pronouns; adverbs describe verbs, adjectives, or other adverbs.
- **Avoid double negatives.** Do not use two negative words, like *no, not, neither, hardly,* or *barely,* in one sentence. See page 198 for a list of other negatives.
- **Keep your verb tense consistent.** Switching tense within a sentence can change its meaning. Generally, a sentence or paragraph that begins in the present tense should continue in the present tense.
- **Review prepositional idioms.** If you have studied the list of prepositional idioms on page 200, you may be able to "hear" whether a preposition (*to, of, about, for, with, about, on, upon*) sounds right with a particular phrase or verb.
- **Check your sentence structure.** Keep an eye out for sentence fragments, run-on sentences, comma splices, and misplaced or dangling modifiers.

11 ▶ LAST Practice Exam 1

CHAPTER SUMMARY

This is the first of the two practice Liberal Arts and Sciences Test (LAST) exams in this book based on the format and content of the official LAST. See Chapter 4 for a complete description of the official exam. Use this practice exam to see how you would do if you were to take the LAST today.

There will be a four-hour time limit when you the take the official LAST. As you take this first practice exam, however, do not worry too much about timing. Just take the test in a relaxed manner to find out which areas you are skilled in and which areas will need extra work.

The answer sheet you should use for the multiple-choice questions is on page 217. (You will write your essay on a separate piece of paper.) After you finish taking your test, you should review the answer explanations found at the end of this test. The answer explanations are followed by information on how to score your exam.

▶ Answer Sheet

1.	ⓐ	ⓑ	ⓒ	ⓓ
2.	ⓐ	ⓑ	ⓒ	ⓓ
3.	ⓐ	ⓑ	ⓒ	ⓓ
4.	ⓐ	ⓑ	ⓒ	ⓓ
5.	ⓐ	ⓑ	ⓒ	ⓓ
6.	ⓐ	ⓑ	ⓒ	ⓓ
7.	ⓐ	ⓑ	ⓒ	ⓓ
8.	ⓐ	ⓑ	ⓒ	ⓓ
9.	ⓐ	ⓑ	ⓒ	ⓓ
10.	ⓐ	ⓑ	ⓒ	ⓓ
11.	ⓐ	ⓑ	ⓒ	ⓓ
12.	ⓐ	ⓑ	ⓒ	ⓓ
13.	ⓐ	ⓑ	ⓒ	ⓓ
14.	ⓐ	ⓑ	ⓒ	ⓓ
15.	ⓐ	ⓑ	ⓒ	ⓓ
16.	ⓐ	ⓑ	ⓒ	ⓓ
17.	ⓐ	ⓑ	ⓒ	ⓓ
18.	ⓐ	ⓑ	ⓒ	ⓓ
19.	ⓐ	ⓑ	ⓒ	ⓓ
20.	ⓐ	ⓑ	ⓒ	ⓓ
21.	ⓐ	ⓑ	ⓒ	ⓓ
22.	ⓐ	ⓑ	ⓒ	ⓓ
23.	ⓐ	ⓑ	ⓒ	ⓓ
24.	ⓐ	ⓑ	ⓒ	ⓓ
25.	ⓐ	ⓑ	ⓒ	ⓓ
26.	ⓐ	ⓑ	ⓒ	ⓓ
27.	ⓐ	ⓑ	ⓒ	ⓓ

28.	ⓐ	ⓑ	ⓒ	ⓓ
29.	ⓐ	ⓑ	ⓒ	ⓓ
30.	ⓐ	ⓑ	ⓒ	ⓓ
31.	ⓐ	ⓑ	ⓒ	ⓓ
32.	ⓐ	ⓑ	ⓒ	ⓓ
33.	ⓐ	ⓑ	ⓒ	ⓓ
34.	ⓐ	ⓑ	ⓒ	ⓓ
35.	ⓐ	ⓑ	ⓒ	ⓓ
36.	ⓐ	ⓑ	ⓒ	ⓓ
37.	ⓐ	ⓑ	ⓒ	ⓓ
38.	ⓐ	ⓑ	ⓒ	ⓓ
39.	ⓐ	ⓑ	ⓒ	ⓓ
40.	ⓐ	ⓑ	ⓒ	ⓓ
41.	ⓐ	ⓑ	ⓒ	ⓓ
42.	ⓐ	ⓑ	ⓒ	ⓓ
43.	ⓐ	ⓑ	ⓒ	ⓓ
44.	ⓐ	ⓑ	ⓒ	ⓓ
45.	ⓐ	ⓑ	ⓒ	ⓓ
46.	ⓐ	ⓑ	ⓒ	ⓓ
47.	ⓐ	ⓑ	ⓒ	ⓓ
48.	ⓐ	ⓑ	ⓒ	ⓓ
49.	ⓐ	ⓑ	ⓒ	ⓓ
50.	ⓐ	ⓑ	ⓒ	ⓓ
51.	ⓐ	ⓑ	ⓒ	ⓓ
52.	ⓐ	ⓑ	ⓒ	ⓓ
53.	ⓐ	ⓑ	ⓒ	ⓓ
54.	ⓐ	ⓑ	ⓒ	ⓓ

55.	ⓐ	ⓑ	ⓒ	ⓓ
56.	ⓐ	ⓑ	ⓒ	ⓓ
57.	ⓐ	ⓑ	ⓒ	ⓓ
58.	ⓐ	ⓑ	ⓒ	ⓓ
59.	ⓐ	ⓑ	ⓒ	ⓓ
60.	ⓐ	ⓑ	ⓒ	ⓓ
61.	ⓐ	ⓑ	ⓒ	ⓓ
62.	ⓐ	ⓑ	ⓒ	ⓓ
63.	ⓐ	ⓑ	ⓒ	ⓓ
64.	ⓐ	ⓑ	ⓒ	ⓓ
65.	ⓐ	ⓑ	ⓒ	ⓓ
66.	ⓐ	ⓑ	ⓒ	ⓓ
67.	ⓐ	ⓑ	ⓒ	ⓓ
68.	ⓐ	ⓑ	ⓒ	ⓓ
69.	ⓐ	ⓑ	ⓒ	ⓓ
70.	ⓐ	ⓑ	ⓒ	ⓓ
71.	ⓐ	ⓑ	ⓒ	ⓓ
72.	ⓐ	ⓑ	ⓒ	ⓓ
73.	ⓐ	ⓑ	ⓒ	ⓓ
74.	ⓐ	ⓑ	ⓒ	ⓓ
75.	ⓐ	ⓑ	ⓒ	ⓓ
76.	ⓐ	ⓑ	ⓒ	ⓓ
77.	ⓐ	ⓑ	ⓒ	ⓓ
78.	ⓐ	ⓑ	ⓒ	ⓓ
79.	ⓐ	ⓑ	ⓒ	ⓓ
80.	ⓐ	ⓑ	ⓒ	ⓓ

Questions 1 and 2 are based on the following paragraph.

The English language premiere of Samuel Beckett's play, Waiting for Godot, took place in London in August 1955. Godot is an avant-garde play with only five characters (not including Mr. Godot, who never arrives) and a minimal setting: one rock and one bare tree. The play has two acts; the second act repeats what little action occurs in the first with few changes: The tree, for instance, acquires one leaf. In a statement that was to become famous, the critic Vivian Mercer described Godot as "a play in which nothing happens twice." Opening night, critics and playgoers greeted the play with bafflement and derision. The line, "Nothing happens, nobody comes, nobody goes. It's awful," was met by a loud rejoinder of "Hear! Hear!" from an audience member. _____ However, Harold Hobson's review in the Sunday Times managed to recognize the play for what history has proven it to be, a revolutionary moment in theater.

1. Which sentence, if inserted in the blank space, would make the best sense in the context of the passage?
   a. The director, Peter Hall, had to beg the theater management not to close the play immediately but to wait for the Sunday reviews.
   b. Despite the audience reaction, the cast and director believed in the play.
   c. It looked as if *Waiting for Godot* was beginning a long run as the most controversial play of London's 1955 season.
   d. *Waiting for Godot* was in danger of closing the first week of its run and of becoming nothing more than a footnote in the annals of the English stage.

2. Which of the following best describes the attitude of the author of the passage toward the play *Waiting for Godot*?
   a. It was a curiosity in theater history.
   b. It is the most important play of the twentieth century.
   c. It represents a turning point in stage history.
   d. It is too repetitious.

Survey Regarding Reading Habits	
Books per Month	**Percentage**
0	13
1–3	27
4–6	32
>6	28

3. Which of the following graphs most accurately represents the information in the previous table?

a.

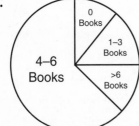

b.

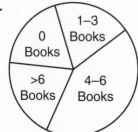

c.

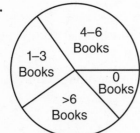

d.

4. During the semester break, Marcus can wax the floors of five classrooms in an hour. Janet can wax four of the same classrooms in an hour. If Marcus works for three hours, and Janet works for two hours, what percentage of the 50 classrooms will be waxed?

    a. 46%

    b. 44%

    c. 23%

    d. 52%

5. Which answer choice best summarizes the following quote?

> *What is history but a fable agreed upon?*
> —Napoleon Bonaparte

    a. History is a set of facts.
    b. History is subjective.
    c. History is irrelevant.
    d. History is the objective study of our collective past.

Questions 6 and 7 refer to the following poem.

The Sun just touched the morning;
The morning, happy thing,
Supposed that he had come to dwell,
And life would be all spring.

She felt herself supremer,—   *5*
A raised, ethereal thing;
Henceforth for her what holiday!
Meanwhile, her wheeling king

Trailed slow along the orchards
His haughty, spangled hems,   *10*
Leaving a new necessity,—
The want of diadems!

The morning fluttered, staggered,
Felt feebly for her crown,—
Her unanointed forehead   *15*
Henceforth her only one.

      —Emily Dickinson

6. This poem predominantly uses which literary device?
    a. personification
    b. alliteration
    c. euphemism
    d. parody

7. The word *diadems* in line 12 means

    a. hammers.

    b. pens.

    c. fences.

    d. crowns.

8. Which of the following would be considered a primary source when researching the reasons for the United States's use of the atom bomb during World War II?

    I. the official bombing order, dated July 25, 1945

    II. a biography of Leo Szilard, Chief Physicist of the Manhattan Project

    III. a documentary about "Fat Man" and "Little Boy," the two atom bombs used by the United States in 1945

    IV. President Truman's diaries from 1944–1945

    a. I and II only

    b. II and III only

    c. IV only

    d. III and IV only

Questions 9 and 10 are based on the following passage.

In 1930, the first military coup in almost 90 years took place in Argentina, underscoring the tension between populist demands and the military. Causes of the coup can be traced to the economic slump following the stock market crash of 1929. The army ousted President Irigoyen, and maintained control for 16 years either by ruling directly or by controlling election results through the use of force. In 1943, a new military group seized power, calling itself the GOU (*Grupo de Oficiales Unidos,* Group of United Officers). Its Secretary of Labor and Social Welfare was Juan Perón. Perón styled himself a man of the people, intervening on behalf of workers in strikes, forming relationships with union leaders, and calling for improvements in working conditions. He became a hero of the working class, or *descamisados* (literally, the shirtless). By 1945 Perón was vice president and minister of war, and in 1946, he was elected president with the help of the *descamisados.*

9. According to the passage, what is one reason for Perón's political success?

    a. He understood the need to reach out to the people.

    b. He was a member of the military.

    c. His wife, Eva, was extremely popular with the Argentinians.

    d. He used the depressed economic status to subjugate the population.

10. What historic event is analogous to Argentina's economic slump and subsequent military coup?

    a. the Great Depression and the election of Herbert Hoover

    b. the Communist Revolution and the reign of Tzar Nicholas I

    c. the end of the Vietnam War and the election of Lyndon Johnson

    d. the war reparations imposed on Germany after World War II and the rise of Adolf Hitler

11. In this painting depicting Marc Antony crowning Julius Caesar as dictator of Rome, the artist suggests that Caesar was
  a. a power hungry man, eager for power.
  b. despised by the citizens of Rome.
  c. uncomfortable with the idea of being appointed dictator.
  d. distrustful of Marc Antony.

12. Choose the underlined section that contains an error in the following sentence. If there is no error, select choice **d.**

After studying the research results, the population rate was expected to rise for the fifth
                    a.   **b.**   **c.**

consecutive year. No error.
                    d.

13. All students at Central High School take math.

Some students at Central High School take art.

Charles takes math.

If the previous statements are true, which of the following statements must also be true?
  a. Charles attends Central High School.
  b. Some students at Central High School take both math and art.
  c. All students at Central High School take art.
  d. Charles does not take art.

Use the following passage to answer questions 14 and 15.

The first alien dynasty to rule China was established in 1279 by Mongol Kublai Khan, a grandson of Genghis Khan. The Yuan dynasty held power for nearly a century, during which the Chinese culture was enhanced and diversified. The use of the written language increased, and as a result drama and the novel were developed. The Mongols' empire reached as far as Western Asia and Europe, and their extensive contacts in these regions brought with them a rich cultural exchange. Western musical instruments were introduced, as well as Islam, which grew as many Chinese converted and became Muslims. But in 1368, the Yuan dynasty collapsed, unable to overcome the strains of imperial rivalries, peasant uprisings, and numerous natural disasters.

14. According to the passage, what positive result was experienced by the Chinese people from being ruled by an alien dynasty?
   a. It forged a bond among peasants that led to eventual uprisings.
   b. It brought wealth to the country.
   c. It suppressed native musical forms in favor of those produced by Western instruments.
   d. It enriched the culture.

15. What can be inferred about the Mongols from the passage?
   a. They established a great empire through successful conquests of other cultures and civilizations.
   b. They converted the Chinese population from Buddhism to Islam.
   c. Their empire was defeated in 1368.
   d. They originated the Chinese drama.

16. Which of the following songs begins with the three bars shown here?

   a. "She'll Be Coming around the Mountain"
   b. "The Star-Spangled Banner"
   c. "Yankee Doodle"
   d. "How Much Is that Doggie in the Window?"

17. *In most of us . . . was the great desire to [be] able to read and write. We took advantage of every opportunity to educate ourselves. [Punishments] were very harsh if we were caught trying to learn or write.*

—John W. Fields

This quotation is an excerpt from Mr. Fields' narrative describing his life as

a. a prison inmate.

b. a slave.

c. a private in the Northern Army during the Civil War.

d. a sharecropper.

Use the following map to answer questions 18 and 19.

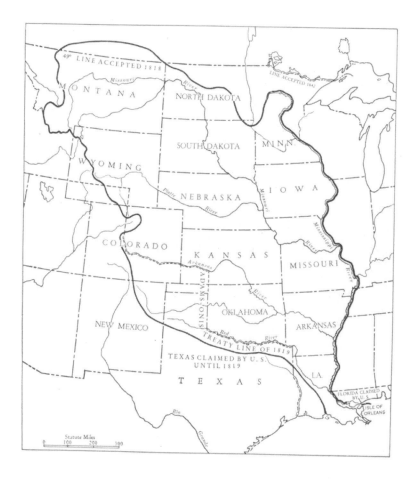

18. What land acquisition of 1803 is represented by the area outlined by the bold line?

a. the Holland Land Purchase

b. the Indian Territory Settlement

c. the French and Mexican Land Purchase

d. the Louisiana Purchase

19. What can you infer from the map about the acquisition?

   a. It caused settlers to be relocated further west.

   b. It almost doubled the size of the United States at the time.

   c. It allowed American manufacturers to use the Colorado River to transport goods.

   d. It included most of what is now the state of New Mexico.

Questions 20 and 21 are based on the following passage.

Sinclair Lewis's novel *Main Street*, published in 1920, examines the stifling effects of small town life. Its protagonist, Carol Kennicott, is a sophisticated outsider in the setting of Gopher Prairie, Minnesota. She brings with her a love of art and literature as well as a desire to enact social reform. Kennicott is rejected by the town's homogeneous population, who view any form of intellectualism as a threat.

20. Lewis's Kennicott would most likely have embraced which historic or cultural event of the 1920s?

   a. prohibition

   b. dance marathons

   c. women's suffrage

   d. industrial mass production

21. What sentence best describes a major theme of *Main Street* according to the passage?

   a. In *Main Street*, Sinclair Lewis presents a critique of Americans who are content with their provincial lives.

   b. Lewis's character, Carol Kennicott, represents the outsider and helps rationalize Americans' fear of immigrants exemplified in the Red Scare.

   c. *Main Street* is a call to citizens of every small town, who are urged to conform rather than face rejection.

   d. Sinclair Lewis captures the joys and sorrows of small town American life in his uplifting novel *Main Street*.

Use the following table to answer questions 22–24.

Country	Population 1960	1985	Today
United Kingdom	52,372,000	57,493,000	60,776,238
India	445,393,000	838,159,000	1,129,886,000
Japan	94,092,000	123,537,000	127,468,000
United States	180,671,000	250,132,000	301,442,000
Total	772,528,000	1,269,321,000	1,619,572,238

22. Which country's population increased by the greatest percentage from 1960 to 1985?

  a. the United States

  b. the United Kingdom

  c. India

  d. Japan

23. Which of the following statements is supported by the data in the table?

  a. The world's population is growing more slowly than that of India.

  b. India is the fastest-growing country in Asia.

  c. Japan's population grew more rapidly between 1960 to 1985 than from 1985 to today.

  d. The United States's population will level off by the year 2015.

24. Which country's population grew the least between 1960 and today?

  a. the United Kingdom

  b. Japan

  c. India

  d. the United States

25. Why did the framers of the U.S. Constitution establish the judicial, executive, and legislative branches of government?

  a. to insist that those best qualified in each field should serve in that capacity

  b. to instill a sense of equality within the government

  c. to ensure that there would be a separation of powers

  d. to undermine the system of checks and balances that had been in place prior to the forming of the United States

Use the following diagram to answer question 26.

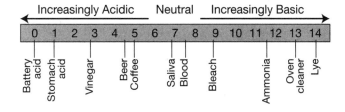

26. In an acid-base reaction, an acid reacts with a base to produce water and a salt. The pH scale can be used to describe the acidity of a liquid. Which two liquids could undergo an acid-base reaction?

   a. bleach and ammonia
   b. lye and ammonia
   c. blood and saliva
   d. bleach and vinegar

Questions 27–29 are based on the following passage and table.

MINERAL	GOOD SOURCES	SYMPTOMS OF DEFICIENCY	FUNCTIONS
Sodium	Table salt, normal diet	Muscle cramps	Water balance, muscle and nerve operation
Potassium	Fruits, vegetables, grains	Irregular heartbeat, fatigue, muscle cramps	Muscle and nerve operation, acid-base balance
Calcium	Dairy, bony fish, leafy green vegetables	Osteoporosis	Formation of bone and teeth, clotting, nerve signaling
Phosphorous	Dairy, meat, cereals	Bone loss, weakness, lack of appetite	Formation of bone and teeth, energy metabolism
Magnesium	Nuts, greens, whole grains	Nausea, vomiting, weakness	Enzyme action, nerve signaling

Minerals are an important component of the human diet. Some minerals are needed in relatively large amounts. These include calcium, phosphorus, potassium, sulfur, chlorine, and magnesium. Others, including iron, manganese, and iodine, are needed in smaller amounts. Humans need 26 minerals all together, but some of them are only required in tiny amounts. Some minerals, such as lead and selenium, are harmful in large quantities. Dietary supplements can decrease the chance of mineral deficiencies listed in the table, but they should be taken with great care, because overdose can lead to poisoning.

27. Taking several iron supplements per day can
   a. decrease the chance of bone loss.
   b. make you stronger.
   c. make up for an unbalanced diet.
   d. cause poisoning.

28. Which of the minerals listed in the table are you most likely lacking if you experience irregular heartbeat?
  a. sodium
  b. potassium
  c. calcium
  d. phosphorous

29. Which two minerals are necessary for formation of healthy bones and teeth?
  a. calcium and magnesium
  b. calcium and phosphorous
  c. calcium and potassium
  d. calcium and sodium

30. Mr. DeLandro earns $12 per hour. One week, Mr. DeLandro worked 42 hours; the following week, he worked 37 hours. Which of the following indicates the number of dollars Mr. DeLandro earned for two weeks?
  a. $12(42 + 37)$
  b. $12 \times 42 + 42 \times 37$
  c. $12 \times 37 + 42$
  d. $12 + 42 \times 37$

Use the following passage to answer question 31.

The roots of the modern-day sport of lacrosse are found in tribal stick and ball games developed and played by many native North American tribes dating back as early as the fifteenth century. The Native American names for these games reflected the bellicose nature of those early contests, many of which went far beyond friendly recreational competition. For example, the Algonquin called their game *Baggattaway,* which meant, "they bump hips." The Cherokee Nation and the Six Tribes of the Iroquois called their sport *Tewaarathon,* which translated into "Little Brother of War." Rules and style of play differed from tribe to tribe and games could be played by as few as 15 to as many as 1,000 men and women at a time. These matches could last for three days, beginning at dawn each day and ending at sunset. The goals could be specific trees or rocks, and were a few hundred yards to a few miles apart. Despite these differences, the sole object of every game was the same: to score goals by any means necessary. Serious injuries caused by blows from the heavy wooden sticks used in the games were not uncommon, and often expected. Not surprisingly, the Native Americans considered these precursors to today's lacrosse excellent battle preparation for young warriors, and games were often used to settle disputes between tribes without resorting to full-blown warfare.

31. Which of the following titles would be the most appropriate for this passage?

  a. Little Brother of War

  b. Lacrosse: America's Most Violent Sport

  c. The Origins of the Modern Lacrosse Stick

  d. The Six Tribes

Question 32 is based on the following figure.

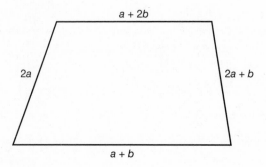

32. What is the perimeter of the figure?

  a. $6a + b$

  b. $5a + 5b$

  c. $6a + 4b$

  d. $3a + 5b$

33. Through friction, energy of motion is converted to heat. You use this in your favor when you

  a. wear gloves to make your hands warm.

  b. rub your hands together to make them warm.

  c. soak your hands with hot water to make them warm.

  d. place your hands near a fireplace to make them warm.

Use the following poem to answer question 34.

The Eagle

He clasps the crag with crooked hands;
Close to the sun in lonely lands,
Ringed with the azure world he stands.
The wrinkled sea beneath him crawls;
He watches from his mountain walls,
And like a thunderbolt he falls.

—Alfred, Lord Tennyson

34. Given the tone of the poem, and noting especially the last line, what is the eagle most likely doing in the poem?

    a. dying of old age

    b. hunting prey

    c. learning joyfully to fly

    d. keeping watch over a nest of young eagles

35. What is the tone of this quote?

> *I'm always making a comeback, but nobody ever tells me where I've been.*
>
> —Billie Holiday

    a. sincere

    b. ironic

    c. humorous

    d. nostalgic

Use the following passage to answer questions 36–38.

The Declaration of Independence was drafted by a committee of the Second Continental Congress, led by Thomas Jefferson. Its purpose was to justify the colonies' break from English rule. In the Declaration, Jefferson, who was the most intelligent of the group, explained that it was within the colonists' rights to be independent, according to the "Laws of Nature and of Nature's God." Jefferson stated that "all men are created equal," and they have the right to "life, liberty, and the pursuit of happiness."

However, the colonists' declaration alone did not give them independence. England was not willing to give up the lucrative colonies that easily. The colonies formed the Continental Army and, led by General George Washington, fought what would later be called the Revolutionary War against England. England's superiority as a naval power gave them the advantage until the French army came to the colonists' aid in 1777. A French naval victory on the Chesapeake, which led to the surrender of British troops, marked the beginning of the colonists' military successes. The United States gained its independence decisively in 1793, with the signing of the Treaty of Paris.

36. According to the passage, why did the English decide to wage war against the colonies?

    a. They wanted to retain the land.

    b. The colonies were a viable revenue source.

    c. They didn't believe that independence was a "law of nature."

    d. They thought General Washington could be easily defeated.

37. Which of the following represents an opinion of the passage's author?

    a. All men are created equal.

    b. The signing of the Treaty of Paris granted independence to the United States.

    c. The purpose of the Declaration of Independence was to justify the colonists' break from English rule.

    d. Thomas Jefferson was the most intelligent of the group of writers who drafted the Declaration.

38. Which statement best reflects a difference between pre-Revolutionary War England and the colonies?

    a. The colonists believed they were born with certain rights, and the English believed they had absolute power over the colonists.

    b. The English had an alliance with France, which was an enemy of the colonists.

    c. The colonists' army was superior to that of the English.

    d. The English believed the "Laws of Nature" meant that stronger powers should dominate weaker ones, and the colonists believed those laws meant they had a right to seek independence.

39. The floor of a walk-in closet measures 7 feet by 4 feet. If the ceiling height is 8 feet, what is the volume in cubic feet of the closet?

    a. 28

    b. 56

    c. 224

    d. 168

Question 40 is based on the following passage.

Moscow has a history of chaotic periods of war that ended with the destruction of a once largely wooden city and the building of a "new" city on top of the rubble of the old. The result is a layered city, with each tier holding information about a part of Russia's past. In some areas of the city, archaeologists have reached the layer from 1147, the year of Moscow's founding. Among the findings from the various periods of Moscow's history are carved bones, metal tools, pottery, glass, jewelry, and crosses.

40. From the passage, the reader can infer that

    a. the people of Moscow are more interested in modernization than in preservation.

    b. the Soviet government destroyed many of the historic buildings in Russia.

    c. Moscow is the oldest large city in Russia, founded in 1147.

    d. Moscow has a history of invasions, with each new conqueror razing past structures.

41. How could this picture best be described?

  a. It is detail-oriented.

  b. It is the work of an Impressionist painter.

  c. It favors symmetry and embraces the concepts of neo-classicism.

  d. Its perspective, that of the boy on the curb, is unique.

Questions 42 and 43 are based on the following passage.

In 1628, English physician William Harvey established that the blood circulates throughout the body. He recognized that the heart acts as a pump and does not work by using up blood as earlier anatomists thought. To carefully observe the beating of the heart and the direction of blood flow, Harvey needed to see the work of the blood in slow motion. Because there was no way for him to observe a human heart in slow motion, he studied the hearts of toads and snakes, rather than the rapidly beating hearts of "warm blooded" mammals and birds. By keeping these animals cool, he could slow their hearts down. The main argument for his conclusion that the blood circulates stemmed from his measurement of the amount of blood pumped with each heartbeat. He calculated that the amount of blood pumped each hour by far exceeds the total amount of blood in the body and proved that the same blood passes through the heart over and over again.

42. What misconception did scientists harbor before Harvey's study?

  a. The heart circulates blood.

  b. The heart pumps blood.

  c. The heart uses up blood.

  d. The heart contains no blood.

43. Which of the following did Harvey do?

    I. observe the heartbeat and blood flow in snakes and frogs

   II. determine that the heart acts as a pump

  III. count the number of blood cells that pass through the heart every hour

  IV. show that the blood circulates

  a. I

  b. I and II

  c. I, II, and IV

  d. I, III, and IV

Questions 44–46 refer to the following excerpt.

What's Wrong with Commercial Television?

Kids who watch much commercial television ought to develop into whizzes at the dialect; you have to keep so much in your mind at once because a series of artificially short attention spans has been created. But this in itself means that the experience of watching the commercial channels is a more informal one, curiously more "homely" than watching BBC [British Broadcasting Corporation].

This is because the commercial breaks are constant reminders that the medium itself is artificial, isn't, in fact, "real," even if the gesticulating heads, unlike the giants of the movie screen, are life-size. There is a kind of built-in alienation effect. Everything you see is false, as Tristan Tzara gnomically opined. And the young lady in the St. Bruno tobacco ads who currently concludes her spiel by stating categorically "And if you believe that, you'll believe anything," is saying no more than the truth. The long-term effect of habitually watching commercial television is probably an erosion of trust in the television medium itself.

Since joy is the message of all commercials, it is as well they breed skepticism. Every story has a happy ending, gratification is guaranteed by the conventions of the commercial form, which contributes no end to the pervasive unreality of it all. Indeed, it is the chronic bliss of everybody in the commercials that creates their final divorce from effective life as we know it. Grumpy mum, frowning dad, are soon all smiles again after the ingestion of some pill or potion; minimal concessions are made to mild frustration (as they are, occasionally, to lust), but none at all to despair or consummation. In fact, if the form is reminiscent of the limerick and the presentation of the music-hall, the overall mood—in its absolute and unruffled decorum—is that of the uplift fables in the Sunday school picture books of my childhood.

—Angela Carter, from *Shaking a Leg* (1997)

44. According to the author, what is the main difference between commercial channels and public television stations like the BBC?

  a. Commercial television is very artificial.

  b. Public television is more informal and uplifting.

  c. Commercial television teaches viewers not to believe what they see on TV.

  d. Commercial television is more like the movies than public television.

45. Which of the following would the author most likely recommend?

    a. Don't watch any television at all; read instead.

    b. Watch only the BBC.

    c. Watch only commercial television.

    d. Watch what you like, but don't believe what commercials claim.

46. According to the author, what is the main thing that makes commercials unrealistic?

    a. Everyone in commercials always ends up happy.

    b. The background music is distracting.

    c. Commercials are so short.

    d. The people in commercials are always sick.

Refer to the following poem to answer questions 47 and 48.

War Is Kind

Do not weep, maiden, for war is kind.
Because your lover threw wild hands toward the sky
And the affrighted steed ran on alone,
Do not weep.
War is kind.
Hoarse, booming drums of the regiment
Little souls who thirst for fight,
These men were born to drill and die
The unexplained glory flies above them
Great is the battle-god, great, and his kingdom—
A field where a thousand corpses lie.
Do not weep, babe, for war is kind.
Because your father tumbled in the yellow trenches,
Raged at his breast, gulped and died,
Do not weep.
War is kind.
Swift, blazing flag of the regiment
Eagle with crest of red and gold,
These men were born to drill and die
Point for them the virtue of slaughter
Make plain to them the excellence of killing
And a field where a thousand corpses lie.

Mother whose heart hung humble as a button

On the bright splendid shroud of your son,

Do not weep. War is kind.

—Stephen Crane, 1899

47. The speaker repeats the line "War is kind" five times in the poem. Why?

   a. He wants to emphasize the truth of this line.

   b. It is the theme of the poem.

   c. He is talking about several wars.

   d. It will take a lot to convince listeners that this line is true.

48. Which of the following best conveys the theme of the poem?

   a. War is unkind, but necessary.

   b. There is no virtue in war.

   c. We should not weep for soldiers, because they died in glory.

   d. Everyone must sacrifice in a war.

49. Which one of the following statements is an opinion, rather than a fact?

   a. All organisms are made of one or more cells.

   b. It's wrong to kill any organism.

   c. All organisms need energy.

   d. Some organisms reproduce asexually.

Questions 50–52 are based on the following passage.

Cuttlefish are intriguing little animals. The cuttlefish resembles a rather large squid and is, like the octopus, a member of the order of cephalopods. Although they are not considered the most highly evolved of the cephalopods, they are extremely intelligent. While observing them, it is hard to tell who is doing the observing, you or the cuttlefish, especially since the eye of the cuttlefish is very similar in structure to the human eye. Cuttlefish are also highly mobile and fast creatures. They come equipped with a small jet located just below the tentacles that can expel water to help them move. Ribbons of flexible fin on each side of the body allow cuttlefish to hover, move, stop, and start. By far their most intriguing characteristic is their ability to change their body color and pattern.

    The cuttlefish is sometimes referred to as the "chameleon of the sea" because it can change its skin color and pattern instantaneously. Masters of camouflage, cuttlefish can blend into any environment for protection, but they are also capable of the most imaginative displays of iridescent, brilliant color and intricate designs, which scientists believe they use to communicate with each other and for mating displays. However, judging from the riot of ornaments and hues cuttlefish produce, it is hard not to believe they paint themselves so beautifully just for the sheer joy of it. At the very least, cuttlefish conversation must be the most sparkling in all the sea.

50. Which of the following is correct according to the information given in the passage?

    a. Cuttlefish are a type of squid.

    b. Cuttlefish use jet-propulsion as one form of locomotion.

    c. The cuttlefish does not have an exoskeleton.

    d. Cuttlefish are the most intelligent cephalopods.

51. Which of the following best outlines the main topics addressed in the passage?

    a. I. general classification and characteristics of cuttlefish

        II. uses and beauty of the cuttlefish's ability to change color

    b. I. classification and difficulties of observing cuttlefish

        II. scientific explanation of modes of cuttlefish communication

    c. I. explanation of the cuttlefish's method of locomotion

        II. description of color displays in mating behavior

    d. I. comparison of cuttlefish with other cephalopods

        II. usefulness of the cuttlefish's ability to change color

52. Which of the following best describes the purpose of the author in the passage?

    a. to describe the chameleon of the sea informatively and entertainingly

    b. to explain the communication habits of cuttlefish

    c. to produce a fanciful description of the chameleon of the sea

    d. to persuade scuba divers of the interest in observing cuttlefish

Use the following graph to answer questions 53 and 54.

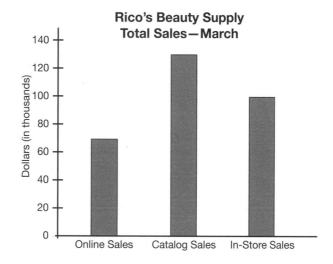

53. Customers of Rico's Beauty Supply can make purchases online, from a catalog, or in the store. About how much more did the company make from catalog sales than from online sales in March?

 a. $35,000
 b. $65,000
 c. $130,000
 d. $195,000

54. Approximately what fraction of the company's total sales came from in-store sales?

 a. $\frac{1}{3}$
 b. $\frac{1}{6}$
 c. $\frac{1}{2}$
 d. $\frac{1}{4}$

Questions 55 and 56 are based on the following passage.

Radiation from radioisotopes can be used to kill cancer cells. Chemist Marie Curie received two Nobel Prizes for her work with radioisotopes. Her work led to the discovery of the neutron and synthesis of artificial radioactive elements. She died of leukemia at 67, caused by extensive exposure to radiation. Curie never believed that radium and other materials she worked with were a health hazard. In World War I, glowing radium was used on watch dials to help soldiers read their watches in the dark and to synchronize their attacks. Unfortunately, women who worked in factories were drawing their radium stained brushes to fine points by putting them between their lips. As a result, their teeth would glow in the dark. But this was an amusement for children more than a cause of worry. About ten years later, the women developed cancer in their jaws and mouths and had problems making blood cells. This exposed the dangers of radiation.

55. Based on the information in the passage, which statement about radioisotopes is false?

 a. Radioisotopes can kill cancer cells.
 b. Radioisotopes can cause cancer.
 c. A radioisotope can glow in the dark.
 d. Einstein received the Nobel Prize for working with isotopes.

56. Which dangers of radiation were mentioned in the passage?

 I. radiation can cause genetic mutations
 II. radiation can lead to leukemia
 III. radiation can cause chemotherapy
 a. I only
 b. II only
 c. III only
 d. I and II

Use the following passage to answer questions 57 and 58.

Beginning in 1958 . . . local NAACP (National Association for the Advancement of Colored People) chapters organized sit-ins, where African Americans, many of whom were college students, took seats and demanded service at segregated all-white lunch counters. It was, however, the sit-in demonstrations at Woolworth's store in Greensboro, North Carolina, beginning on February 1, 1960, that caught national attention and sparked other sit-ins and demonstrations in the South. One of the four students in the first Greensboro sit-in, Joe McNeil, later recounted his experience: ". . . we sat at a lunch counter where blacks never sat before. And people started to look at us. The help, many of whom were black, looked at us in disbelief too. They were concerned about our safety. We asked for service, and we were denied, and we expected to be denied. We asked why we couldn't be served, and obviously, we weren't given a reasonable answer, and it was our intent to sit there until they decided to serve us."

Source: www.congresslink.org and Henry Hampton and Steve Fayer (Eds.) *Voices of Freedom: An Oral History of the Civil Rights Movement from the 1950s through the 1980s.* New York: Vintage, 1995.

57. Joe McNeil has not directly stated, but would support which of the following statements?
   a. Without the sit-in in Greensboro, NC, the civil rights movement would never have started.
   b. Woolworth's served affordable lunches.
   c. Local NAACP chapters were causing trouble and upsetting citizens.
   d. The college students showed courage when they participated in the Greensboro sit-in.

58. What is the author's purpose in including Joe McNeil's quotation?
   a. to show that young people are the most likely to push for societal change
   b. to demonstrate that everyone has a different point of view
   c. to give a firsthand account of what has become a historic event
   d. to discount the importance of the civil rights movement

Credit: India Picture Gallery (http://historylink102.com/india/index.htm)

59. The statue pictured shows
   a. the Hindu God Siva in warrior mode.
   b. the Hindu God Siva representing the threefold qualities of nature: creation, preservation, and destruction.
   c. the Hindu God Siva in benevolent mode.
   d. the Hindu God Siva in androgynous form.

60. A middle school cafeteria has three different options for lunch:
   For $2, a student can get either a sandwich or two cookies.
   For $3, a student can get a sandwich and one cookie.
   For $4, a student can get either two sandwiches, or a sandwich and two cookies.
   If Jimae has $6 to pay for lunch for her and her brother, which of the following is NOT a possible combination?
   a. three sandwiches and one cookie
   b. two sandwiches and two cookies
   c. one sandwich and four cookies
   d. three sandwiches and no cookies

Question 61 is based on the following passage.

Two hundred religious leaders and their followers gathered in front of the Capitol yesterday morning demanding economic justice for all Americans. A spokesperson for the group declared that "budgets are moral documents. They should direct resources towards those who need them most." The rally coincided with the start of budget talks in Congress, in which the senators and representatives must take up the White House's draft budget. As the group entered the Capitol, 115 were arrested for civil disobedience.

61. You can infer from the passage that those in the rally are against what provision in the White House's draft budget?

    a. tax cuts for those earning $200,000 per year or more

    b. a decrease in funding for the Head Start program

    c. tax exempt status given to dividends earned from stock holdings

    d. all of the above

Questions 62 and 63 are based on the following passage.

The Shaker church was founded in America in 1774 by a small group from Manchester, England. They established 19 communities in New York, Massachusetts, Connecticut, New Hampshire, Maine, Ohio, Kentucky, and Indiana where they lived, worked, and worshipped without fear of persecution. The Shakers adhered to strict religious principles that provided guidance for every aspect of their lives. Central to their beliefs were the virtues of simplicity, purity of mind, harmony, and order. The Shakers turned their backs on "worldliness," which to them signified any practice that centered on things of earthly as opposed to heavenly significance. Displays of pride, pleasures of the flesh, and excessive ornamentation were thus shunned.

    The physical manifestation of these principles may be seen in the articles they made for use in everyday life. Everything from boxes to baskets and furniture was designed and made with fine craftsmanship and a deep respect for the integrity of the materials used. Their belief in the sanctity of labor and emphasis of quality led to the creation of objects of austere beauty that are prized by modern collectors.

62. Which practice would a Shaker craftsperson least likely employ?

    a. signing his or her work

    b. oiling wood surfaces

    c. using meticulous joinery techniques

    d. all of the above

63. Based on descriptions in the passage, which item is most likely made by Shakers?

a.

b.

c.

d.

64. Select the answer choice that best corrects the following sentence:

Running toward the gate as the plane took off, leaving Aramis and I standing helplessly in the terminal.

   a. Running toward the gate as the plane took off, leaving Aramis and I standing helplessly in the terminal.

   b. While running toward the gate and watching the plane take off, which left Aramis and me standing helplessly in the terminal.

   c. Left helplessly standing in the terminal after Aramis and me ran toward the gate and watched the plane take off.

   d. As we ran toward the gate, the plane took off, leaving Aramis and me standing helplessly in the terminal.

65. Which would NOT be considered a primary source when researching the history of the Reconstruction period?

   a. texts of the Fourteenth (1868) and Fifteenth (1870) Amendments, which guaranteed citizenship and the right to vote for freed slaves

   b. *A History of Reconstruction,* James Farthing (Scribner's, 1931)

   c. texts of "Jim Crow" laws, enacted beginning in 1876, which mandated "separate but equal" status for African Americans

   d. *My Life as a Free Man*, the memoir of William Brown Cummings (University of Alabama Press, reprint 1970)

Question 66 is based on the following passage.

Effective written communication depends entirely on the ability to choose the right words. To do so, you must not only understand the denotative (literal) meaning of thousands of words, but you must be aware of their connotative meanings as well. Connotations are implied meanings, which involve emotions, cultural assumptions, and suggestions.

     Some connotations can cause confusion in or offense to your reader. You must be aware of inclusive language, proper levels of formality, and the often bewildering jargon of many professions. Words that have a casual tone don't belong in formal correspondence, just as those that are only familiar to a select group of people should not be used when communicating with those outside that group. It is knowledge, awareness, and care in use that will help you choose the words that convey your meaning in a way that is not only clear to your reader, but also makes him or her feel comfortable. Achieving the dual goals of clarity and comfort are hallmarks of effective communication.

66. What is an assumption held by the author of the passage?

   a. that most people don't know the denotative meanings of the words they use

   b. that noninclusive language may be offensive to some readers

   c. that the connotative meanings of words are often impossible to decipher

   d. that being aware of and using proper levels of formality are the best ways to improve your writing

67. While researching a paper on Lewis and Clark, a student located three sources that provide conflicting descriptions of their November 1804 encounter with the Hidatsas Indians. Which source most likely contains the most reliable description?
   a. an account of the encounter given by Sacagawea and recorded by her husband Toussaint Charbonneau, who translated it from Shoshone to French
   b. a transcription of an interview with Jean-Baptiste Charbonneau, son of Sacagawea who was born in 1805
   c. notes made by William Clark during the expedition
   d. an autobiography of Meriwether Lewis written in 1809, three years after the expedition ended, months before he committed suicide

Use the following passage and table to answer question 68.

The amount of solute that can be dissolved in a solvent at a given temperature is called solubility. For most substances, solubility increases with temperature. Rock candy can be made from sugar solutions that have an excess of sugar dissolved. The amount of sugar per 100 grams of water at a given temperature has to be higher than the amount that is normally soluble in order to make rock candy.

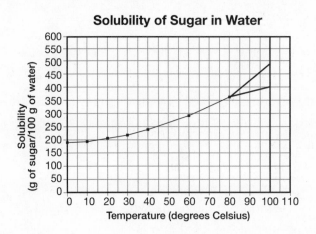

Solubility of Sugar in Water

68. Based on the solubility of sugar in water as a function of temperature, plotted in the graph, how much sugar would you need to dissolve in 100 grams of water to make rock candy at 40° C?
   a. more than 250 grams
   b. between 50 and 100 grams
   c. between 100 and 150 grams
   d. between 150 and 200 grams

Questions 69–71 are based on the following passage.

Ballet has its roots in the Italian Renaissance, during the 1400s. The dukes and other members of the court held lavish parties with entertainment in the form of dance programs (known as "balletti"). The dances were based on the patterns, steps, and rhythms of folk dances, but were staged with elaborate scenery and costumes. When Catherine de Medici, a member of the Italian ruling family, became the Queen of France in 1547, she introduced the dance programs to her adopted country.

The French embraced the new art form, and soon the Ballet Comique de la Reine was established in Paris. King Louis XIV, who reigned during the late 1600s and early 1700s, enjoyed dancing and actually performed in the ballets given at his court. In 1661, he founded the first professional ballet school, the *Académie Royale de Musique et de Danse.* The dancers were trained to perform for the king and his court.

Eventually, however, court dances fell out of favor. Dancers needed to find new venues, and looked to the theater. At first, they were hired to perform between scenes at operas, but by the late 1700s, full ballets were staged. During this period, ballet companies developed in other European cities, including St. Petersburg and Florence.

69. According to the passage, who or what was most responsible for the fostering and development of ballet?
   a. Renaissance Italians
   b. French and Italian ruling classes of the fifteenth and sixteenth centuries
   c. the ballet school founded by King Louis XIV
   d. Catherine de Medici

70. What was a likely consequence of the demise of ballet as a court "fad"?
   a. Ballet reached a wider audience.
   b. The king embraced a new dance form.
   c. Peasant dances returned to favor.
   d. Professional ballet dancers were unemployed.

71. According to the passage, how did early Italian "balletti" differ from the peasant dances on which they were based?
   a. The peasants danced in courts rather than in their rural communities.
   b. They were embellished with costumes and scenery.
   c. They were performed by professional French dancers.
   d. They were performed by Italian noblemen.

72. A bag contains 12 red, 3 blue, 6 green, and 4 yellow marbles. If a marble is drawn from the bag at random, what is the probability that the marble will be either blue or yellow?
   a. 7%
   b. 12%
   c. 16%
   d. 28%

Credit: India Picture Gallery (http://historylink102.com/india/index.htm)

73. The Taj Mahal, pictured, is an example of
   a. perfect symmetry.
   b. classic western architecture.
   c. an historic monument within an urban setting.
   d. how perspective can be distorted when viewing an object from a distance.

Question 74 is based on the following paragraph.

According to the U.S. Department of Labor, elementary school teachers must be able to teach basic skills such as color, shape, number and letter recognition, personal hygiene, and social skills. They are also responsible for establishing and enforcing rules for behavior, and policies and procedures to maintain order among students. Teachers at the elementary level observe and evaluate children's performance, behavior, social development, and physical health. They also instruct students individually and in groups, adapting teaching methods to meet students' varying needs and interests.

74. The purpose of this paragraph is to
   a. persuade.
   b. entice.
   c. argue.
   d. describe.

75. All sources used when writing an academic paper, both for direct quotes and reference, must be included in the
  a. bibliography.
  b. footnotes.
  c. index.
  d. table of contents.

76. Which of the following is NOT a prominent architectural characteristic of medieval castles featured in the engraving shown?
  a. turrets
  b. moats
  c. stone walls
  d. dungeons

77. Longitude and latitude are used to
  a. provide scale on maps.
  b. identify a geographic location on the earth.
  c. locate a constellation in the night sky.
  d. measure the surface of the earth.

Use the following paragraph to answer question 78.

German printer Johannes Gutenberg is often credited with the invention of the first printing press to use movable type. He used handset type to print the Gutenberg Bible in 1455. Although his invention greatly influenced printing in Europe, similar technologies were used earlier in China and Korea. Chinese printers used movable block prints and type made of clay as early as 1040, and Korean printers invented movable copper type about 1392.

78. What is the purpose of the paragraph?

    a. to praise the advances of printing technology

    b. to connect the early advances in printing with today's technological advances

    c. to show that technological advances can develop in different geographical areas over periods of time

    d. to give credit to Gutenberg for the first movable-type printing press

79. The following pie chart illustrates the relative productivity (new plant material produced in one year) of different biomes. Based on the chart, which biome has the largest effect on the overall productivity?

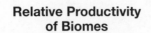

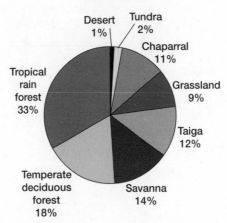

    a. chaparral

    b. savanna

    c. tropical rain forest

    d. desert

Use the following chart to answer question 80.

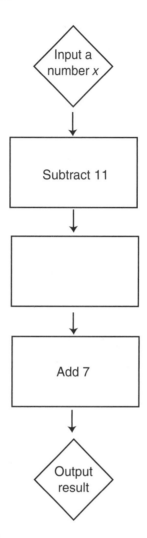

80. When the input is 63, the result is 11. What is the missing step?
   a. divide by 4
   b. subtract 31
   c. divide by 13
   d. subtract 41

Written Assignment

Using the following assignment, write an essay of about 300–600 words. Do not write on any other topic. Essays on other topics, no matter how well written, will receive a rating of U (unscoreable).

Should gambling be legalized in every state?

In favor of allowing legalized gambling to continue: Gambling provides numerous benefits to the states in which it is legal. In the form of lotteries, it produces a revenue stream that is used to fund state education departments. Casinos owned by Native American tribes have helped restore the pride and culture of native peoples, provide thousands of jobs, and increase demand for many types of goods and services. Gambling is also an enjoyable form of entertainment. These kinds of benefits far outweigh any possible negative effects of legalized gambling.

In opposition to allowing legalized gambling to continue: The harmful effects of legalized gambling are felt throughout our society. In towns and cities where casinos are located, crime rates have soared. Gambling addiction rates are also higher in states where gambling is legal. This type of addiction not only harms the addict, but because of debt and job loss can negatively affect his or her family. In addition, although it has been practiced since ancient times, gambling is immoral, and for that reason alone, as with many other immoral activities, it should not be legalized.

In your essay, evaluate the preceding arguments and take a position either for or against the legalization of gambling in every state. Construct a logical argument and back it up with evidence and examples.

▶ Answers

1. **d.** It is logical that a play would close after such a bad first-night reception, and the sentence in choice **d** also uses a metaphor about stage history that is extended in the next sentence. Choices **a, b,** and **c** do not fit the sense or syntax of the paragraph, since the *however* in the next sentence contradicts them.

2. **c.** Although the writer seems amused by the negative criticisms of the play, he or she does give the opinion that it was revolutionary (a word that literally means a turning point). Choice **a** underplays and choice **b** overestimates the importance of the work to the author of the passage. Choice **d** mistakes Vivian Mercer's opinion for the author's.

3. **c.** Because three out of the four sections are each close to 30% (27%, 32%, and 28%), look for the answer choice with three of the four sections about the same size and that together make up about 90% of the circle. Only choice **c** has three sections about the same size that take up most of the circle and the fourth section about half the size of one of the others.

4. **a.** First, find the total number of floors they can wax in the specified time. This is arrived at by multiplying the rate for each person by the amount of time spent by each. Marcus waxes five floors an hour for three hours, or 15 floors; Janet waxes four floors an hour for two hours, or eight floors. Together they wax 23 floors. Because there are 50 classrooms total, the percentage waxed is $\frac{23}{50} = 0.46$, which is equal to 46%.

5. **b.** A fable is a story that is not grounded in fact. Therefore, choices **a** and **d** are incorrect. Choice **c** is also incorrect because, although not based on fact, history is not said to be unimportant. Choice **b** correctly links the terms *fable* and *subjective*.

6. **a.** By referring to the dawn as "she," and the Sun as "he" and "wheeling King," Dickinson is using personification. Alliteration (choice **b**), the repetition of consonant sounds; euphemism (choice **c**), the substitution of an agreeable word or idea for one less pleasant; and parody (choice **d**), ridicule by imitation; are literary devices not used in the poem.

7. **d.** Diadems are described as a necessity of the "wheeling King" with "haughty, spangled hems," making "crown" the most logical choice.

8. **c.** A primary source would be a person who had direct knowledge of the reasons the United States used the atom bomb, or records produced by that person. A secondary source would include information derived from primary sources, and synthesize that information into summary form. To answer this question correctly, you must identify only those primary sources that meet the criteria (those that help one to research "the reasons for the United States's use of the atom bomb"). Therefore, although the original bombing order is a primary source, it is not a correct choice. Only option IV is correct, and it is identified by choice **c.**

9. **a.** The passage clearly states that Argentina's military coups "underscored the tension between populist demands and the military." Perón understood this tension, and mitigated it by becoming, in addition to a high-ranking military officer, a hero of the working class. The last sentence states that the support of this class helped him get elected president.

10. d. Choice **d** is analogous because Germany had a very poor economic situation following the war, due in part to the massive amount of money it was "fined" after World War I. One reason for Hitler's rise to power was the desperation of Germans for a leader who promised to restore economic well-being.

      However, if you were not familiar with pre-World War II history, you could have used the process of elimination to answer this question. The Great Depression occurred during the presidency of Herbert Hoover—he was not elected in response to an economic situation. During the Communist Revolution, the tzar was deposed and murdered, in part because of his role in the dire economic circumstances facing his people. Lyndon Johnson's presidency (1963–1969) took place during the Vietnam War, which did not end until six years after he left office.

11. c. By portraying Julius Caesar turning his back and putting up his hand in an almost defiant gesture toward Antony's offer of the crown, the artist succeeds in conveying the idea that Caesar was uncomfortable with the idea of being appointed dictator.

12. a. The error in this sentence is a dangling modifier. "After studying the research results" is meant to describe something, but the sentence fails to specify anything to which it can refer ("the population rate" is not capable of studying research results).

13. b. Since *all* students at Central High School take math and *some* students take art, then some of the students will take both math and art. Choice **a** is incorrect because there is no information that shows that Charles attends Central High School. Choice **c** is incorrect because the second given statement says that *some* students take art and it cannot be assumed that this includes all students. Choice **d** is incorrect because there is no information given to prove that Charles does not also take art.

14. d. There is no evidence presented in the passage to support choices **a** and **b**. Suppression of native musical forms cannot be viewed as a positive result, so choice **c** is also incorrect. The second sentence of the passage states that during the Yuan dynasty, Chinese culture was "enhanced and diversified," making choice **d** the correct answer.

15. a. The passage states that "the Mongols' empire reached as far as Western Asia and Europe." The other answer choices may be eliminated through careful reading: "many" Chinese converted to Islam, but not the entire population; the Yuan dynasty was defeated in 1368, not the entire Mongol empire; the Chinese drama was developed during the Yuan dynasty, but the passage does not indicate that it was the Mongols who developed it.

16. a. The notes show the beginning of the popular American folk song "She'll Be Coming around the Mountain."

17. b. Prisoners, army privates, and sharecroppers were not forbidden to learn how to read and write. Slave owners imposed this restriction on their slaves in order to maintain their authority.

18. d. The largest and most famous land deal in U.S. history was the Louisiana Purchase, arranged by President Thomas Jefferson in 1803. The Holland Land Purchase involved land in western New York State. The Indian Territory Settlement and French and Mexican Land Purchase are distracters.

19. b. There is no information on the map regarding settlers or manufacturers, therefore choices **a** and **c** are incorrect. The map clearly shows that a small portion of what is now New Mexico was included in the sale, so choice **d** is also wrong. The United States in 1803 was made up of most of the land east of the Mississippi River, so it may be inferred that the enormous amount of territory gained in the acquisition nearly doubled the size of the country.

20. **c.** Kennicott is described as an outsider who has "a love of art and literature and a desire to enact social reform." Dance marathons and industrial mass production have nothing to do with this description. Prohibition was the product of a segment of society who wanted people's rights restricted (specifically, the right to consume alcohol). Kennicott would have more likely embraced women's suffrage, a movement that allowed women to vote in national elections beginning in 1920.

21. **a.** Choices **b** and **c** describe the opposites of *Main Street* themes. Kennicott is an outsider, but her character is used not to rationalize fear of the outsider but to criticize that fear. Similarly, the desire to conform rather than face rejection is also criticized. Choice **d** misses the tone of the novel as captured in the passage. Words such as *stifling*, *rejected*, and *threat* do not describe an "uplifting" novel.

22. **c.** India's population almost doubled during the 25-year period.

23. **c.** The other answer choices refer to information not found in the table, such as the populations of all other Asian countries and world population figures.

24. **a.** The United Kingdom experienced the slowest growth in population of the four countries on the chart between 1960 and today.

25. **c.** The three branches of government were put in place to avoid a power imbalance; the branches were given equal authority, with separate roles to play. No one branch could have more power than the other two.

26. **d.** It is the only pair of liquids listed in which one is acidic (vinegar—pH 3) and the other basic (bleach—pH 9).

27. **d.** Taking too many minerals can lead to poisoning. None of the other choices was discussed in the passage or listed in the table.

28. **b.** No other mineral deficiency has this symptom.

29. **b.** The table lists that the function of both calcium and phosphorous is the formation of healthy bones and teeth.

30. **a.** In two weeks, Mr. Delandro worked a total of (42 + 37) hours and earned $12 for each hour. Therefore, the total number of dollars he earned was 12(42 + 37).

31. **a.** *Little Brother of War* is the best choice for the title of this passage because the games are described as fierce and warlike. At the end of the passage, the author wrote that games were often used to settle disputes between tribes without resorting to full-blown warfare. Therefore, these games could be considered an alternative to war, or war's "little brother." The other choices do not fit because they are unsupported by the passage, or describe only a small portion of the passage.

32. **c.** To find the perimeter of the figure, find the sum of the lengths of its sides: $2a + a + b + 2a + b + a + 2b = 6a + 4b$.

33. **b.** Only the action in choice **b** involves friction (of one hand against the other).

34. **b.** Saying that the eagle watches and then falls *like a thunderbolt* implies alertness and striking, so the most logical choice is that the eagle is hunting.

35. **c.** Holiday jokingly uses the word *comeback* in the second part of the sentence to refer to a physical return, rather than a return to her career. The joke cannot accurately be described as sincere, nor is it nostalgic, because it does not indicate a desire to return to a sentimentalized time in the past. If she was ironic, she would use the word to mean the opposite of its literal meaning.

36. b. The answer is found in the second paragraph: "England was not willing to give up the lucrative colonies that easily."

37. d. Jefferson wrote the Declaration with the help, primarily, of John Adams and Benjamin Franklin. The statement that Jefferson was the "most intelligent of the group" is an opinion of the author. There is no factual basis for it.

38. a. There is nothing in the passage to suggest France's alliance was with the English prior to the war (choice **b**); in fact, the French sided with the colonists in 1777. The passage states that the English had the military advantage until 1777, meaning the colonist army was not superior (choice **c**). Although the second part of choice **d** is correct (the colonists believed the Laws of Nature meant they had a right to seek independence), there is no indication that the English interpreted those laws in the opposite way.

39. c. A closet is the shape of a rectangular solid. To find the volume, multiply: $V = lwh$. $7(4)(8) = 224$ cubic feet.

40. d. Choice **d** is the only inference that can be drawn from the passage, because the first sentence speaks of periods of war. The other choices, whether true or false, are not addressed in the selection.

41. a. Using the process of elimination, choice **a** is the only correct answer. The style and subject indicate it is not the work of an Impressionist, and although the image could possibly be described as neo-classic, symmetry is not a feature. Finally, the perspective is not that of the boy, because he is a part of the wider scene, one that includes much more than simply his perspective.

42. c. The passage explained that other scientists at the time mistakenly thought that the heart uses up blood. Choices **a** and **b** are not misconceptions. Choice **d** was not mentioned in the passage.

43. c. The passage explained that Harvey did I, II, and IV. Although he also calculated the amount of blood that passes through the heart every hour, he did not count the blood cells one by one (III), nor did he have the technology to do that.

44. c. The author states in lines 10–12 that "commercial breaks are constant reminders that the medium itself is artificial" and that "the long-term effect of habitually watching commercial television is probably an erosion of trust in the television medium itself" (lines 20–23). Thus, commercial television teaches viewers not to believe what they see or hear on TV. Commercial television is very artificial (choice **a**), but we do not get a sense from the passage about the level of artificiality of public television stations. Choice **b** is incorrect because line 7 states that watching commercial channels is a "more informal" experience than watching public television. The only comparison to the movies is in lines 12–14, which simply state that the people on television are more "realistic" because they are life size, so choice **d** is incorrect.

45. d. The author doesn't seem to think watching television—whether it is commercial or public—is inherently a bad thing, so choice **a** is incorrect. She doesn't state that we shouldn't watch commercial television and only watch the BBC (choice **b**); rather, she is emphasizing that we should not (indeed, can't) believe everything we see on commercial TV (choice **d**). She does not suggest that we do not watch public television, so choice **c** is incorrect.

46. a. The author writes that "Every story has a happy ending . . . which contributes no end to the pervasive unreality of it all" (lines 25–29) and "it is the chronic bliss of everybody in the commercials that creates their final divorce from effective life as we know it" (lines 29–31). There is no mention of background music, so choice **b** is incorrect. She does not discuss the length of commercials, so choice **c** can be eliminated. The author notes that anyone who is ill in a commercial ends up feeling better by the end, so choice **d** is incorrect.

47. d. Throughout the poem, the speaker shows how war is *not* kind: It kills a lover, a father, and a son; it leaves fields littered with thousands of corpses. That war is kind is therefore not the theme of the poem (choice **b**), and it is not the truth he wants to emphasize (choice **a**). He is talking about war in general—no specific war is mentioned—so choice **c** is also incorrect.

48. b. The tone of the poem makes it clear that war is *not* kind and that there is no virtue in slaughter or excellence in killing. There is no suggestion in the poem that war is necessary, so choice **a** is incorrect. The poem shows that the soldiers did not die in glory (indeed, the glory is "unexplained"), so choice **c** is incorrect. Each of the people the speaker addresses has sacrificed, but the theme of the poem is that such sacrifice is *unnecessary* and wrong, so choice **d** is incorrect.

49. b. This is a statement that can't be tested by scientific means. All the others can.

50. b. The passage describes the cuttlefish's use of a water jet to move. Choice **a** is incorrect because the passage only describes cuttlefish as *resembling* squid. Choices **c** and **d** are not stated in the passage.

51. a. This choice covers the most important ideas in the two paragraphs. All the other choices list minor details from the paragraphs as the main subjects.

52. a. This choice includes both the informational content and light tone of the passage.

53. b. $130,000 (catalog sales) $-$ $65,000 (online sales) = $65,000

54. a. $130,000 + $65,000 + $100,000 = $295,000, which is about $300,000. Working with compatible numbers, $100,000 out of $300,000 is $\frac{1}{3}$.

55. d. There was no mention of Einstein in the passage. All the other statements were made.

56. b. Danger II was mentioned in the passage. Curie died of leukemia because of lifelong exposure to radiation. Danger I is true, but was not discussed in the passage. Danger III is false; radiation does not cause chemotherapy. Radiation is applied in chemotherapy.

57. d. Although McNeil does not state that the college students were brave, the firsthand account notes that the African-American Woolworth's employees "were concerned" about the students' safety. This implies that the students could not be sure of what consequences they would face.

58. c. The author uses Joe McNeil's account to give a firsthand description of what it was like to be a part of a significant event in the civil rights movement.

59. c. This Indian statue clearly shows the Hindu god in a benevolent pose. There is nothing to suggest a warrior (choice **a**), the three qualities of nature (choice **b**), or androgyny (choice **d**).

60. a. It will cost $3 for a sandwich and a cookie. To get two additional sandwiches, it would cost another $4. Therefore, it would cost $7 to get three sandwiches and a cookie. Because she only has $6 to spend, this combination is not possible.

61. **d.** The answer may be found in the group's demand for "economic justice" by means of a "moral" budget that "directs resources to those who need them most." It may be inferred that they would be against any budget provision that aids the wealthy and/or otherwise directs resources from the poor. Choices **a**, **b**, and **c** are such provisions.

62. **a.** According to the passage, Shakers were against displays of pride; therefore it may be inferred that their craftspeople would not sign their works. They did, however, emphasize fine craftsmanship and quality. Choices **b** and **c** would be evidence of this emphasis, and were in fact techniques used by the Shakers.

63. **d.** The ornamentation on the pictured items of choices **a**, **b**, and **c** is not in keeping with the simplicity of design favored by the Shakers. Choice **d** pictures a classic Shaker table.

64. **d.** Choice **d** is the only possible answer that results in a complete sentence.

65. **b.** Primary sources are products of people who have direct knowledge of the events they describe. They are also typically written or produced at or near the time being studied. A history of reconstruction published more than 50 years after the period began cannot be considered a primary source.

66. **b.** The answer may be found in the first two sentences of the second paragraph. The author states that some connotations can be offensive or confusing, and then she cites three examples: inclusive language, proper level of formality, and jargon.

67. **c.** The most reliable sources of information are known as primary sources. They are written or compiled by persons with firsthand knowledge of an event, during or close to the time it occurred. While choices **c** (William Clark) and **d** (Meriwether Lewis) are both primary sources, the most reliable is probably **c**. Sacagawea's account (choice **a**) was told to her husband, who then translated it from her native Shoshone to French. Sacagawea's son (choice **b**) was born after the incident and his interview could therefore only be considered a secondary source. Lewis wrote his autobiography three years after the expedition ended.

68. **a.** According to the graph, at 40° C, about 250 grams of sugar can be normally dissolved in 100 grams of water. In order to make rock candy, this amount has to be exceeded.

69. **b.** Although answer choices **a**, **c**, and **d** are important to the development of ballet, it was the ruling classes of both countries (including Catherine de Medici and Louis XIV) that fostered and helped develop ballet.

70. **a.** The passage states that "court dances," and not ballet specifically, fell out of favor, making choice **b** incorrect. There is no reason to infer that peasant dances regained popularity (choice **c**). The passage also states that once court dances fell out of favor, dancers found work in theaters, thus choice **d** is incorrect. It may be inferred that as ballet dancers performed in theaters instead of courts, they reached wider audiences.

71. **b.** The passage does not state who performed the dances during Italian court parties, making choices **a**, **c**, and **d** incorrect. In addition, there were no French professional dancers at the time (choice **d**). Paragraph 1 clearly states that elaborate scenery and costumes transformed the peasant dances.

72. **d.** Add the number of marbles to get the total number in the bag: $12 + 3 + 6 + 4 = 25$. Therefore, 25 is the number of possible outcomes. Seven marbles are either blue or yellow. Seven is the number of favorable outcomes: $\frac{7}{25} \times \frac{4}{4} = \frac{28}{100} = 28\%$.

73. a. The Taj Mahal is perfectly symmetrical, with each half constructed as the mirror image of the other.

74. d. The factual tone of the paragraph and its lack of opinion mean it is not intended to change the reader's mind. That rules out *persuade* (choice **a**), *entice* (choice **b**), and *argue* (choice **c**). It is a simple description of the duties of an elementary school teacher as reported by the U.S. Department of Labor.

75. a. A bibliography is an alphabetical compilation at the end of a paper in which every source, whether quoted or used for research or reference purposes, is listed.

76. d. While it may be assumed that the pictured castle includes a dungeon, it is not featured in the engraving.

77. b. Longitude (east–west) and latitude (north–south) are the standard coordinates used to locate positions on the earth's surface.

78. c. Although Gutenberg is given credit for the invention of movable type, others in different parts of the world at different time periods had used a similar technique. This does not lessen the great effect that Gutenberg's invention had on European culture.

79. c. Tropical rain forests are the most productive.

80. c. If the input is 63, the first step of the flow chart is 63 – 11 = 52. Because the next step is missing, take a look at the third step and the final result that is obtained. The third step will add 7 to the answer of the missing step and get a result of 11. Therefore, the result of the missing step must be 11 – 7 = 4. To get an answer of 4 from 52, you must divide 52 by 13. Thus, the missing step is to divide by 13.

Written Assignment

Essay 1 (weak)

Some states are considering legalizing gambling for a number of good reasons. They can see from states that already have legal gambling that it is a great source of income. Casinos not only provide jobs (with taxable income), but they earn taxable profits and develop taxable land. Millions of dollars can be made for a state from just one casino.

On the other hand, states that have casinos also have higher crime rates in and around the cities where the casinos are located. They also have more compulsive gamblers than other states. These are two serious problems that affect many people, not just those who work in or visit the casinos.

Casinos have done much to help tribes of Native Americans who have suffered since the founding of this country more than 200 years ago. It is high time our government made decisions that benefited these people to whom so much harm was done. Allowing legalized gambling brings money, jobs, and a new sense of pride to the tribes that own and run casinos.

But is gambling immoral, and should not be allowed for that reason? There is no real agreement in our country on this issue. People base their views of morality on the values they were taught by their parents and on what they were taught in religious institutions. These views vary widely, and one should not be given more weight than another. In other words, morality is not a good argument to be used either in favor of or against legalized gambling.

Should all states legalize gambling? This is a complicated question that brings to mind many different issues. There are obvious benefits as well as serious detriments. Those states considering legalizing gambling should carefully consider all of the issues before making a decision.

Evaluation

The primary reason this essay would receive a low score is its failure to fully address the prompt. The assignment states that the writer should not only evaluate the two arguments presented, but also side with one and construct a logical argument around that position. This writer does a fair job of evaluating the arguments, but never chooses a side, even in the final paragraph.

Essay 2 (strong)

The decision to legalize gambling in states such as Connecticut, Nevada, and New Jersey has provided those states with a wealth of benefits and opportunities that they would otherwise not have realized. States considering a move to legalize gambling should examine these benefits as they deliberate the issue.

Most states today are experiencing budget shortages, and their legislatures must make tough decisions about how to allocate funds. Programs that help the disadvantaged, repair roads and bridges, and provide resources to schools are often cut. But if those states legalized gambling, they would be able to fund all of those programs and more. Gambling produces millions of dollars in profit, as well as providing jobs with taxable income.

In Connecticut, some casinos are owned by Indian tribes that had dwindled to a small number of tribesmen who lived in poverty. Centuries of unfair actions and laws involving property took away native lands, forced migrations of tribes, and eventually began destroying their culture. Casinos have turned that cycle around by providing not only the casino profit for the tribe, but also employment for thousands of Native Americans.

Gambling has been practiced since ancient times, proving that it is an activity that people will pursue whether it is legal or not. In the absence of legalized gambling, criminals and crime organizations take over gambling operations. They pocket millions of dollars made from betting on everything from football games to horse races and political elections. This money is used to reward the criminals who run the operations, and fund more illegal activity such as purchasing drugs for resale.

Those opposed to gambling most often cite addiction and immorality as their strongest arguments. What they don't discuss is the fact that state governments are not charged with legislating morality. Just as they do not regulate the sale and purchase of alcohol to adults, even though it can be addictive, they should not "protect" their citizens from gambling. The issue of morality is a personal one, often based on religious beliefs and values. Those who believe gambling is immoral have the right to choose not to gamble, but they do not have the right to prevent others from enjoying a form of entertainment that they believe has nothing to do with morality.

States considering the legalization of gambling would do well to examine all of the issues surrounding the subject. Such consideration would inevitably show that the benefits of gambling far outweigh any perceived detriments.

Evaluation

This essay would receive a high score because it fulfills each part of the assignment. It evaluates both the pro and con arguments presented in the prompt, and chooses one side on which to take a stand. Its argument is developed and supported by well-chosen examples and evidence. In addition, it is well-organized, uses a sophisticated vocabulary that is appropriate for its audience, and follows the conventions of essay writing, including sentence and paragraph structure and mechanics.

► Scoring Your Practice Test

Your official LAST score is a cumulative score representing all subareas of the test, including all multiple-choice questions and the constructed-response assignment, which will count toward 20% of your total score. Your total score will be reported on a scale between 100 and 300; a passing score for the official LAST is any score of 220 or above.

To take full advantage of this practice test, you should find both your overall score on the multiple-choice questions of this test, as well as your individual scores in each subarea. To find your overall score, simply divide the number of multiple-choice questions you answered correctly by the total number of multiple-choice questions found on the test, which is 80. For example, if you answered 60 questions correctly:

$$\frac{60 \text{ (questions correct)}}{80 \text{ (total questions)}} = .75, \text{ or } 75\%$$

To score your constructed-response question, it is highly recommended that you ask a professional friend or colleague familiar with the area of Written Analysis and Expression to evaluate your essay using the official *Performance Characteristics and Scoring Scale* found at the end of the official LAST Preparation Guide, which can be found on the NYSTCE website at www.nystce.nesinc.com/PDFs/NY_fld001_prepguide.pdf. Your friend or colleague should assign you a score on the constructed-response essay between 1 and 4.

After you have a score for both parts of the practice test, you should use the following guidelines:

- If you get 80% or more of the multiple-choice items correct and score a 4 on the written assignment scoring scale, your preparation for the test is **EXCELLENT.**
- If you get 70% or more of the multiple-choice items correct and score a 3 or 4 on the written assignment scoring scale, your preparation for the test is **VERY GOOD.**
- If you get 60% or more of the multiple-choice items correct and score a 3 on the written assignment scoring scale, your preparation for the test is **GOOD.**
- If you get less than 60% of the multiple-choice items correct and score a 2 or 1 on the written assignment scoring scale, you should probably do some additional preparation before taking the actual test.

This practice test also offers you the opportunity to diagnose your areas of strength and weakness, to target your preparation for the official test. Following is a table that breaks down the questions in this practice test by subarea and their corresponding objectives. You can use this table to identify the areas in which you may need to concentrate more of your study time. For this practice test you should score at least 75% or higher in each subarea. You can find out your individual subarea scores by dividing the number of questions you answered correctly in a particular subarea by the total number of questions in that subarea.

Use your scores in each subarea in conjunction with the LearningExpress Test Preparation System in Chapter 7 to help you devise a study plan using the prep materials found in this book along with the materials from your classes and courses.

LAST Practice Exam 1 for Review

SUBAREA AND OBJECTIVE	CORRESPONDING QUESTION	
Subarea I: Scientific, Mathematical, and Technological Processes		Total # of questions in Subarea I: 22
0001	60, 72, 80	
0002	3, 13, 53, 54, 68	
0003	4, 30, 32, 39	
0004	26, 27, 28, 29	
0005	42, 43, 55, 56	
0006	33, 79	
Subarea II: Historical and Social Scientific Awareness		Total # of questions in Subarea II: 18
0007	10, 17	
0008	5, 9, 14, 25, 58	
0009	36, 38, 61	
0010	8, 37, 57	
0011	18, 19, 22, 23, 24	
Subarea III: Artistic Expression and the Humanities		Total # of questions in Subarea III: 19
0012	11, 16, 35, 41, 59, 73	
0013	69, 70, 71, 76	
0014	6, 7, 34, 47, 48	
0015	20, 21	
0016	62, 63	
Subarea IV: Communication and Research Skills		Total # of questions in Subarea IV: 21
0017	44, 46, 50, 51	
0018	15, 31, 40, 45, 52, 74, 78	
0019	2, 49, 66	
0020	1, 12, 64	
0021	65, 67, 75, 77	
Subarea V: Written Analysis and Expression		Total # of questions in Subarea V: 1
0022	Written Assignment	

12 ▶ Elementary ATS-W Practice Exam

CHAPTER SUMMARY

This practice Elementary Assessment of Teaching Skills—Written (ATS-W) is based on the format and content of the official Elementary ATS-W. See Chapter 5 for a complete description of the official exam. Use this practice exam to see how you would do if you were to take the Elementary ATS-W today, and to diagnose your strengths and weaknesses to help you study more effectively for the official test.

To simulate the test-taking experience, give yourself the time and the space to work. Because you won't be taking the real test in your living room, you might take this one in an unfamiliar location, such as a library. Use a timer or stopwatch to time yourself, allowing ample time for preparing and writing your essay; you'll have four hours to complete your official exam. If you would prefer to take this test for more diagnostic purposes, just take the test in a relaxed manner to find out which areas you are skilled in and which areas will need extra work. After you finish taking your test, you should review the answer explanations found at the end of this test. The answer explanations are followed by information on how to score your exam and diagnose your strengths and weaknesses.

The answer sheet you should use for the multiple-choice questions is on page 263. (You will write your essay on a separate piece of paper.)

▶ Answer Sheet

	a	b	c	d		a	b	c	d		a	b	c	d
1.	ⓐ	ⓑ	ⓒ	ⓓ	28.	ⓐ	ⓑ	ⓒ	ⓓ	55.	ⓐ	ⓑ	ⓒ	ⓓ
2.	ⓐ	ⓑ	ⓒ	ⓓ	29.	ⓐ	ⓑ	ⓒ	ⓓ	56.	ⓐ	ⓑ	ⓒ	ⓓ
3.	ⓐ	ⓑ	ⓒ	ⓓ	30.	ⓐ	ⓑ	ⓒ	ⓓ	57.	ⓐ	ⓑ	ⓒ	ⓓ
4.	ⓐ	ⓑ	ⓒ	ⓓ	31.	ⓐ	ⓑ	ⓒ	ⓓ	58.	ⓐ	ⓑ	ⓒ	ⓓ
5.	ⓐ	ⓑ	ⓒ	ⓓ	32.	ⓐ	ⓑ	ⓒ	ⓓ	59.	ⓐ	ⓑ	ⓒ	ⓓ
6.	ⓐ	ⓑ	ⓒ	ⓓ	33.	ⓐ	ⓑ	ⓒ	ⓓ	60.	ⓐ	ⓑ	ⓒ	ⓓ
7.	ⓐ	ⓑ	ⓒ	ⓓ	34.	ⓐ	ⓑ	ⓒ	ⓓ	61.	ⓐ	ⓑ	ⓒ	ⓓ
8.	ⓐ	ⓑ	ⓒ	ⓓ	35.	ⓐ	ⓑ	ⓒ	ⓓ	62.	ⓐ	ⓑ	ⓒ	ⓓ
9.	ⓐ	ⓑ	ⓒ	ⓓ	36.	ⓐ	ⓑ	ⓒ	ⓓ	63.	ⓐ	ⓑ	ⓒ	ⓓ
10.	ⓐ	ⓑ	ⓒ	ⓓ	37.	ⓐ	ⓑ	ⓒ	ⓓ	64.	ⓐ	ⓑ	ⓒ	ⓓ
11.	ⓐ	ⓑ	ⓒ	ⓓ	38.	ⓐ	ⓑ	ⓒ	ⓓ	65.	ⓐ	ⓑ	ⓒ	ⓓ
12.	ⓐ	ⓑ	ⓒ	ⓓ	39.	ⓐ	ⓑ	ⓒ	ⓓ	66.	ⓐ	ⓑ	ⓒ	ⓓ
13.	ⓐ	ⓑ	ⓒ	ⓓ	40.	ⓐ	ⓑ	ⓒ	ⓓ	67.	ⓐ	ⓑ	ⓒ	ⓓ
14.	ⓐ	ⓑ	ⓒ	ⓓ	41.	ⓐ	ⓑ	ⓒ	ⓓ	68.	ⓐ	ⓑ	ⓒ	ⓓ
15.	ⓐ	ⓑ	ⓒ	ⓓ	42.	ⓐ	ⓑ	ⓒ	ⓓ	69.	ⓐ	ⓑ	ⓒ	ⓓ
16.	ⓐ	ⓑ	ⓒ	ⓓ	43.	ⓐ	ⓑ	ⓒ	ⓓ	70.	ⓐ	ⓑ	ⓒ	ⓓ
17.	ⓐ	ⓑ	ⓒ	ⓓ	44.	ⓐ	ⓑ	ⓒ	ⓓ	71.	ⓐ	ⓑ	ⓒ	ⓓ
18.	ⓐ	ⓑ	ⓒ	ⓓ	45.	ⓐ	ⓑ	ⓒ	ⓓ	72.	ⓐ	ⓑ	ⓒ	ⓓ
19.	ⓐ	ⓑ	ⓒ	ⓓ	46.	ⓐ	ⓑ	ⓒ	ⓓ	73.	ⓐ	ⓑ	ⓒ	ⓓ
20.	ⓐ	ⓑ	ⓒ	ⓓ	47.	ⓐ	ⓑ	ⓒ	ⓓ	74.	ⓐ	ⓑ	ⓒ	ⓓ
21.	ⓐ	ⓑ	ⓒ	ⓓ	48.	ⓐ	ⓑ	ⓒ	ⓓ	75.	ⓐ	ⓑ	ⓒ	ⓓ
22.	ⓐ	ⓑ	ⓒ	ⓓ	49.	ⓐ	ⓑ	ⓒ	ⓓ	76.	ⓐ	ⓑ	ⓒ	ⓓ
23.	ⓐ	ⓑ	ⓒ	ⓓ	50.	ⓐ	ⓑ	ⓒ	ⓓ	77.	ⓐ	ⓑ	ⓒ	ⓓ
24.	ⓐ	ⓑ	ⓒ	ⓓ	51.	ⓐ	ⓑ	ⓒ	ⓓ	78.	ⓐ	ⓑ	ⓒ	ⓓ
25.	ⓐ	ⓑ	ⓒ	ⓓ	52.	ⓐ	ⓑ	ⓒ	ⓓ	79.	ⓐ	ⓑ	ⓒ	ⓓ
26.	ⓐ	ⓑ	ⓒ	ⓓ	53.	ⓐ	ⓑ	ⓒ	ⓓ	80.	ⓐ	ⓑ	ⓒ	ⓓ
27.	ⓐ	ⓑ	ⓒ	ⓓ	54.	ⓐ	ⓑ	ⓒ	ⓓ					

1. Alberta is an effective third-grade teacher with enthusiasm for teaching science. She decides to incorporate more activities in her science class that improve students' skills in communication. How might she take advantage of her fondness of science to improve this part of her teaching?
   a. Use student writings in science as a basis for creating formal grammar lessons for her language arts instruction.
   b. Provide multiple means (pictures, songs, physical models) for students to communicate what they have learned in science activities.
   c. Do interesting science activities and allow students to participate if they score at passing levels on language arts assessments.
   d. Do a variety of exciting demonstrations, have the students write about them, and then assess their writing.

2. New York State requires that all school districts have a mentoring program for new teachers and also participate in professional development for teachers holding professional certification. The development of the components of the required mentoring programs for teachers and the models and criteria for professional development are the responsibility of
   a. the State Professional Standards and Practices Board for Teaching appointed by the Board of Regents.
   b. the Legislative Committee on Teaching Practices selected from state representatives.
   c. the Mentoring and Professional Development Commission of the State Education Department.
   d. the Deputy Commissioner of Mentoring and Professional Development who is selected by the State Senate.

Use the following information to answer questions 3 and 4.

Adam implements a system of awarding improvement points for group work in his sixth-grade class. He calculates his student's average "base score" from assessments in the previous marking period. Students then receive improvement points based on how much above their base score they reach on current assessments. They receive zero points if their assessment score is below their base score. Adam groups the students in teams and sets goals for the total number of improvement points the students earn each week. At the end of three weeks, teams that gain 100 points are recognized as "Stars." Teams that gain 200 points are "All-Stars," and teams that gain 300 points are "Superstars."

3. In considering the impact of this teaching method on motivation, Adam needs to be aware that
   a. girls will be more motivated than boys by this kind of system.
   b. by assigning points individually but granting rewards to the groups, this tends to focus students on their own work.
   c. he should not tell his students how the system works so they do not "low ball" the base scores.
   d. the use of such external reinforcers is controversial and reduces student independence.

4. In forming and maintaining the groups, Adam should

    a. form the groups homogeneously, since points are awarded for gains and having all of the best students together won't matter.

    b. allow the students to form their own groups so that students will be motivated by working with their friends.

    c. change the groups every four or five weeks so that students on low-scoring teams have a better chance to succeed.

    d. assign students to same-sex groups because research shows this fosters communication and improves performance.

5. Teachers should have a variety of models of instruction available for various learning outcomes. In choosing a model of teaching that one might use to involve students in the community at large and the community in the classroom, the teacher might use

    a. problem-based learning, as it draws on real-life, authentic problems that can be contexted in the community.

    b. direct instruction, because it is the most time efficient and can be used to teach the most community-related information.

    c. cooperative learning, because the feedback structure is most closely matched to real-life rewards, such as job salaries.

    d. mastery learning, because all students learn to keep to the same pace as they will have to do in real life.

6. Ms. Petersen is a kindergarten teacher and is having difficulty in making transitions between activities. She receives several suggestions for improving this aspect of her teaching.

    I. Reduce the use of group activities so that the children will have fewer distractions when activity transitions are taking place.

    II. Work on the children's time-telling skills so they will be better able to follow the posted schedule and prepare for transition activities.

    III. Actively warn students about upcoming transitions and establish efficient transition routines.

    IV. Clearly end the first activity, announce the transition expectations, allow time for getting attention, and begin the new activity.

Which of the recommended practices are supported by classroom management research?

    a. I and III only

    b. I, II, and III only

    c. III and IV only

    d. II, III, and IV only

7. In a suburban primary school, the faculty has decided to adopt a predesigned parent education program. They review the Parent Effectiveness Training (PET) program, the Systematic Training for Effective Parenting (STEP) program, and Active Parenting Today (APT). All of the following are factors the faculty should consider in choosing a program EXCEPT
   a. the nature of the local program and the social networks and support that already exist in the community.
   b. maintaining the dominant role of the teacher in making the decisions about goals and classroom activities.
   c. matching the program to the socioeconomic status and similar characteristics of the intended parent population.
   d. encouraging parents to share their experiences with other parents and mutually support each other.

8. Bert Cobb has been teaching fifth grade for seven years. In response to changes in the school population, Bert was asked, and agreed, to take a new assignment in third grade. Having a good experiential base, Bert wants to advance his teaching practice to a higher level and he sees this as a good opportunity. Reading some professional development materials, Bert decides to build more subject integration into his teaching when he moves to the third grade. Although subject integration has been shown to improve student achievement in some cases, Bert should be aware that
   a. integration requires additional planning, which can be time consuming.
   b. integrating curriculum requires more transitions within lessons and therefore more opportunities for students to go off task.
   c. integrating reading with other subjects improves subject achievement, but leads to lower reading scores.
   d. integrated instruction improves pupil performance on achievement tests, but lowers positive attitudes toward school.

9. In classrooms where the instruction is based on constructivist principles, the teacher takes on more of a role of facilitator than a presenter of knowledge and skills. In such a classroom, communication practices that are effective in promoting student learning include
   a. giving directions orally only one time, thereby minimizing student questions and freeing the teacher to circulate.
   b. using lavish praise so that students who do not do as well are not discouraged.
   c. taking a neutral position to student responses, but using what is heard to plan subsequent instruction.
   d. grouping students with similar communication styles so that they can help each other.

10. Grace grew up in a middle-class home in a suburban area. While preparing in college to be a teacher, she worked in a diverse urban school. She decided that this was the setting where she wanted to build her career. She took a job right out of college in an urban elementary school. Her students are predominantly black and Hispanic with about 10% white and a few students from families who have recently immigrated from Asia or Eastern Europe. In assessing what she can do to enhance the understanding of her students, her best strategy would be to first
   a. learn about her cultural background and reflect on how it impacted her education.
   b. identify the holidays and foods representing all of the children in her class.
   c. focus on gender roles, because they are usually more important to making curricular decisions.
   d. learn about the local community and the community's expectations regarding the role of education.

11. Richard learned a vivid demonstration about air pressure when he was in college. It starts by putting a small amount of water in a soda can and putting the can on a hot plate. The can is picked up with tongs, turned over, and quickly touched to a pan of water. The change in air pressure dramatically crushes the can. Richard decides to use this demonstration to teach his third graders about air pressure. Before he does the demonstration, he tells the students, "Don't do this at home without adult supervision." Which of the following should Richard be aware of?
   a. Richard has protected himself adequately from a lawsuit if a student repeats the activity and is injured.
   b. Richard will be protected adequately only if he notifies his principal and records the activity in his plan book.
   c. The disclaimer will not provide any protection in case of student injury because of the age of the students.
   d. Richard should record the disclaimer in his plan book and take attendance of the children who were present when he stated it.

12. Bypass or compensatory strategies are a form of instructional accommodations that help students gain full access to classroom content and instruction and to demonstrate their mastery of skills and content. Which of the following would be considered a bypass strategy?
   a. allowing a student to use a spell-checker while completing a social studies assignment
   b. having a teacher's aide instruct a student on the use of a calculator while peers are learning computational skills
   c. giving a student intensive instruction through a pullout program in an area of weakness
   d. excusing a student with a learning disability from a class in Spanish to allow for more instruction in English

13. Coaching (sometimes called *collegial coaching*) is a professional development system providing one-on-one interactions leading to reflection on one's own, and possibly an experienced teacher's practice. Typically, the purpose of coaching models is to help new or experienced teachers use new materials, curricula, or strategies. A key element to collegial coaching is

   a. the materials or strategies that are being implemented must have been selected by those in the program.

   b. the techniques or strategies that are focused on should be selected by the more experienced teacher-coaches.

   c. the teachers focus more on student learning and improvement than on "inputs" or teaching practices.

   d. coaching requires that all of the members of the group have large blocks of common planning time.

14. Candace is planning a lesson in a guided discovery model so that she can develop the general concept of democracy. She focuses her learning objectives on identifying the common characteristics of various democracies in history and on the differences between democracy and other forms of government. With her learning objectives specified, what is the next element that will be essential to her planning?

   a. choosing a classroom technology that will be appropriate to help individual students in her class

   b. knowing how many of the students in her class have cultural backgrounds to use as examples of the concept of democracy

   c. finding reading materials on the subject that match up with the reading comprehension levels of her pupils

   d. the selection of examples that illustrate the concepts of the lesson, as well as non-examples that will set the limit of the concepts

15. Research has revealed several different frameworks of learning-styles analysis. While researchers differ in the number and kinds of "styles" they use for analysis, they all agree that which of the following must occur for classroom learning to be maximized?

   a. Because it is not possible to know which modality is strongest for every student in every situation, lessons should accommodate all modalities.

   b. Teachers should design lessons that move children from their innate learning styles into academic modalities that work better in school.

   c. Teaching styles are based on preferred learning styles of teachers and teachers limit their effectiveness in trying to teach other ways.

   d. Lessons should be designed to move students from concrete learning styles to more abstract learning styles.

16. Of the many possible applications of computers in the classroom, there is a wide variety of drill-and-practice programs for basic reading skills and basic math skill instruction. While drill-and-practice programs have been criticized for their overuse and focus on low-level learning objectives, such programs can be effective, as long as they
   a. provide high rates of responding relevant to the skill being learned.
   b. have negative reinforcements, such as explosions or "dings" when students give wrong answers.
   c. are used in the same way with every student so that no one feels singled out for remediation.
   d. do not store information about performance as this would embarrass students who don't do well.

17. The New York Code of Ethics for Educators calls on teachers to do all of the following EXCEPT
   a. nurture the intellectual, physical, emotional, social, and civic potential of each student.
   b. take authority over parents and community members in designing educational environments.
   c. commit to their own learning in order to develop their practice.
   d. advance the intellectual and ethical foundation of the learning community.

18. A relatively large suburban district has a significant turnover in top administration. The new administration is led by a superintendent whose prior experience was as the Assistant Superintendent for Instruction of an urban district in another state. As part of instituting new professional development programs, the new administration seeks to create "subcultures" which focus on some aspect of high-quality teaching and research about teaching practices. Teachers can move into and out of these groups as their professional development needs change. Which of the following is a supportable observation about this effort?
   a. Research has shown that such a system provides social and organizational support for teacher development.
   b. Such a system is effective in sustaining an existing school culture but not in supporting change.
   c. Such a system would work only with senior teachers because they would dominate the groups.
   d. The administrators of the district would have to become part of the groups to keep them focused.

19. Discussion is an effective teaching strategy for promoting cognitive growth in children. Discussions promote students linking their background knowledge to the topic under discussion. To plan for discussions teachers should identify a clear goal and select an appropriate topic. Topics for discussions that foster cognitive development are those that
   a. allow the teacher to present all of the basic knowledge to the students before they discuss.
   b. bring the students back to one "acceptable" answer by the end of the lesson.
   c. deal with controversial topics so that emotional response is maximized.
   d. are open-ended and in low-consensus areas so that multiple answers are appropriate.

20. In the town of Lomberg, the cultural makeup of the community has changed significantly in the past 20 years. At Lomberg Elementary School, the teachers decide to move the curriculum toward a more multi-cultural perspective. They meet and brainstorm a number of possible strategies for changing the curriculum. The most powerful step they might take is

   a. purchasing materials with culturally diverse role models that they can use in different areas of the curriculum, as this will have the most visible effect.

   b. putting celebrations of culturally diverse holidays into the school calendar, as the school year is organized around holidays.

   c. focusing on one subject area and examining the values and structure on which it is based, because this can be used to bring a truly culturally diverse viewpoint to teaching.

   d. investing in computer databases that have information about the achievements of culturally diverse individuals to be used in all subject areas.

21. According to research into psychosocial development, which of the following is an indicator of normal development in the elementary grades?

   a. The child learns to measure success in comparison to standards.

   b. The child thinks about how his or her actions impact the future.

   c. The child learns to commit to long-term relationships.

   d. The child learns to trust parents or others to meet his or her needs.

22. In Dana Xu's fifth-grade class there are consistently distracting conversations among about one-third of the children. One day Dana starts the day by telling the students they need to work on this problem. He lists nine ideas that he thought of on the board, which include:

   - rearrange the desks to keep chronic talkers separated
   - allow everyone to talk any time they want to
   - have a free time in which talking is allowed
   - allow students to talk only when the teacher is not talking

He leads the children in discussions, deleting items off of the list until only one remains (they choose having a free time). They then make a plan to implement this and identify a way that they can evaluate the success of the plan. According to research on classroom management, Dana's plan suffers from what weakness?

   a. By allowing the students to choose a strategy for solving the problem, the solution may not be consistent with school policy.

   b. The option chosen is extrinsically motivating the students to talk and they will be unable to limit themselves.

   c. The children should have helped brainstorm the list of alternatives so they would have ownership.

   d. The students should have tried each alternative before choosing one.

23. Joan Kuminsky takes her first job in a primary school that has a high population of students placed at risk. The main risk factors among the student population are poverty and students for whom English is a second language. There is also a lot of student mobility as parents move from one low-paying job to the next. Joan researches strategies to adapt her instruction for the students in her classroom. Her best first step would be to do which of the following?

    a. Adopt a passive teaching model where the teacher is a facilitator but does not actively present new information.

    b. Use pictures, videos, and other representations so that students will become adept at learning from abstractions.

    c. Reduce teacher questions during learning activities and focus on accurate presentations of material.

    d. Give students ample opportunities to practice the skills and concepts they are learning in a variety of contexts.

24. Jane is developing a plan to increase parent involvement in her classroom. She plans to survey her students' parents and create a resource file of interests and willingness to help with classroom activities. Jane should also keep in mind which of the following?

    a. She should provide little specific information when inviting parents and save details for when they arrive.

    b. The teacher should confirm arrangements with parents in writing with specific information about the visit.

    c. She should keep invitations open-ended so parents can arrive early or stay later after the activity they assist with.

    d. Parents prefer activities where they can just join in as they see fit rather than being given specific jobs.

25. Communicating with parents has been demonstrated to lead to a variety of academic benefits. Which of the following is a benefit of communicating academic expectations to parents?

    a. While parent conferences have a positive impact on parental academic support, report cards and letters home are less effective.

    b. Conferences should be used to give strict rules for parents to follow so they will put their children's needs first.

    c. Parents tend to become involved in reading activities in the lower grades and subject-specific homework at the higher grades.

    d. With effective communication practices, parental involvement increases as the level of schooling increases.

26. The No Child Left Behind Act (NCLB) requires that children be tested each year in grades 3–8 and at least once in grades 10–12 to see if they are meeting state standards. Children with disabilities are entitled to accommodations when they are taking these high-stakes tests to assure that their performance indicates their mastery of material. When reporting results, which of the following is true?

   a. The scores of students with disabilities must be reported publicly both separated from other students and also as a part of the aggregate scores of a district.

   b. The scores of students with disabilities must be separately reported from the scores of other students.

   c. The scores of students with disabilities may not be publicly reported separated out from the scores of their peers.

   d. Districts may decide whether or not they include the scores of students with disabilities with their aggregate score or separately.

27. Immersion experience is a professional development model based on adult learning research indicating that learning is enhanced through direct experience in content and processes. As a professional development strategy, immersion experiences benefit teachers in developing content-area skills because

   a. teachers learn by the same principles they are expected to implement with students.

   b. by pretending that they are elementary-school children, the teachers gain the perspective of child learners.

   c. by reading about processes in science and social studies, adult learners can develop process skills.

   d. teachers learn best how to teach when they are modeling student behavior in simulated lessons.

28. Karen is teaching a third-grade lesson on sinking and floating. The students make boats out of aluminum foil and then sink them by adding pennies. As the boats are weighted, the children watch a scale on the side of the container to measure how much volume the boat displaces. After the boat sinks they take it out, empty the water, and weigh the boat and pennies. They then divide the volume by the weight to get the density. Which of the following is the most accurate observation about this lesson?

   a. This lesson is good because, developmentally, the children need experience with density to understand other concepts.

   b. This lesson is poor because density is learned by age six through observing sinking and floating.

   c. The lesson is good because density explains sinking and floating in a more abstract but age-appropriate way.

   d. The lesson is poor because children this age are not developmentally ready to grasp volume or density.

29. One of the disparities among schools today is their access to instructional technologies, especially up-to-date computers and efficient links to the Internet. Research has shown that in classrooms where there are culturally and linguistically diverse learners

    a. language-intensive computer programs provide maximum benefit to English Language Learners.

    b. graphics and visually intensive computer applications can make students overly dependent on pictorial images.

    c. multimedia approaches provide visual cues that help children activate prior knowledge and assimilate new knowledge.

    d. diverse students gain the most from using tutorial programs to give them the same frame of reference as other students.

30. According to social development theorists, children's play is the primary means of their cultural development. Through play, children, from a young age, take on adult roles appropriate to their culture and rehearse the values they will hold and roles they will play in the future. Teachers need to be aware of the role of play in motivation to participate in social activities because

    a. children of beginning school age have not yet been firmly socialized and must develop school ways of learning.

    b. children must be guided into independent learning before they become overly dependent on groups.

    c. by the time children enter school they have developed a way of learning that is based on their culture of origin.

    d. children of non-European cultures use egocentric speech where they announce things that older children will only think.

31. Bruce is an eight-year-old in a third-grade classroom. Bruce commonly says things like, "I am going to lunch now," "I'm a good boy," and "I have to pick up the toys now." As Bruce's teacher interprets this behavior, she should be aware that

    a. this is a common attention-seeking behavior of eight-year olds and is of no concern.

    b. Bruce is showing excessive reliance on extrinsic motivation and should be helped to seek intrinsic rewards.

    c. this egocentric, thinking out loud usually ends by age seven and may be evidence of a developmental delay.

    d. Bruce should be encouraged to use inner speech because this leads to all higher mental functioning.

32. Developmental theories posit that all individuals pass through a series of stages and that these stages are the same for everyone and are achieved in the same order. Most research shows that several factors influence the development of an individual and determine how he or she moves from one stage to the next. Which of the following is NOT identified as influencing such development?
   a. biological maturity, which is the development of the structure of the brain and body
   b. physical experience, which is sensory contact with the natural environment
   c. metacognitive learning, which is instruction that moves the child away from being egocentric
   d. social experience, which is composed of opportunities to develop social concepts such as competition and cooperation

33. Jason has been effective in his fifth-grade classroom for the two years he has been teaching. His practice is based mostly on teacher-oriented models. He decides that because he has a foundation established, he wants to move to more group-oriented teaching models. What would be his best strategy for establishing group work into his class?
   a. He should teach his students metacognitive strategies so they can share effectively in groups.
   b. He must teach students to engage in group formative assessment so they can work independently after being given tasks.
   c. He should assess the cultural backgrounds, as children with non-Western cultural backgrounds tend to be more adept at group work.
   d. He could institute think-pair-share activities, as this is the simplest model that develops group skills.

34. Computer technology can be used in classrooms for tutoring applications (drill-and-practice, tutorials, remediation), interactive applications (word processing, spreadsheets, simulations) and experimentation applications (interfaced lab sensors, data gathering programs, Web-based resources). If a school wants to institute computer use to help teachers present information at the beginning of units in ways that help children organize their thinking, they will probably find the most effective applications to be
   a. interactive applications, such as word processing, so the children can think through what they are learning.
   b. tutoring programs that are integrated into advance organizers to present overviews of what will be studied.
   c. experimentation programs that allow students to search the Web to find all of the available resources on a topic.
   d. either interactive or experimentation applications, as tutoring programs have almost no positive effect on learning.

35. A fifth-grade team wants to add more group work into their classes. They do some research on the model and visit other classes where veteran teachers have been using the model. In implementing the model, they should be sure that they develop

   a. goals individualized to each student and individual accountability.

   b. goals individualized to each student and group accountability.

   c. goals set for each group and individual accountability.

   d. goals set for each group and group accountability.

36. The mother of one of your sixth-grade students comes to see you about her daughter's grade information. The mother tells you that her sister is a lawyer and is preparing a custody case for her. One of the issues in the case is about the school performance of the children. The mother states that she wants you to give her sister any information about her daughter's school performance if she should call. Which of the following applies?

   a. Because grades are public information, you can give the lawyer any information she requests.

   b. Because the request was made orally, you should make a note with the date and time of the request and put it in the student's file.

   c. The mother must make the request in writing and through the school administration.

   d. You should tell the mother that all requests have to come from her and you can only release information to her.

37. Which of the following describes an important consideration for deciding how to use textbooks in your classroom?

   a. Most textbooks have not been coordinated with state and local standards.

   b. Textbooks in mathematics traditionally require a teacher-directed approach and so should be discarded.

   c. Most social studies textbooks are written at a reading level 1–2 years above grade and should be adjusted accordingly.

   d. Good lessons have multiple entry points and a textbook approach only appeals to one learning style.

38. Both demographics and career expectations have changed over the years so that family structure and parental involvement in schools are different from even a generation ago. Many studies have looked at the impact of family patterns on the achievement of children in schools. Which of the following is an accurate description of what we can expect of parental involvement in classrooms today?

   a. Children from two-parent families are slightly more likely to be expelled or suspended from school.

   b. School participation of mothers in two-parent households is equal to that of single-parent households.

   c. While families are getting smaller and more diverse, parents are becoming younger and more involved with their schools.

   d. While the employment of married mothers with preschool children is down, the employment of mothers with K–6 age children is up.

39. Teachers model behavior when they act in certain ways that are then imitated by children. In a second-grade classroom, the teacher models how she sometimes struggles with math problems but can solve them through persistence. In this case, the teacher should be aware that

 a. she is more likely to trigger the stereotype that math is hard and not for girls.

 b. she would be better off modeling someone who enjoys math and finds it easy.

 c. while she may encourage students to attempt to solve math problems, they are less likely to follow through.

 d. the children will see characteristics they can apply to their own learning and are likely to adopt them.

40. The faculty in an elementary school is working on improving their instruction for English Language Learners (ELL) in grades 4–6. While the population of ELL students is currently about 5%, that population is expected to triple in the next 10–15 years. Which of the following factors should the teachers keep in mind as they adapt their curriculum to accommodate these changes?

 a. Research indicates that ELL students' use of nonstandard English can result in a teacher's lowered expectations, which itself may lower performance.

 b. Historically, ELL students have naturally learned to bridge their school lives and their home lives.

 c. They should avoid group work as much as possible, as the ELL students will slip back to their first language with peers.

 d. all of the above

41. Learner's tendencies to persist in the face of difficult or challenging tasks are affected by their inherent motivation. One system for considering students' motivation is whether they are *performance oriented* or *learning oriented*. Which of the following is an accurate description of this concept?

 a. Students who are performance oriented are more worried about making errors and how these errors affect their grades.

 b. Students who are learning oriented tend to be equally motivated by all areas of the curriculum.

 c. Students who are performance oriented tend to be better suited to work in group activities.

 d. Students who are learning oriented tend to be more motivated by extrinsic rewards.

42. A medium-sized school district is in the fourth year of implementing a comprehensive teacher leader mentoring model. Two lead teachers who train mentors, serve as administrative liaisons, and manage logistics are identified in each of four elementary schools. A key goal of the mentoring program is to develop self-reflection skills in new teachers. Which of the following would be an effective practice in helping reach this goal?

 a. The mentor should give the new teacher lots of free time to practice reflection.

 b. The mentors should be prepared so that they have all of the answers to mentees' questions.

 c. The new teacher should be able to change mentors if the relationship is not working out.

 d. The mentors should rely on their experience rather than research for the first year.

43. Equitable school funding is an important issue in New York and across the United States. New York and most other states rely on local property taxes as the major funding mechanism for local schools. This system has its origin in
  a. reductions in federal support of schools following World War II as the country rebuilt.
  b. historical school funding from local land owners because property ownership indicated taxable wealth.
  c. shared governance, whereby the state government sets policy and requires local boards to implement it.
  d. the Morrill Act after the Civil War, which established the first system of public schools.

44. Shared reading, used mainly at the primary grades, allows children to become more familiar with a book as they "share" the reading. Which of the following describes the best books for use in shared reading?
  a. predictable books with repeated patterns pictures and rhymes
  b. stories that have memorable, surprise endings
  c. books with new words that "stretch" the child's vocabulary
  d. books that tell stories from different cultures

45. One of the areas of controversy in the application of technology to the classroom is the use of calculators in elementary mathematics instruction. Over more than 30 years, the National Council for Teachers of Mathematics (NCTM) has published many research findings on the subject. In general, this body of research shows that
  a. calculator use should be permitted only after students have learned to perform operations without them.
  b. children who are introduced to calculator use in the primary grades are less likely to become fluent in mathematics.
  c. the regular use of calculators at all grade levels leads to the development of a variety of computational skills.
  d. children who begin to use calculators after grade 4 show marked improvement in reasoning and problem solving.

46. Bethany teaches intermediate-level students with disabilities and over several years has become proficient at using direct instruction to explicitly teach subject matter content and skills. Because she is proficient in the use of direct instruction she modifies or omits steps in the model as she sees fit. This year she is working with several children with behavior disorders in her classroom. She needs to be aware that
  a. intermediate-level students with behavior disorders generally cannot maintain focus, so independent practice should be omitted from lessons.
  b. children with behavior disorders tend to learn skills more readily than content, so the teacher needs a more content-oriented model.
  c. by keeping each lesson in the same structure and not omitting steps, she provides structure which will help her students.
  d. direct instruction is more effective at teaching content than skills and this matches the learning style of learners with behavior disorders.

47. Paula's colleague is expressing her views on bringing parents into her classroom in the high-needs, urban intermediate school (grades 4–6) in which they both teach. Paula's colleague strongly states that because many of her children come from single-parent and other nontraditional families, she does not want much parent involvement. Her reasoning is that these parents are not good role models of effective families and she believes that the school should provide more positive images of family life. What would be a good, research-supported response by Paula to her colleague?

    a. At the intermediate level, children benefit less from parental involvement in their classrooms anyway.

    b. Children, even at the intermediate level, gain their sense of self-worth in part from how their families are respected and valued.

    c. Such parents can still be effective in the classroom if they are given strict guidance on how to act and what to say.

    d. Parental involvement in schools is decreasing anyway because there has been little demonstrated beneficial effect.

48. In Gerry's school, the science program has a lot of process skills being taught. The children in Gerry's class have a wide range of abilities to manipulate the physical materials used in the various activities. To assess and provide feedback, Gerry keeps notes and at the end of each week writes narrative comments about each child's performance and improvement. However, this becomes very time-consuming and Gerry looks for a way to give feedback without taking up so much time. Which of the following would be a good tool to accomplish this?

    a. A portfolio, because a lot of the assessment process can be shifted to having the students assess each other.

    b. A rubric, because rubrics help shape the teacher's thinking so he or she is able to recognize different levels of skill.

    c. A checklist, because research has shown checklists to be more valid and reliable than other forms of skills assessment.

    d. Periodic hands-on practical tests would allow the teacher to see how different students would perform on the same assessment tasks.

49. Historically, the relationship between democratic institutions and public schools in the United States regarding public education as a cornerstone of democracy traces its origins to

    a. the civil rights movement, which sought to educate minority children for political empowerment.

    b. the GI Bill following World War II, which provided for the education of children of soldiers.

    c. reformers from the North who remade public schooling in the South following the Civil War.

    d. the Founders, particularly Jefferson, who asserted that a minimum education should be a prerequisite to vote.

50. Matt and Tina have been working together for four years in a rural district with a moderate level of students from homes of poverty. Tina attends a conference and learns about a grant program for rural schools targeted at providing technology to assist in math instruction for students with learning disabilities. Tina and Matt decide to apply for a grant. Which of the following ideas would be a valid basis for such a grant?

  a. They could target development of PreK/K students' abilities to count using visually oriented software.

  b. They should use a broad range of software that includes problem-solving situations as well as drill-and-practice.

  c. They should limit the use of technology to drill-and-practice exercises, as these are the basic skills that students with learning disabilities need most.

  d. They should fund the acquisition of computers for the students' homes so that they would have access to math-oriented websites from home.

Use this lesson description to answer questions 51–53.

The first-grade teacher gathers the students in a small circle on the floor. She shows them a pet mouse and asks them for observations about it. She lists their answers on a sheet of poster paper. She then produces a rabbit and repeats the process. This is also done with a real hamster, cat, and dog. She uses a computer projector to show pictures several students brought to class of animals they have at home including a cow, a horse, a goat, and a sheep. Each child leads a discussion of the characteristics of his or her animal. The teacher tells the children that each of these animals is a kind of mammal. They then create a list of common characteristics of mammals, and finally, decide on the wording for their definition.

51. Which of the following is an appropriate description of this lesson?

  a. The lesson is an example of a deductive lesson which has the strength of teaching the way children naturally learn.

  b. The lesson is an example of an inductive lesson which has the strength of teaching the way children naturally learn.

  c. The lesson is an example of a deductive lesson which has the weakness of not linking to the background knowledge of all of the children.

  d. The lesson is an example of an inductive lesson which has the weakness of not linking to the background knowledge of all of the children.

52. Suppose the teacher began the lesson by presenting the definition of mammal to the children, using the rabbit as an example of the definition, and then had them apply the definition on their own to other examples. This change in the model is appropriately described as

  a. the lesson is now a direct instruction model, which has the advantage of being more time efficient.

  b. the lesson is now a deductive lesson, which has the advantage of stronger links to students' prior knowledge.

  c. the lesson is now inductive, which has the advantage of stronger vocabulary development.

  d. the lesson is now an inquiry model, which has the advantage of teaching by use of the scientific method.

53. How could the lesson described have strengthened the concept being taught while still applying the teaching model selected?

    a. The teacher should have had some examples of animals that were not mammals so the children could contrast them to mammals.

    b. The teacher should have introduced the scientific definition of mammal after the children developed their own, nonstandard definition.

    c. The children should have been presented a mix of mammals and non-mammals, allowing them to make up their own groups.

    d. The teacher should be sure to guide the student responses to regular descriptors, e.g., fur, backbones, four-chambered heart, etc.

54. Mr. Garcia prepares a test for his sixth-grade language arts class. Because he wants to assess whether the students can organize information and make an effective argument, he uses 25 multiple-choice items. The test covers two weeks of instruction, but he draws his questions only from the last three days' lessons because they were the most important. Because it is multiple-choice test, he can score it and return the tests the next day. He is somewhat disappointed with the results. He tells the class that they were especially weak on the parts of a persuasive paragraph. He tells them to keep the test and review the questions they missed because this subject will be used in the next unit. Which of the following would be research-supported analysis of Mr. Garcia's test?

    a. Essay or short-answer questions would have been a better choice of evaluation of the skill he was interested in assessing.

    b. He should select material from the unit randomly to be sure that students learn to study everything equally and completely.

    c. Having the students keep their papers was good because research shows students learn from reviewing tests after time has passed.

    d. Focusing the students on the parts they had trouble with is good because it will make them be responsible for their own improvement.

55. Dean Simms is planning over the summer for some changes to his fourth-grade classroom. In particular he wants to increase the variety of ways that he assesses student learning. He reads several articles and reviews a collection of assessment materials he gathered from his colleagues. One assessment he decides to add is a set of publisher-made tests that go with the science book series the district uses. While these tests can be used effectively, Dean must be aware that

    a. publisher-made tests are highly valid, but because of the unpredictability of fourth-grade students' attention, are often unreliable.

    b. such normed, standardized tests are generally highly reliable and usually free from bias, but they may not be valid measures.

    c. research has shown that despite awareness of the importance of culture, publisher-made tests still retain cultural bias.

    d. publisher-made tests in science tend to underestimate the reading level of science content and therefore may be too high for his students.

56. Bonnie Moses is a part-time teacher working in a second-grade classroom where the regular teacher has release time to work on coordinating the district reading program. Bonnie is responsible for teaching math in the afternoons. The regular teacher has the desks arranged in clusters because she does a lot of group work and cooperative learning tasks. Bonnie tends to use more individual tasks. Which of the following research-based findings would most affect Bonnie's approach?

a. The arrangement should be fine as long as Bonnie keeps the students busy with learning tasks throughout the lesson.

b. The classroom physical environment is less important with the second graders because they tend to be field independent.

c. The seating arrangement will impede the type of instruction Bonnie plans because second-grade boys only average seven minutes of time on task.

d. The seating arrangement allows too much eye contact and close proximity to expect the children not to distract one another.

Use the following information to answer question 57.

Alice is reviewing with her students for an upcoming test. She starts off by talking about individual items and then goes into a general overview of the test—the kinds and number of different items. She tells the class, "This is going to be a hard test, but I know you will do well. The last couple of tests have been on tough material, but I have seen how hard you have worked and you keep doing better."

She puts a transparency on an overhead projector with a short reading on it. She has the students take out paper and gives them five minutes to write an answer. She has three students share their responses and they discuss them as a class. She explains, "On the test you are going to do one question just like this, but with different material. In your responses, be sure to give the kinds of examples to support your answer like the ones we did today."

57. Which of the following is a valid observation about this review session?

a. She set up expectations for her class that the students may not be able to deliver and risks alienating them.

b. By being so precise about what the test would cover, she reduced the likelihood they would study other important material.

c. It is good that they practiced the kinds of items that demonstrate the skills that would be on the test.

d. Research shows that classroom review sessions tend to increase test anxiety more than they prepare students to do well.

58. Rachel is apprehensive about her first round of parent conferences. She discusses this with her colleagues who offer her a variety of suggestions on how to prepare. Among the suggestions, Rachel is told to

   I. assemble a collection of student work, including tests quizzes and homework

   II. allow the parent(s) to set the agenda and choose the topics for discussion

   III. set a business-like tone and pace and have a fixed ending time

   IV. be clear about if and when follow-up contact and communication will occur

The best research-supported advice is

a. I and II only

b. II and III only

c. II and IV only

d. I and IV only

Use the information below to answer questions 59 and 60.

Alex is developing a third-grade unit on equivalent fractions. His math instruction has moved relatively slowly this year and based on the district's math curriculum, he has to cover the related concepts in a relatively short amount of time. The concepts themselves are relatively well defined and he is comfortable with the content. His key concern is that his students develop the automaticity to use the concepts fluently when they learn more fractional concepts next year.

59. Which of the following models would work best in this case for Alex?

  a. Cooperative learning, so that the students can support each other with the differences in their background knowledge.

  b. Guided discovery, because linking to next year's curriculum requires an open-ended teaching approach.

  c. Peer tutoring, because the involvement of the students in the teaching increases the total instruction in the short time period.

  d. Direct instruction, because the instructional goals are well-defined and he has to address this content in a short time frame.

60. In the previous scenario, Alex will have to pay extra attention to what particular aspects of the instruction?

  a. There is sufficient attention to applying of the concepts that the students can transfer the learning to new contexts.

  b. Children must engage in sufficient classroom dialogue that they develop applications of the concepts in the context of their backgrounds.

  c. He must rely on summative assessment to determine if his children have developed the level of automaticity to be effective.

  d. He must have a sufficient task analysis of the skills he is teaching and have students memorize the steps in the various processes.

61. When Liz is deciding how to manage behavior in her third-grade classroom, she thinks back to the teachers she remembered in school. She uses some of the practices of these role models, including:

- a child who is constantly whispering to her neighbor is made to stay after school and clean out the hamster cage
- a student who made a mess in the social studies learning center is not allowed to go out for recess for three days
- a child who forgets his reading book must do an additional assignment in math, the subject he likes least

Classroom management research would say that Liz's penalties are NOT appropriate because
  a. the consequences of the offenses are not logically related to the misbehavior.
  b. the penalties are extrinsic, whereas the motivation for the misbehavior is intrinsic.
  c. the penalties are too far removed in time and should be more immediate.
  d. the penalties are too harsh and may damage the children's self-concepts.

62. During the school day, a fifth-grade teacher has his students working on some practice math problems. One of his students had complained of nausea and was sent to the school nurse. The teacher wonders how the ill student is doing and goes down the hall—about 40 feet away—to see how he is doing. When the teacher returns, he finds that Billy poked Sonny, sitting in the seat ahead of him, with a pencil. Sonny, went after Billy, who tried to run away. In doing so, Billy's feet got tangled up in the desk legs, and he fell into the heater, breaking his wrist. Which of the following apply?
  a. Billy is substantially at fault here because he started the events, which might not have happened if the teacher had been present.
  b. Sonny's parents would be liable for Billy's injuries because Sonny's actions were intentional.
  c. The teacher is guilty of nonfeasance because he was out of the classroom when the event occurred.
  d. No one is at fault because the students are minors and the teacher was performing an appropriate duty in checking on the ill student.

63. The level of difficulty of a lesson or learning activity is related to the motivation of the learner to complete the task. Which of the following appropriately describes the relationship between motivation and level of difficulty?
  a. Intrinsically motivated students do not like to be bored but do not mind being asked to do tasks above their competence level.
  b. Students with ADHD are motivated by having lots of very easy tasks to keep them occupied.
  c. Extrinsically motivated students will stay engaged in very difficult tasks as long as the teacher provides verbal praise.
  d. Difficulty depends on the individual and must be hard enough not to be boring but not so hard as to cause frustration.

64. A teacher's use of which of the following classroom practices can best support the literacy of students for whom English is a second language?

    a. Spend most of their time working individually so they do not rely on others for their reading and writing help.

    b. Use picture walks and other visual activities that prepare students for reading that they will do.

    c. Use unpredictable text so that the students have to focus on the basic ideas of the text and not just word translation.

    d. Only use graphic organizers as discussion aids after reading and writing tasks have been completed.

Use the following information to answer question 65.

Kelli wants to make a more focused effort to work with the students and families who attend the school in her very diverse community. Over the summer she develops a three-part plan that includes the following:

    1. She prepares a survey for the parents of her students to find out what they need to help their children and has it translated into all of the languages spoken in the students' homes.

    2. She develops home learning activity packets that match key learning objectives, being sure that only basic supplies are needed for the activities.

    3. She plans to have a student-created newsletter describing important classroom activities to send home.

65. Which of the following is true of the practices Kelli proposes?

    a. The survey implies that the parents are not capable of helping their children without assistance from the teacher, which will be seen as offensive.

    b. The home learning activity packets intrude on family time and will be seen in some cultures as uninvited meddling.

    c. The newsletter will have to be translated just as the survey was and this will make it too complicated.

    d. All of the proposals encourage collaboration and invite participation, which would be helpful in the classroom.

66. A fourth-grade teacher is planning to use discussions in her classroom to get students to apply the concepts they are learning in social studies lessons to their own lives. Because the teacher has not used discussion format before, she should be aware that the teacher's role must

    a. reduce the amount of teacher talk and use it to focus the discussion, encourage thoughtful responses, and maintain momentum.

    b. be to initiate the lesson with a short, focused presentation and then step aside while the students carry the rest of the lesson.

    c. be a provider of the basic information that the students need so that they can apply it in the discussion context.

    d. be to wait until the discussion dies out of its own momentum rather than cut it off too soon.

67. Most teacher preparation programs include the study of sociological trends regarding family structure. In preparing to be an effective classroom teacher, which of the following is an important reason for including this area of study?

    a. The roles of men and women in child rearing have stabilized in recent years and teachers must contrast these with historic roles.

    b. The movement of families from well-paying urban jobs to lower-paying information and service jobs affects classroom performance.

    c. Recent trends have shown that families want schools to leave education about moral and social issues to the family.

    d. In working with families, it is important to focus on the functioning of the family unit and not on family composition.

68. Several intermediate grade teachers get together to try to motivate their students to read more. Which of the following is a research-supported practice to motivate reading at the 4–6 grade level?

    a. reducing the practice of the teacher reading aloud to the class so that students internalize the motivation to read

    b. bringing more female reading role models into the classroom, as most poor readers tend to be girls

    c. making an extra effort to bring real-world reading materials, for example, newspaper articles, into the classroom

    d. creating a reading incentive program where students get prizes for reading lots of books

69. Fred Curtis is concerned about his ability to adapt instruction for students with exceptionalities in his classroom. In particular, reading assignments have been problems in the past for his inclusion students. The materials the school provides for his classroom are inappropriate for the reading levels of his students. He makes several adaptations to try to help the students to be more independent readers. These include:

- using advance organizers that structure or summarize the reading passages
- reviewing key concepts and terms after students read the text
- providing study guides with questions that focus on important information
- asking students to summarize information in their own words

In talking with a reading teacher in his school, Fred finds out that these practices are mostly supported by reading research with the exception of

    a. advance organizers can make students overly dependent on the teacher.

    b. key concepts and terms should be introduced before reading, not after.

    c. the study guide questions will complicate the reading for the students.

    d. students may summarize incorrectly and not know it.

70. A teacher's use of which of the following practices is most likely to result in oral language development in her third-grade students?

   a. having the children listen to radio programs and audio tapes regularly so they have excellent role models.

   b. implementing literature circles in which students have the opportunity to share their ideas

   c. having students make oral reports on reading, tape their presentations, and play them back for each child

   d. having them make up and sing songs that help them remember content and are set to popular music

71. Chris goes to a professional development program on portfolio assessment. He likes the idea that portfolios are a more valid measure of the learning that takes place in his classroom. He implements a portfolio system for evaluating his social studies program. For each activity, he helps students decide what work samples to collect and has them work in groups to design how their work will be presented. However, when he collects and assesses the work, he is very disappointed that what he got was far less than what he expected. Which of the following could have helped his use of portfolios?

   a. The students should not have been allowed to design the presentations of their work, as they are not good judges of quality.

   b. He should have added a formal assessment at the end of the portfolio process where the students were tested on their learning.

   c. He should have had the students work in groups and submit one portfolio per group so that the quality of the work would be higher.

   d. He should have established some preset criteria which would be shared with the students as they developed their portfolios.

72. Mark Kelly starts the school year with his first-grade class by discussing with the children what rules they should have in the classroom. This year, they decided on several, including:

   ■ Be polite.
   ■ Raise your hand to talk.
   ■ Listen when someone else is talking.
   ■ It is never acceptable to hit.

   While this list is generally workable, he may have problems because

   a. "Be polite" is too vague and rules need to be clear and understandable.

   b. "Raise your hand" is too controlling and schools should foster independence.

   c. "Listen . . ." is not culturally sensitive and will discriminate against some backgrounds.

   d. the "no hitting" rule should have an exception for defending oneself.

73. A second-grade teacher is working with a science curriculum package that has activities designed to teach inference—the ability to discern a cause when presented with an effect. In one example, the children are shown a picture of a boy, fully dressed and dripping wet. The children are asked to infer what might have happened that caused what they see. The children offer such explanations as: "The boy probably went to see his Grandmother," "The boy's mother was worried that he would be too hot," and "He is wet just because he is wet." Sue may want to abandon this activity because her children are demonstrating which of the following characteristics of typical second graders?

   a. short attention spans that prevent them from concentrating on the task at hand, causing poorly thought out answers

   b. precausal thinking that does not allow a grasp of cause-effect relationships in the physical environment

   c. phenomenism, which causes children to think that their answers are true because they want them to be true

   d. inductive reasoning, which leads the children to derive an explanation from a mechanical explanation they misunderstand

74. Brain development has been linked to a variety of factors including social interactions. Which of the following describes the role of social interaction in brain development?

   a. Learning in a social context can substitute for direct physical contact with the learning environment.

   b. Social interaction benefits the learner only if it occurs after direct experiences with the environment.

   c. Learning in a social context also requires direct physical contact with the learning environment.

   d. Appropriate social interaction must be carefully moderated between too much and too little.

75. Phillip is a sixth-grade student who teachers suspect has a behavioral disorder, but his parents refuse to have him tested. Over a period of two weeks, Philip's behaviors are growing increasingly problematic. On returning from lunch, the teacher notices pages torn from several books in a pile next to Phillip's desk. In the far corner of the room, several destroyed books are found. The teacher takes the student to the principal, arguing that the seriousness of this incident warrants suspension. The principal concurs and suspends him for one week. This action is

   a. appropriate, assuming that the teacher is willing to testify that Phillip was guilty beyond a reasonable doubt in the teacher's mind.

   b. inappropriate, because the school did not provide adequate due process rights, including the right to tell his side of the story.

   c. appropriate, if the value of the books in question had a value of over $100, making their destruction a misdemeanor crime.

   d. inappropriate, because suspensions over three days require that formal procedures be in place to protect the student's rights.

76. Peer mentors and tutors are used in many classrooms. The use of peers working with other peers has been shown to be effective in a wide range of teaching situations, especially for skill learning. Teachers who wish to adopt peer tutoring systems in their classrooms should be aware that, regarding the motivational value of such programs,

   a. cross-age tutoring is motivational for the older tutors, but requires extrinsic motivation to keep the younger tutees involved.

   b. same-age tutoring is only motivational where the tutoring partners are at about the same skill level.

   c. helping someone is intrinsically motivating for the tutors and increased success motivates the tutees.

   d. peer tutoring is not generally successful when used with students with disabilities or developmental delays.

77. Abraham Maslow is associated with research into basic needs that are common to all people. Maslow presented these in a hierarchy expressing that individuals must meet their lower ranked needs before they can be motivated to meet their higher needs. The base is composed of four *deficiency needs* at the bottom and three *growth needs* at the top. Which of the following represents a growth need?

   a. love and belonging needs: satisfactory relationships with others

   b. aesthetic needs: the ability to express oneself creatively

   c. self-esteem needs: positive feelings of self-worth

   d. safety needs: physical, emotional, and mental security

78. Jennifer usually has students in her class who have speech and language problems. She has the help of a speech therapist and a teacher's aide in her classroom. In creating a classroom where all of her students can be successful, Jennifer should try for all of the following EXCEPT

   a. use praise and other reinforcements to create a positive atmosphere.

   b. when students make errors, model for them rather than correct them directly.

   c. actively encourage and teach listening skills.

   d. remove language instruction from other contexts to focus on skills.

79. Group identity is a product of cultural identity (e.g., ethnicity and race) and other factors that help students determine who they are. Group identity goes beyond cultural identity and includes all of the following EXCEPT

   a. food preferences.

   b. gender.

   c. religion.

   d. ethnicity.

80. A fourth-grade teacher takes her students on a field trip to a nearby city park to gather plants they will identify in science class. While there, two students climb up and walk on the railing of a footbridge. The teacher tells them to come down, but then turns to work with other children working on their assignment. One of the children falls and is seriously injured. Which of the following applies?

    a. The teacher is protected from lawsuits because the class was on a school-related outing.

    b. The teacher would be protected if the student's parents had signed a permission form waiving liability.

    c. The liability falls on the city park managers because the railing was an "attractive nuisance."

    d. The accident was foreseeable and therefore the teacher is liable for any injuries.

Written Assignment

Census and projected demographic data show that teachers in all settings—rural, suburban, urban—must expect to have to address the needs of a more diverse student population in the coming years. Your district has been proactive in moving toward a curriculum that meets the needs of all students, including those from diverse cultural backgrounds. You have been asked to lead a committee in formulating a plan for your grade level to achieve the goal expressed in the district's adopted position statement:

> Our goal is to transform the curriculum so that students may learn concepts and ideas from the perspective of diverse cultural and ethnic groups and apply their learning to real-life issues and themes.

Frame your response in the essay by:

- Identifying a grade level and a subject area
- Stating a position, grounded in the professional literature, for the importance of achieving the goal as described by the district
- Describing two specific actions your team should take to implement the goal, supporting each with proven concepts from the teaching profession
- Describing two ways that have been shown to work to communicate to all stakeholders so that they might support this initiative

▶ Answers

1. **b.** Allowing students to use multiple methods of communicating what they learn in science lessons is beneficial to all students, but culturally diverse students in particular will benefit from such practices.

2. **a.** Future teachers should be aware of the existence of the State Professional Standards and Practices Board for Teaching and its responsibilities. The Board is composed of 28 members and includes K–12 teachers and administrators, higher education representatives, public representatives, and one teacher-education student.

3. **d.** Any assessment and grading system is an external reinforcement system and disproportionately motivates achievement motivated students (those motivated by rewards of the system, as opposed to learning motivated students who are motivated by the interest of learning). Choice **a** is incorrect because boys are actually more likely to be motivated by the competition of the system. Choice **b** is incorrect because as rewards are granted to groups, team members become motivated to help each other. Choice **c** is incorrect because the teacher *should* tell his students how the system works so that they will be more motivated to take on a challenge they understand.

4. **c.** Teams should be changed periodically to give students on low-scoring teams a chance to be successful. Choice **a** is incorrect because to maximize the academic and social benefits of group work, students should be assigned heterogeneously. Students should not form their own groups (choice **b**), because this leads to management problems with students talking and playing. Choice **d** is incorrect because there is no research to support that same sex groups working in mixed gender classrooms foster communication and improve performance.

5. **a.** Problem-based (or project-based or anchored) instruction is anchored in the real world in which the learners live. It should draw interesting problems or challenges from the community and bring students in contact with real people and resources to apply to creating their solutions.

6. **c.** In Option I, the teacher is allowing a pedagogical weakness change how she delivers instruction. Option II is not appropriate for the age range of the children. Only choice **c** does not include I or II.

7. **b.** Parent education programs are based on the trend to work collaboratively between parents and school personnel in facilitating goals and activities, which contrasts with the statement found in choice **b**.

8. **a.** Bert should be aware that one of the principal drawbacks of subject integration is that it may greatly increase planning time requirements. Choices **b**, **c**, and **d** are incorrect because integrated instruction actually reduces transitions and chances for off-task behaviors, has been shown to improve reading scores, and improve attitudes toward school.

9. **c.** In the constructivist classroom, student talk is a source of feedback that reveals student thinking. The teacher is engaging in *active listening* whereby he or she gathers information while promoting communication as a tool for refining ideas. When the teacher affirms "right" answers, the students no longer have a reason to keep processing the ideas under discussion.

10. **d.** Learning about the local community and the community's expectations regarding the role of education would be the most logical starting point because that is the area where the teacher has the least experience. While choices **a**, **b**, and **c** have some value, effective instruction should relate school learning to the everyday lives of the students.

11. c. In cases of student injury from what they learn in the classroom, courts take into account the age and maturity of the students. In this case, the teacher demonstrated a fun and exciting activity, and it is not reasonable to assume that young children would remember and obey the disclaimer.

12. a. A bypass strategy is an alternative way for a student to gain access to the curriculum. A child with difficulty spelling would have a hard time demonstrating mastery of social studies content with an assignment full of spelling errors. The spell-checker does not substitute for the student's knowledge of social studies.

13. c. The purpose of coaching is to improve student performance. Choices **a**, **b**, and **d** are incorrect because the new curriculum or materials may come from the administration or elsewhere, topic selection for coaching should be done collaboratively, and in some cases, coaching may be relatively unstructured and require little common time.

14. d. Guided discovery is a model that builds concepts inductively from the consideration of examples. However, to distinguish what makes the examples included in the concept, non-examples help distinguish between closely related concepts.

15. a. Children vary in their preferred learning styles and an individual child may use different learning styles in different situations. Without the ability to assess all children in all manner of learning tasks, learning is maximized by accommodating all learning styles in every activity as much as possible.

16. a. High rates of responding translate to time on task, which is a benefit of drill-and-practice programs. Negative reinforcements (choice **b**) are actually at times more motivating to children; software should provide individualized instruction (not the same for everyone, as in choice **c**); and the best programs store information the teacher can use as formative assessment (choice **d**).

17. b. Future teachers in New York are bound by the Code of Ethics and should be aware of its contents. Of the options in the question, choice **b** is not one of the six principles; in fact, Principle 5 calls on teachers to collaborate with, not take authority over, parents and community members.

18. a. Research has shown that such a system provides social and organizational support for teacher development. Choices **b**, **c**, and **d** are all false statements. In building capacity for change, districts of sufficient size may use the mechanism of professional development "subcultures" to implement change and bring teachers of different levels together for improving practice. In addition, such systems can be managed collaboratively by teachers.

19. d. Discussions that enhance cognitive growth get students to identify relationships among concepts they grasp and apply them to novel situations. Because making meaningful links among internalized concepts is individual, the topics must permit learners to apply their knowledge in a variety of ways.

20. c. Only choice **c** is an example of creating a culturally diverse viewpoint that truly transforms the nature of the curriculum. Choices **a**, **b**, and **d** are all examples of additive models or practices of diversifying the curriculum.

21. a. A child learning to measure success in comparison to standards is an indicator of normal development in the elementary grades. The other answers are indicative of middle adulthood (choice **b**), young adulthood (choice **c**), and infancy (choice **d**).

22. **c.** Drawing on research into effective conflict resolution, after defining the problem, the teacher should lead students in brainstorming possible solutions. Dana did help the students evaluate the solutions, choose one to try, and make a plan to implement and evaluate the choice, but the students do not have ownership of the alternatives because they were not involved in identifying them.

23. **d.** Only choice **d** is good advice—to give students many opportunities to practice what they are learning in different contexts. The other choices are all false: Students placed at risk need active teaching, concrete examples, and lessons structured by teacher questions. All of these make learning more effective for the students concerned.

24. **b.** Specific information confirmed in writing helps parents to feel more comfortable about what is expected of them and sets boundaries for their participation that help in teacher planning. Choice **c** takes flow of the classroom away from the teacher. Choice **d** takes the control of the parental activity from the teacher and gives it to the parents.

25. **c.** Parental involvement tends to support reading activities at the lower grades and subjects at the higher grades. Choice **a** is incorrect because all three forms of communication (report cards, letters, and conferences) are effective in building parental support of their children. Choice **b** is incorrect because conferences should be used to side with parents, not to lecture or pressure them. Choice **d** is incorrect because the opposite is true: Parental involvement shows a decline as level of school increases.

26. **a.** Both IDEA and NCLB require that students with disabilities be included in the overall scores of every district and also disaggregated and reported separately.

27. **a.** Immersion is an intensive learning experience dealing with the content and processes of a particular subject area. Teachers benefit from becoming a learner of the content.

28. **d.** Children normally develop the ability to conceive mass and volume by fifth or sixth grade. The lesson is not developmentally appropriate.

29. **c.** Thought and language are closely linked and language is closely related to culture. Therefore, classroom learning can be maximized for all students by presenting information visually when appropriate.

30. **c.** Because children are socialized into cultural patterns about learning and school, they may have been socialized to learn one way at home and need to develop a new skill set for learning in school.

31. **c.** Using verbalized statements to guide one's own behavior typically ends around age seven. While this may be within the normal range of language development, the child should be observed for other signs of developmental delay. While choice **d** correctly describes the relationship between inner speech and higher cognitive functioning, the child will not make this transition by simply being told not to talk out loud.

32. **c.** Metacognition is not an important factor of intellectual development and the description as written in the choice is not an effective definition of metacognitive learning.

33. **d.** In think-pair-share, students learn to think about what they are learning, as well as develop skills in communicating ideas with others and sharing with the larger group. This is the simplest model to introduce students to working together on learning tasks.

34. **b.** Tutoring programs are effective in presenting information and testing to see if children have mastered it. Current versions of tutoring programs are designed to provide well-designed expository instruction (gain attention, provide objectives, give immediate feedback, etc.).

35. **c.** Goals set for the group give the entire group a motivation, help them focus on shared learning tasks, and give them a stake in each other's success. Individual accountability holds each member of the group responsible for learning the material and ensures that the work is not simply being done by the most able students.

36. **c.** According to the Family Educational Rights and Privacy Act of 1974 (also known as the Buckley Amendment) parents can determine what confidential information about their children is released and to whom, but that request must be made in writing through the administration.

37. **d.** Choice **d** describes an appropriate consideration of the use of textbooks in classrooms. Choices **a** and **b** are incorrect because most publishers have coordinated their textbooks to national (and many to state) standards, and carefully match their reading levels to grade levels. Choice **b** describes a problem with traditional mathematics textbooks, but they still serve as a resource even in a problem-solving teaching approach and should not be abandoned.

38. **b.** The involvement of women in outside-of-school activities has reduced the potential for mothers to be involved in school functions and volunteer for classroom activities. This has also led to increased needs for preschool and other child care.

39. **d.** The teacher is modeling that no one is good at all things but that effort and persistence are positive and desirable traits. Students are more likely to pick up on this than they would false enthusiasm.

40. **a.** The legitimate concern of the choices offered is that some teachers lower their expectations for ELL students.

41. **a.** Performance-oriented students are more worried about receiving praise and good grades (extrinsic motivations) than learning. Choice **b** is incorrect because students may be learning oriented in some subjects and performance oriented in others; choice **c** is incorrect because there is no reason why either orientation is better suited to working in groups.

42. **c.** Mentors need to be selected to closely match content areas, grade levels and, if possible, personal interests. If the mentor/mentee relationship is not effective, there should be an option to change the mentor.

43. **b.** School funding through local property taxes is the historical model of school support in New York and most other states. The state and federal roles in school funding have been to even out the disparities in resources between wealthy and poor districts, although this has not always worked effectively.

44. **a.** Predictable books allow children to "pretend read" from which they develop confidence in their ability to read.

45. **c.** NCTM's position statements, research articles, and books on the topic all advocate the use of calculators in teaching mathematics at all grade levels.

46. **c.** Students with learning and behavior disorders have been shown to benefit from a high level of classroom structure like that which is provided by direct instruction.

47. **b.** Children's perceptions of their own self-worth are linked to how they believe their family is appreciated and respected.

48. **b.** A rubric is designed to help the teacher consistently identify levels of performance among learners. Choices **a**, **c**, and **d** are all incorrect: Portfolios typically increase time spent in assessment, checklists are no more or less valid or reliable than rubrics, and practical tests are usually less valid assessments because they remove skill performance from its context.

49. d. The role of public schools in providing an educated electorate for the democratic processes goes back to the founding of the country. Jefferson is the archetype of early advocates of public schools as a support for democratic institutions.

50. b. Research shows that technology used to help students with learning disabilities should go beyond drill-and-practice software so that students can practice problem-solving skills in a math context.

51. b. Inductive lessons work from particular examples to create general rules. This is the way that people learn naturally in situations outside of school.

52. a. With a teacher presentation of the definition and example application and student-guided practice, the lesson is now more like (but not entirely) a direct instruction lesson. Direct instruction is more time efficient because the teacher can cover more concepts in a given amount of time.

53. a. Concepts are developed by comparing a set of examples against non-examples. The non-examples help to set the limits of the concept.

54. a. With the goal of teaching students to organize information and make effective arguments, the teacher needs to match the assessment to the instructional goal. Multiple-choice items are better for low-level outcomes and demonstrating the ability to recognize correct answers, not constructing them.

55. b. Validity is the degree to which an assessment measures the learning of what was actually taught. While publisher-made tests match the book content itself, teachers usually draw on other learning activities and the background of their students. This variance from what might be in the book usually reduces the validity of the test.

56. d. Research shows that, while the use of clusters is widespread in K–5 classrooms, such a seating arrangement cues students that talking to one another is permissible or even encouraged.

57. c. Instruction should match the form of assessment students are expected to use to demonstrate their learning.

58. d. Option II is not supportable, as the teacher is the professional and should set the agenda for the meeting. Option III is not desirable, as the pace and tone of the meeting should be friendly and collaborative. Options I and IV are research-supported practices.

59. d. Direct instruction is an appropriate model for teaching well-defined concepts in a short amount of time.

60. a. Recent research in direct instruction recommends the use of real-world examples and applications, teacher scaffolding of concept development, and assessment of understanding to assure that concepts learned can be transferred to new contexts.

61. a. Research shows that, as much as possible, the consequences of misbehavior should be logically related to the error; for example, the student who made the mess in the social studies learning center should have to fix it, or clean it up.

62. c. The teacher has a contractual duty to supervise students under his or her care. Failure to meet this duty is nonfeasance or failure to perform. The ill student was under the appropriate care of the school nurse. The teacher's obligation was to the students in the classroom.

63. d. Learning tasks are motivating when they are challenging enough not to be boring, but not so hard as to cause frustration (appropriately challenging).

64. **b.** Having students interpret and create visual images gives them rich connections to text material. Choice **a** ignores the benefits of pair or group activities. ESL students benefit from predictable text (choice **c**), and graphic organizers before reading tasks is more beneficial (choice **d**).

65. **d.** All of the proposals show concern on the part of the teacher and demonstrate that she wants to involve parents and families, but not that the families have to participate. These have all been shown to be effective practices.

66. **a.** In leading discussions the teacher's role is reduced but focused. The lesson should not need much presentation as discussions depend on student background knowledge (in contrast to choices **b** and **c**.) Choice **d** is incorrect because it is better to cut off discussions too soon than to let them go until all students have talked themselves out.

67. **d.** Sociological research provides research to allow teachers to focus on the issues that make a difference in how families function. Research separates those aspects of family life that make a difference in beliefs, values, and behaviors.

68. **c.** The teacher as a role model of real-world reading is the only option that is a recommended practice. To motivate reading, teachers should continue to read to intermediate grade children, and not stop as suggested in choice **a**. While choice **b** suggests poor readers are female, the opposite is true, and male role model readers will help. Choice **d** is incorrect: Reading incentive programs have been criticized because they provide external motivation to read and lead some children to read "easy" books just to win incentives.

69. **b.** Reading research recommends the teacher practice all of the choices, with the exception of choice **b**.

70. **b.** Only choice **b** has a body of research that recommends it as an effective technique to develop oral language skills.

71. **d.** Portfolios should be developed with the end in mind. As such, there should be preset criteria against which the final product will be reviewed. Students should be involved in deciding what goes into the portfolio and how it is presented because that is part of the learning process.

72. **a.** "Being polite" is too abstract for first-grade children. Rules at the primary level should focus on specific illustrative behaviors so that children do not have to make decisions about whether or not they are obeying the rule.

73. **b.** The children's descriptions reflect forms of precausal thinking, including phenomenism, participation, and finalism, which are all typical of children this age. Further, phenomenism (choice **c**) and inductive reasoning (choice **d**) are described incorrectly.

74. **c.** Studies have shown that the gross structure of the cerebral cortex is maximized by physical (sensory) interaction with a learning environment in the context of social interaction.

75. **b.** Even if the teacher is fully convinced of the student's guilt, the school did not appear to exercise any due process activities to protect the student's rights. The value or amount of the damage is immaterial. Choice **d** misstates the correct legal circumstance—suspensions over ten days require a formal due process hearing and/or other procedures.

76. **c.** The motivational aspect of peer tutoring has been well researched and demonstrates a motivational effect on both the tutors and tutees.

77. b. Even if you are only somewhat familiar with the hierarchy, safety, belonging, and self-esteem are needs that, if they are not met, can prevent higher learning. Aesthetics is a need we all share, but most individuals cannot address this if their lower needs are not met.

78. d. Rather than the advice offered in choice **d**, language skills should be taught in contexts that are meaningful for the children.

79. a. Of the four factors offered, food preferences are not recognized by sociologists and educators as significant factors of group identity.

80. d. In choice **a**, it is true that the teacher is an agent of the school and therefore in New York, the district would be required to defend her; however, she can still be found liable. Permission forms (choice **b**) do not bar parents from suing if the teacher's actions were negligent. Attractive nuisance is a valid concept in the law, but it does not apply here. The accident was foreseeable and the teacher should have made sure the students complied with her orders.

Written Assignment

Essay 1 (weak)

America and New York are becoming more diverse. Addressing the needs of culturally and ethnically diverse students will continue to become more important. I have been asked to describe how our school district might prepare to address the needs of these students better.

It is important for teachers to incorporate diversity in their classroom. As our district stated, it is important to show how the ethnic groups can be applied to real-life situations. By teaching students about different cultures, it helps them realize the importance their culture has in the real world. The curriculum is also an important way to express the importance of culture. It is important that the school and teachers apply these cultures in the classroom and curriculum.

As a team, I believe we should include literature which exemplifies different cultures in the curriculum. The students will learn better when the culture shown in the book is one the students can relate to. I think when students read, they better understand the situation if they can relate to the culture in the book. These books will also help students understand other cultures and respect the differences in their school and classroom. These books could also be translated into languages that are native to the students in the classroom. Therefore, the students could learn the same material but in their primary language.

As a team, the teachers should decide on a way to incorporate culture into their classroom. I would like to see the teachers each create a culture bulletin board. Each student should contribute to the board by exemplifying their culture. Throughout the year, the students should bring in food, clothes, or other things which exemplify their culture. I feel the teachers should welcome all of the cultures and include all of the cultures in their classroom when possible.

The school should have workshops to teach teachers how to incorporate different cultures into their classroom. By showing teachers different ways that could work for them will help teachers accept the ways which are most convenient for their classroom. The school should also create committees that attempt to incorporate culture including administrators, teachers, and parents. The committees will create a community of understanding and will come up with many new ideas that can be implemented in the school.

Evaluation

The weak response is apparently based mostly on the opinion of the author and does not incorporate ideas of the profession nor use the vocabulary that would be associated with these ideas. The answer apparently missed the third prompt in the question and fails to deal with the issues of building effective communication with families. It also did not identify the grade level and subject(s) as required. The essay is a collection of commonsense suggestions with no evidence of understanding the knowledge of the teaching profession.

Identifying a grade level and a subject area. The writer did not specify the grade level or subject(s) in the response. (The writer may have felt the subjects were implied to be all subjects, but this is not stated.)

Stating a position, grounded in the professional literature, for the importance of achieving the goal as described by the district. The ideas expressed in the response demonstrate only a limited knowledge of practices that would be effective in this setting. While some connection to the body of knowledge of the teaching profession is implied, it has to be read into the essay. The author does not use professional language or the concepts to which such vocabulary refers. In several places ideas are stated as fact but only seem to have the opinion of the author to back them up, for example, "It is important that the school and teachers apply these cultures in the classroom and curriculum." While it is correct that this is important, as stated, it appears that this is simply the opinion of the author.

Describing two specific actions your team should take to implement the goal, supporting each with proven concepts from the teaching profession. The author makes two vague suggestions that appear to be drawn from his or her commonsense thinking about teaching. The writer makes the first recommendation because "I believe we should include literature . . ." and the second is something "I would like to see . . ." Other evidence comes from what the author "thinks" or "feels." The first recommendation is to "include literature which exemplifies different cultures," but this is followed by several thoughts about what this might do and does not reflect research-based practice.

Describing two ways that have been shown to work to communicate to all stakeholders so that they might support this initiative. This part of the question is probably missed. The last paragraph of the essay talks about professional development, but it does not focus this activity on communication with students' homes and therefore misses the purpose of the prompt. If it is meant to address the communication portion of the question, it does not do so explicitly. In the end it seems that some committees are given the task of coming up with the specific recommendations missing in the essay.

The essay also begins with a paragraph that restates the question. This continues into the second paragraph. This is seen as padding and will not strengthen the essay. Even with this filler, the essay runs about 350 words. Some of the phrases and wording in the essay are awkward or confusing. There is a consistent mismatch of the pronoun "their" and plural nouns: their classroom, their language, their culture when the usage required their classrooms, their languages, and their cultures.

Essay 2 (strong)
Grade level: third grade; Subject area: all subjects

Educators and theorists contend that teachers must develop new strategies to assure that all children learn at high levels including increasing numbers of students from diverse backgrounds. The No Child Left Behind legislation requires that states demonstrate that all children are performing at grade level in academics. New York has both a history of diverse students and also programs for helping all children demonstrate their achievement. Multicultural education has been built on principles of diversity, social justice, equality, and personally relevant instruction. These are important values for teaching all children.

One practice that the team might take is to share information about students so that the group collectively sets expectations for every student. In the past, teachers did not expect much from certain racial or ethnic groups. Because of this they taught these children differently or assessed their work with a different perspective. This is especially important when the assessment is qualitative. This leads to a cycle of self-fulfilling prophesy in which student failure leads to ever-decreasing lower expectations. It has been shown that academic performances of children can be gained by increasing teacher expectations and modifying their behavior.

Another practice would be to improve the cross-cultural understanding of the teachers. Because teacher knowledge and behavior is the quality that the teacher team has most direct control over, this could be very effective. In prior cases teachers studied the cultural gaps that separated the home and school. By determining the cultural expectations, roles, and values each child brings to the school setting, resources can be reassigned to meet the needs of all. Classroom practices might include increased use of learning centers, cross-age or same-age peer tutoring, or changing available reading materials.

In the past, there have been difficulties in communicating between monolingual teachers and families who may be English Language Learners or not speak English at all. Communication between teachers/schools and families is vital to get the cooperation of parents and family members in supporting the educational activities designed for the students. This helps students to relate their school experiences to the lives they live at home. In this case it would be important to have a home-school coordinator who is capable of making phone calls home, translating written communications, and participating in parent-teacher conferences. It is sometimes possible to involve other parents, bilingual teachers, or older siblings in facilitating communication, but involving these individuals can place an undue burden on them, especially siblings who have their own educational issues to deal with.

Evaluation
The strong essay demonstrates a grasp of professional concepts and an understanding of current issues in the field. The writer applies these ideas to the situation posed by the question and uses the words and phrases of the education profession in communicating about them: NCLB, qualitative assessment, social justice, equality of results, and English Language Learners. The essay further creates a strong response by complying with the specific directives of the question: to identify a grade level and subject area, to state a position grounded in the

professional literature, to describe two specific actions as requested, and to describe two ways that have been shown to work in addressing this issue.

Identifying a grade level and a subject area. The writer specified that he or she is responding to the circumstances in the third grade and addressing all subjects.

Stating a position, grounded in the professional literature, for the importance of achieving the goal as described by the district. The author showed a grasp of the issues related to diversity in the elementary grades, including increasing diversity and NCLB. After describing the situation nationally and in New York, the author clearly explained why the goal of multicultural education is an important one, e.g., that the values of multicultural education (diversity, social justice, equality, and relevance) are important for teaching all children.

Describing two specific actions your team should take to implement the goal, supporting each with proven concepts from the teaching profession. The author demonstrated a grasp of the implications for planning and delivering instruction that is based on what the profession has learned about teaching diverse student groups. In describing the first action, the writer expresses how all of the teachers at the grade level can incorporate diversity into preparing and delivering instruction. This explanation includes demonstrating a grasp of the current state of thinking in the profession about diversity and how this impacts practice. In the case of the second action, the author explains how a classroom teacher can use the principle of equality in planning for an effective classroom. This portion of the essay links the idea of "equality of results" to practice that can make a difference in classrooms.

Describing two ways that have been shown to work to communicate to all stakeholders so that they might support this initiative. The author gives a sound rationale that shows a grasp of communication issues in working with the families of students from diverse backgrounds. In the essay, the writer focuses on the language issue and identifies ways that this barrier may be overcome. The author also suggests other ideas, but describes the possible problems associated with these suggestions. In all, the writer demonstrates a grasp of the issues raised by the question prompt and uses professional ideas and vocabulary in crafting the response.

Finally, the essay is concise. It is about 450 words, it does not restate the question at the beginning or have an extensive summary at the end, as essayists will often do.

▶ Scoring Your Practice Test

Your official ATS-W score is a cumulative score representing all subareas of the test, including all multiple-choice questions and the constructed-response assignment, which will count toward 20% of your total score. Your total score will be reported on a scale between 100 and 300; a passing score for the official ATS-W is any score of 220 or above.

To take full advantage of this practice test, you should find both your overall score on the multiple-choice questions of this test, as well your individual scores in each subarea. To find your overall score, simply divide the number of multiple choice questions you answered correctly by the total number of multiple-choice questions found on the test, which is 80. For example, if you answered 60 questions correctly:

$$\frac{60 \text{ (questions correct)}}{80 \text{ (total questions)}} = .75, \text{ or } 75\%.$$

To score your constructed-response question, it is highly recommended that you ask a professional friend or colleague familiar with the area of Instruction and Assessment to evaluate your essay using the official *Performance Characteristics and Scoring Scale* found at the end of the official Elementary ATS-W Preparation Guide, which can be found on the NYSTCE® website at www.nystce.nesinc.com/PDFs/NY_fld090_prepguide.pdf. Your friend or colleague should assign you a score on the constructed-response essay between 1 and 4.

After you have a score for both parts of the practice test, you should use the following guidelines:

- If you get 80% or more of the multiple-choice items correct and score a 4 on the written assignment scoring scale, your preparation for the test is **EXCELLENT**.
- If you get 70% or more of the multiple-choice items correct and score a 3 or 4 on the written assignment scoring scale, your preparation for the test is **VERY GOOD**.
- If you get 60% or more of the multiple-choice items correct and score a 3 on the written assignment scoring scale, your preparation for the test is **GOOD**.
- If you get less than 60% of the multiple-choice items correct and score a 2 or 1 on the written assignment scoring scale, you should probably do some additional preparation before taking the actual test.

This practice test also offers you the opportunity to diagnose your areas of strength and weakness, to target your preparation for the official test. Following is a table that breaks down the questions in this practice test by subarea and their corresponding objectives. You can use this table to identify the areas in which you may need to concentrate more of your study time. For this practice test you should score at least 75% or higher in each subarea. You can find out your individual subarea scores by dividing the number of questions you answered correctly in a particular subarea by the total number of questions in that subarea.

Use your scores in each subarea in conjunction with the LearningExpress Test Preparation System in Chapter 7 to help you devise a study plan using the prep materials found in this book along with the materials from your classes and courses.

ELEMENTARY ATS-W Practice Exam for Review

SUBAREA AND OBJECTIVE	CORRESPONDING QUESTION	
Subarea I: Student Development and Learning		Total # of questions in Subarea I: 26
0001	1, 19, 32, 73, 74	
0002	15, 21, 28, 77	
0003	6, 24, 47, 66	
0004	44, 63, 67, 69	
0005	10, 20, 64, 79	
0006	12, 26, 46, 50, 78	
Subarea II: Instruction and Assessment		Total # of questions in Subarea II: 37
0007	5, 22, 54, 59, 71	
0008	8, 23, 40, 68	
0009	48, 52, 53, 70	
0010	35, 55, 57, 58	
0011	3, 7, 33, 65	
0012	37, 51, 60, 72	
0013	30, 41, 62, 76	
0014	9, 14, 31, 39	
0015	16, 29, 34, 45	
Subarea III: The Professional Environment		Total # of questions in Subarea III: 17
0016	2, 17, 43, 49	
0017	13, 18, 27, 42	
0018	4, 25, 38, 56	
0019	11, 36, 61, 75, 80	
Subarea IV: Instruction and Assessment: Constructed-Response Assignment		Total # of questions in Subarea IV: 1
0020	Written Assignment	

13 ▶ Secondary ATS-W Practice Exam

CHAPTER SUMMARY

This practice Secondary Assessment of Teaching Skills—Written (ATS-W) is based on the format and content of the official Secondary ATS-W. See Chapter 5 for a complete description of the official exam. Use this practice exam to see how you would do if you were to take the Secondary ATS-W today, and to diagnose your strengths and weaknesses to help you study more effectively for the official test.

To simulate the test-taking experience, give yourself the time and the space to work. Because you won't be taking the real test in your living room, you might take this one in an unfamiliar location, such as a library. Use a timer or stopwatch to time yourself, allowing ample time for preparing and writing your essay; you'll have four hours to complete your official exam. If you would prefer to take this test for more diagnostic purposes, just take the test in a relaxed manner to find out which areas you are skilled in and which areas will need extra work. After you finish taking your test, you should review the answer explanations found at the end of this test. The answer explanations are followed by information on how to score your exam and diagnose your strengths and weaknesses.

The answer sheet you should use for the multiple-choice questions is on page 305. (You will write your essay on a separate piece of paper.)

▶ Answer Sheet

1.	ⓐ	ⓑ	ⓒ	ⓓ	28.	ⓐ	ⓑ	ⓒ	ⓓ	55.	ⓐ	ⓑ	ⓒ	ⓓ
2.	ⓐ	ⓑ	ⓒ	ⓓ	29.	ⓐ	ⓑ	ⓒ	ⓓ	56.	ⓐ	ⓑ	ⓒ	ⓓ
3.	ⓐ	ⓑ	ⓒ	ⓓ	30.	ⓐ	ⓑ	ⓒ	ⓓ	57.	ⓐ	ⓑ	ⓒ	ⓓ
4.	ⓐ	ⓑ	ⓒ	ⓓ	31.	ⓐ	ⓑ	ⓒ	ⓓ	58.	ⓐ	ⓑ	ⓒ	ⓓ
5.	ⓐ	ⓑ	ⓒ	ⓓ	32.	ⓐ	ⓑ	ⓒ	ⓓ	59.	ⓐ	ⓑ	ⓒ	ⓓ
6.	ⓐ	ⓑ	ⓒ	ⓓ	33.	ⓐ	ⓑ	ⓒ	ⓓ	60.	ⓐ	ⓑ	ⓒ	ⓓ
7.	ⓐ	ⓑ	ⓒ	ⓓ	34.	ⓐ	ⓑ	ⓒ	ⓓ	61.	ⓐ	ⓑ	ⓒ	ⓓ
8.	ⓐ	ⓑ	ⓒ	ⓓ	35.	ⓐ	ⓑ	ⓒ	ⓓ	62.	ⓐ	ⓑ	ⓒ	ⓓ
9.	ⓐ	ⓑ	ⓒ	ⓓ	36.	ⓐ	ⓑ	ⓒ	ⓓ	63.	ⓐ	ⓑ	ⓒ	ⓓ
10.	ⓐ	ⓑ	ⓒ	ⓓ	37.	ⓐ	ⓑ	ⓒ	ⓓ	64.	ⓐ	ⓑ	ⓒ	ⓓ
11.	ⓐ	ⓑ	ⓒ	ⓓ	38.	ⓐ	ⓑ	ⓒ	ⓓ	65.	ⓐ	ⓑ	ⓒ	ⓓ
12.	ⓐ	ⓑ	ⓒ	ⓓ	39.	ⓐ	ⓑ	ⓒ	ⓓ	66.	ⓐ	ⓑ	ⓒ	ⓓ
13.	ⓐ	ⓑ	ⓒ	ⓓ	40.	ⓐ	ⓑ	ⓒ	ⓓ	67.	ⓐ	ⓑ	ⓒ	ⓓ
14.	ⓐ	ⓑ	ⓒ	ⓓ	41.	ⓐ	ⓑ	ⓒ	ⓓ	68.	ⓐ	ⓑ	ⓒ	ⓓ
15.	ⓐ	ⓑ	ⓒ	ⓓ	42.	ⓐ	ⓑ	ⓒ	ⓓ	69.	ⓐ	ⓑ	ⓒ	ⓓ
16.	ⓐ	ⓑ	ⓒ	ⓓ	43.	ⓐ	ⓑ	ⓒ	ⓓ	70.	ⓐ	ⓑ	ⓒ	ⓓ
17.	ⓐ	ⓑ	ⓒ	ⓓ	44.	ⓐ	ⓑ	ⓒ	ⓓ	71.	ⓐ	ⓑ	ⓒ	ⓓ
18.	ⓐ	ⓑ	ⓒ	ⓓ	45.	ⓐ	ⓑ	ⓒ	ⓓ	72.	ⓐ	ⓑ	ⓒ	ⓓ
19.	ⓐ	ⓑ	ⓒ	ⓓ	46.	ⓐ	ⓑ	ⓒ	ⓓ	73.	ⓐ	ⓑ	ⓒ	ⓓ
20.	ⓐ	ⓑ	ⓒ	ⓓ	47.	ⓐ	ⓑ	ⓒ	ⓓ	74.	ⓐ	ⓑ	ⓒ	ⓓ
21.	ⓐ	ⓑ	ⓒ	ⓓ	48.	ⓐ	ⓑ	ⓒ	ⓓ	75.	ⓐ	ⓑ	ⓒ	ⓓ
22.	ⓐ	ⓑ	ⓒ	ⓓ	49.	ⓐ	ⓑ	ⓒ	ⓓ	76.	ⓐ	ⓑ	ⓒ	ⓓ
23.	ⓐ	ⓑ	ⓒ	ⓓ	50.	ⓐ	ⓑ	ⓒ	ⓓ	77.	ⓐ	ⓑ	ⓒ	ⓓ
24.	ⓐ	ⓑ	ⓒ	ⓓ	51.	ⓐ	ⓑ	ⓒ	ⓓ	78.	ⓐ	ⓑ	ⓒ	ⓓ
25.	ⓐ	ⓑ	ⓒ	ⓓ	52.	ⓐ	ⓑ	ⓒ	ⓓ	79.	ⓐ	ⓑ	ⓒ	ⓓ
26.	ⓐ	ⓑ	ⓒ	ⓓ	53.	ⓐ	ⓑ	ⓒ	ⓓ	80.	ⓐ	ⓑ	ⓒ	ⓓ
27.	ⓐ	ⓑ	ⓒ	ⓓ	54.	ⓐ	ⓑ	ⓒ	ⓓ					

Use the following information to answer question 1.

Carolyn is complaining to Maria about the results of the quiz she gave after yesterday's eighth-grade lesson on *A Tale of Two Cities.* "I can't believe that the answers are so superficial. They unload a lot of information about the story, but they can't pull it together into a cogent thesis." Carolyn shows the quiz question, an essay prompt, to Maria.

"How effective was Dickens' use of vivid imagery in foreshadowing the revolution that was about to start in France?"

Maria asks Carolyn about the prior performance of the students and the lesson from the day before. Maria knows that Carolyn makes up detailed lesson plans. She asks to see yesterday's and notices several discussion questions listed:

- Why was Sidney Carton in Paris?
- What was Carton's occupation?
- Where was Dr. Manette imprisoned?
- Why does the Marquis say, "Repression is the only lasting philosophy?"

1. Which of the following would be an effective observation that might help Carolyn?
  a. Her lesson questioning is convergent, but she is asking divergent questions on the assessment.
  b. The quiz question is so vague that the students probably do not know how to deal with it.
  c. The lesson questions are at the application level while the quiz question is at the comprehension level.
  d. Eighth graders cannot be expected to answer application-level questions such as she used on the quiz.

2. At one time, the processes and systems set up to address the education of students with disabilities were left up to state or local decision makers. Today there are both court precedents and federal law that establishes procedural protections for these individuals. Which of the following describes how this change occurred?
  a. Reforms set off in response to the Russian Sputnik satellite expanded educational opportunities for all.
  b. Courts in the 1970s established the principle of "appropriate" education, which was coalesced by PL 94-142 in 1975.
  c. Title IX, which prohibits discrimination against individuals with disabilities, was passed by Congress in 1999.
  d. *Brown v. Board of Education* in 1953 extended equal opportunity to all regardless of race, gender, ethnicity, or handicapping condition.

3. An English teacher is having her twelfth-grade Advanced Placement (AP) class do critical analyses of films. Each student must bring in a 3–5 minute clip of a movie, show it to the class, and then offer a critique. The teacher asks for the titles and a summary from the student for each film, but does not screen them beforehand. One student uses a movie that the teacher has not heard of. The movie is rated R but the teacher did not ask about the rating. When the student is showing the clip, a graphic scene of a violent rape is presented. The student critiques the scene as a statement that society is not doing enough to prevent rape and prosecute rapists. Which of the following applies?

   a. Because the clip validly related to the critique and the students were older, there is no problem.

   b. While the clip should not have been shown to these students, teaching practices are protected by academic freedom.

   c. The clip should not have been shown without warning the students and allowing anyone who objected to be excused.

   d. The teacher violated the law by showing R-rated movie scenes to minors.

Use the information below to answer questions 4 and 5.

Juanita Fiore poses the following situation to her tenth-grade biology class: Alex is a water quality control agent for the Department of Environmental Conservation. Alex's best friend from high school, Tim, owns a restaurant in the town where they grew up. While monitoring a stream, Alex finds that small amounts of kitchen wastes from Tim's restaurant are draining into the stream. Alex tells Tim, who replies that he knows about the situation but he cannot afford to fix it now. Tim asks Alex not to report the situation for a while and he will fix it next spring when the restaurant is doing better.

Ms. Fiore poses the following questions:

- Which is more important, honesty or friendship?
- What might happen to Alex if he does this favor?
- What other choices does Alex have?

4. Which of the following principles should Juanita consider in guiding the discussion?

   a. The students should not state personal positions during the discussion.

   b. The teacher must make the environment safe for different value positions.

   c. The teacher should push students to participate in the discussion.

   d. The teacher would bias the discussion by asking questions.

5. In class, a student, Ojas, argues that the small amount of waste in the stream is probably not hurting anything, and Alex should help Tim. He argues that one's good motives are important. Ojas is demonstrating his priority for which level of moral development?

   a. Good Interpersonal Relationships

   b. Maintaining the Social Order

   c. Social Contract and Individual Rights

   d. None of these: Ojas's position is immoral

6. Safety in schools is a great concern in the twenty-first century. Schools have engaged in a variety of practices to address the root causes and impacts of violence among students in schools. These include:

   I. school-wide programs designed to identify and reduce harassment and bullying
  II. peer mediation programs that involve students in a system to reduce overall conflict
 III. discovering rumors and threats and keeping them from becoming public
 IV. using classroom instruction to teach respect and responsibility as important values

Which of the following correctly identifies proven effective strategies?
a. I and II only
b. I, II, and III only
c. I, II, and IV only
d. I, III, and IV only

7. Cooperative learning is one of the most researched models of instruction. Which of the following has NOT been shown to be a positive effect of cooperative learning?
a. Students demonstrate more verbal and nonverbal support for their classmates and acceptance of their ideas.
b. Students who participate in cooperative classrooms show more tolerance for other races and ethnicities.
c. Students' academic achievement in all subjects and at all grade levels is usually higher than in traditional classrooms.
d. More content can be covered in a shorter amount of preparation time.

8. The social studies teachers in a rural school are concerned about the learning outcomes their curriculum is achieving. While their students perform well on district achievement tests, the teachers feel the students do not demonstrate the ability to use what they learn in school in outside settings. Four teachers are advocating for the expanded use of four different models of instruction. If you were an outside consultant advising this school, which of the following arguments could you say has empirical evidence behind it?
a. Problem-based learning develops students' investigative skills and gives them the chance to model these in adult roles.
b. Direct instruction shows the greatest transfer of learning when complex skills are involved.
c. Role playing requires students to take positions contrary to their personal beliefs and is the most effective.
d. Mastery learning requires the most in-depth exploration of topics and therefore has the greatest transfer.

9. In her social studies class this year, Joan has decided to include more information about diverse cultures. She gives her students an outline of upcoming topics every two weeks. They are encouraged to bring in materials or share information from their own cultural background. About one-third of her students actively participate in this. Which of the following is an accurate observation of Joan's practice?

   a. This *additive approach* integrates information into the existing curriculum, but the dominant culture is still central.

   b. This *contributions approach* will end up focused on holidays and not have a meaningful impact on her students.

   c. This *transformational approach* changes the basic perspective of study because it uses multiple points of view.

   d. This *social action approach* puts responsibility on the students, therefore helping them to become change agents.

10. New York State has created Learning Standards that identify the goals of instruction in every major subject area. These Learning Standards documents are supported by a collection of Resource Guides and core curricula in the various subject areas. Which of the following accurately describes the role of Learning Standards in classroom curricular decision making?

   a. The Learning Standards give detailed information about the scope and sequence of the curriculum.

   b. The Learning Standards establish the scope and sequence and the core curricula provide daily planning objectives.

   c. The Learning Standards provide broad guidance that is elaborated in the scope and sequence outlined in the core curricula.

   d. The Learning Standards provide specific daily learning objectives and the Resource Guides organize these into scope and sequence.

11. Ron's parents are seeking advice on how to work with Ron as he moves into the upper grades. Ron was identified in fourth grade as a student with a learning disability. His parents have noticed several characteristics of Ron's school work. He does not seem to notice that when he reads and comes to information he does not understand, he simply continues reading. Ron has been taught strategies for remembering information, such as asking himself questions about what he learned, however, he almost never uses these strategies. Based on this information, what is most likely the situation Ron's parents and teachers will have to address?

   a. Ron has become unmotivated, probably from lack of success in school.

   b. Ron appears to have trouble with visual tasks and needs alternative modes of instruction.

   c. Ron lacks reasoning skills and should not expect success in academic work.

   d. Ron is a passive learner, which is typical of students with learning disabilities.

12. Access to technology is changing all aspects of education, including the student assessment process. Of the following practices, which is the most important application as it impacts student assessment practices?
   a. tracking students so they can be homogeneously grouped for instruction
   b. making it easier to send information home to parents, especially regarding behavior
   c. allowing teachers to have access to test banks of items when they create tests
   d. addressing the needs of individual students by providing personalized data to teachers

Use the information below to answer questions 13–15.

Mr. Fowler teaches eighth-grade science. He likes to use a problem-based approach to motivate his students by providing a context of how science applies to their everyday lives. He begins a new unit by dividing the class into groups of three or four and giving each a collection of written materials to guide them. Part of the activity requires that the students collect data from home about physical characteristics that are indicators of genetic traits, for example, earlobe shape, dimples, freckles, nose shape, and three other characteristics. In the written materials the students are told how to approach family members about gathering the information and informing them what it is to be used for. Anyone can opt out of participating. After the information is collected, the students put the data into a spreadsheet and do a series of three-dimensional exploding pie charts to represent their information. After the fourth day of the unit, Mr. Fowler is called to the office. There he is confronted by the principal and an angry parent. He is informed that one child, Liz, gathered her information about her parents from photos and did not talk to or inform them of the project. Liz is now asking questions about why she does not have any of the physical characteristics Mr. Fowler says she should have based on her parents' features. Liz is an adopted child but has never been told this.

13. From the standpoint of instructional design, which of the following is an appropriate description of how the teacher used the relationship between student motivation and practices that sustain student cooperation in learning?
   a. The activities were well-designed because the students were extrinsically motivated by the data from their families.
   b. The activities were well-designed because the students used data about themselves, which is intrinsically motivating.
   c. The activities suffered from a design problem in that students could opt out of bringing in the data.
   d. The activities were poorly designed because the teacher should have assumed that personal data might lead to problems.

14. What problem did the use of the computer program have from an instructional design perspective?
   a. They could have obtained data for the activity from the Internet easier than from home.
   b. The data could have been more clearly expressed by a more simple chart format.
   c. The students entered the data and would have been likely to make mistakes.
   d. Students learn more from data summaries when they graph data by hand.

15. While the teacher obviously would feel terrible about the family situation, has he placed himself in any legal jeopardy?

  a. No, because this activity is typical of what other science teachers do in many other classrooms.

  b. No, because the Family Educational Rights and Privacy Act (FERPA) does not cover data used for educational purposes.

  c. No, because the proximate cause of the situation was the student not following the directions to inform her family.

  d. Yes, because he should have had a release form signed by the parents before he asked the students to gather the data.

16. Learning styles (also called cognitive styles) are preferences for particular approaches students have for learning tasks, problem solving, and processing information. When accounting for learning styles in adapting instructional practices, teachers need to take into account that

  a. learning styles are culturally based and therefore not using them to adapt instruction is culturally insensitive.

  b. if you cannot adapt your lessons to account for all of the learning styles of your students some of them are likely to fail.

  c. learning styles are relatively stable, which makes a useful planning tool for designing lessons.

  d. learning styles change suddenly during adolescence and you need to reassess them often.

17. Sue Markam divides her class into groups of four for a discussion exercise and gives each group a list of 12 statements about *Macbeth*. The students in the groups are designated A, B, C, or D. In turn, a student has to pick a statement, read it to the group and then restate it so that it is true and explain his or her reasoning. Sue sees the educational value of this exercise in that each student has to verbalize to his or her peers an important idea about the play. Which of the following theories supports Sue's practice?

  I. Motivational Theory, which recommends using the student's desire to please the teacher to encourage participation.

  II. Developmental Theory, which states social interaction encourages learning because students re-evaluate their views of the world.

  III. Elaboration Theory, which says by putting our ideas into words we organize and restructure them.

  IV. Behaviorist Theory, because the small steps in the lesson give students many chances for positive reinforcement.

  a. I and II only

  b. I and III only

  c. II and III only

  d. II and IV only

SECONDARY ATS-W PRACTICE EXAM

18. At the end of the first marking period, Bill is disappointed with the assessment results from his ninth- and tenth-grade classes. In talking to some of the students about what might be going on, the students express frustration with trying to prepare for Bill's tests and quizzes. Several good students explain that they find themselves studying a lot of material that never shows up on the assessments. Which of the following is most likely to help Bill with his planning?

   a. He should assess the students more often so that everything presented in class is assessed at least once.

   b. Most beginning teachers go through this phase of student frustration with assessment, and it will pass.

   c. Most beginning teachers include too much irrelevant information, so he should focus on critical ideas.

   d. He should have the students read an assignment and then cover the material the same way in class for better reinforcement.

Use the following information to answer questions 19 and 20.

Dan is using a computer program in teaching a high school economics class. The program has a tutorial section that teaches "annual depreciation" as a function of cost divided by expected life. The program poses this question to the user:

   A company buys new computers at a cost of $1,600 per unit. The technology staff for the company tells the manager that they will be expected to last four years. What is the annual depreciation?

   One student responds "$400," receives a message of "Good Work" and is sent on to the next part of the tutorial. Another student responds "$1,600," and gets a message "Sorry, try again." After the student misses the question three times, the computer explains the right answer and sends the student back to the tutorial.

19. Which of the following is a valid observation about this program?

   a. The program should have had a section on guided practice between the tutorial and the test.

   b. Tutorial programs should not be used to teach new material because teachers are still superior in covering new learning.

   c. The program is effective because it allows faster students to move on while remediating those who need help.

   d. The program is effective because it gave the learner three chances before it cycled back to the tutorial.

20. Implementing technology into existing or new curriculum plans is one of the fastest-moving areas of teacher planning. Teachers must develop methods and strategies to maximize student learning through the use of technology. Which of the following is NOT a valid goal of implementing technology into teaching and learning?

    a. facilitating technology-enhanced experiences that address content standards and student technology standards

    b. using technology to support user-centered strategies that address the diverse needs of students

    c. applying technology to develop students' higher-order skills and creativity while managing student learning activities

    d. maximizing the available technologies in the classroom, as research shows any technology in the classroom will provide positive results

21. Julia is a new eighth-grade science teacher in a rural 7–12 school. Her mentor, Al, has been teaching there for 19 years. At the end of the year, Julia is called in to the principal's office to discuss her annual professional performance review. The review is much less than what she had expected and she is shocked to see statements that were based on comments from Al. She protests that what she shared with her mentor was candid in hopes that he would help her to improve, and she did not know that Al might be a part of the performance review. Which of the following applies?

    a. Under New York State Law, mentor information is confidential and may not be used in annual performance reviews.

    b. Under Regulations of the Commissioner of Education, a novice teacher must be informed in writing if a mentor is a part of the review process.

    c. While it is beneficial to beginning teachers that their mentors not be part of the review, Julia should have asked before they began.

    d. As an employee of the district, her mentor was an agent of the school board and must share any requested information with administrators.

22. Which of the following is likely to be the greatest concern regarding diversity that a teacher should consider in relying heavily on group work and partner activities?

    a. Immigrant parents may object because they see the teacher as the one who ensures that students learn.

    b. Students from broken homes have most likely already been taught to rely on groups.

    c. Girls most often take on passive roles in mixed-gender groups.

    d. Students from low socioeconomic status (SES) homes tend to be unmotivated in group settings.

23. Darius is a teacher in a low-income urban neighborhood. In his student teaching, Darius's supervisor had him keep a reflective log. Each day he documented the events of the day, selected one to write about in detail, and then wrote an analysis of the episode applying the principles of effective teaching he learned in his classes. He decides to continue this into his beginning teaching practice. After several weeks, though, he finds that he is simply documenting his frustrations and not really improving his classroom performance. According to reflective practice as defined by the practice of reflection-in-action, what should Darius be doing to use reflection to improve as a teacher?

   a. He should abandon reflection until he has a year or two under his belt so that he has experience to draw upon.

   b. He should form a study group of other beginning teachers as a framework of mutual support.

   c. He must link what he recognizes from reflection to actions he can implement in his classroom.

   d. Now that he has access to experienced teachers, he should use them, not educational research, as his basis for reflection.

24. *Resocialization* is a tool used in motivating underachieving students who may be resistant to the educational process or apathetic toward school achievement. To cultivate interest in students who have developed poor attitudes and habits toward school, the teacher may engage in

   a. reducing the expectations on the students until they start to have success in academic tasks.

   b. using extrinsic rewards for a period until students begin to engage in tasks they initially consider irrelevant or boring.

   c. pairing students with others who are high achieving and can help them focus on academic skills.

   d. allowing students to spend more time in activities they like if they meet minimums in subjects they do not like.

25. Using inquiry strategies in the classroom actively involves students in lessons designed around questions about how the real world operates. Inquiry strategies are valuable because they develop critical thinking skills when the instruction is designed to do which of the following?

   a. Teachers do not explicitly teach critical thinking so the students can figure it out for themselves.

   b. Students are given only one or two situations to engage critical thinking so they can do it right.

   c. Teachers separate out the critical thinking and teach it before engaging real-world problems.

   d. The usefulness of critical thinking skills is discussed, especially when and where they are used.

26. Analysis of classroom instruction at the secondary level shows that 70–95% of instructional time centers on material from textbooks. Advantages of textbooks include the planning framework they provide teachers, the summary of information in the field, and that they are a convenient, common resource for student use. However, the use of textbooks has been legitimately criticized because

  a. they tend to focus on current, controversial topics and incite excessive reactions in students.

  b. some states require certain reading levels, so content gets modified in ways that compromise the integrity of the ideas.

  c. they tend to be written for the above average-performing student with remedial material for others.

  d. textbooks are written by content experts and they tend to go too deeply into a few topics.

27. Secondary education in the United States traces its existence back to 1635 in Boston, Massachusetts. After nearly 200 years of development, the first schools that resembled modern high schools appeared. The motivation for developing the public high school was primarily because

  a. the enrollments in middle schools became more than they could handle, and so older children got a separate system.

  b. colleges, seeking to prepare and enroll more students from poor families, developed a system of feeder public schools.

  c. existing grammar schools for college preparation and private academies were inadequate to prepare an educated workforce.

  d. many students were graduating from public junior high schools and they needed a place to continue their education.

28. In deciding how to structure reading groups in her class, a ninth-grade language arts teacher decides to emphasize opportunities for her students to develop relationships with children who are different from themselves; therefore, she applies a heterogeneous grouping strategy. In doing so, she assigns her four nonnative students (all English Language Learners) to four different groups (or the five in the class). She will have to be careful to be aware that

  a. if the nonnative students are successful in their reading groups they will become less comfortable with their nonnative peers.

  b. these groups will have to be focused by particular problems the students are having in language arts.

  c. such assignments can cause the nonnative students to be perceived as stereotypes of their heritage and not as individuals.

  d. regardless of the cultural issues, the groups should all contain some high, medium, and low-ability students.

Use the following information to answer question 29.

In a lesson on the structure of water molecules, Mr. Wilkins presents a series of PowerPoint® slides by a computer projector onto a screen. One of the slides is shown here:

The water molecule

- Consists of two hydrogen atoms covalently bonded to a single oxygen atom.
- The hydrogen atoms constantly pull at the electrons of the covalent bonds.
- This attraction for the shared electrons is called the electronegativity.
- The higher the electronegativity of the atom the more it pulls shared electrons toward its center of mass
- The electronegativities of the hydrogen and oxygen atoms are very different.
- Oxygen has one of the highest electronegativities of all elements
- Oxygen pulls the electrons closer to it than the hydrogen does.
- The unequal sharing of the electrons causes the water molecule to have a positive side and a negative side.
- This type of bond is called a polar covalent bond.

---

29. From an instructional design standpoint, what would be a proper assessment of this slide?

   a. Black on white color scheme is too harsh and should be yellow letters on a dark background.

   b. Putting the text over a picture of a water molecule would have made the information more memorable.

   c. Using the advantages of the computer, the teacher should have animation and exciting graphics.

   d. There is too much information for this single slide, and multiple slides should be used.

30. Which of the following are benefits of using small-group instruction to provide academic support to students with disabilities?

   I. Students can be grouped for basic skill practice when they are performing well below the rest of the class.

   II. Students can be grouped if they are having trouble mastering a specific skill.

   III. Students with disabilities can be put in small groups with higher performing students who provide role models for academic and social behavior.

   IV. Research shows that students with disabilities function better when they spend less time under the direct supervision of the teacher, as in whole-class instruction.

   a. I, II, and III

   b. I, II, and IV

   c. I and III only

   d. II and IV only

31. Daniel spent years collecting real-life examples of how math is used every day. He has an extensive collection of newspaper articles, food packages, travel situations, sports examples, and more. Every day he comes into class and poses a problem to his students. They must try to figure out, in their own way, how to solve the problem. He then relates the example to the math concept that is being learned that day. Which of the following is an accurate description of Daniel's practice?

    a. He is using anticipatory sets to link to real life and intrinsically motivate the students.

    b. He is using a scaffolding process which requires that the problems all be a little above the students' abilities.

    c. While these activities may motivate his students a little, the loss in effective use of class time offsets the benefit.

    d. If the problems require high-level thought they will be intrinsically motivating, but if they are low level, they will de-motivate the students.

32. Mr. Brophy has had a meeting with the mother of a student in his tenth-grade English class. The parent was bothered by Mr. Brophy's practice of calling on students randomly during class discussions. The mother expressed that her son says he always knows the answers to the questions, but he is shy and too embarrassed to speak in front of peers. Being a former teacher, the mother says that she never had problems running her class by offering questions to volunteers. Mr. Brophy, being familiar with the research behind classroom questioning, might offer which of the following in defense of his practice?

    a. The only way for the student to overcome his shyness is to be required to speak in front of peers.

    b. When students know they do not have to participate in discussion, they become passive and learning drops.

    c. If he allows one student to opt out of participating the students will single him out anyway.

    d. If he allows one student to opt out of participating he has to make the offer to others, which will reduce participation.

33. Metacognition is a teaching strategy that develops in students their ability to monitor their level of understanding of a topic and decide whether it is sufficient. Incorporating activities that develop metacognition is useful because

    a. it requires students to engage in the process of fitting new knowledge into one's existing background.

    b. it supports students so that they are able to achieve at higher levels than they could without support.

    c. it gives students a framework going into the lesson so that they know how to categorize new learning.

    d. it increases students' abilities to transfer learning to new situations without explicit prompting.

34. A middle school teacher provides her students with selective reading guides to assist them when they are expected to learn new material from their textbooks. This is a good strategy because it helps students to

  a. learn to apply metacognitive techniques to adjust the approach they take to reading different kinds of text.

  b. learn to acquire text information and interact with written materials when reading and studying.

  c. work in groups when reading is required to participate in the group discussions.

  d. develop the vocabulary they need for a reading assignment before they begin reading.

35. Transitions between parts of lessons are an important factor in maintaining good activity flow and effective instruction. Michael and his mentor, Liz, are focusing on the transition times in his lessons to help him improve in this area. Liz observes the following about Michael's classes:

   I. Michael gets students highly engaged in each activity and then they have difficulty switching to new activities.

  II. His transitions are highly structured—sometimes even more than the learning activities.

 III. Students save problems, e.g., searching for homework or asking to get books from their lockers, for lesson transitions.

 IV. Michael gives a lot of individual help in the activities and some students get off-task waiting for the next segment.

  Which of these are problems that make Michael's transitions vulnerable to disruptions?

  a. I, III, and IV

  b. I, II, and IV

  c. II, III, and IV

  d. I, II, III, and IV

36. A relatively large suburban district has a significant turnover in top administration. The new administration is led by a superintendent whose prior experience was as the Assistant Superintendent for Instruction of an urban district in another state. As part of instituting new professional development programs, the new administration seeks to create "subcultures" which focus on some aspect of high-quality teaching and research about teaching practices. Teachers can move into and out of these groups as their professional development needs change. Which of the following is a supportable observation about this effort?

  a. Research has shown that such a system provides social and organizational support for teacher development.

  b. Such a system is effective in sustaining an existing school culture but not in supporting change.

  c. Such a system would work only with senior teachers because they would dominate the groups.

  d. The administrators of the district would have to become part of the groups to keep them focused.

37. Quinn was having a discussion with a colleague about an article he read about direct instruction. Quinn's colleague shared several arguments against direct instruction, including that it decontextualizes learning and that *natural learning* comes from having experiences and then making sense, or *constructing learning*. Quinn responded by sharing the research support from the article, which included

  a. classical behaviorism demonstrates humans learn by reward systems that are the basis of direct instruction.

  b. most human behavior is learned through modeling, which is the theoretical basis of direct instruction.

  c. constructing knowledge requires significant related background experience and direct instruction does not.

  d. direct instruction works well when the teacher shows the students how to give feedback to each other.

38. Kerry is a high school math teacher. One of the students in Kerry's class has an Individualized Education Program (IEP) that allows him to have extended time on tests. One of the testing mechanisms Kerry uses is a power test—a timed test in which a student is scored based on how many problems she or he gets right in the given amount of time. Kerry calls the student aside at the end of the first day of class and says that he will have to take the power tests unmodified. The timing is the point of the test. Which of the following applies?

  a. Federal law obligates Kerry to meet the provisions of the IEP.

  b. If no other compromise can be found, Kerry must excuse the student from this form of testing.

  c. Kerry is within his rights to insist that the student maintain the academic integrity of the testing.

  d. Power testing is identified in federal law as a prohibited practice for students with disabilities.

39. Fred was assigned as a mentor to Mike when Mike joined the school district as a new teacher. Fred has been teaching the same subject as Mike, but for 17 years. After a year and a half, Mike feels he is not making much progress in planning ways to make his lessons go more effectively. He is especially concerned that his lessons do not focus on, or achieve the objectives of the district's curriculum. Which of the following is likely at work in this scenario?

  a. Teaching is fundamentally an art based on intuition and Fred cannot impart his intuitive actions to Mike.

  b. Experienced teachers plan for long, complex transitions between segments of their lessons, which keep them coherent.

  c. Mike and Fred need to recognize that new and experienced teachers approach planning and interactive decision making differently.

  d. Experienced teachers do not need to have internal structure in their lessons because they are better able to maintain students' attention.

40. After wrestling with classroom management issues in her first year, Mary decides to discuss the situation with her mentor. Mary believes that a rapid pace of instruction, especially during recitations, will help her to manage the classroom better. As students become distracted or off-task, she always tries to increase the pace of the lesson. Her mentor suggests that she look at professional development literature that discusses *wait time*. At the beginning of the next year, Mary uses some of the ideas she learned from the material she read. After every teacher question she makes the students wait at least three seconds before anyone can raise a hand to answer. After three weeks of seeing no improvement in student attention, she abandons the technique. Based on what you know, what would be the appropriate advice for this teacher?

   a. Wait time research showed promise in the 1970s but has largely been disproved since that time.

   b. The wait time period should be about three seconds for easy questions but 10–15 seconds for hard questions.

   c. Wait time is an effective method in early grades, but does not work with high school-aged students.

   d. Wait time is not appropriate after all questions, only for leading questions asking for high-level thought.

41. Mr. Bender teaches eleventh-grade social studies. In reflecting on his classroom practices, he is concerned about how much students are getting out of class discussions. In a recent discussion of the causes leading up to World War II, he found that the students answered all of his discussion questions quickly and fully in class. However, in an assessment essay right after the lesson, few students demonstrated a grasp of the material. In comparing his experience to research in effective questioning techniques, which of the following might he add to his practice to make discussions more effective?

   a. By offering points on the next test or quiz to students who answer questions in class, they will show more extrinsic motivation.

   b. By adding wait time to his low-level questions, he can read the faces of the students who are participating and those who are not actively involved.

   c. By making his questions more vague, his students will have to work harder to figure out what the question is asking.

   d. Repetition questions, asking different students to reconsider offered answers, focuses the students and maintains interaction with the teacher.

42. In preparing for parent-teacher conferences, high school teachers can maximize the effectiveness of the process by

   a. presenting written copies of the rules of the school and classroom and making the parents sign a copy.

   b. having examples of student work available and being prepared to discuss how this work reflects the student's learning against instructional goals.

   c. focusing on the problems that the student has and presenting a written list of needs for improvement.

   d. deflecting any criticism of the student and emphasizing his or her good traits and valuing the student's work.

43. Walt is a third-year biology teacher in a suburban district. He has been notified that this year he will have a student in his classes who has ADHD. Walt is given a collection of background materials, some of them dating back to the 1980s, to read to help him prepare to meet the needs of this student. Among the advice, Walt reads:

   I. Teachers should help ADHD students attend to what they eat because diet, food sensitivity, and sugar consumption make ADHD symptoms worse.
   II. Poor parenting is often a cause of ADHD and teachers must provide more classroom structure to compensate for the structure students do not receive at home.
   III. In designing instructional activities, teachers should keep in mind that ADHD students respond well to academic activities that have high personal relevance and substantial feedback on performance.
   IV. Variety of learning activities and high levels of challenge are likely to help keep ADHD students focused.

Based on more up-to-date research, which of the above is NOT true?
   a. I and III only
   b. II and III only
   c. II and IV only
   d. III and IV only

44. Ms. Englund is a novice teacher who has been assigned to Mr. Reeves as her mentor as she begins teaching high school math. Each week they sit down together and Ms. Englund talks through her plans for the lessons she expects to teach the following week. Mr. Reeves then critiques what he hears and offers refinements that he thinks might improve the planning process for these lessons. Ms. Englund then uses the planning forms required by the district to plan and document her lessons. Based on research-supported practices of the profession, this activity
   a. shows that the mentor does not value the opinions of the novice because he is always second-guessing her.
   b. should reverse the phases of giving and receiving information so that the mentor gives his advice first.
   c. is a form of *oral blueprinting* and is helpful prior to final, formal lesson planning for beginning teachers.
   d. is a form of *opinion substitution* whereby the novice teacher benefits from having bad decisions solved before they impact practice.

45. The role of using school activities to have an impact on the local community has been studied as a factor in student motivation. In general, the role of applying school learning in the context of the students' community is
   a. students are motivated by lessons that relate to them personally, but care less about how such things impact their community.
   b. adolescents are more motivated by learning if they see how it impacts the community in which they live.
   c. elementary students tend to be more motivated by lessons linked to their community and secondary students by lessons linked to their personal lives.
   d. learners of all ages are motivated when they see both the personal usefulness of what they are learning and how it impacts their community.

46. Moving from a private school to a medium-sized rural public school, Myra notices a difference in motivation of the students. She decides to try actively to promote interest in class. She decides to do an inventory of student attitudes and use this to increase academic motivation of the group. The inventory includes the following items:

- How do you like activity-oriented lessons such as field work or projects?
- What issues do you feel are important to you?
- How much would you like to do an assignment that includes making a presentation to a group outside of school?
- Has completing schoolwork ever given you a sense of pride? If so, when?

Based on the concepts and principles of student motivation, which of the following best describes this inventory?
   a. The teacher is trying to identify extrinsic motivational factors so that she can design an effective reward structure in the class.
   b. The teacher is trying to identify intrinsic motivational factors so that she can decide how to structure self-motivating lessons.
   c. The inventory assesses a mix of intrinsic and extrinsic motivational factors that can be applied in a variety of ways.
   d. The inventory assesses extrinsic motivational factors, but they are low on the needs scale and may not be effective.

47. Dan has been an early adopter of just about every form of teaching technology that he has become aware of in the last 12 years he has been in the classroom. When the school needed to hire a replacement technology coordinator, he eagerly applied and got the position. He worked with several other like-minded teachers to come up with a technology plan for the district. Which of the following should be the next logical step in implementing their plan?

   a. They should seek outside funding so that they can implement technology solutions without cost to the district.

   b. They should offer workshops to the teachers who have not shown high levels of interest in technology in the past.

   c. They should incorporate technology into all of the IEPs of students with special needs because the law requires schools to provide these resources.

   d. They should involve the administration of the school, which research shows is essential to the success of technology plans.

48. The social studies department of a large semi-rural school district has been using a commercially produced, nationally normed achievement test for ten years. In a cost-cutting move, the district has decided to stop using this testing service. The teachers get together over the summer and develop a test plan that is coordinated with the local curriculum (which is based on the state Learning Standards). Each teacher is to use the test plan to individually develop the tests and quizzes used in his or her classroom. Which of the following is a concern about how this plan might be carried out?

   a. The testing is likely to increase in validity, but teacher-made tests usually have low reliability.

   b. The testing is likely to decrease in validity, but teacher-made tests are usually gender-biased based on the gender of the teacher.

   c. The test plan is likely to assure test reliability, but validity and bias will be ongoing issues.

   d. The adherence to the state Learning Standards will assure that the tests have adequate reliability and validity.

49. A new teacher gets a job in a high school where the teaching practice has been a traditional teacher-centered approach. During student teaching, the new teacher worked in a classroom where cooperative learning was the dominant model of instruction. The new teacher starts off the year with two units built on cooperative learning projects. Based on data produced by many years of research into cooperative learning, what potential problems might this new teacher anticipate?

   a. Engagement of the students in learning may be limited as they adjust to a student-centered teaching model.

   b. Student competition for grades initially increases when cooperative learning practices are introduced.

   c. Achievement differences between majority culture students and minority students generally increase in cooperative classrooms.

   d. While social skills generally improve in cooperative classrooms, academic achievement usually goes down.

50. Jeffrey has moved from teaching life science for three years in a middle school to a high school assignment teaching tenth-grade biology. One of the students in his class is Mary Ellen, who is gifted with talents in mathematics, science, and music. Mary Ellen has participated in several summer programs, including a summer science research program at a local college. When the year begins, Mary Ellen consistently challenges Jeffrey on minutiae and irrelevant details about the concepts he is teaching. He decides to offer her an option—at the beginning of each unit, she can take the unit test. If she gets an 80 or above, she can spend four days a week on special projects that Jeffrey will create for her. She agrees. Which of the following would be an appropriate analysis of Jeffrey's plan?

a. Research has shown such curriculum compacting to work with students who are gifted and talented.

b. The 80 or above score that Jeffrey has set is too low to challenge Mary Ellen.

c. Jeffrey has probably created a problem for Mary Ellen's other teachers as she will expect the same treatment.

d. Jeffrey should offer the same option to all of his other students or he will be in violation of the IDEA act.

51. A consortium of English teachers from several different districts obtains a federal grant to improve assessment at the participating schools. Using the state Learning Standards, the teachers decide to create test banks that any of the participating schools can draw on to use in their classrooms. To develop the test bank, the teachers are paid to work in the summer. The test-writing group first prepares a broad overview of the content that should be covered in the 9–12 grade levels. They then decide to look at how the courses are taught at the member schools, but they find a wide variation in practices. Rather than try to do too much with the tests, they decide to survey the content, but not use information about how this content is covered in the individual schools. It is likely that this test bank will

a. have predictive validity for performance on the state tests, but will not have content validity.

b. have limited usability because the students will get different directions when they take the tests.

c. have curricular validity because it was prepared by teachers, but it will have low predictive validity.

d. have good content validity, but not have comparable curricular validity for each school.

52. Mr. Sauer is a tenured high school biology teacher. He is also a community activist and opposes the military and foreign policies of the president and administration. Every day he spends about 15–20 minutes of each class telling the students that the administration is corrupt and evil and that they need to begin to work for reforms "or you won't have a world to grow up in." Students complain to the school administrators, who meet with Mr. Sauer. They inform him that he must stop making political comments and teach the curriculum. Which of the following apply?

a. The teacher has the right of academic freedom to teach how he sees fit and the interference is illegal.

b. As long as his students are passing Regents exams at a rate equal to the state average, he can do what he wants.

c. The administrators can require him to minimize his comments to 5–10 minutes, but they cannot stop him entirely.

d. The teacher is responsible to teach the curriculum and cannot force his political views on a captive audience.

Use the information in the description that follows for questions 53 and 54.

Arni took a class in college which used portfolios for assessment. She wants to do the same for evaluating her tenth-grade English class. She convinces her principal to pay for an online electronic portfolio service as a pilot for one year.

53. Arni decides to use the portfolios for both formative and summative assessment in her class. Which of the following should she consider?
    a. The entries in a portfolio used for formative assessment are usually chosen by the student and those for summative assessment are usually required by the teacher.
    b. If she is going to use the portfolio for summative assessment she should evaluate it against a standard rubric that has been developed from national norms.
    c. Electronic portfolios have been shown to work for demonstrating factual and conceptual knowledge, but not for procedural or metacognitive knowledge.
    d. A portfolio is an effective assessment technique for higher-level skills but cannot effectively capture low-level, declarative knowledge.

54. At some point, Arni will have to convert her subjective evaluation into a score that can be reported on a grade report. The best method to do this in keeping with her choice to use portfolios would be
    a. having tests or quizzes in addition to the portfolio for numerical scoring.
    b. having tests or quizzes that will be included in the portfolio.
    c. using a rubric similar to one developed to score other performance tasks.
    d. allowing the students to make up assessment questions and testing them on those.

55. The physical environment, including spatial arrangements, affects a variety of classroom management factors including psychological security, that is, the feeling that the classroom is safe and comforting. Which of the following is a factor that can be used to create a psychologically secure environment?
    a. People tend to feel more secure and comfortable with items and surfaces that are soft to the touch.
    b. Placing desks near high-traffic areas tends to make users slow down and walk more carefully.
    c. Allow students to choose to sit near the walls or corners to maintain a feeling of privacy.
    d. Reduce decorations and other distractions that could cover walls or floors.

56. Eric teaches biology in a culturally diverse community. Which of the following is likely to be an effective strategy for working in a classroom in this community?
    a. use one main teaching strategy so that all students can adjust to it
    b. have the students all read literature from his culture so they can relate to him
    c. talk to teachers of the cultures represented in his school to build his own cultural understanding
    d. use norm-referenced grading so students learn how to compete for grades

57. Wally's classroom is an active center of projects, discussions, and active learning. Wally creates options for projects for his students and then helps them recognize the skills they need to accomplish the necessary tasks. Together they decide how the students will attain the skills and knowledge they require. They usually have the autonomy to choose how they will build their skill set and accomplish the tasks given. Which of the following is an observation about this teaching practice?

   a. This is a problem-based model that is based on the principles of classical behaviorism and will achieve low-level outcomes.

   b. This is a teacher-centered model because the teacher mediates all of the activity and can therefore control the outcomes.

   c. This is a content-heavy model of teaching, which puts the responsibility for learning the subject matter on the students.

   d. This is a student-centered model based on principles of constructivism, which assume that knowledge is personal, social, and cultural.

58. Roberta is teaching a unit from the district curriculum on the separation of Church and State. Her assessment is an essay in which the students compare the preambles of the U.S. Constitution with those of Australia and the Bahamas. The latter two documents declare the role of religion in the establishment of the state, while the U.S. Constitution makes no reference to God or any religion. The students generally write personal opinions to the effect that they feel God is important and therefore don't agree that government should be separated from organized religion. As Roberta reflects on these results, which of the following would be an appropriate basis for reflecting to improve her practice?

   a. She needs to know her students better so she can overcome their personal objections through her instruction.

   b. She needs to be more sensitive to the obvious feelings of the local community and possibly avoid this issue in the future.

   c. She needs to change her instruction to better focus on the key concepts and how they would be applied in the assessment.

   d. She needs to change the assessment so that the students have more structure to narrow their answers to what she wants to see.

59. A new social studies teacher accepts a job in a school district where there is a high proportion of English Language Learners (ELLs). Which of the following concepts should this teacher be aware of in planning to work with these students?

   a. Vocabulary should be focused on by separate instruction out of the context of the textbook.

   b. Readings should be selected that reduce unfamiliar content and vocabulary but teach the same concepts.

   c. Literacy learning is one area where scaffolding ELL students only makes them more dependent on the teacher.

   d. Information in textbooks often assumes background knowledge that may be different or lacking in ELL students.

60. Historically, children of diverse cultural backgrounds have encountered school subjects usually taught in both (1) an unfamiliar language, and (2) a culturally unfamiliar manner. Culturally diverse learners can find that their ways of thinking and interacting are regarded as deficits in the classroom. Teachers need to be aware that this can contribute to problems with which of the following?

    I. desired levels of language proficiency
   II. desired conceptual understanding of content
  III. physical maturation of the brain
  IV. multiple means of knowledge representation

    a. I and II only
    b. I, II, and III only
    c. I and IV only
    d. III and IV only

61. Ari is preparing to revise his courses of study. He will be teaching the same three classes he taught last year, which was his first year of teaching. He asks for and receives updated data on the following:

    I. needs assessment data from the school district
   II. pre-assessment and placement data: reading tests, aptitude tests, etc.
  III. instructional objectives from the local curriculum plans in his discipline.

In addition, which of the following would best aid Ari in preparing course of study documents?
    a. The goals of the school or district in his area and the grades above and below.
    b. The unit plans of the teacher he replaced: a 20-year teaching veteran.
    c. The grades of the students who will be taking his class this year.
    d. The instructional objectives from the other subjects at the same grade levels.

62. Sexual harassment and sex discrimination have long been problems in public education. Federal law requires that public schools have clear policies to combat sexual harassment and have grievance procedures for handling sex discrimination and sexual harassment complaints. These laws apply to
    a. anyone, including all students, who engage in sexual harassment or discrimination.
    b. adults and students over the age of 14 who engage in sexual harassment or discrimination.
    c. students who harass other students who are younger and any adults who engage in sexual harassment or discrimination.
    d. only adults who engage in sexual harassment or discrimination.

Use the following information to answer question 63.

The mission statement of a high school is posted on the wall where students and visitors can see it as they enter. It reads, in part:

> Our school uses an active learning educational program to teach the academic skills required by New York State Learning Standards. Our programs are based on (1) a student-centered curriculum that accommodates student interests and learning styles, and (2) a belief that learning requires a commitment to learning by students and their parents. The daily schedule is focused on students' needs and interests. The curriculum integrates the areas of citizenship, physical, intellectual, social, aesthetic, and career development into lessons that take place in the classroom and the community beyond.

63. This mission statement expresses an educational philosophy of
   a. behaviorism, where the focus is on student behavior, assuming that the academic skills will evolve from learning.
   b. constructivism, in which the student is active, learning is less structured, and authentic assessment is likely to be used.
   c. progressivism, where the teacher, not the curriculum, is the primary source of authority and evaluator of student learning.
   d. humanism, in which external motivations and controls assure that the students are engaged in authentic learning.

64. According to the cultural deficit theory of minority achievement, the social, cultural, and language backgrounds of children from minority cultures hold them back from performing well academically. In this view of multicultural education, minority children enter school without the "cultural capital" on which teachers, textbooks, and administrators build academic learning. Which of the following are valid observations about cultural deficit theory?

   I. This theory "blames" children and their families for the lack of success of the school program.
   II. The only solution to the problems the theory implies would be to revise the entire curriculum.
   III. Cultural deficit implies the schools must help children catch up, when this approach usually widens achievement gaps.
   IV. Schools who subscribe to cultural deficit almost always track students, which lowers teacher expectations and student performance

   a. I and II only
   b. II and IV only
   c. I and III only
   d. II and III only

65. The school faculty is developing a plan to deal with several recent events of cyber-bullying. Several proposals generate considerable discussion among the teachers and administrators. An expert brought in to help the school develop its policies advises that all of the following have significant problems EXCEPT
   a. advising students to delete messages from individuals who have bullied them in the past before they even read them.
   b. creating a public list of students found to have bullied others and posting it on a website.
   c. involving the police in cases where bullying messages contain physical threats.
   d. not taking action against students who only use words, as statements are protected by the First Amendment.

Use the following information to answer question 66.

One of the useful strategies in developing reading strategies is to use a think aloud procedure. Layla creates a series of lessons where she uses a series of short readings through which she demonstrates reading strategies. She puts a transparency on the overhead that has the steps of the strategy for the students to follow. She then takes them through the process—providing explanations and asking questions to check for understanding.

66. The next step she should use in modeling by using the think aloud procedure would be to
   a. read a passage out loud to the class while stopping at key points to prompt thinking or ask questions.
   b. have all of the students read different parts of the text out loud and tell how they relate to what they read.
   c. have the students all read the same text passage and then share their thinking with a partner.
   d. have the students read a passage, write a response in their journals, and then read their journal entries out loud to the class.

Use the following information to answer question 67.

Jackie's parents divorced when she was five. At that time, her mother got custody of Jackie and her father moved out of state. After years of little contact, Jackie's father moved back to the area and wants to establish a relationship with his daughter. She is now in eleventh grade. Her father wants to know how she is doing in school and so makes a request to see her records. When Jackie's mother finds out, she calls the school and demands that they not release any records without her approval, which she will not give.

67. Which of the following best describes this situation?

    a. As a parent, even though he does not have custody, her father has a legal right to see his daughter's records.

    b. Because she is over 14, Jackie can give permission for her father to see her records.

    c. The school could have allowed the father to have the records until the point where the custodial parent opposed it.

    d. Jackie's mother, as custodial parent, can deny access to records by the noncustodial parent.

68. A great deal of time is spent in most classrooms in recitation or the initiation-response-evaluation pattern of communication. Although this is a model of instruction that is in use in most classrooms, it suffers from the limitation that

    a. the active role of the teacher allows him or her to easily foster conversations and interactions among the students in the class.

    b. the teacher usually manages the conversation in a way that emphasizes higher-level thinking about key concepts.

    c. it grew out of white, middle-class values and does not match the discourse styles of students with different cultural backgrounds.

    d. the teacher can minimize gender and cultural differences by deciding which students get to participate in the discussion.

69. Jean came from a teacher education program with a strong background in developmental theories. After several weeks of observing students, she feels she has a pretty good idea of the degree to which each one uses concrete or abstract operations, as well as their varied problem-solving approaches. Jean prepares a unit of instruction with tasks aligned with her assessment of the developmental levels of her students. The unit has mixed results. What possibly explains the limited success with such a carefully designed unit of instruction?

    a. Student development and readiness can vary widely over a period of days or weeks.

    b. Because the unit introduced new material, the teacher must anticipate a drop of two years in student developmental levels.

    c. Developmental levels can tell the teacher how well students think abstractly but not how they deal with low-level information.

    d. Informal assessment of student development is not as precise as Jean would like.

70. Paul is an English teacher in a suburban high school. Newly out of college, he sees it as important to relate to his students and have them relate to him. In teaching a unit on poetry, he asks several students to bring in music that they listen to. After screening the songs and selecting interesting ones, he uses this material in teaching poetry and poetry interpretation. He is disappointed when the effort has limited results. The same students show interest and participate in class with the addition of only a few others. In trying to motivate performance in his activity, what has Paul overlooked?

    a. Motivation requires that students perceive a need and see an educational action as meeting that need. The lesson did not establish that need.

    b. Students are most highly motivated by aesthetic needs and not all students perceive the same music as aesthetically pleasing.

    c. High school students are so highly motivated by social and belonging needs and they do not see the attention of a teacher as significant.

    d. High school teachers must first establish a system of extrinsic rewards to capture students' interest and then move to intrinsic rewards.

71. Ling is struggling to help her students read the textbook independently in her science class. She reads an article in a professional journal about using vocabulary-building strategies to help struggling readers in content area instruction. She should be aware that a factor that limits students' ability to use context as a vocabulary strategy is

    a. context cues are dependent on the text itself and not the background of the reader.

    b. the context material that reveals an unfamiliar word must be close to the word.

    c. good context cues are subtle and require the reader to work hard to discern them.

    d. footnotes, boldface type, or parenthetical definitions are the most effective context cues.

Use the following information to answer question 72.

The tenth-grade class is going on a field trip to a local museum. In preparation, the students must get a parent to sign a permission form and return it to the school. The permission form states:

> We will be going on a field trip to the City Science Museum on April 20. Before your child can participate, he or she must have a signed permission form on file. By signing this permission form, you agree that neither the school nor any of its employees may be held responsible for any accident or injury that occurs on the trip.

All of the students return their forms. When they get to the museum, the two chaperoning teachers give all of the students an assignment sheet that they can complete by examining the exhibits. The teachers go to the snack bar for coffee.

72. While they are there, a student falls from a balcony and is seriously injured. Which of the following applies?

  a. The teachers are fully protected by the permission forms the parents signed.

  b. The teachers are liable because they did not supervise the students in a reasonably responsible way.

  c. The teachers share responsibility with the museum because they had reason to believe the students would be safe.

  d. The teachers are partially liable because the students were old enough to assume partial responsibility for their safe conduct.

73. Steve is a second year teacher who has had a formal observation by his principal. In the class of juniors, Steve was trying to implement a discussion model lesson. There are 13 girls in the class and 14 boys. In the follow-up conversation, the principal shows Steve the following data chart:

	High-level questions	Low-level questions
Boys	|||	卌 卌 |||
Girls	||||	卌 卌 ||||

Which of the following is a valid observation about Steve's lesson?

  a. The ratio of low-level questions shows this was more of a recitation lesson than discussion and not likely to achieve the outcomes he wants.

  b. The ratio of low-level questions is appropriate for a discussion model and if he wants higher-level outcomes he should use direct instruction.

  c. The ratio of questions between boys and girls shows a bias against boys which is likely to affect the classroom climate.

  d. The question ratios are appropriate and Steve can achieve higher-level thinking by asking application-level questions on his test.

74. Bob Anderson discovers that several of his seventh-grade science students believe that air pushing down on things causes gravity. He explains that gravity is a function of mass and that the size of the earth is what gives it its gravity. The students stick doggedly to their belief, arguing that there is no gravity in space because there is no air in space. His further explanations do little to persuade the students. Which of the following factors most likely contribute to this situation?

    a. Cause-effect thinking is underdeveloped at this age and the concepts of gravity and mass are abstract.

    b. While students this age are capable of abstract thought, they revert to concrete thought under stress.

    c. Students this age have a stronger social awareness than self-concept and they go along with their peer's stated beliefs.

    d. Students this age cluster their learning and unless they have sufficient real experience, they can't grasp abstract ideas.

75. When fully integrating curricula, subject matter boundaries become unclear and may even disappear. Students engage topics holistically and are more likely to engage real-life problems in meaningful ways. However, before engaging in the time and coordination required for integrated planning, teachers need to be aware of which drawback?

    a. While the integration of content may make it seem more relevant to students, there is greater responsibility on them to connect concepts.

    b. Because there are more subjects involved in each lesson, more transitions are required, making less time available for instruction.

    c. Integration often leads to de-emphasis of content because the integration may lead teachers into content in which they are not experts.

    d. Teacher planning time is limited and efforts to integrate instruction and content will lead to decreased communication among teachers.

76. In constructing knowledge of the real world into knowledge structures of the mind, students take in information through experience or learning activities. When the new learning does not match the predictions of the student based on prior learning, disequilibrium occurs. To bring their understanding back into balance students must

    a. scaffold the new experience so that it can be incorporated into the old.

    b. modify existing mental structures so that they match to the new experience.

    c. take in additional data from the learning situation until balance is restored.

    d. all of the above

77. Dale has taught junior high general science for 11 years. This year, because of a retirement, he has been reassigned to teach biology because he is certified and the school cannot find another teacher. As a conservative Christian, Dale does not believe in the theory of evolution. When it comes up in the curriculum, he only assigns the reading in the book and in class explains why evolution is false. He offers in place of instruction on evolution, lessons on intelligent design, the idea that living creatures were designed by a higher, supernatural power which he does not name. Which of the following apply?
  a. In that he does not identify God as the designer, he is within his rights to teach alternate theories to evolution.
  b. As a certified biology teacher, he is entitled to teach the subject any way that he sees fit.
  c. As an agent of the school board, he must teach the approved curriculum which cannot, by federal law, include intelligent design.
  d. If the school board had approved a curriculum including intelligent design his actions would have been acceptable.

78. Katie is mentoring a new colleague, Brenda. In their discussions of classroom management, they discuss the issues using a framework of direct versus indirect environmental effects. Select the one of the following four factors that is an indirect environmental effect.
  a. The teacher uses a lot of small group work with students tested individually to assess their learning.
  b. The students periodically complete self-assessments that help them to recognize their learning strengths and weaknesses.
  c. The teacher posts a list of rules for what is required of all reports, essays, and other written work.
  d. The students assume, from the arrangement of the desks, that the teacher does not really want them to interact and discuss.

79. A middle school faculty has decided to try portfolios as a way to assess their progress in improving reading scores through their content classes. Sharon has been using portfolios in some limited ways in her classroom for several years and she has found them to be a powerful tool. To convince her colleagues to make more use of portfolio assessment, she needs to bring more than her personal experience to the discussion. She does some research and finds that portfolio assessment of reading has shown benefits including:

  I. matching the activities where the students learned the material on which they are being assessed.
  II. the assessment measures all of the students on the same learning objectives in the same way.
  III. providing a collaborative approach to assessment, which can lead to better self-assessment.
  IV. linking the assessment process more closely to teaching and learning than tests do.

  a. I, III, and IV
  b. II, III, and IV
  c. I and III only
  d. I, II, III, and IV

Use the following information to answer question 80.

Marion had fond memories of an English professor she had in college. The professor would have the students read a work and write a reaction paper, usually with a vague prompt or none at all. He would then read their papers before class and then lead a discussion based on examples he gleaned from their essays. Each lesson would come together at the end with a concise explanation of an important principle of writing. Marion tried this approach in her ninth-grade English class for a lesson on foreshadowing with disappointing results. The student writings had weak examples from which she could draw and they could not make the connection among the examples until Marion directly pointed them out.

80. Which of the following explains what occurred in this lesson?
   a. Such a concept attainment lesson depends on students having a basic understanding of the examples from which the idea is refined.
   b. Ninth graders are in the developmental stage of concrete operations and not capable of the deductive thought required in the lesson.
   c. To be sure such a deductive lesson works effectively, she needed to "plant" some students with correct responses before class.
   d. Foreshadowing is not a concept, and therefore students would not be able to see the pattern even if it were stronger.

Written Assignment

There is ongoing controversy around the inclusion of students with special needs in regular education classrooms. In some cases, parents worry about the presence of students with special needs affecting academic performance in classes. Alternately, full inclusion implies that "regular" classes are the best placement for students with special needs. Imagine that your school district has adopted a mission statement that includes the following goal statement:

Our goal is to provide full inclusion of all students with disabilities in every classroom setting through person-centered and family-centered planning, maximizing student success and resulting in skill in student self-determination.

Write an essay for New York State educators, framing your response by:

- Identifying the grade level and subject area in which you are preparing to teach
- Explaining how research has demonstrated that full inclusion is a desirable goal for students with disabilities

- Describing one potential drawback of the district's plan for students with disabilities and one potential drawback for "regular" students
- Describing for each potential drawback a strategy you could use in your classroom to minimize or eliminate problems
- Using sound educational principles, explaining why you expect that the strategies you recommended could help achieve the district's educational goal.

►Answers

1. a. Convergent questions have one simple correct answer. Divergent questions have many right answers. The students only get to practice their thinking on convergent questions in the lessons while they are assessed with a divergent question on the quiz. Choice **c** incorrectly identifies the levels of the questions: The lesson questions are knowledge level and the quiz question is synthesis.

2. b. PL 94-142 and the court decisions of that era ushered in the reforms in the educational rights of persons with disabilities that continue today. Choices **a**, **c**, and **d** are incorrect: Sputnik led to reforms in math and science education, Title IX was passed in 1972 and prohibits sex discrimination, and *Brown v. Board of Education* struck down the "separate but equal" policy in public education.

3. d. Academic freedom at the secondary school level allows teachers to make instructional decisions about how to implement the approved curriculum. The R rating of the movie precluded showing it to minors, whether or not they were allowed to excuse themselves. The teacher should have never allowed the movie to be shown without determining the film rating and content.

4. b. In such a discussion, students *should* take personal positions, but not be forced to publicly participate if they do not want to. Teacher questions are the tool by which the teacher shapes and advances discussions. By making the environment safe for various positions, more students will voluntarily participate and feel free to take personal positions.

5. a. Students in Kohlberg's Good Interpersonal Relationships stage of moral development believe that good behavior means having good motives and interpersonal feelings such as concern for others.

6. c. The only strategy among the four offered that has not been shown to be effective is III. Schools should provide ways for students to communicate with adults about rumors and threats and the school should deal with them publicly.

7. d. While choices **a**, **b**, and **c** describe research-supported benefits of cooperative learning, the model does not allow for rapid acquisition of the kind of low-level content traditionally tested by high-stakes tests.

8. a. Problem-based learning provides students with real-world problems in a limited context. The students must create the method by which they will solve the problem before they can work on the solution itself. The responsibility for their learning is similar to roles they will have to play in adult life.

9. a. The practice described is an *additive approach*. While it does include more cultural perspectives, the dominant culture is still the focus of instruction and students perceive the implied value judgment that the majority culture is more important. The *contributions approach* described in choice **b** is similar, but the teacher did not ask the students to limit what they bring to class to holiday and food-related materials.

10. c. The Learning Standards provide broad guidance in the subject area, core curricula develop this guidance into a scope and sequence of topics and skills, and the resource guides provide supporting examples and assessment guidance.

11. d. Ron's inability to react to information he does not understand and his failure to use strategies for remembering information are indicative of passive learners. Being a passive learner is often a characteristic of students with learning disabilities.

12. **d.** Individualizing the curriculum and differentiating instruction have driven educational progress in the past 20 years. While a case could be made for choice **c** due to the emphasis on high-stakes testing, choice **d** is the better answer because it serves as a link both to improved instruction and better assessment.

13. **b.** Students are intrinsically motivated to engage in topics that relate to themselves directly.

14. **b.** Data should be presented graphically in the simplest form possible that allows for the concept being learned to be expressed. The remaining choices are incorrect because data from the Internet (choice **a**) would have defeated the motivational intent of the activity and student data entry (choice **c**) is positive because it engages more active learning, and far outweighs the concern about accurate entry.

15. **a.** One of the defenses a teacher may use to justify classroom practices is to follow the practices of the profession. Knowing about identical or similar lessons that are available at professional conferences, journals, or valid websites can help a teacher justify a controversial practice.

16. **c.** Learning styles are relatively stable personal (not cultural) characteristics. While it is not possible to adapt every lesson for all of the learning styles of your students, learning styles are a useful planning tool.

17. **c.** Choice **c** is the only option that excludes both incorrect responses. Motivational Theory is incorrectly described in I; Behaviorist Theory (IV) does not apply to the situation.

18. **c.** Beginning teachers typically lack economy in their lesson presentations. They include both too much information and irrelevant content about a concept. As teachers gain experience and feedback, they can present material in more straightforward and logical ways.

19. **c.** One major strength of tutorial programs is the ability to allow students to work at their own pace. None of the other options have evidence to support their efficacy.

20. **d.** Putting technologies into classrooms for the sake of having them there does not provide educational benefits. Many times in the past, computers and certain types of programs were implemented in classrooms in an "answer seeking a question" way. Technologies should be implemented as the best possible solution to a clearly-defined problem. Choices **a**, **b**, and **c** are all recommendations taken directly from the International Society for Technology in Education.

21. **c.** Guidelines provided by the New York State Education Department state that the district may define the role of mentors as strictly guidance or of evaluation. This designation must be within any requirements set forth in the collective bargaining agreement. The novice teacher should clarify the role of his or her mentor at the beginning of the process.

22. **c.** Research shows that girls tend to take on passive roles in small groups or partner situations especially when hands-on activities are involved. The remaining choices are examples of inappropriate stereotyping, and are not valid concerns.

23. **c.** Reflection must not only be thinking about what is happening in one's classroom. While it is good that Darius is comparing his experience to the body of research of the profession, he must also use it to plan future action by linking to actions he will take.

24. **b.** To resocialize students, the teacher must find ways to motivate students without reducing expectations. While extrinsic rewards will make students teacher-dependent in the long run, they can be used to reengage students as a short-term solution.

25. d. Only choice **d** accurately describes a benefit of teaching critical thinking. Choices **a**, **b**, and **c** are incorrect: Teachers should explicitly teach critical thinking skills, students should have many opportunities to apply them, and critical thinking should be fully integrated into the inquiry problem.

26. b. Concerns about reading level have caused textbook material to be written for reading levels in ways that oversimplify or create improper emphasis on important topics. Choices **a**, **c**, and **d** are incorrect: Textbooks have been shown to focus on noncontroversial, bland topics, written for the average student, and treat topics too superficially, not deeply.

27. c. In 1821, a school that became the English High School opened in Boston. The idea spread in response to the need to educate more children than could be handled by existing Latin grammar schools and private academies.

28. c. The teacher will have to work to be sure the non-native students do not become "token" representatives of their culture for the other students. In choice **d**, research shows that such arrangements cause middle-level achievement students to get left out of interactions. Achievement levels in groups should be medium-low with low and medium-high with high.

29. d. Using an electronic medium, it takes no more expense and very little extra time to put less information on more slides. In the case in question, the students surely would be struggling to read and take notes from the slide while the teacher is explaining the material. In such a presentation, it is more effective to present one key idea at a time.

30. a. Options I, II, and III are all supported by research. Option IV is incorrect because research shows that students with disabilities function better when they spend *more* time under the direct supervision of the teacher, as in whole-class instruction.

31. a. Interesting questions, anecdotes, or problems can motivate students to attend to lessons if the students can relate to the situation. These activities are anticipatory sets and can help the teacher link lessons to students' lives and have a powerful motivational effect.

32. b. Research into classroom questioning shows that there must be equitable distribution of questions to maintain active learning and communicate high expectations for all. The teacher and parent should try to find other strategies to help the student learn to participate in class.

33. d. Choice **d** is an accurate description of a benefit of metacognition. Choice **a** describes assimilation, choice **b** describes scaffolding, and choice **c** describes advanced organizers.

34. b. Selective reading guides help students learn to respond selectively to text. This aids them in knowing how to process information in subject areas.

35. a. Choice **a** leaves out item II—highly structured transitions. Transitions should be carefully structured to reduce the chances of students beginning to socialize or move around the room.

36. a. Research has shown that such a system provides social and organizational support for teacher development. Choices **b**, **c**, and **d** are all false statements. In building capacity for change, districts of sufficient size may use the mechanism of professional development "subcultures" to implement change and bring teachers of different levels together for improving practice. In addition, such systems can be managed collaboratively by teachers.

37. b. Social learning theory works as a basis for direct instruction and proposes that much of what humans learn is done by observing others and then modeling their behaviors. Choices **a**, **c**, and **d** are incorrect: Social learning theory goes beyond classical behaviorism; direct instruction must also link to students' prior knowledge, and requires the teacher to provide significant feedback on performance.

38. a. Kerry is obligated to make adjustments as described in the student's Individualized Education Program (IEP). Kerry should participate in IEP meetings to make a case for this testing practice if it is important. However, Kerry cannot simply tell the student he will not receive his IEP-prescribed modification.

39. c. Research has shown that experienced teachers plan in different ways from novice teachers including: (1) they think differently about planning, (2) they do more planning informally, and (3) they rely less on overt objectives.

40. d. *Wait time* gives students time to think of answers to questions requiring application, analysis, or other high-level thought. The scenario implies that the teacher did not change the kind of questions she asked, only that she added wait time to each question. She should be asking fewer, but higher level, questions.

41. d. Repetition questions, as described in the answer, simply ask another student to reconsider the answer offered by a classmate. Repetition questions are better than repetition statements by the teacher because they provide informal feedback to the teacher as to the depth of understanding of the students.

42. b. The parents need to understand what the goals of instruction are and how their child is performing. Choices **a** and **c** are needlessly negative practices. Choice **d** does not advance any important educational objective.

43. d. Although dietary issues (I) and poor parenting (II) have historically been attributed to causing or exacerbating ADHD, more recent research has proven that these are not contributing factors.

44. c. Oral blueprinting allows the initial planning to be controlled by the novice teacher and to have guidance provided by a supportive mentor. This benefits the novice by getting the advice of the mentor before the lessons and also to establish a basis for reflection with the mentor after teaching the lessons.

45. d. When considering the use of the local community in providing context for school learning, research shows that this increases motivation both from the standpoint of personal interest and also because students feel useful to their communities.

46. b. The teacher is trying to find out what motivates these students from within (intrinsic). By using these to structure lessons, she should spend less time externally motivating the students.

47. d. Research has shown that active support by administrators, especially superintendents, is required for reform efforts, particularly regarding technology implementation. The actions described in choices **a**, **b**, and **c** would ultimately commit district resources.

48. a. Validity is a measure of how well the assessment matches the expectations of the instruction. Because the teachers are teaching the classes and making up the tests, they are likely to be more valid than commercially produced tests. However, commercially produced tests have their items tested and refined against field data, so they are more reliable than teacher-made tests.

49. a. Students need time to develop the skills necessary to learn in a cooperative learning setting. In that they have not seen cooperative learning before this (as implied in the question) it is likely to take these students longer to adjust. Effects on grades (choice **b**), cultural differences (choice **c**), and academic achievement (choice **d**) depend on effective implementation of the model and are not linked to the newness of the model for students.

50. a. Curriculum compacting such as Jeffrey is doing helps when students do not find the regular curriculum challenging. Mary Ellen is demonstrating that she has a grasp of required material before she has access to advanced study projects.

51. d. The process described is likely to assure coverage of the content (content validity). Curricular validity is a reflection of the knowledge and skills as they are presented in the curriculum of the course. The process as described would most likely lead to weak curricular validity.

52. d. The teacher is an agent of the school board and is required to teach to the curriculum the board approves. While the teacher could make occasional comments outside the curriculum, the law regards students as a captive audience, and they are protected against non-instructional actions such as those described.

53. a. Portfolios used for formative (instructional) assessment generally use student-chosen artifacts. The students demonstrate their judgment and understanding of their own work by the artifacts they choose. In summative assessment, students must be assessed against the same norms or criteria, so usually the teacher must require entries that illustrate performance.

54. c. If the teacher uses portfolios for assessment but bases evaluation on tests and quizzes (choice **a** or **b**) the students devalue the portfolios, which reduces or eliminates their effectiveness. A rubric allows the teacher to quantify (within a range of reliability) the subjective assessment of the portfolio.

55. a. Items that are soft and responsive to touch have been shown to generate feelings of security and comfort. All of the other choices are the opposite of practices that increase psychological security in the classroom.

56. c. Only choice **c** is an effective practice in culturally diverse classrooms. Choices **a**, **b**, and **d** are incorrect: Eric should *vary* his teaching strategies to aid all students. *He* should read literature *from the cultures of his students*, and be sensitive to cultures that de-emphasize competition.

57. a. This is a problem-based model, but does not build on behaviorism (choice **a**) rather, on constructivism. It is student-centered (not choice **b**) and process-oriented (not choice **c**). Constructivism utilizes the philosophy of John Dewey and theorists who emphasize the social, culturally influenced personal construction of meaning.

58. c. The central goal of teaching is student learning and the students substituted their personal opinions from the content they were taught (but obviously disagreed with). Roberta already knows, as implied in choice **a**, what the objections will be on this topic. Choice **b** implies changing the curriculum, which has already been approved by the district (as stated in the stem of the question). Choice **d** is incorrect because the assessment is already aligned with the instructional objective and does not need to be changed.

59. d. Teachers should be aware of needed background knowledge and the differences ELL students bring to their classrooms. Choices **a**, **b**, and **c** are incorrect: ELL students benefit from learning vocabulary in context, they should not have their academic expectations lowered by "easy" materials, and scaffolding is appropriate instructional support.

60. a. Research shows that when taught without regard to their backgrounds, culturally diverse students do not attain a desired level of language proficiency (I) and they do not understand concepts in the same way as their peers (II).

61. a. All schools should have identified goals that are to be accomplished in each course over the academic year. These should already be aligned with state Learning Standards in the discipline.

62. **a.** Title IX, passed in 1972, is intended to protect anyone from sexual harassment from any other individual in settings where federal funding is received.

63. **b.** The active learning, student-needs centeredness, flexibility, and authentic learning implied by the mission statement are hallmarks of constructivist philosophy. In addition, none of the other schools of philosophy are described appropriately.

64. **c.** Cultural deficit theory would suggest that remediation for minority students occurs, not wholesale change in the curriculum (II). There is no connection between cultural deficit theory and the practice of tracking (IV).

65. **c.** Students should not delete bullying messages but show them to a trusted adult. Naming names publicly may violate federal privacy rights, especially those of minors. Speech meant to intimidate or harm children is not protected speech. Only choice **c** is appropriate policy advice for schools.

66. **a.** The think-aloud strategy is a technique of modeling the thinking process by an expert (the teacher). Options other than choice **a** do not include any teacher modeling.

67. **a.** The Buckley Amendment (P.L. 93-380 amended by P.L. 93-568), also called the Family Education Rights and Privacy Act (FERPA), requires that either parent, even the noncustodial parent, has a right to see the records of his or her child. If the student was 18 or over, she could request to see records on her own.

68. **c.** The initiation-response-evaluation model assumes that the students will listen quietly to teacher presentations and respond individually in turn to teacher questions. Students with different cultural backgrounds may bring a more active and participatory discourse pattern to the classroom, be peer-oriented rather than teacher-oriented, or decide for themselves when to participate.

69. **d.** Most teachers rely on informal assessments of students' cognitive capabilities. These may be generally good, but other factors confound one's abilities to identify the abilities of individual students. Further, experienced, expert teachers demonstrate a more effective ability to read subtle cues and adapt lessons to what they see.

70. **a.** Motivation is the connection between the students' perception of needs and how they see possible actions as meeting those needs. The teacher did not establish what need his students have as regards the subject and further, does not seem to have tried to link actions to meeting those needs.

71. **b.** Choices **a** and **c** are incorrect because context cues *are* dependent on reader background and have a clear—not subtle—connection. Footnotes, boldface type, and parenthetical definitions, described in choice **d**, are not context cues.

72. **b.** Even with a signed permission form, teachers have a responsibility to act as reasonably responsible adults in supervising the students in their care. If a teacher's behavior is negligent, he or she is liable for damages. Tenth graders may be responsible to act in ways appropriate to their age, but to leave a group completely unsupervised is almost certainly negligent.

73. **a.** A discussion model is designed to build conceptual understanding, engage the students, and build communication skills and thinking processes. This is achieved by asking higher-level questions that allow the students to practice these skills with feedback. The use of low-level, factual questions to check for understanding is an indicator of a recitation lesson.

74. **a.** A strong grasp of cause-effect relationships normally develops in adolescents around age 15, older than the seventh graders in question.

75. **c.** Integrated instruction may cause teachers to cover content in which they are not expert so as to match subjects more closely. Choices **a**, **b**, and **d** are incorrect: Integrated planning is shown to make more explicit connections for students, require fewer transitions, and increase communication among teachers.

76. **b.** The modification of existing, limited knowledge structures is accommodation, which is the process of cognitive growth.

77. **c.** In a series of Supreme Court and lower federal rulings, theories of supernatural creationism, including intelligent design, are religious, not scientific teachings. As such, they, or any other religious positions in any classes, may not be included in the public school curriculum. While public schools may teach about religions from an historical, sociological, or other perspective, they may not teach the precepts of any religion as fact.

78. **d.** An indirect effect is one that leads to a behavior that impacts learning. The conditions of the environment themselves do not impact learning.

79. **a.** Portfolios measure individual students' achievements in ways that allow for individual differences, which makes II inappropriate. All of the other descriptors are supported by research.

80. **a.** Concept attainment lessons are based on inductive reasoning and require that students attend to critical attributes of the concept being learned. To do so, they must be familiar with the examples that are used in the lesson.

Written Assignment

Essay 1 (weak)

As educators we know that each of our classes will include some disabled students. I believe it is our responsibility as educators to meet the needs of all students in the best way possible. As I will be teaching high school English, I have to be ready to deal with these students who will be in my classes.

Research has shown that full inclusion is a desirable goal in high school classes. In my classroom, I will do everything I can to see that disabled students achieve as much as regular students in learning lessons about literature, grammar, and writing. This is desirable because in American schools we educate each student to the best of their ability and this includes special needs students.

One potential drawback to the district's goal is they do not say what they will do when the special education students cannot keep up. As teachers, we have 30 or more students in every class we teach and we have to get them ready to pass tests at the end of the year. Special education students have to take the same tests as the rest of the kids and they cannot always keep up. This will be bad for the school's test scores and bad for the self-esteem of the special ed students.

One potential drawback for the regular students is that they will get frustrated by being held back by the special ed students trying to keep up. I remember in my own school we had three students in my tenth-grade English class who had a hard time keeping up. My teacher told us that she had to stay on a lesson until these kids got it because that is what the principal wanted.

I think that I could help these kids keep up with the rest of the class if I had them stay after school or come in during their free time to make up work. By spending more time with the special education kids, they would be able to better keep up with the rest of the class and then the regular students would not get mad at them.

I would also tell the other students that the district has a goal of full inclusion and we all have to help them keep up with the class.

Evaluation

While the writer identified the subject he or she is preparing to teach, the grade level was not specified as requested by the question prompt. In the answer, the author does not refer to professional educational concepts nor use the vocabulary of the profession. The ideas expressed come from the author's common sense analysis of teaching and at one point the writer uses a personal anecdote as evidence for a claim made in the essay. Anecdotes are not evidence and should be avoided in your essay.

Explain how research has demonstrated that full inclusion is a desirable goal for students with disabilities. The author's response is vague and based on a common sense analysis of classroom issues. It restates the phrasing of the question saying that "inclusion is a desirable goal" without providing any professional defense of the assertion. It does not demonstrate a grasp of learner characteristics, instruction, assessment, or the professional environment. It does not refer to any research-validated educational concepts. Further, the current language of the profession is not used. The author refers to *special education students*, *disabled students*, and *special ed students*.

Describe one potential drawback of the district's plan for students with disabilities and one potential drawback for "regular" students. Neither of the proposed drawbacks demonstrates a grasp of the professional issues. The assertions that are made are not supported by the professional literature in the field. The answer also demonstrates a rather unprofessional concern about getting students ready to pass standardized exams. In describing the drawback for "regular" students, the author relies on a personal anecdote.

Describe for each potential drawback a strategy you could use in your classroom to minimize or eliminate problems. The author offers two different solutions, extra help and talking to the other students, but neither is linked to either of the identified problems. The idea of providing extra help has some potential benefit, but it is vaguely described and is not linked to either of the stated problems. The proposal to talk to the other students to make them more tolerant as described is unprofessional. Educational research has shown that in classrooms where students with special needs are included, all students learn to be more tolerant of others. However, this will not be achieved by identifying some students as the source of problems for others and then telling the others simply to be patient or by laying the blame for the issue on the faceless district.

Essay 2 (strong)

As a teacher preparing to teach science, I will discuss how I would plan to implement the district's goals in a tenth-grade biology class.

In the past, students with disabilities were segregated from the regular students and classes. However, evidence has shown that students with disabilities can achieve at the same level as their peers in academic classes. More than 20 years of research has shown that these students need accommodations that allow them access to the benefits of the instruction all students receive in the classroom. This has led to improved student outcomes and these benefits also help students without disabilities in many ways, including being more responsive to the needs of others.

One potential drawback of the district's plan may be to make the commitment to full inclusion of all students in every classroom setting. Depending on the needs of any particular student, it may not be appropriate to place him or her in regular classes for every subject. This should be addressed appropriately in preparing the IEP for each individual student. This is the same potential drawback for the "regular" students in the district. For the district to assure that every student will be accommodated in every class, they may have to commit a disproportionate amount of resources to include some students for whom an alternative placement or services would be best. This would draw resources, including teacher time, away from providing instruction to all students.

The strategy I would use to help assure that student placements in my classes would be appropriate would be to participate in the IEP planning process. As a classroom teacher, I can be a part of the team that works to appropriately place students based on their needs. I can communicate what my class has to offer and learn how I might accommodate and support these students. I can also help to plan when special services or "pull out" services might be needed. Science can be a very good class for learners who need hands-on experiences, but Regents biology demands a high level of vocabulary skill and some students may need pull out services to assist them with this.

The strategy I would use to assure that all students, including those with special needs, get their fair share of resources, would be to individualize my instruction as much as possible. This means careful assessment of the needs and achievement of every student and designing classroom activities that meet each student at his or her level. To deliver this instruction, I will need materials at different reading levels; hands-on, inquiry-based lessons, and group work that builds on peer interactions and learning.

Evaluation

In the strong response, the author has demonstrated a grasp of the three subareas of teacher competence delineated by the test framework: student development and learning characteristics, instruction and assessment, and the professional environment. The response follows the construction of the essay as required by careful reading of the question prompt: identifying the grade level and subject, demonstrating knowledge of inclusion research, identifying a potential drawback for included and "regular" students, describing strategies for minimizing problems, and explaining how the recommendations help to meet the district's goal.

Explain how research has demonstrated that full inclusion is a desirable goal for students with disabilities. The author specifically and correctly referred to the educational research about the benefits of inclusion. The essay also uses vocabulary that expresses professional concepts, for example, IEP, inclusion, accommodations, inquiry-based lessons, and peer interactions. The description focuses on what makes inclusion a desirable goal as required by the question prompt.

Describe one potential drawback of the district's plan for students with disabilities and one potential drawback for "regular" students. The author identified specific drawbacks for both students with special needs and for regular students. The essay not only names or describes the drawback, but also explains in sufficient detail that the reader can infer that the writer has a professional grasp of the issues and the ideas leading to solutions.

Describe for each potential drawback a strategy you could use in your classroom to minimize or eliminate problems. The writer used parallel construction in addressing the solutions in the same order as they were presented in the preceding paragraph. Again, the author demonstrates a grasp of the professional concepts and vocabulary in describing the proposed solutions, for example, the vocabulary load of Regents biology classes, the benefits of inquiry-based lessons, and the role of the classroom teacher in participating in the IEP process. The answer also is specific in prescribing classroom practices, for example, having materials at different reading levels and using group work that will be used to solve the problem.

▶ Scoring Your Practice Test

Your official ATS-W score is a cumulative score representing all subareas of the test, including all multiple-choice questions and the constructed-response assignment, which will count toward 20% of your total score. Your total score will be reported on a scale between 100 and 300; a passing score for the official ATS-W is any score of 220 or above.

To take full advantage of this practice test, you should find both your overall score on the multiple-choice questions of this test, as well your individual scores in each subarea. To find your overall score, simply divide the number of multiple-choice questions you answered correctly by the total number of multiple-choice questions found on the test, which is 80. For example, if you answered 60 questions correctly:

$$\frac{60 \text{ (questions correct)}}{80 \text{ (total questions)}} = .75, \text{ or } 75\%.$$

To score your constructed-response question, it is highly recommended that you ask a professional friend or colleague familiar with the area of Instruction and Assessment to evaluate your essay using the official *Performance Characteristics and Scoring Scale* found at the end of the official Secondary ATS-W Preparation Guide, which can be found on the NYSTCE website at www.nystce.nesinc.com/PDFs/NY_fld091_prepguide.pdf. Your friend or colleague should assign you a score on the constructed-response essay between 1 and 4.

After you have a score for both parts of the practice test, you should use the following guidelines:

- If you get 80% or more of the multiple-choice items correct and score a 4 on the written assignment scoring scale, your preparation for the test is **EXCELLENT**.
- If you get 70% or more of the multiple-choice items correct and score a 3 or 4 on the written assignment scoring scale, your preparation for the test is **VERY GOOD**.
- If you get 60% or more of the multiple-choice items correct and score a 3 on the written assignment scoring scale, your preparation for the test is **GOOD**.
- If you get less than 60% of the multiple-choice items correct and score a 2 or 1 on the written assignment scoring scale, you should probably do some additional preparation before taking the actual test.

This practice test also offers you the opportunity to diagnose your areas of strength and weakness, to target your preparation for the official test. Following is a table that breaks down the questions in this practice test by subarea and their corresponding objectives. You can use this table to identify the areas in which you may need to concentrate more of your study time. For this practice test you should score at least 75% or higher in each subarea. You can find out your individual subarea scores by dividing the number of questions you answered correctly in a particular subarea by the total number of questions in that subarea.

Use your scores in each subarea in conjunction with the LearningExpress Test Preparation System in Chapter 7 to help you devise a study plan using the prep materials found in this book along with the materials from your classes and courses.

SECONDARY ATS-W Practice Exam for Review

SUBAREA AND OBJECTIVE	CORRESPONDING QUESTION	
Subarea I: Student Development and Learning		Total # of questions in Subarea I: 25
0001	4, 5, 17, 74	
0002	16, 25, 33, 76	
0003	6, 28, 45, 65	
0004	34, 59, 66, 71, 79	
0005	9, 22, 60, 64	
0006	11, 30, 38, 50	
Subarea II: Instruction and Assessment		Total # of questions in Subarea II: 38
0007	24, 35, 55, 68, 78	
0008	10, 26, 43, 75	
0009	12, 48, 51, 53, 54	
0010	18, 39, 61	
0011	7, 8, 37, 57, 73	
0012	40, 49, 69, 70, 80	
0013	13, 31, 46	
0014	1, 32, 41	
0015	14, 19, 21, 29, 47	
Subarea III: The Professional Environment		Total # of questions in Subarea III: 17
0016	16, 27, 62, 63	
0017	20, 23, 36, 44, 58	
0018	42, 56	
0019	3, 15, 52, 67, 72, 77	
Subarea IV: Instruction and Assessment: Constructed-Response Assignment	Written Assignment	Total # of questions in Subarea IV: 1

14▶ LAST Practice Exam 2

CHAPTER SUMMARY

This is the second of the two practice Liberal Arts and Sciences Test (LAST) exams in this book based on the format and content of the official LAST. This practice exam gives you another chance to master your test-taking skills and get ready for your official exam.

For this second practice LAST, pull together all the tips you've been practicing since the first practice exam. Give yourself the time and the space to work. Because you won't be taking the real test in your living room, you might take this one in an unfamiliar location, such as a library. Use a timer or stopwatch to time yourself, allowing ample time for preparing and writing your essay. Remember, you'll have four hours to complete your official exam. In addition, use what you've learned from reading the answer explanations on previous practice tests. Remember the types of questions that caused problems for you in the past, and when you are unsure, try to consider how those answers were explained. Once again, use the answer explanations and scoring review table at the end of the exam to understand questions you may have missed.

The answer sheet you should use for the multiple-choice questions is on page 353. (You will write your essay on a separate piece of paper.) After the exam, use the answer explanations to learn about why you missed certain questions. Then, use the scoring section and table at the end of the exam to see how you did overall.

▶ Answer Sheet

1. ⓐ ⓑ ⓒ ⓓ
2. ⓐ ⓑ ⓒ ⓓ
3. ⓐ ⓑ ⓒ ⓓ
4. ⓐ ⓑ ⓒ ⓓ
5. ⓐ ⓑ ⓒ ⓓ
6. ⓐ ⓑ ⓒ ⓓ
7. ⓐ ⓑ ⓒ ⓓ
8. ⓐ ⓑ ⓒ ⓓ
9. ⓐ ⓑ ⓒ ⓓ
10. ⓐ ⓑ ⓒ ⓓ
11. ⓐ ⓑ ⓒ ⓓ
12. ⓐ ⓑ ⓒ ⓓ
13. ⓐ ⓑ ⓒ ⓓ
14. ⓐ ⓑ ⓒ ⓓ
15. ⓐ ⓑ ⓒ ⓓ
16. ⓐ ⓑ ⓒ ⓓ
17. ⓐ ⓑ ⓒ ⓓ
18. ⓐ ⓑ ⓒ ⓓ
19. ⓐ ⓑ ⓒ ⓓ
20. ⓐ ⓑ ⓒ ⓓ
21. ⓐ ⓑ ⓒ ⓓ
22. ⓐ ⓑ ⓒ ⓓ
23. ⓐ ⓑ ⓒ ⓓ
24. ⓐ ⓑ ⓒ ⓓ
25. ⓐ ⓑ ⓒ ⓓ
26. ⓐ ⓑ ⓒ ⓓ
27. ⓐ ⓑ ⓒ ⓓ
28. ⓐ ⓑ ⓒ ⓓ
29. ⓐ ⓑ ⓒ ⓓ
30. ⓐ ⓑ ⓒ ⓓ
31. ⓐ ⓑ ⓒ ⓓ
32. ⓐ ⓑ ⓒ ⓓ
33. ⓐ ⓑ ⓒ ⓓ
34. ⓐ ⓑ ⓒ ⓓ
35. ⓐ ⓑ ⓒ ⓓ
36. ⓐ ⓑ ⓒ ⓓ
37. ⓐ ⓑ ⓒ ⓓ
38. ⓐ ⓑ ⓒ ⓓ
39. ⓐ ⓑ ⓒ ⓓ
40. ⓐ ⓑ ⓒ ⓓ
41. ⓐ ⓑ ⓒ ⓓ
42. ⓐ ⓑ ⓒ ⓓ
43. ⓐ ⓑ ⓒ ⓓ
44. ⓐ ⓑ ⓒ ⓓ
45. ⓐ ⓑ ⓒ ⓓ
46. ⓐ ⓑ ⓒ ⓓ
47. ⓐ ⓑ ⓒ ⓓ
48. ⓐ ⓑ ⓒ ⓓ
49. ⓐ ⓑ ⓒ ⓓ
50. ⓐ ⓑ ⓒ ⓓ
51. ⓐ ⓑ ⓒ ⓓ
52. ⓐ ⓑ ⓒ ⓓ
53. ⓐ ⓑ ⓒ ⓓ
54. ⓐ ⓑ ⓒ ⓓ
55. ⓐ ⓑ ⓒ ⓓ
56. ⓐ ⓑ ⓒ ⓓ
57. ⓐ ⓑ ⓒ ⓓ
58. ⓐ ⓑ ⓒ ⓓ
59. ⓐ ⓑ ⓒ ⓓ
60. ⓐ ⓑ ⓒ ⓓ
61. ⓐ ⓑ ⓒ ⓓ
62. ⓐ ⓑ ⓒ ⓓ
63. ⓐ ⓑ ⓒ ⓓ
64. ⓐ ⓑ ⓒ ⓓ
65. ⓐ ⓑ ⓒ ⓓ
66. ⓐ ⓑ ⓒ ⓓ
67. ⓐ ⓑ ⓒ ⓓ
68. ⓐ ⓑ ⓒ ⓓ
69. ⓐ ⓑ ⓒ ⓓ
70. ⓐ ⓑ ⓒ ⓓ
71. ⓐ ⓑ ⓒ ⓓ
72. ⓐ ⓑ ⓒ ⓓ
73. ⓐ ⓑ ⓒ ⓓ
74. ⓐ ⓑ ⓒ ⓓ
75. ⓐ ⓑ ⓒ ⓓ
76. ⓐ ⓑ ⓒ ⓓ
77. ⓐ ⓑ ⓒ ⓓ
78. ⓐ ⓑ ⓒ ⓓ
79. ⓐ ⓑ ⓒ ⓓ
80. ⓐ ⓑ ⓒ ⓓ

Use the following graph to answer question 1.

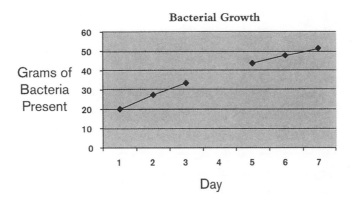

Bacterial Growth

1. What is the best approximation of the amount of bacteria (in grams) present on day 4?
   a. 38
   b. 30
   c. 41
   d. 40

Questions 2 and 3 are based on the following passage.

According to scientists, the sun has existed for 4.6 billion years. The sun produces energy by a nuclear conversion of hydrogen into helium. When hydrogen runs out, according to this theory, the sun will expand, engulfing the earth and other planets. Not to worry—the expansion will not affect us, since the sun has enough hydrogen for another 4.6 billion years. When it expands, the sun will become what is called a red giant star. In another 500 million years, the sun will shrink to the current size of the earth and will be called a white dwarf, cooling down for several billion years.

2. According to the passage, the sun will eventually
   a. expand and then shrink.
   b. shrink and then expand.
   c. shrink and then run out of helium.
   d. expand because it ran out of helium.

3. Based on this theory, the sun will, at some point, be a

a. blue star.

b. red dwarf star.

c. white dwarf star.

d. asteroid.

4. Choose the best correction for the underlined part of the sentence. If no correction is needed, choose **d.**

Before we can complete the science experiment, <u>we will need to check with the professor to find out when the lab is free and deciding who will collect the necessary materials.</u>

a. we will need to check with the professor to find out when the lab is free and decide who will collect the necessary materials.

b. we will need to check with the professor, find out when the lab is free, and then deciding who will collect the necessary materials.

c. we will need to check with the professor to find out when the lab is free, and then deciding who will collect the necessary materials.

d. no correction needed

Question 5 is based on the following painting.

Lucas Cranach the Elder, Portrait of Johannes Cuspinian, 1502–03. (Dr. Oskar Reinhart Collection, Winterthur, Switzerland.)

5. Typical of portraits painted in the sixteenth century, Cranach's subject is

    a. a fellow painter.

    b. a member of the Court.

    c. a writer.

    d. a commoner.

Use the following graph to answer question 6.

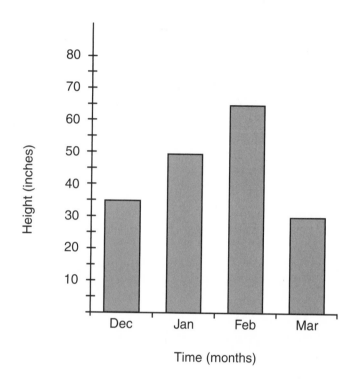

6. Which of the following represents the best choice for the title of the graph?

    a. Average Rainfall per Month for Winter Months in the Northern United States

    b. Average Number of Hours of Sunlight for Winter Months in the Northern United States

    c. Daily Snowfall Rates for Winter Months in the Northern United States

    d. Average Snowfall per Month for Winter Months in the Northern United States

Use the following table to answer questions 7–9.

World Energy Consumption, 1970-2020

Year	Quadrillion Btu Consumed
1970	207
1975	243
1980	285
1985	311
1990	346
1995	366
2000	382
2005	439
2010	493
2015	552
2020	612

Sources: History—Energy Information Administration (EIA), Office of Energy Markets and End Use, International Statistics Database and International Energy Annual 1999, DOE/EIA-0119(99), Washington, DC, February 2001. Projections—EIA, World Energy Projection System (2002).

7. In which five-year period in the past was the increase in the world's energy consumption the greatest?

   a. 2010–2015

   b. 1970–1975

   c. 2000–2005

   d. 1985–1990

8. What is the table's estimate of world energy consumption for the year 2015?

   a. 540 quadrillion Btu

   b. 552 quadrillion Btu

   c. 555 quadrillion Btu

   d. 557 quadrillion Btu

9. What is the trend of the world's energy consumption?

   a. It is increasing.

   b. It is decreasing.

   c. It is remaining constant.

   d. It is increasing, but will level off by the year 2015.

Question 10 refers to the following paragraph.

Why has the school decided to ban the chewing of gum on their grounds? The answer is obvious to anyone who has inadvertently placed his or her hand beneath a seat or desktop, or who has stepped into a sticky wad on the floor. Administrators have a right to put any rules into place that they see fit. The ban will not only help to keep the school and its grounds cleaner, but will cut down on the hours our custodians must work, and increase the lifespan of school furniture.

10. What is the best way to improve the paragraph?
   a. Eliminate the first sentence.
   b. Switch the placement of sentences 2 and 3.
   c. Eliminate the third sentence.
   d. No improvement is needed.

Questions 11 and 12 refer to the following passage.

Mental and physical health professionals may consider referring clients and patients to a music therapist for a number of reasons. It seems a particularly good choice for the social worker who is coordinating a client's case. Music therapists use music to establish a relationship with the patient and to improve the patient's health, using highly structured musical interactions. Patients and therapists may sing, play instruments, compose music, dance, or simply listen to music. The course of training for music therapists is comprehensive. In addition to their formal musical and therapy training, music therapists are taught to discern what kinds of interventions will be most beneficial for each individual patient. Because each patient is different and has different goals, the music therapist must be able to understand the patient's situation and choose the music and activities that will do the most toward helping the patient achieve his or her goals. The referring social worker can help this process by clearly articulating each client's history. Although patients may develop their musical skills, that is not the main goal of music therapy. Any client who needs particular work on communication or on academic, emotional, and social skills, and who is not responding to traditional therapy, is an excellent candidate for music therapy.

11. Which of the following would be the most appropriate title for this passage?
   a. The Use of Music in the Treatment of Autism
   b. How to Use Music to Combat Depression
   c. Music Therapy: A Role in Social Work?
   d. Training for a Career in Music Therapy

LAST PRACTICE EXAM 2

12. Which of the following inferences can be drawn from the passage?

    a. Music therapy can succeed where traditional therapies have failed.

    b. Music therapy is a relatively new field.

    c. Music therapy is particularly beneficial for young children.

    d. Music therapy probably will not work well for psychotic people.

13. Some soccer players like to play in the rain.

All soccer players take science.

Sheila likes to play in the rain.

Based on this information, which of the following statements is true?

    a. Some science students play soccer.

    b. Only soccer players take science.

    c. Sheila plays soccer.

    d. Sheila takes science.

Refer to the following passage to answer question 14.

Before I had left America, that is to say in the year 1781, I had received a letter from M. de Marbois, of the French legation in Philadelphia, informing me he had been instructed by his government to obtain such statistical accounts of the different states of our Union, as might be useful for their information; and addressing to me a number of queries relative to the state of Virginia. I had always made it a practice whenever an opportunity occurred of obtaining any information of our country, which might be of use to me in any station public or private, to commit it to writing. These memoranda were on loose papers, bundled up without order, and difficult of recurrence when I had occasion for a particular one.

        —Thomas Jefferson, *Paris*

14. The passage may be identified as part of an autobiography by

    a. its use of the third person.

    b. its use of specific details known only by the author.

    c. its use of the first person.

    d. its references to actual persons and places.

Questions 15 and 16 are based on the following passage.

We sailed from Peru (where we had continued by the space of one whole year), for China and Japan, by the South Sea; taking with us victuals for twelve months; and had good winds from the east, though soft and weak, for five months space, and more. But then the wind came about, and settled in the west for many days, so as we could make little or no way, and were sometimes in purpose to turn back. But then again there arose strong and great winds from the south, with a point east, which carried us up (for all that we could do), towards the north; by which time our victuals failed us, though we had made good spare of them. So that finding ourselves, in the midst of the greatest wilderness of waters in the world, without victuals, we gave ourselves for lost men and prepared for death. Yet we did lift up our hearts and voices to God above, who showeth his wonders in the deep, beseeching him of his mercy, that as in the beginning he discovered the face of the deep, and brought forth dry land, so he would now discover land to us, that we might not perish.

—Francis Bacon, *The New Atlantis*, 1627

15. *The New Atlantis* shows evidence of Bacon's inspiration from
   a. Western European society.
   b. the King James Bible.
   c. contemporary explorers of the New World.
   d. ancient survivor myths.

16. Bacon's vision of Atlantis, an ideal world, may have been based on all of the following EXCEPT
   a. Eden.
   b. Thomas More's *Utopia* (1516).
   c. the Elysian Fields of Greek mythology.
   d. Hades, Roman mythology's underworld.

17. By 1878, the Standard Oil Company, owned by John D. Rockefeller, had bought out most of its business rivals and controlled 90% of the petroleum refineries in the United States. Which of the following was a likely effect of Standard Oil's business practices?
   a. The company set limits on its prices.
   b. The company increased oil prices.
   c. Competition in the oil market flourished.
   d. Standard Oil increased its efforts to attract needed customers.

18. During the spring bowling season, a bowler achieves the following scores: 116, 100, 104, 104, 114, 109, and 109. The bowler's three best scores are averaged for her final score of the season. What is her final score?

    a. 105

    b. 107

    c. 113

    d. 111

19. Bruce Springsteen's song, "The Promised Land" refers to a major tenet of what religion?

    a. Christianity

    b. Buddhism

    c. Mormonism

    d. Judaism

20. Which of the following energy sources causes the least pollution to the environment?

    a. coal

    b. nuclear power

    c. gasoline

    d. solar

Refer to the following photograph to answer question 21.

Child Laborers in Indiana Glass Works, Midnight, Indiana, 1908.

Source: The National Archives and Records Administration.

21. Which of the following conclusions can you draw from the photo and its caption?
  a. Laws in the early 1900s protected children from long working hours.
  b. The photographer believed that children could make significant contributions to the economy.
  c. Children in 1908 worked in occupations where they would not be permitted today.
  d. The progressives fought to create labor laws that would protect children.

Use the following information to answer questions 22–24.

The cost of tickets to the school play is $7.50 for adults and $5 for children ages 12 and under. On Saturday and Sunday afternoon, there is a special matinee price: $5.50 for adults and $3 for children ages 12 and under. Special group discounts are available for groups of 30 or more people.

22. Which of the following can be determined from the information given in the passage?
  a. how much it will cost a family of four to buy tickets for the school play on Saturday afternoon
  b. the difference between the cost of two tickets for the school play on Tuesday night and the cost of one ticket on Sunday afternoon
  c. how much tickets to the school play will cost each person if he or she is part of a group of 40 people
  d. the difference between the cost of a ticket for the school play for an adult on Friday night and a ticket for the school play for a 13-year-old on Saturday afternoon

23. According to the passage, how much will tickets to the school play cost for two adults, one 15-year-old child, and one 10-year-old child on Sunday night?
  a. $27.50
  b. $19.50
  c. $25
  d. $26.50

24. Using the passage, how can you find the difference in price between a ticket for the school play for an adult and a ticket for a child under the age of 12 if they are attending the show on Saturday afternoon?
  a. subtract $3 from $7.50
  b. subtract $3 from $5.50
  c. subtract $5 from $7.50
  d. subtract $7.50 from $5.50

Use the following quote to answer question 25.

As this long and difficult war ends, I would like to address a few special words to the American people: Your steadfastness in supporting our insistence on peace with honor has made peace with honor possible.

—Richard Nixon

25. What does this quote refer to?

    a. the Vietnam War

    b. the Korean War

    c. the Gulf War

    d. World War II

Question 26 refers to the following paragraph.

President Polk had to react quickly to the impending crisis between Mexico and the United States. Mexico had ended the diplomatic relationship between the countries and demanded the return of Texas. Thinking quickly, Polk sent special envoy John Slidell to Mexico City to inform the Mexican government of U.S. intentions to honor the original Nueces River boundary of Texas, and their desire to purchase California. In anticipation of the Mexicans not honoring Slidell's proposal, Polk amassed the U.S. Army, led by Zachary Taylor, along the disputed southern border of Texas at the Rio Grande River in January of 1846. In April, an unprovoked and ruthless Mexican force crossed the border and savagely attacked Taylor's men, killing several American troops. Despite a small opposition of Whigs led by Abraham Lincoln, a large majority of congressmen voted to declare war on Mexico.

26. Which sentence represents an opinion of the author?

    a. 5

    b. 2

    c. 6

    d. 4

Refer to the following poem to answer question 27.

Crossing the Bar

Sunset and evening star,
And one clear call for me!
And may there be no moaning of the bar,
When I put out to sea.

But such a tide as moving seems asleep,
Too full for sound and foam,
When that which drew from out the boundless deep
Turns again home!

Twilight and evening bell,
And after that the dark!
And may there be no sadness of farewell,
When I embark;

For though from out our bourn of Time and Place
The flood may bear me far,
I hope to see my Pilot face to face
When I have crost the bar.

                        —Alfred, Lord Tennyson

27. Who is the "Pilot" Tennyson refers to in the next to last line of the poem?
    a. his lover
    b. his muse
    c. God
    d. the commander of his ship

Question 28 refers to the following bibliography entry.

    —*The United States and the Principle of Manifest Destiny*. Princeton, N.J.: Princeton University Press, 1985.

28. The dash in the entry signifies
    a. that the author is unknown.
    b. that there are multiple authors.
    c. that the author is the same as for the entry above it.
    d. that there is no author identified in the book.

29. What is one example of how humans are delaying evolutionary changes in their population?
    a. the use of eyeglasses and contact lenses
    b. a reliance on fast food
    c. the availability of birth control
    d. increasing births as a result of in vitro fertilization

Use the following chart to answer questions 30 and 31.

Type of Government	Characteristics	Examples
Monarchy	■ One person from a royal family is ruler. ■ Power is inherited from generation to generation. ■ *Absolute monarchs* have complete authority. ■ *Constitutional monarchs* have limited authority; a representative democracy governs.	■ Saudi Arabia ■ Morocco *Absolute monarchy:* ■ Swaziland *Constitutional monarchies:* ■ Great Britain ■ Japan ■ Sweden
Dictatorship	■ It is ruled by one leader who has absolute power over many aspects of life, including social, economic, and political. ■ Leader is not elected by the people.	■ Nazi (National Socialist) government of Adolf Hitler ■ General Augusto Pinochet in Chile from 1973–1990
Oligarchy	■ It is governed by a small upper-class group. ■ Leaders are not elected by the people.	■ City-state of Sparta in ancient Greece
Democracy	■ In *direct democracy,* decisions are made by the people. ■ In *representative democracy,* people elect officials to represent their views.	*Representative democracies:* ■ United States ■ Canada ■ Most European nations

30. A military leader uses his power to overthrow a country's government and names himself the absolute leader of the government. He takes over all the nation's television stations and newspapers. What kind of government has he set up?
   a. absolute monarchy
   b. dictatorship
   c. oligarchy
   d. direct democracy

31. In which of the following political systems would citizens have the most influence over law-making?
   a. absolute monarchy
   b. dictatorship
   c. oligarchy
   d. direct democracy

32. Jacob pays a $19 flat fee for his cellular phone service each month, which includes the first 120 minutes of airtime he uses. He is then charged $0.32 per minute for each minute after that. If x represents the total airtime he uses each month, and he always uses more than 120 minutes of airtime each month, which of the following expressions can be used to calculate his monthly cellular phone bill?
   a. $19 + 0.32x$
   b. $19 + 0.32(x - 120)$
   c. $19(x - 120) + 0.32x$
   d. $19x + 0.32$

Question 33 refers to the following passage.

Peel three large russet potatoes and cut them into small, uniform pieces. Put them in a saucepan and fill with water until potatoes are submerged. Bring to a boil and simmer for 2–3 minutes. Drain potatoes. Put 4 tablespoons of olive oil in a large roasting pan. Place potatoes in the pan, and add kosher salt and a few sprigs of fresh rosemary. Roast in a 400° oven for about 45 minutes, stirring occasionally, until beginning to brown.

33. The best summary for this passage is
   a. New Uses for Fresh Rosemary
   b. Roasting: A Healthier Way to Cook
   c. How to Roast Potatoes
   d. An Easy Side Dish for Company

Questions 34 and 35 refer to the following passage.

The tango originated in Argentina in the mid 1800s, but has its roots in the dances of Europe that developed decades before. Prior to the 1830s, dancing between men and women was done with little or no physical contact. That changed with the introduction of the Viennese waltz, in which couples faced one another and embraced. The dance became a craze in Europe, and was followed a decade later by another popular dance employing an embrace, the polka.

European immigrants brought their dances to Argentina, where they quickly caught on. The Argentines adapted the dances, incorporating Spanish Flamenco music, which was one of the most popular forms of music in Buenos Aires in the mid-1800s. By 1857, the name tango appeared, describing not only the new dance form, but also the music used to accompany it. The tango took the embrace of the waltz and the polka a step further, as dancers pressed their cheeks and chests together, and entwined their legs during the complicated footwork.

One reason the exact origins of the tango are unknown is the fact that the dance developed not in literary society, which might be counted on to record the development, but rather in the dance halls and brothels. These venues were frequented by the less privileged and uneducated classes who left little evidence of their existence, let alone their dance habits. But by the 1890s, the tango had reached the theater and was established in mainstream society.

34. According to the passage, what do the polka and the tango have in common?
   a. They both originated in Europe.
   b. They both use Flamenco music.
   c. They both gained popularity in brothels.
   d. They both involve an embrace by the dancers.

35. With which idea would the author of the passage most likely agree?
   a. The tango remains a dance of the less privileged classes.
   b. The dances of Europe were superior to those of South America.
   c. Cultural developments are recorded by literary society.
   d. Literary society did not embrace the tango.

Question 36 refers to the following figures.

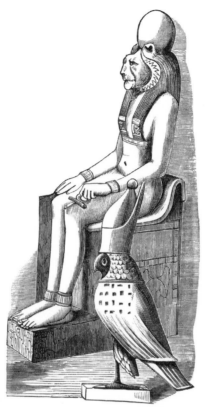

PASHT, THE CAT-HEADED GOD.

36. What conclusion can be drawn about a similarity between ancient Egypt and ancient Greece, based on the images?

    a. The mythologies of both cultures included figures that were part human and part animal.

    b. They both worshipped women.

    c. They both used imposing figures at the entrance of tombs.

    d. The artists of both cultures worked exclusively in limestone.

Question 37 refers to the following passage.

I had almost given up hope of finding a mouthwash that kept my breath fresh all morning. My medicine cabinet was full of bottles of once-used elixirs, all of which promised the desired result. Then I found out about Morning Bright. I was skeptical of its claims, having believed so many similar assertions before. The first time I tried it, I was amazed! My breath was still fresh when it was time to meet colleagues for a lunch meeting. I'll never use another mouthwash again, and you shouldn't either.

37. The author's purpose is to

    a. describe.

    b. convince.

    c. dissuade.

    d. argue.

Questions 38 and 39 are based on the following passage.

Farm animals can carry salmonella, a kind of bacteria that can cause severe food poisoning. However, animals fed antibiotics can carry especially deadly strains of salmonella. In Minnesota in 1983, 11 people were hospitalized with salmonella poisoning. This number itself was not striking at all. Every year, 40,000 Americans are hospitalized with salmonella poisoning. What was striking about the cases in Minnesota was that each patient had severe symptoms and all the patients were infected with the same, rare strain of salmonella, resistant to several common antibiotics. A young scientist, Scott Holmberg, noted that eight patients were taking the same antibiotics for sore throats. He ruled out the possibility that the antibiotics themselves were infected with the bacteria because three of the patients were not taking antibiotics at all. He later showed that the people were infected with salmonella prior to taking the antibiotics, but that the antibiotics triggered the onset of salmonella poisoning. He postulated that salmonella suddenly flourished when the patients took antibiotics, because the antibiotics killed off all other competing bacteria. He was also able to trace the antibiotic resistant salmonella to the beef that was imported to Minnesota from a farm in South Dakota, at which cattle were routinely fed antibiotics and at which one calf died of the same strain of salmonella.

38. As a result of this finding, the Food and Drug Administration should
   a. carefully regulate the prescription of antibiotics for sore throats.
   b. prevent the export of meat from South Dakota to Minnesota.
   c. limit the practice of feeding antibiotics to cattle.
   d. take the antibiotic that caused salmonella off the market.

39. Based on the passage, which one of the following statements is false?
   a. Salmonella poisoning is a common bacterial infection.
   b. Some strands of bacteria are resistant to antibiotics.
   c. Antibiotics kill off bacteria that are not resistant to antibiotics.
   d. Antibiotics transmit salmonella.

40. Which of the following would be used as a secondary source by a student researching the effects of the dust bowl?
   I. President Roosevelt's 1933 National Industrial Recovery Act that established the Soil Erosion Service (SES)
   II. photographs of dust bowl survivors by Dorothea Lange
   III. John Steinbeck's novel, *The Grapes of Wrath*
   IV. 1940 article in *Time* magazine citing the research findings of the Soil Erosion Unit of the U.S. Department of Agriculture
   a. I and II
   b. I and III
   c. II and III
   d. III and IV

41. Which of the following most accurately depicts the information in this graph?

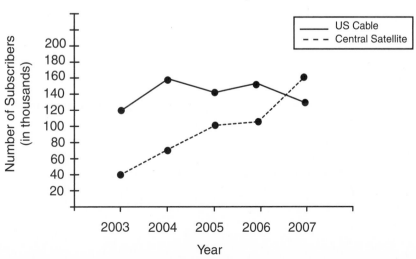

Number of Subscribers
at Two Television Companies

a.

Number of Subscribers at
Two Television Companies

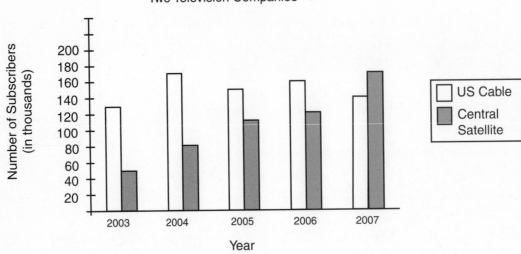

b.

Number of Subscribers at
Two Television Companies

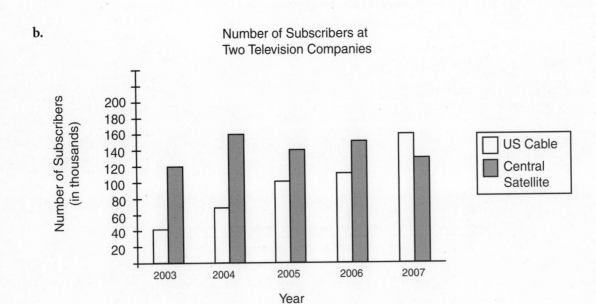

c.

Number of Subscribers at Two Television Companies

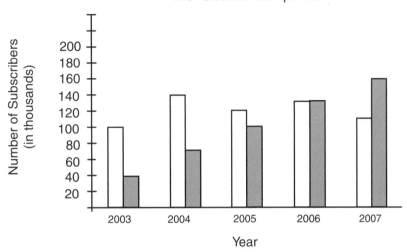

d.

Number of Subscribers at Two Television Companies

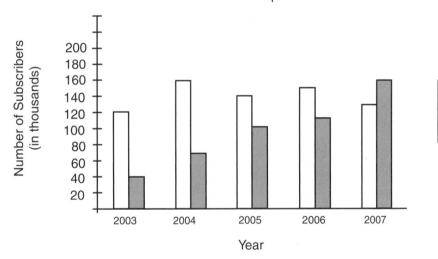

Refer to the following passage to answer question 42.

Orchids grow slowly in comparison with houseplants. Most houseplants require repotting annually to account for growth during the previous year. Orchids, however, need repotting just once every two years. This may be done by selecting a pot that is about the size of the orchid's roots. Fill it about two-thirds with orchid potting medium, and set the plant in the pot with its roots spread out. If the orchid is monopodial (growing upward from a single point), the growing tip should be centered. If it is sympodial (growing laterally), place the growing tip two fingers from the pot rim. Add additional growing media to hold the plant firmly in place.

42. What information in the passage supports the assertion in the first sentence?
  a. The right size pot for an orchid is one that is about the size of its roots.
  b. The roots of an orchid should be spread out in the pot.
  c. To repot an orchid, you must determine whether it is monopodial or sympodial.
  d. Orchids need repotting just once every two years.

43. In past presidential elections, television networks have made predictions about which candidate is likely to win *before* the polls closed throughout all of the nation's time zones. Which of the following statements explains why this would anger some voters?
  a. Predictions based on voting in eastern time zones influence those who have not yet voted in the more western time zones.
  b. Voters in the Central Time Zone want to know who won in the eastern states.
  c. Polls in the Pacific Time Zone open earlier if voters want their votes to be counted.
  d. Polls close one hour later in the Mountain Time Zone than in the Central Time Zone.

Questions 44 and 45 refer to the following passage.

Many years ago there lived an Emperor, who was so excessively fond of grand new clothes that he spent all his money upon them, that he might be very fine. He did not care about his soldiers, nor about the theatre, and only liked to drive out and show his new clothes. He had a coat for every hour of the day; and just as they say of a king, "He is in council," so they always said of him, "The Emperor is in the wardrobe." *1*

In the great city in which he lived it was always very merry; every day came many strangers; one day two rogues came: they gave themselves out as weavers, and declared they could weave the finest stuff anyone could imagine. Not only were their colors and patterns, they said, uncommonly beautiful, but the clothes made of the stuff possessed the wonderful quality that they became invisible to any one who was unfit for the office he held, or was incorrigibly stupid. *2*

"Those would be capital clothes!" thought the Emperor. "If I wore those, I should be able to find out what men in my empire are not fit for the places they have; I could tell the clever from the dunces. Yes, the stuff must be woven for me directly!" *3*

And he gave the two rogues a great deal of cash in hand, that they might begin their work at once. *4*

As for them, they put up two looms, and pretended to be working; but they had nothing at all on their looms. They at once demanded the finest silk and the costliest gold; this they put into their own pockets, and worked at the empty looms till late into the night. *5*

—Excerpt from Hans Christian Andersen's *The Emperor's New Clothes*

44. Paragraph 3 uses which literary device?
   a. foreshadowing
   b. irony
   c. metaphor
   d. alliteration

45. Which sentence best describes the dominant theme of the passage?
   a. Vanity blinds a man to truth.
   b. Cleverness can make one rich.
   c. The clothes make the man.
   d. Rulers can be easily manipulated.

Questions 46 through 49 refer to the following definitions of political beliefs and policies. For each question, read the quote and identify the label that best describes it.

Isolationism: a national policy of avoiding political alliances with other nations
Nationalism: a sense of allegiance to the interests and culture of a nation
Jingoism: extreme nationalism characterized by a warring foreign policy
Pacifism: the belief that nations should settle their disputes peacefully
Regionalism: a political division between two regions within an area

46. *This whole nation of one hundred and thirty million free men, women, and children is becoming one great fighting force. Some of us are soldiers or sailors, some of us are civilians. . .A few of us are decorated with medals for heroic achievement, but all of us can have that deep and permanent inner satisfaction that comes from doing the best we know how—each of us playing an honorable part in the great struggle to save our democratic civilization.*
   —Radio address of President Franklin D. Roosevelt, October 12, 1942
   a. isolationism
   b. nationalism
   c. jingoism
   d. pacifism

47. *The . . . parties solemnly declare in the names of their respective peoples that they condemn recourse to war for the solution of international controversies, and renounce it as an instrument of national policy in their relations with one another.*

—Kellogg-Briand Pact, Article I, 1928

    a. isolationism
    b. nationalism
    c. regionalism
    d. pacifism

48. *The great rule of conduct for us in regard to foreign nations is, in extending our commercial relations to have with them as little political connection as possible. So far as we have already formed engagements let them be fulfilled with perfect good faith.*

—President George Washington, Farewell Address, 1796

    a. isolationism
    b. regionalism
    c. pacifism
    d. jingoism

49. *The free States alone, if we must go on alone, will make a glorious nation. Twenty millions in the temperate zone, stretching from the Atlantic to the Pacific, full of vigor, industry, inventive genius, educated, and moral; increasing by immigration rapidly, and, above all, free—all free—will form a confederacy of twenty States scarcely inferior in real power to the unfortunate Union of thirty-three States which we had on the first of November.*

—Rutherford Birchard Hayes, January 4, 1861

    a. isolationism
    b. nationalism
    c. jingoism
    d. regionalism

Question 50 is based on the following passage.

Is Pluto a Planet?

Based on perturbations in Neptune's orbit, the search for a ninth planet was conducted and Pluto was discovered in 1930. Pluto orbits the sun just like the other eight planets, and it has a moon, Charon, and a stable orbit. Based on its distance from the sun, Pluto should be grouped with the planets known as gas giants. In addition, Pluto, like the planet Mercury, has little or no atmosphere. Pluto is definitely not a comet because it does not have a tail like a comet when it is near the sun. Pluto is also not an asteroid, although its density is closer to an asteroid than to any of the other planets. Pluto is a planet because it has been classified as one for more than 60 years since its discovery.

50. Which argument supporting the classification of Pluto as a planet is the weakest?
   a. Pluto has been classified as a planet for more than 60 years since its discovery.
   b. Pluto has a moon.
   c. Pluto has a stable orbit.
   d. Pluto, like the planet Mercury, has little or no atmosphere.

51. What is a good method for determining the reliability of an Internet site?
   a. Verify its information using two additional sources.
   b. Check to see when the site was last updated.
   c. Verify the author or sponsor of the site.
   d. all of the above

Questions 52 and 53 refer to the following passage.

The United States is often referred to as a "melting pot," a place where people from many other countries, for many reasons, came to live. These people brought with them their cultures, languages, and customs, and came together to form one nation. The original colonies were settled by English immigrants seeking religious freedom. By the time they founded the United States, other English immigrants, such as the Quakers, and thousands from Germany and Ireland had joined them, and there were hundreds of thousands of Africans, brought to America by force in the slave trade. Because of famines in Ireland, millions of Irish immigrants arrived in the 1800s. Poverty and the wish to practice their religion freely brought millions of Swedes and Norwegians here at the same time. Persecution was the reason about two million European Jews came to America beginning in 1880, and poverty caused the same number of Italians to seek a better life in America.

52. What is the main idea of the passage?

    a. A "melting pot" is made up of people from many countries.

    b. Immigrants came to the United States for different reasons.

    c. The United States is one nation formed by people from many countries.

    d. Adversity is the major reason immigrants came to the United States.

53. Which group in the "melting pot" had the most difficult time assimilating?

    a. Africans

    b. Italians

    c. Jews

    d. Quakers

Question 54 is based on the following passage.

Over the past 20 years, worldwide illiteracy rates have consistently declined. The main reason for this decline is the sharp increase in the literacy rates of young women, which is the result of campaigns to increase educational opportunities for girls. For example, between 1970 and 1990, the literacy rate among women in the United Arab Emirates increased from 7% to 76%.

54. This passage is mainly about

    a. the cause of illiteracy among women.

    b. the effects of illiteracy among women.

    c. the cause of reduced illiteracy rates among women.

    d. the effect of educational opportunities for girls.

55. Complete the two missing parts of the following food chain: X $\rightarrow$ plant $\rightarrow$ X $\rightarrow$ snake

    a. water, owl

    b. water, mouse

    c. sunlight, deer

    d. sunlight, mouse

Questions 56 and 57 are based on the following figure.

56. This Aztec work represents an art form used throughout civilization by many cultures, called
   a. decorative columns.
   b. relief sculpture.
   c. utilitarian pottery.
   d. religious painting.

57. Which answer choice represents the best description of the sculpture's composition?
   a. The headdresses on the two figures anchor the middle of the sculpture.
   b. The decorative friezes on the top left and side left provide symmetry.
   c. Although the two gods are dissimilar in size, they are balanced through use of the large stick-like object that bisects the image diagonally.
   d. The open book at the bottom of the work provides balance.

Questions 58 and 59 are based on the following passage.

In the past, people thought that the earth was flat and that a ship that sailed too far would fall off the edge of the world. The earth appears flat because the earth is too large for humans on earth to see its curvature. Several events helped shed the misconceptions. For one, during a lunar eclipse, the earth is positioned between the sun and the moon. It eclipses the moon by casting a shadow on it. The shadow the earth casts is round. When Magellan circumnavigated the earth, he proved that one could not fall off the edge of the earth, because the earth was round and had no edges. Finally, space missions provided us with images of our round earth from far away and showed us how beautiful our planet looks, even from a distance.

58. In the passage, what was cited as proof that the earth is round?

    I. the earth casts a round shadow on the moon during a lunar eclipse

    II. the earth revolves around the sun

   III. Magellan circumnavigated the earth

   IV. images from space

    a. I and II

    b. I, II, and III

    c. I, II, and IV

    d. I, III, and IV

59. With which misconception about the earth is the passage concerned?

    a. that the earth turned

    b. that the earth was in the center of the solar system

    c. that the earth was flat

    d. that the earth was created at the same time as the sun

60. Select the underlined section that contains an error in the following sentence. If there is no error, select choice **d**.

Climate change, <u>including ice ages and interglacial periods,</u> <u>has</u> <u>effected</u> the earth for
                                    a.   **b.**   **c.**

millions of years. <u>No error.</u>
              d.

Refer to the following passage to answer questions 61 and 62.

Stephen Sondheim is one of the preeminent American composers and lyricists of the twentieth century. His craft was honed at the feet of a master, Oscar Hammerstein II, for whom he worked as a personal assistant while in his early twenties. A subsequent collaboration as lyricist with Leonard Bernstein resulted in one of the most popular musicals in history, *West Side Story*. But Sondheim's innovations and true genius were best revealed in later works, in which he stretched the genre of musical theater in two important ways. First, his desire to explore and reveal psychological truths found voice in unforgettable characters whose depth and vitality were unheard of in a genre that relies heavily on two-dimensional, stereotypical characters. Second, he drew his material from various and startling art forms, time periods, and subjects, ranging from Japanese poetry to ancient Rome and the nineteenth century English class system.

61. According to the passage, Sondheim used the genre of musical theater to communicate
  a. psychological truths.
  b. stereotypical characters.
  c. startling art forms.
  d. the legacy of Oscar Hammerstein.

62. What is one way in which Sondheim's musicals differ from the works of other artists?
  a. He used Japanese poetry as a subject.
  b. He relied on the guidance he received from the legendary Oscar Hammerstein and Leonard Bernstein.
  c. His characters had more depth than the typical two-dimensional musical figures.
  d. He created the most popular musical of all time, *West Side Story*.

Refer to the following passage to answer question 63.

The information on a standard compact disc (CD) is contained in a single spiral track of pits, starting at the inside of the disk and circling its way to the outside. This information is read by shining light from a 780 nm wavelength semiconductor laser. Information is read as the laser moves over the bumps (where no light will be reflected) and the areas that have no bumps, also known as *land* (where the laser light will be reflected off the aluminum). The changes in reflectivity are interpreted by a part of the compact disc player known as the *detector*. It is the job of the *detector* to convert the information collected by the laser into the music that was originally recorded onto the disk.

63. What is the author's purpose in writing the passage?
  a. to dissuade
  b. to describe
  c. to argue
  d. to convince

Use the following passage to answer question 64.

A study conducted by the Centers for Disease Control (CDC) found that high school students who take part in team sports or are physically active outside of school are less likely to engage in risky behaviors, like using drugs or smoking. Physical activity does not need to be strenuous to be beneficial. The CDC recommends moderate, daily physical activity for people of all ages, such as brisk walking for 30 minutes or 15–20 minutes of more intense exercise. A survey conducted by the National Association for Sport and Physical Education questioned teens about their attitudes toward exercise and about what it would take to get them moving. Teens chose friends (56%) as their most likely motivators for becoming more active, followed by parents (18%) and professional athletes (11%).

64. Which of the following techniques is used in the last sentence of the passage?

a. illustration by example

b. comparison of different arguments

c. contrast of opposing views

d. generalized statement

65. Jacqueline was one-third as young as her grandmother 15 years ago. If the sum of their ages is 110, how old is Jacqueline's grandmother?

a. 80

b. 75

c. 65

d. 60

Questions 66 and 67 are based on the following passages.

Gun rights groups, including the National Rifle Association, argue that they should be able to possess any type of gun based on the Second Amendment to the Constitution, which protects "the right of the people to keep and bear arms." They oppose bans on weapons sales, maintaining that bans on the sale of certain types of weapons have not proven effective in reducing violent crime. They are also against background checks of those wishing to buy guns and against mandatory safety locks on guns.

Gun control advocates have an opposing view, believing that the Second Amendment does not grant the right to own military-style firearms (also known as assault weapons). To bolster their argument, they cite incidents such as the Columbine High School massacre in 1999, in which assault weapons were used to kill 14 students and one teacher. They are in favor of a number of measures intended to curb gun-related violence, including mandatory child safety locks, background checks, limits on the number of guns a person can buy, and raising the age limit for gun ownership.

66. Based on the passages, what do gun rights advocates and gun control advocates have in common?

a. a belief that bans on gun sales do not reduce violent crimes

b. a belief that background checks will keep guns out of the hands of criminals

c. support for child safety locks on guns

d. none of the above

67. Gun rights advocates would most likely describe the Columbine High School massacre as

a. an inevitable result of the ease with which people can purchase assault weapons.

b. a tragedy.

c. a good reason to support bans on the sale of assault weapons.

d. evidence that rights granted in the Second Amendment should be modified.

Refer to the following poem to answer questions 68 and 69.

A Parting Guest
What delightful hosts are they—
Life and Love!
Lingeringly I turn away,
This late hour, yet glad enough
They have not withheld from me
Their high hospitality.

So, with face lit with delight
And all gratitude, I stay
Yet to press their hands and say,
"Thanks.—So fine a time! Good night."
                        —James Whitcomb Riley

68. Riley uses which literary device in his poem?
 a. hyperbole
 b. personification
 c. imagery
 d. oxymoron

69. Who is the Parting Guest?
 a. Life
 b. the poet
 c. Love
 d. a friend of the hosts

70. Which of the following is an example of natural selection?
 a. the development of flies that were resistant to the chemical DDT after it became widely used to kill household pests
 b. an increase in the average yearly egg production by chickens that were selected by breeders because of their high egg production
 c. an inherited characteristic, such as long necks in giraffes, that is passed on and occurs generation after generation
 d. the development of penicillin and other antibiotics for the treatment of bacterial infections

71. Choose the best revision of the underlined part of the sentence.

The soccer team won their seventh of seven games during this the month of May.

a. In this month of May, the soccer team won their seventh game.

b. The soccer team won their seventh of seven games during May.

c. The soccer team won their seventh game in May.

d. The soccer team won their seventh game during this the month of May.

72. Which source of information should you consult when researching the causes of the Civil War?

a. the diaries of Abraham Lincoln

b. a history of the abolitionist movement

c. an encyclopedia entry for the Civil War

d. all of the above

Question 73 is based on the following passage.

More than 2,000 researchers in 42 countries are actively involved in the study of happiness. Within that group, the work of Richard Davidson, a professor of psychology at the University of Wisconsin, stands out. Davidson observed patterns of brain activity as they related to a subject's mental and emotional states, using new technologies, such as quantitative electrophysiology, positron emission tomography, and functional magnetic resonance imaging. He concluded what western science once believed to be impossible: that the brain is not a static organ—it is able to change and develop over time. This capacity is known as neuroplasticity. From his studies, Davidson was also able to conclude that other areas of the body, including the liver and abdominal muscles, exhibit the same dynamic propensity.

73. Which sentence represents an example of faulty reasoning?

a. 3

b. 2

c. 6

d. 4

Questions 74 and 75 are based on the following passage.

An island in the Adriatic Sea was overpopulated with snakes. Sailors who came to the island brought and let loose mongooses, animals that feed on snakes. The population of snakes started decreasing because the mongooses were eating them. The mongoose population started increasing because there was ample food around. The mongooses were not native to the island and there was no predator on the island to keep the mongoose population in check. At some point, there were hardly any snakes left on the island, and people started populating it. The mongoose, facing a shortage of snakes, started eating chickens that people kept for their eggs and meat. However, people caught on and protected the chickens from getting eaten. The mongoose population decreased. Some remain on the island, but their number is now at equilibrium, kept in check by the availability of food.

74. The passage illustrates
   a. the interdependence of organisms.
   b. the fragility of an ecosystem.
   c. the ability of humans to change an ecosystem.
   d. all of the above

75. There were hardly any snakes left on the island because
   a. mongooses had eaten them.
   b. people had killed them.
   c. there was no predator for the mongooses.
   d. sailors brought them prey.

Refer to the following passage to answer questions 76 and 77.

It is a melancholy object to those who walk through this great town or travel in the country, when they see the streets, the roads, and cabin doors, crowded with beggars of the female sex, followed by three, four, or six children, all in rags and importuning every passenger for an alms. These mothers, instead of being able to work for their honest livelihood, are forced to employ all their time in strolling to beg sustenance for their helpless infants. . . .

I think it is agreed by all parties that this prodigious number of children in the arms, or on the backs, or at the heels of their mothers, and frequently of their fathers, is in the present deplorable state of the kingdom a very great additional grievance; and, therefore, whoever could find out a fair, cheap, and easy method of making these children sound, useful members of the commonwealth, would deserve so well of the public as to have his statue set up for a preserver of the nation . . .

I shall now therefore humbly propose my own thoughts, which I hope will not be liable to the least objection.

I have been assured by a very knowing American of my acquaintance in London, that a young healthy child well nursed is at a year old a most delicious, nourishing, and wholesome food, whether stewed, roasted, baked, or boiled; and I make no doubt that it will equally serve in a fricassee or a ragout.

I do therefore humbly offer it to public consideration that . . . children . . . may, at a year old, be offered in the sale to the persons of quality and fortune through the kingdom; always advising the mother to let them suck plentifully in the last month, so as to render them plump and fat for a good table. A child will make two dishes at an entertainment for friends; and when the family dines alone, the fore or hind quarter will make a reasonable dish, and seasoned with a little pepper or salt will be very good boiled on the fourth day, especially in winter.

—from Jonathan Swift, *A Modest Proposal*

76. In this excerpt, Swift is both
   a. acknowledging a societal problem and using satire to address it.
   b. using humor and being satirical.
   c. acknowledging a societal problem and proposing a feasible solution.
   d. using humor and venting frustration with the monarchy.

77. The Ireland that Swift is writing about
   a. needs more affordable housing.
   b. needs the mothers and children who are begging in the streets to join the labor force and become "useful members of the commonwealth."
   c. could be improved through the implementation of his proposal.
   d. is being governed by "persons of quality and fortune" who are doing nothing to help the less fortunate.

Question 78 refers to the following list.

Tidewater region featured wide coastal plain, wide rivers, and rich soil particularly well-suited to tobacco farming.

Only children of planters were educated and higher education was only for those who could afford it.

Two Major Regions of Early Colonies

New England

Came in groups and settled in self-governing towns. Town meeting as center of power at first, but shifted to selectmen in time.

Plantation owners became the leading economic, political, and social forces of the South. Occupations included farming (scarce labor, tough conditions), fishing, and commerce.

Terrain remarkable for rapid rivers and rocky soil.

Plantation South

78. Which choice represents the best way to outline the information in the list?

a.

I. Two Major Regions of Early Colonies

    A. Plantation South

        1. Tidewater region featured wide coastal plain, wide rivers, and rich soil particularly well-suited to farming.

        2. Only children of planters were educated and higher education was only for those who could afford it.

        3. Came in groups and settled in self-governing towns. Town meeting as center of power at first, but shifted to selectmen in time.

        4. Plantation owners became the leading economic, political, and social forces of the South.

    B. New England

        1. Terrain remarkable for rapid rivers and rocky soil.

        2. Occupations included farming (scarce labor, tough conditions), fishing, and commerce.

b.

I. Two Major Regions of Early Colonies

    A. Plantation South

        1. Tidewater region featured wide coastal plain, wide rivers, and rich soil particularly well-suited to farming.

        2. Only children of planters were educated and higher education was only for those who could afford it.

        3. Plantation owners became the leading economic, political, and social forces of the South.

    B. New England

        1. Terrain remarkable for rapid rivers and rocky soil.

        2. Came in groups and settled in self-governing towns. Town meeting as center of power at first, but shifted to selectmen in time.

        3. Occupations included farming (scarce labor, tough conditions), fishing, and commerce.

c.

I. Two Major Regions of Early Colonies

    A. Plantation South

        1. Tidewater region featured wide coastal plain, wide rivers, and rich soil particularly well-suited to farming.

        2. Came in groups and settled in self-governing towns. Town meeting as center of power at first, but shifted to selectmen in time.

        3. Plantation owners became the leading economic, political, and social forces of the South.

    B. New England

        1. Terrain remarkable for rapid rivers and rocky soil.

        2. Only children of planters were educated and higher education was only for those who could afford it.

        3. Occupations included farming (scarce labor, tough conditions), fishing, and commerce.

d.

I. Two Major Regions of Early Colonies

A. Plantation South

  1. Terrain remarkable for rapid rivers and rocky soil.

  2. Only children of planters were educated and higher education was only for those who could afford it.

  3. Plantation owners became the leading economic, political, and social forces of the South.

B. New England

  1. Tidewater region featured wide coastal plain, wide rivers, and rich soil particularly well-suited to farming.

  2. Came in groups and settled in self-governing towns. Town meeting as center of power at first, but shifted to selectmen in time.

  3. Occupations included farming (scarce labor, tough conditions), fishing, and commerce.

Questions 79 and 80 refer to the following engraving.

Paul Revere made and sold this engraving depicting the "Boston Massacre," a pre-Revolutionary encounter between British troops and American colonists, in which five colonists were killed.

Source: HistoryCentral.com.

79. Which of the following messages did Paul Revere most likely want to convey in his engraving?

  a. American colonists should not protest the presence of British troops in Boston.

  b. The British troops were defending themselves against rowdy gangs of colonists.

  c. British troops savagely killed unarmed citizens.

  d. Americans should willingly pay British taxes on imports of glass, paper, paint, and tea.

80. What can you infer was Revere's purpose in creating and selling the engraving?
   a. to fuel the revolutionary cause
   b. to calm the rebellious spirit of Boston citizens
   c. to create support for the British empire
   d. to represent both sides of the event

Written Assignment

Using the following assignment, write an essay of about 300–600 words. Do not write on any other topic. Essays on other topics, no matter how well-written, will receive a rating of U (unscoreable).

Should high school students be required to pass a standardized test to graduate?

In favor of requiring high school students to pass a standardized test to graduate. The best way to make both high school students and their schools accountable is to create and administer a standardized test for all seniors. Those who pass the test can graduate, and those who don't must remain in school. This requirement will cause students to take their coursework more seriously during the four years of high school in order to prepare for the test. It will also cause high schools to make sure they are teaching at least an agreed upon minimum curriculum to every student.

In opposition to requiring high school students to pass a standardized test to graduate. Using a standardized test as a graduation requirement will do nothing to improve education in this country, and will, in fact, do much to worsen it. There has been a marked increase in the number of standardized tests given to this country's students since the No Child Left Behind act was signed into law. These tests not only take up time that could be spent teaching curriculum, but also change the curriculum as teachers are urged to spend class time "teaching to the test." Studies of standardized tests have also shown them to be biased; affluent suburban students traditionally perform better, and would therefore graduate at higher rates, effectively causing an exploding school population in urban schools that have to retain high school seniors until they pass the test.

In your essay, evaluate the preceding arguments and take a position either for or against a high school graduation requirement of a passing grade on a standardized test. Construct a logical argument and back it up with evidence and examples.

► Answers

1. **a.** The best approximation of the amount of bacteria present on day 4 is 38. The line representing bacteria growth does not reach the line representing 40 grams on day 4, but rather intersects just beneath it.
2. **a.** The passage states that the sun will first expand (not shrink—choices **b** and **c**) when it runs out of hydrogen (not helium—choice **d**), and then 500 million years later, it will shrink.
3. **c.** White dwarf star is the correct answer based on the passage.
4. **a.** The problem with the underlined part of the sentence is parallel structure. "Check with the professor" should be followed by "decide who will collect" rather than "deciding who will collect." Only choice **a** corrects the error.
5. **b.** Portraits during this time period were typically of royal or noble subjects.
6. **d.** In the bar graph, the horizontal axis is labeled with four different months and the vertical axis is labeled with height in inches. The title of this graph is then related to a quantity measured in inches and would occur during the winter months. The title in choice **d** represents a quantity (snowfall) that would be measured in inches during the winter. The amounts in the graph are not reasonable for rainfall amounts in choice **a**.
7. **c.** In the period between 2000 and 2005, consumption increased by 57 quadrillion Btu. The years in the left-hand column are divided by five-year increments. To answer this question, find the greatest difference between each of the first eight rows in the right-hand column. Choice **a** is a distracter; the question states that the correct answer must be a five-year period "in the past."
8. **b.** The table clearly shows the amount of energy estimated to be consumed in 2015 to be 552 quadrillion Btu.
9. **a.** The trend of world energy consumption is increasing. You can answer this question by simply observing that the numbers in the right-hand column are increasing.
10. **c.** The third sentence is out of place; it does not support the main idea as stated in the first sentence ("Why has the school decided . . .").
11. **c.** This passage provides information to social workers about music therapy, as the title in choice **c** indicates. Choice **d** is possible, but does not summarize the passage as well as choice **c**. Choices **a** and **b** refer to topics not covered in the passage.
12. **a.** Based particularly on the last sentence of the passage, **a** is the best choice. The other choices are beyond the scope of the passage.
13. **a.** Because all soccer players take science, then at least some of the science students are also soccer players. We cannot conclude from this information that *only* soccer players take science. The fact that Sheila likes to play in the rain does not give you any information as to whether she is a soccer player or whether she takes science. Thus, there is not enough information to draw a conclusion about choices **b, c,** or **d**.
14. **c.** An autobiography is an author's account of his or her own life. The use of first person pronouns (I and me) is a common device in the genre.

15. c. Bacon was writing during the "Age of Discoveries," in which European explorers sailed around the globe, encountering previously unknown cultures and continents. There is no evidence to support the other answer choices.

16. d. Hades is the underworld, or Hell, of Roman mythology, and as such is the opposite of Atlantis.

17. b. Choice **b** is the most likely effect. By eliminating its competitors, Standard Oil controlled most of the production of oil and could artificially drive up prices.

18. c. The bowler's three best scores are the highest three scores. These are 116, 114, and 109. To find the average, divide the sum of these three scores by 3; $\frac{116 + 114 + 109}{3} = \frac{339}{3} = 113$.

19. d. In Genesis, God promises Abraham a land that will be an eternal possession, where he and his descendants can create a nation that is a model for the rest of the world.

20. d. There is no pollution or waste associated with solar energy.

21. c. This is the only choice supported by the caption and photo. The photo contradicts choice **a**—clearly, laws did not protect children from working as late as midnight. The photo does not support choice **b**—the image does not express a positive opinion about child labor. Choice **d** is true—the progressives did seek to heighten awareness about working children—but the photo does not supply evidence of their involvement.

22. d. Choices **a** and **b** can be ruled out because there is no way to determine how many tickets are for adults or how many are for children. Choice **c** can be ruled out because the price of group tickets is not given.

23. a. Because the 15-year-old requires an adult ticket, there are three adult tickets at $7.50 each and one child's ticket at $5; 3 × $7.50 = $22.50; $22.50 + $5 = $27.50.

24. b. The adult price on Saturday afternoon is $5.50; the child's price is $3. By subtracting $3 from $5.50, you can find the difference in price.

25. a. Nixon was president from 1969–1974, during the Vietnam War.

26. a. The modifiers *unprovoked, ruthless,* and *savagely* signal the opinion of the author.

27. c. The entire poem uses figurative language to compare death to being "put out to sea." The "Pilot" the poet hopes to see face to face when he dies is God.

28. c. A dash is used in a bibliography when an entry is authored by the same person as the entry immediately preceding it.

29. a. Evolutionary changes are those that result from natural selection; that is, changes that perpetuate characteristics that help a species better adapt to its environment. Without intervention, the process of natural selection would eventually eliminate poor eyesight. The use of eyeglasses and contact lenses is therefore an example of how humans are delaying this process.

30. b. Because the military has total control of the nation's media and he has declared himself the sole leader, he has created a dictatorship.

31. d. Citizens in a direct democracy vote on every law. They would have the most influence over law-making decisions.

32. **b.** His total bill will include the $19 flat fee plus $0.32 × the number of minutes of airtime over 120. If $x =$ total airtime minutes, then $x - 120 =$ total airtime minutes over 120. Therefore, the expression becomes $19 + 0.32(x - 120)$.

33. **c.** The question asks for the best summary of the passage. While the other answer choices could work as titles, only **c** accurately summarizes the text.

34. **d.** The end of the first paragraph states that the polka was "another popular dance employing the embrace."

35. **c.** In the last paragraph, the author writes that the tango was not developed "in literary society, which might be counted on to record the development," and that the less privileged and uneducated classes ". . . left little evidence of their existence."

36. **a.** Both images are of figures that are part human and part animal. The images provide no solid evidence of worship practices (choice **b**), and do not appear to be at the entrance of tombs (choice **c**). There is also no indication of the materials used by ancient Greek and Egyptian artists (choice **d**).

37. **b.** The last line of the passage ("I'll never use another mouthwash again, and you shouldn't either") reveals the author's motive, which is to convince the reader to try Morning Bright.

38. **c.** Choice **a** is already being done. There is nothing that indicates that all meat from South Dakota has salmonella or that meat from everywhere else is always healthy, so choice **b** would not be necessary. Choice **d** is wrong because antibiotics are not resistant to salmonella; some salmonella is resistant to antibiotics.

39. **d.** The statement, as noted in the previous question, is false.

40. **d.** Primary sources are documents and other items produced by people with first-hand knowledge of the dust bowl. Those include Roosevelt's Act, which was established in response to the first major dust storm, and Lange's photographs. Steinbeck's novel, a fictional account of the dust bowl migrations, and the *Time* magazine article are considered secondary sources. That means they rely on primary sources, but are not themselves products of first-hand knowledge of the event.

41. **d.** Only answer choice **d** shows the heights of the bars at the same values for each year in the double-line graph. Choice **a** has each company's values by year increased by 10,000. Choice **b** has the values for US Cable and Central Satellite switched. Choice **c** has each of the values for US Cable each decreased by 10,000.

42. **d.** The first sentence reads, "Orchids grow slowly in comparison with houseplants." This assertion about orchids is supported by the fact that they must be repotted just once every two years. The other answer choices are details about how to repot an orchid.

43. **a.** Some voters in the Pacific Time Zone have not yet cast their votes when the polls close in the east. Critics feel that early predictions can affect elections in this time zone.

44. **b.** The Emperor states that with his new clothes, he could "tell the clever from the dunces." But it is clear to the reader that *he* is the dunce, for believing the rogues about their ability to make invisible clothing. This discrepancy between what the character says and what the reader knows to be true is known as *irony*.

45. a. The passage, an excerpt from Hans Christian Andersen's *The Emperor's New Clothes,* centers on a ruler whose obsession with his wardrobe prevents him from seeing the truth (that the rogues are lying). Choices **b** and **d** refer to the rogues, rather than the Emperor who is the major character. Choice **c** is a common saying that goes against the theme of the passage.

46. b. The purpose of Roosevelt's address was to inspire a spirit of nationalism during World War II.

47. d. Signed by the United States and 15 other nations, the Kellogg-Briand Pact of 1928 tried to promote pacifism. However, because there was no way to enforce the pact, it was not effective.

48. a. Washington advocates avoiding political attachments with other nations, which is an isolationist view.

49. d. This comment demonstrates the political division between the North and the South before the outbreak of the Civil War.

50. a. This is the weakest argument because it is justified with authority, tradition, and past belief, rather than scientific facts. People have been wrong in the past, and noting that something has been done a certain way for years does not mean that there are no better ways. It is not a convincing scientific argument.

51. d. All of the answer choices are good methods for determining the reliability of an Internet site.

52. c. The other answer choices are true, based on the passage, but they are not inclusive enough to be the main idea.

53. a. Africans were brought to America against their will and forced to work as slaves. Assimilation for this group was not possible until after slavery was abolished.

54. c. This passage is mainly about the cause of reduced illiteracy rates among women.

55. d. The food chain can be described as a single direction to the flow of energy, in the form of chemical bonds, from photosynthetic organisms that rely on sunlight, like green plants or algae, to animals that eat the plants or other animals.

56. b. The work is clearly a sculpture, and is referred to as "relief" because its features or form stand out from a background.

57. c. The correct answer is choice **c** because the stick-like object, with its thin shaft and large decorative top, bisects the work diagonally and provides balance for the unequally sized figures. Choice **a** is incorrect because the headdresses are found at the top and middle of the work and do not stand out as anchoring features. Because the friezes are found only at the left top and left side of the work surrounding the larger figure, they cannot be said to provide symmetry (choice **b**). The open book at the bottom of the sculpture (choice **d**) is barely noticeable, and does not provide balance.

58. d. Statements I, III, and IV were made in the passage. Statement II is true, but it does not prove that the earth is round and was not discussed in the passage.

59. c. The whole passage is focused on listing evidence that the earth is round, not flat. Choice **a** is not a misconception. Choices **b** and **d** were not discussed in the passage.

60. c. The word *effect* is a noun meaning "a result," and is used erroneously. The correct word is *affect*, a verb meaning "to have an influence on."

61. a. Toward the end of the passage, the author writes that Sondheim had a "desire to explore and reveal psychological truths." The other answer choices are based on information in the passage, but do not relate to the message Sondheim wished to communicate through his art.

62. c. There is nothing in the passage to suggest that no other artists used Japanese poetry (choice **a**), or that other artists did not receive guidance from Hammerstein and/or Bernstein (choice **b**). Sondheim did not create *West Side Story* (choice **d**), but rather wrote its lyrics.

63. b. The tone of the passage does not convey the author's desire to change the mind of the reader; therefore, choices **a** (to dissuade); and **d** (to convince) are incorrect. The factual content does not contain an issue on which to take sides, so choice **c** (to argue) is also wrong.

64. a. The last sentence illustrates factors that motivate teenagers to exercise by using the results of a national survey to provide specific examples.

65. b. This uses two algebraic equations to solve for the age. Jacqueline (J) and her grandmother (G) have a sum of ages of 110 years. Therefore, $J + G = 110$. Jacqueline was $\frac{1}{3}$ as young as her grandmother 15 years ago. Therefore, $J - 15 = \frac{1}{3}(G - 15)$. Solve the first equation for J and substitute that value into the second equation; $J = 110 - G$; $(110 - G) - 15 = \frac{1}{3}(G - 15)$. This simplifies to $95 - G = \frac{1}{3}G - 5$. Add G and 5 to each side; $100 = \frac{4}{3}G$. Multiply each side of the equation by $\frac{3}{4}$ to get $G = 75$.

66. d. Choices **a**, **b**, and **c** do not apply to both groups, according to the passage.

67. b. Gun rights advocates do not want to restrict sales of assault weapons and believe that the Second Amendment to the Constitution grants the right to own any type of weapon, making choices **a**, **c**, and **d** incorrect.

68. b. The poet endows the abstract concepts of Love and Life with human characteristics. They are hosts who provide hospitality and have hands that are held by the poet.

69. b. The poet uses the first-person pronouns *I* and *me* to indicate that he is the guest who has enjoyed the hospitality of his hosts, Life and Love, and turns away to bid them good night.

70. c. Natural selection refers to the process in nature by which species that are best adapted to their environment survive, therefore transmitting their superior genetic characteristics to future generations, while those that are not as well-adapted die out. The long neck of a giraffe is an example of such a genetic characteristic.

71. c. This sentence suffers from wordiness and redundancy. Only choice **c** removes the extra words.

72. d. All of the answer choices represent good sources of information regarding the causes of the Civil War.

73. c. Davidson's study of brain activity patterns could not be used to draw conclusions about the liver and abdominal muscles; therefore the last sentence includes an example of faulty reasoning.

74. d. Statements **a** through **c** were illustrated in the passage. Mongooses depend on snakes for food, choice **a**. The balance in the ecosystem was disturbed when a new predator was introduced, choice **b**. Humans entirely changed the ecosystem when they brought the mongooses, choice **c**.

75. a. There was no mention of choice **b** in the passage. Choice **c** is true, but not as directly related to snake disappearance as choice **a**. Choice **d** is false. Sailors did not bring prey for the snakes; they brought a predator.

76. a. Choice **b** is redundant, as satire is a form of humor. Choice **c** is incorrect because it is not feasible to suggest that the Irish eat their own children to avoid poverty. Choice **d** is incorrect because there is no evidence in the excerpt that Swift is frustrated with the government.

77. **d.** Swift's satire highlights the grave situation facing Ireland's growing impoverished population. The kingdom is in a "deplorable state," and no one has stepped forward to offer a solution (one who did, Swift writes, would "have his statue set up for a preserver of the nation"). Choices **a** and **b** cannot be inferred from the passage; the problem Swift writes about cannot be solved by additional low-income housing or by adding women and children to the labor force. His proposal is satirical, therefore choice **c** is also incorrect.

78. **b.** The other answer choices correctly identify the major points, but fail to correctly attribute minor points.

79. **c.** By depicting the British troops firing into an unprotected crowd, Revere most likely wanted to show them as savage killers.

80. **a.** Revere most likely made and distributed this powerful image to further incite American colonists against the British.

Written Assignment

Essay 1 (strong)

Many state legislatures are considering adopting a new requirement for graduation from their public high schools: a passing score on a standardized test. Standardized testing is nothing new; in fact, since the No Child Left Behind Act was passed in 2001, a record number of such tests are given at many grade levels in order to hold schools accountable. But do these tests deliver what they promise, and is a graduation testing requirement a good idea?

First, let's examine what standardized tests aim to achieve. Because they are based on a "standard," they purport to measure achievement based not on grading discrepancies, curriculum differences, and varying teaching styles, but based on one set of questions and answers. That's the theory. But how well does it hold up in practice? Studies show that standardized tests are biased—white, affluent, suburban students perform better than their non-white, underprivileged urban counterparts. In addition, some tests are poorly written, and grading procedures (including computer grading) have sometimes been found to be faulty. Should eligibility for high school graduation be based on these kinds of inequities?

But what if a test that was fairly written, administered, and graded could be used? There are still other problems with standardized testing. The high stakes involved with a high school graduation requirement test could cause a number of undesired results. Schools, wanting to maintain their reputations through high graduation rates, would redesign curriculum to emphasize the material on the tests. Teachers would have to "teach to the test," leaving little or no time for lessons not directly included on the test. Students with special needs and those experiencing academic difficulties, who could be at greater risk for failure, could be encouraged to drop out of school.

The idea that standardized tests would help the education system by highlighting those schools in need of extra help is simply wishful thinking. Poor test results are used to punish schools in our current system, including reducing or cutting off funding, taking over control of schools from local school boards, and replacing administrators. The threat of these punitive measures increases pressures to perform some of the measures described in the previous paragraph, including teaching to the test and removing students who could perform poorly.

In summary, requiring high school seniors to pass a standardized test in order to graduate will do nothing to improve the educational standards of our country. In fact, it will produce a number of undesired results that will inevitably weaken the very system that testing was designed to better.

Evaluation

This is a strong argumentative essay that fully meets the requirements of the assignment. The author evaluates the arguments presented in the prompt and takes a firm stand on one side of the issue. His argument is logical, well-developed, and backed up by appropriate examples and evidence. He also shows a strong command of written English and the conventions of essay writing. Word choice suggests an excellent vocabulary, and there are few errors in grammar and mechanics.

Essay 2 (weak)

I believe it is a good idea to make high school students pass a standardized test in order to graduate. Sure, we have grades and course requirements that help tell us how good a student is doing, but right now there is no way to figure out how our high school's do against each other. A standard test would do just that.

If students knew that they would have to pass this test in order to graduate, they would work real hard during there four years in high school. The test would be like a kind of carrot thats held out in front of them. If they want it, they have to work for it. Schools would also work harder if they knew their kids had to pass the test. I mean, what would they do with a bunch of seniors who failed the test? The next year, they'd have to teach them again? I can just imagine how crowded some schools would get with all those seniors coming back every year! How old would you have to be before a school said you were to old to come there?

So the schools that had a lot of students who didn't pass would obviously need some help. With the test, they would stand out and help would be given to them. This would be another positive benefit of the test.
I think the standardized test idea is a good one. It will help kids and help schools, and who could argue with that?

Evaluation

While this essay does fulfill the requirements of the prompt by evaluating the pro and con arguments and taking a side, its ideas are not well-developed and the evidence used in support are weak. It appears to have been written in haste, with little or no planning involved. The essay also does not demonstrate an appropriate level of formality. Slang terms, a conversational style, and errors in grammar and mechanics all contribute to its low score.

▶ Scoring Your Practice Test

Your official LAST score is a cumulative score representing all subareas of the test, including all multiple-choice questions and the constructed-response assignment, which will count toward 20% of your total score. Your total score will be reported on a scale between 100 and 300; a passing score for the official LAST is any score of 220 or above.

Once again, to take full advantage of this practice test, you should find both your overall score on the multiple-choice questions of this test, as well as your individual scores in each subarea. To find your overall score, simply divide the number of multiple-choice questions you answered correctly by the total number of multiple-choice questions found on the test, which is 80. For example, if you answered 60 questions correctly:

$$\frac{60\text{(questions correct)}}{80\ \text{(total questions)}} = .75, \text{or } 75\%.$$

To score your constructed-response question, it is highly recommended that you ask a professional friend or colleague familiar with the area of Written Analysis and Expression to evaluate your essay using the official *Performance Characteristics and Scoring Scale* found at the end of the official LAST Preparation Guide, which can be found on the NYSTCE website at www.nystce.nesinc.com/PDFs/NY_fld001_prepguide.pdf. Your friend or colleague should assign you a score on the constructed-response essay between 1 and 4.

After you have a score for both parts of the practice test, you should use the following guidelines:

- If you get 80% or more of the multiple-choice items correct and score a 4 on the written assignment scoring scale, your preparation for the test is **EXCELLENT**.
- If you get 70% or more of the multiple-choice items correct and score a 3 or 4 on the written assignment scoring scale, your preparation for the test is **VERY GOOD**.
- If you get 60% or more of the multiple-choice items correct and score a 3 on the written assignment scoring scale, your preparation for the test is **GOOD**.
- If you get less than 60% or more of the multiple-choice items correct and score a 2 or 1 on the written assignment scoring scale, you should probably do some additional preparation before taking the actual test.

This practice test also offers you the opportunity to diagnose your areas of strength and weakness, to target your preparation for the official test. Following is a table that breaks down the questions in this practice test by subarea and their corresponding objectives. You can use this table to identify the areas in which you may need to concentrate more of your study time. For this practice test you should score at least 75% or higher in each subarea. You can find out your individual subarea scores by dividing the number of questions you answered correctly in a particular subarea by the total number of questions in that subarea.

Use your scores in each subarea in conjunction with the LearningExpress Test Preparation System in Chapter 7 to help you devise a study plan using the prep materials found in this book along with the materials from your classes and courses.

LAST Practice Exam 2 for Review

SUBAREA AND OBJECTIVE	CORRESPONDING QUESTION	
Subarea I: Scientific, Mathematical, and Technological Processes		Total # of questions in Subarea I: 22
0001	13, 22	
0002	1, 6, 23, 32, 41	
0003	18, 24, 65	
0004	20, 50, 58, 59, 70, 74	
0005	29	
0006	2, 3, 38, 39, 55	
Subarea II: Historical and Social Scientific Awareness		Total # of questions in Subarea II: 20
0007	52	
0008	25, 46, 47, 48, 49, 54	
0009	53, 67	
0010	17, 40, 43, 79, 80	
0011	7, 8, 9, 21, 30, 31	
Subarea III: Artistic Expression and the Humanities		Total # of questions in Subarea III: 19
0012	5, 56, 57	
0013	34, 35, 36, 61, 62	
0014	14, 27, 44, 45, 68, 69	
0015	76, 77	
0016	15, 16, 19	
Subarea IV: Communication and Research Skills		Total # of questions in Subarea IV: 19
0017	11, 33, 42	
0018	12, 37, 63, 66, 75	
0019	26, 64, 73	
0020	4, 10, 60, 71	
0021	28, 51, 72, 78	

LAST Practice Exam 2 for Review (Continued)

SUBAREA AND OBJECTIVE	CORRESPONDING QUESTION	
Subarea V: Written Analysis and Expression		Total # of questions in Subarea V: 1
0022	Written Assignment	

The key to success in almost any pursuit is to prepare for all you're worth. By taking the practice LAST exams in this book, you have made yourself better prepared than other people who may be taking the exam with you. You have diagnosed where your strengths and weaknesses lie and learned how to deal with the various kinds of questions that will appear on the test. So, go into the exam with confidence, knowing that you're ready and equipped to do your best.

NOTES

NOTES

NOTES

NOTES

NOTES

NOTES

NOTES

NOTES